MODERN HUMANITIES RESEARCH ASSOCIATION

DISSERTATION SERIES

VOLUME 1

Editors:

F. J. STOPP   R. A. WISBEY

(*Germanic*)

T. J. Rogers, Techniques of Solipsism

TECHNIQUES OF SOLIPSISM

A Study of
Theodor Storm's Narrative Fiction

by

TERENCE JOHN ROGERS

Formerly Lecturer in German in the University of Durham

Published by
THE MODERN HUMANITIES RESEARCH ASSOCIATION
CAMBRIDGE
1970

CONTENTS

ACKNOWLEDGEMENTS

All my quotations from Storm's works are taken from a modern edition: *Theodor Storm, Sämtliche Werke,* hrsg. Peter Goldammer, 4 vols, Aufbau-Verlag Berlin 1956. This splendid edition, with its fine and comprehensive *apparatus criticus,* has been a delight to work from and a mine of information; in particular, my reading of the various volumes of correspondence has uncovered almost nothing of importance which is not contained in the extracts quoted by Goldammer in his notes to particular stories. I refer throughout to this edition as 'SW'; thus, for example, 'SW I 462' means *'Sämtliche Werke,* hrsg. Goldammer, vol. I, p.462'.

My visits to the Schleswig-Holsteinische Landesbibliothek, Kiel, in the summer of 1964, were made largely profitable through the experienced and friendly guidance of Frau Wetzenstein, who, among many other kindnesses, was good enough to show me the Storm manuscripts lodged at the library; I take this chance to thank her.

I count it a privilege to have been supervised by Dr J.P. Stern of St John's College and by Dr P.A. Roubiczek of Clare College. My many conversations with both have given me countless insights; the contact with such learning and such sensitivity has been an incalculable stimulus and enrichment. What is good in this study will be found to bear their mark; the barbarisms that remain are all my own.

Mr T.D. Jones, of Jesus College, has smoothed the rough path in innumerable ways since 1959. My debt to him is recorded, emblematically, in a footnote to p.161; for it is in such places, as he once said, that he most likes his name to be found. I am deeply grateful to the Electors to the Tiarks Scholarship in the University of Cambridge for their generous and welcome award for the academic year 1962-3. What I owe to Dr Ruth Young is immeasurable, or perhaps measured by the fact that this thesis has been completed at all.

September 1966.   T.J.R.

EDITORIAL NOTE

Mr T.J. Rogers was tragically killed in a car accident little more than a year after taking up his first academic post as University Lecturer in the Department of German, University of Durham. The manuscript of this book is therefore as originally approved for the Ph.D. degree of the University of Cambridge in February 1967. No attempt has been made to revise the text in the light of subsequent research.

I CONTOURS OF LONELINESS

To suggest that Storm's early work (or for that matter the bulk of his work) is 'about' loneliness is to say nothing very new; the best[1] of Storm criticism makes the point, and so does the worst.[2] But opinions are less united when we come to ask the more interesting questions which the 'suggestion *that*' brings with it; in what, if anything, lies the uniqueness of Storm's enactments of the lonely condition? Does his creative concern with that condition legitimise it, make it worth while, as a subject for art? Does it show through to us convincingly as another possible or actual way of being alive? What is it like to be lonely, and why do people become lonely, in Storm's world? An adequate answer to this last pair of questions will take us, I think, most of the way towards answering the others; so I shall try in what follows to give an account, based on a number of his early stories, of 'what it is like and why it happens' in the world of Storm's fiction at this time. The state seems to me to be delineated in a curiously pure way in the first story; and the others enlarge upon it, adding new aspects and above all hinting at reasons, which run deep into the nature of human living.

1. MARTHE UND IHRE UHR

Marthe und ihre Uhr (1847) is Storm's first prose effort.[3] To call it a Novelle would be to stretch even that elastic term to breaking-point; in essence it is a portrait, a half-dozen pages long, of the person and life of Marthe, the elderly woman with whom the narrator lodges during his last years at school. Storm conceived the sketch as a sort of literary tribute to Christine Brick, the old lady who had kept house for him in 1845-6: Marthe's characteristics and experiences are closely modelled on those of 'Tante Brick'.[4]

More than anything, this is a study of loneliness, as a state or way of life, and of the various means of overcoming it or at least adapting oneself to it. Already in the first six lines of the piece, Marthe is introduced to us as 'eine alternde *unverheiratete* Tochter';[5] a moment later we hear that her parents and brothers are dead, and that her sisters have married and gone away: 'so blieb denn Marthe *allein* in ihrem elterlichen Hause' (SW I 395). The theme is sounded: Marthe is celibate and she is alone. She is the first of a long line of Storm's figures placed in that situation.

Solitude is the central fact of Marthe's life; it is a kind of reference-point to which all her actions, emotions and experiences are directed. Each tiny happening, each small thing described in these few pages is important only insofar as it reinforces or counteracts her loneliness — important, that is, both to us and to

Marthe. Her solitary life is, in a very quiet way, a battleground on which the desire for contentment is at war with the forces of unhappiness; and if this is so, we are faced with an ambiguity. The mood throughout is one of comparative calm and serenity; it seems that we are asked to accept that contentment wins the day, that Marthe is able to come to terms with her condition and find usefulness and peace within it. But I want to suggest that the facts of the story lead us to the opposite conclusion; we must conclude that the battle goes the other way, that all Marthe's efforts to come to terms are defeated and her hopes shown in the last resort to be illusory, that her solitude is ultimately a humanly unsatisfactory way of life which leaves her unhappy and must leave us unhappy as well.

The portrait of Marthe shows her engaged at various times in a number of activities, or sets of experiences; the description of each is heralded by a reference which indicates that the particular activity is intimately connected with, indeed arises from, her state of solitude; each activity is shown as an attempt to escape from, or 'make use of', her loneliness. The first activity, briefly examined, is reading. The fact that Marthe is not surrounded by people gives her the chance to read widely and educate herself; above all, she has time to reflect on what she has read:

> so hatte das Nachdenken ihrer späteren *einsamen* Stunden . . . sie doch . . . auf eine für Frauen, namentlich des Bürgerstandes, ungewöhnlich hohe Bildungsstufe gehoben. (SW I 395)

But Marthe herself recognizes that reading is not enough; it directs her back into herself, and she needs to turn outwards in order to assure herself that her life has some purpose; so she takes the occasional lodger. Again, the form in which this second activity is announced suggests how closely it is bound up with her awareness that she is alone:

> Die Langeweile drückte Marthen in ihrer *Einsamkeit* nicht, wohl aber zuweilen ein Gefühl der *Zwecklosigkeit* ihres Lebens nach außen hin; sie bedurfte jemandes, für den sie hätte arbeiten und sorgen können. Bei dem *Mangel näher Befreundeter* kam dieser löbliche Trieb ihren jeweiligen Mietern zugute . . . (SW I 396)

Then there is another activity, a willed experience, which is yet more closely woven into the fabric of Marthe's everyday life; it is really her principal attempt to accept her loneliness for what it is and come to terms with it, and as such it is accorded a good deal of space and attention in the story. Marthe comes to make friends with the inanimate objects around her, to invest them with individual identities, to bring them to life as (once more) a consolation for the lack of people; contact with things seems to her even to have its advantages over contact with people:

> Da Marthe seit dem Tode ihrer Eltern *wenig Menschen um sich* sah und namentlich die langen Winterabende fast immer *allein* zubrachte, so lieh die regsame und gestaltende Phantasie, welche ihr ganz besonders eigen war, den

Dingen um sie her eine Art von Leben und Bewußtsein. Sie borgte Teilchen ihrer Seele aus an die alten Möbeln ihrer Kammer, und die alten Möbeln erhielten so die Fähigkeit, sich mit ihr zu unterhalten; meistens freilich war diese Unterhaltung eine stumme, *aber sie war dafür desto inniger und ohne Mißverständnis.* (SW I 396)

Her spinning-wheel has its own personality and caprices, and so does her brown carved armchair; but the thing which comes alive for her most of all is her old clock. Its ticking and chiming become speech; it involves itself in her feelings with sympathy and a sort of understanding. It seems that with the clock Marthe has won her battle; she has found a positive solace, a real companion in her solitude. Alone, she could never have a yardstick for her actions or a brake on her emotions; with the clock she has both. The clock reminds her of her duties: often in the night it goes wrong and chimes incessantly; and it seems to Marthe, as she gets up to put it right, that it is trying to tell her of some omission of which she has been guilty during the day; and at Christmas, when she wants to accept the invitation to celebrate with her sister's family, the clock warns her that she has a duty to stay at home in memory of her dead mother. Best of all, the clock can lift her out of the moods which assail her in her loneliness; and to have the possibility of being lifted out of a mood is no longer to be lonely. The way in which the clock intervenes to break Marthe's mood is described in a passage which develops into a sort of hymn of praise and affirmation. The passage is one of sights and sounds; it treats them on the one hand with the hard plastic realism which is Storm at his best, and on the other with a certain untoward sweetness. The combination is curious, but the effect is somehow moving:

Diese Uhr war die beredteste Gesellschaft ihrer Besitzerin; sie mischte sich aber auch in alle ihre Gedanken. Wenn Marthe in ein Hinbrüten über ihre Einsamkeit verfallen wollte, dann ging der Perpendikel tick, tack! tick, tack! immer härter, immer eindringlicher; er ließ ihr keine Ruh, er schlug immer mitten in ihre Gedanken hinein. Endlich mußte sie aufsehen; — da schien die Sonne so warm in die Fensterscheiben, die Nelken auf dem Fensterbrett dufteten so süß; draußen schossen die Schwalben singend durch den Himmel. Sie mußte wieder fröhlich sein, die Welt um sie her war gar zu freundlich. (SW I 397)

When the clock 'tells' Marthe to stay in her home at Christmas, it directs her to another of her common experiences, another activity engaged in with a view to overcoming her solitude: she moves back into the past, to relive former, happier Christmases, when her family had filled this house with tranquil gaiety. The memory is introduced in terms which suggest, as before, that it is directly consequent on her being alone, and also that the return to the past is total, a reliving and not a mere recalling:

Marthe durfte sich *ungestört* der Erinnerung aller Weihnachtabende ihres Lebens überlassen: ihr Vater *saß wieder* in dem braungeschnitzten Lehnstuhl ... (SW I 398)

Sights and sounds predominate here as well, not dimmed at all by time, but perhaps even more plastic, 'real' and present than the things to which Marthe is woken by the clock in the passage quoted above — here we see the bright glow of the candles and hear 'das Prasseln der Apfelkuchen' and the singing of 'Der Heiland ist gekommen'.

But then we are brought to a halt. Something happens which throws the 'success' of this fourth activity — and by implication the 'success' of all the others — into doubt. Marthe's dream-memory is short-lived: she is brought back from the brightness of the peopled past into the darkness of the solitary present:

> Tick, tack! ging es wieder; tick, tack! immer härter und eindringlicher. Marthe fuhr empor; da war es fast *dunkel* um sie her, draußen auf dem Schnee nur lag *trüber Mondschein.* Außer dem Pendelschlag der Uhr war es *totenstill* im Hause. Keine Kinder sangen in der kleinen Stube, kein Feuer prasselte in der Küche. Sie war ja *ganz allein* zurückgeblieben; die andern waren alle, alle fort. (SW I 399)

So reliving the past is an inadequate escape; the world of memory is so frail a structure that it can be demolished by the ticking of a clock. And then it emerges that the past itself holds things that are bitter and not consoling. The clock sends Marthe back in time again, but now to that Christmas Eve when her mother died, leaving her entirely alone. That same imaginative vividness, which had served to make the earlier Christmas such a joyful memory, now calls up with utter clarity and immediacy all the bitter details of her mother's death. Memory has become a return *to* suffering, not an escape *from* it. This situation occurs again and again in Storm's stories; it makes nonsense of the frequent criticism that Storm stops short of the full working-out of suffering and allows his characters to evade the harsh realities of the present by slipping back into rosy dreams of the past. The relived past is itself often so harsh that the real evasion would be to *forget* it.

Memory, then, is shown to be doubly ineffective as a counterweight to loneliness. And how is it shown to be ineffective? — by the ticking of the clock, Marthe's supposed companion and comforter. As a comforter, the clock's record is unprepossessing: certainly, it lifts her out of the depression caused by her solitude; but it does a great many other things to her as well. As we have seen, it destroys the memory of a happy Christmas and forces Marthe to recollect an unhappy one; and between the one memory and the other it has shown her the emptiness of her present life. Thus it prevents her from making her own kind of contact with her dead family; and it has already prevented her from seeking contact with the living family of her sister, by 'reminding' her of her duty to stay at home in memory of her mother. Its eccentric behaviour in the middle of the night makes her re-examine the omissions and insufficiencies of her life during the previous day. It is a strangely fickle companion — and the same goes for the other furniture. When Marthe is woken from her happy dream, what has happened to the personalities with which she has invested her spinning-wheel and her chair? At the moment when she most needs their company and living support, they seem to have become inanimate objects again, and she wakes up to find herself 'ganz allein'; the 'friends' she invented are proved once for all to be things and not people.

Her memories have betrayed her, and now her furniture has given her no steadier assurance; so there remain those other activities, reading and taking lodgers. Reading she has known to be inadequate from the start — useful in warding off boredom, but unable to lessen her consciousness of the 'Zwecklosigkeit ihres Lebens nach außen hin'. So only the lodgers remain; there, surely, some valuable human relation must exist. But again the limitation is severe: the landlady-lodger relationship is inherently tenuous enough, and what is more, at the times when the contact is most needed (above all at Christmas), it is denied to Marthe. The narrator, like most lodgers, goes away; he spends Christmas 'in einer befreundeten, kinderreichen Familie' (SW I 397); *his* search for contact makes Marthe's search fruitless. It is a sad irony that at the festival of love Marthe is once more placed unequivocally in a situation which in reality she has never escaped: she is left alone.

These activities are not ends but means: they have always the quality of being designed for a purpose — to console or support or even justify Marthe in her lonely state. It seems to me that they do not achieve the desired effect; but there is also a sense in which they are not merely ineffective, but also unacceptable, as answers to solitude. None of them is a real challenge or a proper human alternative; none takes issue with solitude itself; the only thing they ever achieve is to push the awareness of solitude just under the surface for a little while. The possible exception here is the taking of lodgers; we can accept that the presence of another living person in Marthe's home is at least a basis on which a challenge could be made; at least a relationship is created. But what weaker link could Storm have forged between Marthe and other people? The encounter between landlady and lodger stands right on the edge of the area covered by our common definition of 'human relations'; indeed, it threatens to fall, and in the story is shown at the critical moment actually to fall, right outside that area. Storm would have been hard put to it to find for Marthe a relationship which is nearer to being no relationship at all; if this is her most direct means of overcoming her loneliness, then we cannot be very satisfied by it.

What then *could* we be satisfied by? Marthe's solitude is clearly shown as an impoverishment, a condition about which something has to be done; given that I suppose we can accept as valid two possible ways of dealing with it. On the one hand, the solitude could be quite simply eliminated, for example by marriage or by some extensive contact with or commitment to other people. On the other hand, it could be accepted on its own terms, embraced and transmuted, so that we can be convinced that a worthwhile existence may be carved out within its boundaries, and even that achievements or qualities may emerge from it which would be impossible in other circumstances. The first possibility, the elimination of solitude, does not exist for Marthe; her only human commitment is to her lodgers, and I have suggested that as a contact this is so inadequate as to be unacceptable.

So we are left with the second possibility, accepting solitude and turning it to good account; and Marthe's other activities (reading, relating with her furniture, and remembering) are all essays in this possibility, since none of them involves any actual contact with living people — they are all activities performed within the context of her loneliness. And each of them, in one way or another, is curiously invalidated.

It is of Marthe's reading that we can say with most justice, 'This may perhaps make it worth while'. It is not a total consolation, we know, for it cannot fulfil the need for a purpose 'nach außen hin'; but if the autodidactic process results in a refined appreciation and a mature literary judgement, then solitude will have been turned to real account, the enclosed life of the oyster will have produced its pearl. The narrator claims that this has happened, that Marthe has reached an 'ungewöhnlich hohe Bildungsstufe': she can, he says, form 'ein richtiges Urteil' about what she reads, and she is able to distinguish the good from the bad. Yet immediately after asserting that this is so, the narrator goes on to describe Marthe's reactions to a particular work (Mörike's *Maler Nolten*, as it happens) in terms which seem flatly to contradict his assertions:

> Die Gestalten des Dichters wurden für sie selbstbestimmende Wesen, deren Handlungen nicht mehr an die Notwendigkeit des dichterischen Organismus gebunden waren; und sie konnte stundenlang darüber nachsinnen, auf welche Weise das hereinbrechende Verhängnis von so vielen geliebten Menschen dennoch hätte abgewandt werden können. (SW I 396)

Where is the 'Urteil' here? Where is the ability to distinguish good from bad? And above all, is a response of such naivety to be taken as evidence of appreciation on a 'hohe Bildungsstufe'? Surely not: what impresses us about such a response, if anything, is its pristine innocence, the very lack of maturity and experience it displays, for it breaks down the 'artistic organism' and sentimentally abstracts the 'geliebte Menschen', seeking to avert the suffering which is integral to their existence as figures in the work of art. One is forced to the conclusion that loneliness has merely enabled Marthe to read a more than usually large number of books; qualitatively, it has hardly developed her literary responses beyond those of a child. This is one of the curious cases, common in Storm's work,[6] where the first-person storyteller suddenly comes into focus for what he is, a fallible human being. We are forced to look beyond his judgements and to make our own, knowing that he may be wrong; and we realise that Storm recognizes Marthe's naivety (though his narrator may not) and knows it to be inadequate, while of course remaining in sympathy with her throughout.

And what of the furniture? Once again, the narrator seems to be asserting that the chair and spinning-wheel and clock offer lasting companionship and solace, that Marthe has achieved a satisfying relationship with 'things'. But the manner in which these things are described is undeniably wry; it is hardly likely that we are meant to applaud a relationship with objects whose principal characteristics seem to be old age and almost grotesque oddity:

> Ihr Spinnrad, ihr braungeschnitzter Lehnstuhl waren gar sonderbare Dinge, die oft die eigentümlichsten Grillen hatten, vorzüglich war dies aber der Fall mit einer altmodischen Stutzuhr, welche ihr verstorbener Vater vor über funfzig [sic] Jahren, auch damals schon als ein uraltes Stück, auf dem Trödelmarkt zu Amsterdam gekauft hatte. Das Ding sah freilich seltsam genug aus: zwei Meerweiber, aus Blech geschnitten und dann übermalt, lehnten zu jeder Seite ihr langhaariges Antlitz an das vergilbte Zifferblatt; die schuppigen Fischleiber, welche von einstiger Vergoldung zeugten, umschlossen dasselbe nach unten zu; die Weiser schienen dem Schwanze eines Skorpions nachgebildet zu sein. Vermutlich war das Räderwerk durch langen Gebrauch verschlissen; denn der Perpendikelschlag war hart und ungleich, und die Gewichte schossen zuweilen mehrere Zoll mit einem Mal hinunter. – (SW I 396f.)

A passage like this makes it impossible for us to be happy with the idea of Marthe deriving 'companionship and solace' from such things; and how can we be anything but repelled when we read that the peculiar old clock has usurped the functions of Marthe's conscience, reminding her of her duties and omissions?

Even without this – even if the attempt *were* made to instil in us some kind of affection for these pieces of furniture and some sympathy with Marthe's relationship with them – the battle could still never be won; we should still have to make the objection which finally nullifies the value of this relationship, and with it the value of Marthe's remaining activity, that of reminiscence. I have suggested that there are two ways of reacting to solitude which we can recognize as satisfying and illuminating human possibilities: the first is to see to it that one is no longer solitary, and the second (if the first is impossible) is to accept one's solitude for what it is, and to create an integrated and useful life within the realities of one's situation. Only the second possibility is open to Marthe; but she fights this second battle by pretending that she has won the first; her weapons are types of an illusion.

Marthe invests her furniture with personalities in order to delude herself that she has other human beings around her; the pieces of furniture are surrogates for persons, not personalities *as furniture*. Her reminiscing is not simply the recollection of a peopled past, but the attempt to create the illusion of a peopled present ('Ihr Vater *saß wieder* in dem braungeschnitzten Lehnstuhl . . .'), literally to live experiences twice over,[7] in defiance of the sad reality that two into one won't go. She is like the vegetarian who finds consolation for a meatless existence in dressing his food to look like meat and calling it a 'nut cutlet'; she finds consolation for a friendless existence in dressing up her furniture and the shadows of her memory to look like people and calling them 'friends and family'. What we want to know from the vegetarian is whether it is possible to live happily without meat, not how to pretend that one is not living without it at all; and what we want to know from Marthe is whether one can live alone and yet live an integrated human life, not how to pretend one is not alone at all. When Marthe personifies her furniture or returns to the past, she is not in any real sense coming to terms with her loneliness; she is merely clutching at the illusion (clearly shown to be very fragile and very transitory) that she is not alone. And as if to punish her for her self-deception, her two major weapons combine against her: the clock jolts her back from her dreams of happy Christmases, waking her to the empty present, and then memory reclaims her and compels her to witness again the death of the last person who kept her from being quite on her own.

So the whole edifice crumbles. It seemed strong enough at first; the narrator certainly seemed satisfied that Marthe's life was a contented one, that her various activities were sufficient to give her balance and purpose. But then it became evident that the activities were never quite successful in giving her what she needed. And then it became evident that there was never any hope that they *could* give her what she needed, because all of them were rotten at the core, unacceptable, false and illusory. So she is alone and unhappily aware of her loneliness; she cannot find any peace within it, and there is no way out of it; Marthe is a latter-day Ixion. She is condemned to her solitude for Storm's brand of eternity, that is, until death, after which there is nothing. And the bitterness of it all is yet more strongly confirmed when we go outside the story and read what Storm says in a letter about Marthe's prototype, 'Tante Brick':

> Tante Brick sitzt einsam in ihrer Kammer und weint über ihre Verlassenheit am Weihnachtabend; ihre einzige Erinnerung ist der Tod ihrer Mutter, der am Weihnachtabend um zwölf erfolgte; nun sitzt sie und durchlebt noch einmal alles, jede Minute bis zur Todesstunde, dann geht sie zu Bett. — Wie glücklich sind wir doch, daß wir gefunden, was wir lieben! . . . Es muß wohl das Herz vor Wehmut brechen können, dies ahnungsreiche, süße Kinderfest, wenn die Kinderträume verblichen sind und die Jugend ohne Liebe dahingegangen ist, so ganz allein verleben zu müssen. Ich habe die alte Jungfer — es ist mit dem gewöhnlichen Klang ein gar hartes Wort — so gut ich konnte, getröstet . . . [8]

And Stuckert says of *Marthe und ihre Uhr*, 'Das schlichte Leben einer bürgerlichen Frau wird hier mit einfachen Mitteln verklärt und geadelt';[9] Pitrou sees in the story 'la transfiguration . . . des choses du foyer, l'exaltation des humbles, la divinisation du souvenir'.[10] It is left to Böttger to point out that this is the portrait of

> eine alte Frau . . . , der vom Leben nichts mehr geblieben ist als das einsame, freudlose Warten auf den Tod.[11]

Marthe und ihre Uhr seems to me to be a preliminary definition: Storm is using it to sketch out the contours of that area of experience which in later stories he constantly refers to as 'Einsamkeit' or 'Alleinsein' and integrates into an epic process and a causal scheme. It is an essay in loneliness, rather as Harold Pinter's *The Birthday Party* is an essay in fear:[12] a more or less abstract examination of a state, untrammelled by considerations of plot or development. The subsequent stories will provide that.

2. IMMENSEE

Ein schwaches Stäbchen ist die Liebe,
Das deiner Jugend Rebe trägt,
Das wachsend bald der Baum des Lebens
Mit seinen Ästen selbst zerschlägt.

Und drängtest du mit ganzer Seele
Zu allerinnigstem Verein,
Du wirst am Ende doch, am Ende
Nur auf dir selbst gelassen sein.[13]

M.A. McHaffie and J.M. Ritchie conclude their painstaking and perceptive examination of *Immensee*[14] with the words:

In the last analysis this story is an extraordinary mixture of 'Kitsch' and 'Kunst', sentimental rubbish and masterly technique, 'eine Verniedlichung und Verbürgerlichung der deutschen Romantik' — with sexual undertones.

The note of slight desperation in the tone here is interesting, because it reflects the kind of effect this story commonly has on its readers. We are not quite sure what to make of it; the issues seem clear enough at first, but they slip away when we try to fix them; we take fright at the number of unanswered questions and are left with the desire to compensate for the lack of answers by arriving at some decisive form of words, some forthright and unequivocal conclusion. This 'bringing to earth' is misleading, because it is out of character with the quality of the story. But that we feel the need to make the bold judgement, the final flourish, is a good indication of the kind of ground we enter when we come to examine *Immensee*; 'bringing to earth' as a substitute for answers suggests how puzzling are the questions the narrative raises.

Immensee (1849) is a collection of scenes; only the most perfunctory concessions are made in the text to the fact that the scenes are components of a narrative development. Storm gives us ten points on a graph; it is our job as readers to draw the curve which connects them. Indisputably, the curve we draw bears the shape of an unhappy love-affair; almost as indisputably, the process at work is one of alienation. I do not wish to imply a dwindling of affection, a falling out of love on one side or the other, or both; indeed, the indications point the other way. The process is involuntary — Reinhard and Elisabeth are progressively separated by things independent of, indeed running generally counter to, their desires. The separation is defined when Elisabeth marries another man, and recognized to be insuperable when Reinhard visits Elisabeth and her husband Erich some years after the marriage; but though definition and recognition come at a late stage, the process is present and discernible throughout. Its existence (I am leaving aside for the moment the question of its origins) is adumbrated in a series of descriptive, symbolic or premonitory passages.

The tensions in the relationship between Reinhard and Elisabeth are suggested in the earliest encounter we are allowed to witness, a scene in the turf house which the ten-year-old boy has built for the five-year-old girl who is his constant companion. Reinhard tells Elisabeth of his plan to go to India when he is grown up; will she go with him? he asks. Elisabeth is quite agreeable to the idea, so long as their mothers can come too — her own mother particularly. But Reinhard will not have this at any price, and Elisabeth is near to tears when she finally consents to go with him alone.

Seven years are passed over in a single paragraph, of which about half is devoted to a small (though characteristic) incident, and then the next scene, 'Im Walde', is introduced. The occasion is a communal picnic in the woods on the day before Reinhard's departure for the university. It is a turning-point for Reinhard in more ways than one: it stands at the end of an old life and the start of a new one, but more significantly, its events awaken in him an increased (though still by no means total) consciousness of his love for Elisabeth. Storm conveys the nature and quality of this consciousness in a single sentence:

> So war sie nicht allein sein Schützling; sie war ihm auch der Ausdruck für alles Liebliche und Wunderbare seines aufgehenden Lebens. (SW I 416)

That (in passing) is a very fine piece of writing. Storm has set himself a large task here: he must convey Reinhard's youth and promise, the fact that his awareness of his love has not yet reached the stage of complete conscious perception, the gentleness of his feelings for Elisabeth, the association of these feelings with what is good in his life, the way in which Elisabeth is so much a part of him as to become a reference-point for his experience, a sense of wonder at the relationship. All these things are communicated in a manner which triumphantly fulfils the obligations of an artist to his art. Storm refuses to think in categories; his duty is to describe realities as they are. He will not allow himself the glib evasion of recourse to the blurred and conceptualised *idée reçue* of 'love' ('Liebe' and 'lieben' do not occur once in *Immensee*). He must, like every creative artist, redefine and re-interpret, and he does so here with the most wonderful economy and conscientious accuracy. The sentence fits exactly, with perfect rightness, into its context; it does what it has to do finally and comprehensively. It has about it the thrill of the absolutely appropriate, the absolutely precise, and to that extent reading it is a model of the aesthetic experience.

But Reinhard's realisation comes (and it will come twice more in the same way)[15] at the very point where there is a symbolic premonition that the relationship will end in failure: Reinhard and Elisabeth look for strawberries, but they find none — and they lose their way in the forest. The old man who has sent them (and the other young people) on the hunt has already pointed the moral and crystallised the premonition:

> Es stehen genug Erdbeeren im Walde, das heißt für den, der sie zu finden weiß. Wer ungeschickt ist, muß sein Brot trocken essen; so geht es überall im Leben. (SW I 413)

So Reinhard goes away to the university; and the letter Elisabeth sends him there at Christmas (SW I 419f.) gives more hints of something wrong. First, she upbraids him for not keeping his promise to send her fairy-tales; his mother, she says, has told her that he is busy and has no time for 'solche Kindereien', but Elisabeth does not believe her: 'Es ist wohl anders', she writes. Then, she tells him that the linnet he gave her has died.[16] And then, she mentions that Erich has taken to visiting her and is drawing a portrait of her; she seems to have no great admiration for Erich, but he is there, and the warning is sounded.

When Reinhard returns home for the Easter vacation, the estrangement is fully in evidence; characteristically, it is expressed in small physical gestures and the half-formulated emotions of the moment:

> Am Morgen nach seiner Ankunft ging er zu Elisabeth. 'Wie groß du geworden bist!' sagte er, als das schöne schmächtige Mädchen ihm lächelnd entgegenkam. Sie errötete, aber sie erwiderte nichts; ihre Hand, die er beim Willkommen in die seine genommen, suchte sie ihm sanft zu entziehen. Er sah sie zweifelnd an; das hatte sie früher nicht getan; nun war es, als träte etwas Fremdes zwischen sie. — Das blieb auch, als er schon länger dagewesen and als er Tag für Tag immer wiedergekommen war. Wenn sie allein zusammensaßen, entstanden Pausen, die ihm peinlich waren und denen er dann ängstlich zuvorzukommen suchte. (SW I 421)

The sense of strain is further reinforced when Elisabeth reads, more or less by chance, the poems which Reinhard has composed about her. Or rather, she does not really read them; she turns over page after page of the 'Pergamentbuch' in which they are written, seeming only to scan the titles. A blush spreads over her cheeks — is this the moment when we shall see a declaration and a response? But no, she hands the book back to Reinhard without saying a word. When he protests, she takes the book, puts a specimen of his favourite flower in it — and once more hands it back to him.

The time comes for Reinhard to go back to the university. Elisabeth accompanies him to the coach, and the tension mounts. He is more than ever aware of the depth of his feelings for her (though he has still not wholly formulated them to himself), but the more convinced he becomes, the harder it seems to communicate his feelings to her:[17]

> Je näher sie ihrem Ziele kamen, desto mehr war es ihm, er habe ihr, ehe er auf so lange Abschied nehme, etwas Notwendiges mitzuteilen — etwas, wovon aller Wert und alle Lieblichkeit seines künftigen Lebens abhänge, und doch konnte er sich des erlösenden Wortes nicht bewußt werden. Das ängstigte ihn; er ging immer langsamer. (SW I 424)

Finally he tells her that he has a secret (presumably that he wants to marry her, though we cannot be sure that he even knows himself what it is). He will reveal it to her on his return in two years' time, he says; and he asks her not to forget. But her response is ambiguous — she merely shakes her head. Does this mean 'I will not forget' or 'I cannot do what you ask'? Reinhard gets into the coach, and before it has reached the corner, Elisabeth has already turned her back on it and is walking home.

Nearly two years later Elisabeth accepts Erich's proposal at the third time of asking; so now Reinhard's love will never be fulfilled. The visit to Immensee years later is a final attempt to work out some kind of possible relationship; but true to form, Reinhard comes to realise — now that it is impossible — that a full union in love is the only envisageable relation between himself and Elisabeth. It is quite clear to him (and to us, thanks to the lily episode) that he must go away and never come back. The process of alienation is complete.

That is about as far as one can get without controversy. As soon as one starts looking for the causality behind the process, problems arise. Two factors are more or less suggested in the text as immediately contributory. First, Reinhard seems to forget his implicit responsibilities towards Elisabeth in the rush and bustle of a (possibly) somewhat dissipated student life: he does not keep his promise to send her Märchen, he flirts with a gypsy girl, and he has an attack of conscience and a sense of danger narrowly averted when he receives Elisabeth's letter. And second, there are clear indications that Elisabeth's mother exercises a domination over her daughter and forces her into a 'good match' with Erich:[18] apart from the childhood scene I mentioned, and Elisabeth's reaction to the folk-song 'Meine Mutter hat's gewollt', there are a half-dozen hints in the text pointing to the subjection of daughter to mother, the mother's suspicion of Reinhard and her preference for Erich, particularly after the latter has inherited the estate on Immensee. But both these factors are open to objection; there is as much that speaks against them as for them.

First, the dissipation of Reinhard's student life, the imminent danger of irrevocable committal to sinfulness, and the attendant neglect of his duties towards Elisabeth. To give weight to this as a causal factor we need to adduce passages like this one:

> Reinhard hatte in einer entfernten Stadt die Universität bezogen. Der phantastische Aufputz und die freien Verhältnisse des Studentenlebens entwickelten den ganzen Ungestüm seiner Natur. Das Stilleben seiner Vergangenheit und die Personen, welche dahinein gehörten, traten immer mehr zurück; die Briefe an seine Mutter wurden immer sparsamer, auch enthielten sie keine Märchen für Elisabeth. So schrieb denn auch sie nicht an ihn, und er bemerkte es kaum. Irrtum und Leidenschaft begannen ihr Teil von seiner Jugend zu fordern.

The fact is, however, that this passage does not occur at all in the text as we have it — it is part of the first version of the story;[19] Storm eliminated it from the final version.[20] Moreover, the passage stands at the head of a long section, also elided, which gives a much more graphic and highly-coloured description than the one we have of the drinking-party in the cellar on Christmas Eve (after which Reinhard finds Elisabeth's letter). In this first version the party is wild and drunken, the foul-mouthed celebration of a Studentenkorps. The mood is bawdy; the joking contains a certain amount of erotic innuendo connecting Reinhard and the gypsy girl and centring round the tuning pegs on her zither. Reinhard, we learn has gambled away his money and has even forfeited the silver decorations on his coat. His reason for returning to his lodgings is not (as in the second version) that a friend tells him a parcel has arrived for him, but — horror of horrors — that he remembers the money he has put aside for a present for Elisabeth and decides to go back and collect it so as to have money for gambling! All this is cut out, and replaced by a scene very much in a minor key.[21] The Ratskeller is quiet; there are a few students and the odd stranger or two; the waiters are standing around idly. The bawdy student drinking-song is replaced by the gypsy girl's passionate but melancholy lament, 'Heute, nur heute . . .' Reinhard stops flirting with the girl as soon as he hears that a parcel has arrived at his lodgings, even though the gypsy girl begs him to stay and the flirtation definitely looks like being crowned with success (it is much more promising, oddly enough, than the one described in the first version). There is absolutely no mention of gambling, and no hint at all that Reinhard is connected with a Korps. (SW I 417f.)

Why should this section have been changed so drastically? I would suggest that among other reasons[22] Storm rewrote the section because he felt that in its original form it centred the causality too firmly on this one element and closed the reader's mind to whatever other factors he felt to be playing a role. The removal from the section of almost all that is direct, explicit, interpretative, explanatory — or above all moralising — has the effect of warning us off this particular piece of causal territory. We are being told that we must not delude ourselves that this is the whole story — we must keep our eyes open and look further.

What, then, of the mother? Can we find the real cause in her power over, and mercenary ambition for, her daughter? Her reasons for considering Erich the better match for Elisabeth are presumably social and financial ones; that at least would make a good, dull, sensible plot — pure love conquered through base materialism. But in social and financial terms, Reinhard's credentials are at least as good as Erich's. There is no suggestion of any class difference between the two; the fact that they are friends indicates equality in this respect, and anyway, the fact that a massive picnic is organised to mark Reinhard's departure for the university suggests the high standing of his family in the town. Erich's family are well-to-do, certainly (the property on Immensee is 'der zweite Hof seines Vaters'); but he does not seem to have been to the university, whereas Reinhard has. The mystic phrase 'er hat studiert' counts for a lot with the nineteenth-century Bürger as a social asset; and having studied, Reinhard has the prospect of a career which is highly lucrative, or highly respectable, or both. Socially, then, he has the edge on Erich; financially, he is not far behind and may well catch up. If there is so little to choose between the two men, is it a sufficient explanation to say that it is the mother's ambition which leads her to press Erich's suit as single-mindedly as she does? If she is as hard-headed and calculating as this interpretation makes her out to be, surely she would have realised that Reinhard and Erich are both equally far from being disastrous matches? Yet she plumps wholeheartedly for Erich. One can only hazard the guess that her animosity towards Reinhard may spring from a different ground, and such a guess finds unexpected support in the text. I mentioned earlier that Elisabeth's Christmas letter to Reinhard contains three hints of the threatened estrangement, one of which is the death of the bird he had given her. The passage giving the news runs like this:

> Nun ist auch vorigen Sonntag der Hänfling gestorben, den Du mir geschenkt hattest; ich habe sehr geweint, aber ich hab ihn doch immer gut gewartet. Der sang sonst immer nachmittags, wenn die Sonne auf sein Bauer schien; *Du weißt, die Mutter hing oft ein Tuch über, um ihn zu geschweigen,* wenn er so recht aus Kräften sang. (SW I 419; my italics.)

It is clear from the context that the linnet died soon after Erich appeared on the scene; but it is also clear that the mother was in the habit of covering the linnet's cage with a cloth well *before* Erich's entrance — indeed, the 'Du weißt' clearly suggests that she did this even before Reinhard went away. I want to take the italicised words at more than their face value, and their implications about 'timing' as more than purely fortuitous; it is dubious, I know, to attach so much symbolic value to so slight a reference, but what else is there to go on? Slight references are the only currency the conventions of *Immensee* allow us to use. It seems to me, then, that the covering of the bird with a cloth is the mother's attempt to silence this daily reminder of Reinhard, symbolic of her desire to remove his personality and influence from her daughter's experience; and the desire is therefore present well before Erich, the alleged 'better match', ever really appears. So the animosity cannot be grounded in any unfavourable specific comparison between Reinhard and Erich. What *is* it grounded in? The text gives no clear indication. I want to reserve judgement on this problem; I have introduced it here so as to stress its negative value; it is yet further proof that we *still* cannot sit back and say that we have found the cause.

Dissipation and maternal domination, then, are too full of ambiguities to be satisfactory or exhaustive explanations. Can we look for a causality in the wider social situation? Böttger, the East German, is obviously the man to consult for a 'sociological' interpretation, and sure enough, we find a very nice one, substantiated with a text from one of the gospels:

> Seit den Tagen, da die Menschenrechte proklamiert wurden, gehörte die Freiheit der Gattenwahl zum Programm des sich emanzipierenden Bürgertums. 'Auf dem Papier', sagt Friedrich Engels in seinem Werk *Der Ursprung der Familie, des Privateigentums und des Staats,* 'in der moralischen Theorie wie in der poetischen Schilderung, stand nichts unerschütterlicher fest, als daß jede Ehe unsittlich, die nicht auf gegenseitiger Geschlechtsliebe und wirklich freier Übereinkunft der Gatten beruht'. In der Wirklichkeit regierten

die Interessen der Familie und ökonomische Rücksichten, ein Widerspruch, an dem die gesamte bürgerliche Jugend des 19. Jahrhunderts dahinkränkelte. *Immensee* enthüllt die Krankheit einer Jugend, die unentschlossen zwischen dem revolutionären Ideal freier Liebesentscheidung und dem reaktionären Argument der angeblichen Notwendigkeiten praktischen Lebens hin und her pendelte, sich schließlich immer der herkömmlichen Praxis fügte und damit ihr Leben vergiftete . . .

Wir haben es also in der Novelle *Immensee* weder mit einer Selbstdarstellung noch mit der Gestaltung eines Wunschbildes zu tun, sondern mit der epischen Widerspiegelung objektiver Verhältnisse. Für Storm war *Immensee* eine Liebesgeschichte aus der 'guten alten Zeit' vor dem Jahre 1840, ehe die liberalen Ideen in voller Breite das Bürgertum ergriffen. Sie beruht auf dem Widerspruch zwischen dem bürgerlich-humanistischen Ideal und der reaktionären bürgerlichen Praxis, wie er sich für die Restaurationsperiode als Allgemeinerscheinung herausgebildet hatte.[23]

There are a number of reasons for rejecting this interpretation; I want to single out one here. Böttger's case ultimately rests on the (factual, not ideological) assumption that Erich has a clear social and financial advantage over Reinhard; but this assumption, as I said earlier, seems to me misguided, so all that Böttger says is thrown into question. Nonetheless, there is one sense in which social demands could be said to play their part in preventing the 'wirklich freie Übereinkunft' of Reinhard and Elisabeth; the alienation is hastened and exacerbated by physical separation; it is during Reinhard's absence that the rift becomes explicit and irreparable. Whether it is the mere fact of separation, or Reinhard's preoccupation with his new way of life, that makes the rift widen so much, need not concern us here; either way, we can say fairly safely that the rift widens 'because' Reinhard is away at the university.

I mean that the decision that Reinhard should go away to study is not really his decision, is not an act of conscious choice or will on his part. This is how we hear of it:

> Sieben Jahre waren vorüber, Reinhard *sollte* zu seiner weiteren Ausbildung die Stadt verlassen.

and a few lines later:

> Es war im Juni; Reinhard *sollte* am andern Tage reisen. (SW I 412; my italics.)

The repetition of 'sollte', and the emphasis on leaving the town, travelling away (rather than going *to* anywhere) are striking; they seem to me to imply that Reinhard does not have very much say in the matter; that the step is more or less imposed on him by what society considers to be the right thing for intelligent young men to do; and also that the principal feature of this social demand is shown to be the way it pushes Reinhard *away*. Again, this is much ado about very little; but again, I think the narrative conventions of the story make this sort of examination necessary. One could say, then, that social pressures bring about a separation without which Reinhard and Elisabeth might have had a better chance of coming together. But still the whole story has not been told. If this separation were at the root of the estrangement, we should expect any 'pre-separation' scenes to show at least the promise of what things could have been like if Reinhard had never had to go away. The equation 'separation = alienation' needs to be brought into sharper relief by its corollary, 'non-separation = non-alienation'. But this is not what happens: the childhood scene ('Die Kinder') is notable precisely for the way it suggests tensions already present in the relationship.[24] So even before Reinhard leaves, before his departure is even contemplated, all is not well. The separation is arguably a catalyst — but we have yet to find the cause.

We have tried the individual and particular, and then the general and social, and we have found both of them wanting. But the recognition of their inadequacy is useful because it helps to throw new light on the nature of the alienation; certain features emerge which were hidden before. From the start, the relationship between Reinhard and Elisabeth seems to carry the seeds of its own destruction. The first stage we are allowed to see is fraught with tension, and none of the other stages is free of it; each move towards union has its attendant obscurities and ill omens. Elisabeth agrees to go alone with Reinhard to India, but is near tears in doing so; Reinhard recognizes the extent of his feelings after the picnic, but he and Elisabeth find no strawberries and lose themselves; she sends him cakes at Christmas, together with an affectionate letter, but the letter says that he has not kept his word, that the bird has died and that Erich is visiting; Reinhard's approach to a declaration, as the two walk to the coach, is received ambiguously. The signs of failure are always there. Furthermore, the process of estrangement has an air of inevitability; we fail to find a viable and unambiguous root cause because there is no single thing in this story of which we can say 'if it had not been for that, everything would have been all right'. There is no room for an 'if only' in *Immensee*; all we can say is 'nothing else could have happened'. I would claim for the story that we are made to *feel* this inevitability below the level of conscious working-out and statistical elimination; but the claim is hard to substantiate without conscious working-out of the kind I have indulged in over the last few hair-splitting pages.

The relation contains the seeds of its own destruction from the beginning, and destruction is inevitable. What this means in effect is that the process is organic: it proceeds to its end as a plant proceeds out of a seed, it is indistinguishable from the relation as a canker is indistinguishable from the cells it destroys. The alienation is inherent in the fact that Reinhard and Elisabeth are in intense relation with one another. They are drawn apart, not because of what they do or what is done to them, but because of what they are.

Things now begin to fall into place. When we take the little causal formula 'They are drawn apart because of what they are' (leaving it for the moment in those general and cryptic terms), a rationale takes shape behind the manifold ambiguities and contradictions of this (apparently so simple) story. Again and again, we have followed a signpost to a possible causality and have ended up in a cul-de-sac; but the cul-de-sacs are *meant*. The way we have said 'This might be the cause' and have then been forced to say 'No, it is not', is a pattern of experience as Storm sees it. The same process of examination and rejection is being carried out at three levels: in Reinhard as he recalls once more the details of the broken relationship and tries to work out the reasons for the break (for this is why he remembers); in Storm, as he creates a fictional structure in an attempt to formulate and make sense of his own unhappy experience;[25] and in us, as we search for the aesthetic and experiential coherence of the story and its relevance as illumination. It is almost as if the aid of Reinhard and the reader were being enlisted to help Storm solve his problem. All three have to take up, and then discard as insufficient, the various possible causes; all three are brought gradually into a position where the only possible explanation lies, not in action or reaction, but in existence. The tensions in the relationship are present from the first because, from the first, Reinhard and Elisabeth are what they are; the mother is suspicious of Reinhard even before the appearance of Erich because, even before the appearance of Erich, Reinhard is what he is. Separation, university life, material considerations may seem to play their part in widening the rift, but Storm hedges them around with reservations and inconsistencies because he has found them to be just so hedged around in his own experience, and wants Reinhard (and us) to be dissatisfied with them, as he has been, and look beyond them, as he has done. They are the visible part of the iceberg; the submerged part, which really does the damage, is the fact of the nature and existence of Reinhard and Elisabeth.

What *is* their nature and existence? What are the peculiar qualities inherent in these two people which single them out for the kind of treatment they receive? There seems to be no real answer to this question. Reinhard and Elisabeth are unexceptional, very ordinary people. It has been argued that they are abnormal in their diffidence and reticence, their unwillingness or inability to communicate.[26] But are they? Surely this degree of reticence is one of the norms of 'real life'; many people just don't talk about their emotions very much. Reinhard and Elisabeth are abnormally reticent in comparison with *other literary characters* — and that is where the confusion lies. We are used to accepting the literary convention of personages who are articulate and communicative beyond verisimilitude; this is one of the areas in which our suspension of disbelief is so ready as to be automatic. We know that the 'untrue' articulateness is a necessary vehicle for the revelation of other 'truths' about the character in question or about human character in general; in the interests of 'truthfulness' about what the writer considers major, we are prepared to sacrifice the minor 'truth' about the way people express themselves. But what happens when a writer (and I think Storm is such a writer) wants to convey a re-interpretation of experience which says that the way people communicate or fail to communicate is *not* a minor issue, but on the contrary a basic ingredient in the human condition and a 'truth' much further-reaching in its consequences than men commonly suppose? Are we to demand that he makes his characters articulate about their inarticulateness? Surely he must be exempted from this convention, and we must accept his characters' reticence for what he intends it to be — not an abnormality but a norm. We must, as it were, suspend our suspension of disbelief. The reticence of Reinhard and Elisabeth not only hides the realities of their characters from us and from each other;[27] it *is* a reality of their characters, and a compelling reality about 'life'. Here is a most remarkable case of the (literary) exception proving the (experiential) rule.

These two people, then, are unexceptional in this way as in every other. In addition, each event, and above all each character, in this story is enveloped in a mist which prohibits the perception of any but the barest outlines.[28] These two factors combine to bring us inescapably to one conclusion: all that distinguishes Reinhard and Elisabeth from empty space, all that marks their step from non-existence to existence, is their humanity and their relationship; we know almost no more about them, and indeed, that is more or less all there is to know about them; and so we have arrived at a specification which makes our causal formula as precise and explicit as it will ever be. Now it runs: 'Reinhard and Elisabeth are drawn apart because they are human beings and because they are seeking a union in love'. We have exposed the root.

> Und drängtest du mit ganzer Seele
> Zu allerinnigstem Verein,
> Du wirst am Ende doch, am Ende
> Nur auf dir selbst gelassen sein.

The statement is metaphysical, and the implications of an extra-individual force are clear. Whether one can speak of it in terms of 'fate', 'the gods', 'God' or 'the human condition', I don't know. The force is certainly alluded to twice in the text in terms which suggest the supernatural. During the symbolic search for strawberries (a fruitless search, as the love will be fruitless), Reinhard says:

> 'Hier haben (die Erdbeeren) gestanden, . . . aber die Kröten sind uns zuvorgekommen, oder die Marder, oder vielleicht *die Elfen*'. (SW I 414; my italics.)

and when Reinhard comes home for his first vacation, the strain between him and Elisabeth is described like this:

> nun war es, als träte *etwas Fremdes* zwischen sie . . . (SW I 421; my italics.)

But one can obviously not give much weight to these allusions as evidence of the postulating of an observably supernatural agency: the first specifies somehow too narrowly and is anyway lighthearted in tone, and the 'etwas' of the second could be replaced by 'the way things are' just as meaningfully as, for instance, by 'the gods'. It seems to me that Storm may at these two points be positing and then discarding possible definitions of the force, in the same way (and with the same effect) as we have already seen him positing and then discarding possible causalities. It is quite likely that he himself has no clear idea about the precise nature of the force; but he has no doubts about its existence.

I would be inclined to offer a definition (subjective, but with foundation) of this force in terms of 'the way things are', 'the human condition'. What seems to be present here is the force of human limitation as Storm sees it. The position taken up in the story might be expressed like this: because human beings are built in the way they are, very few people are able to jump over a seven-foot-high wall; most of us are simply not equipped to do it. In the same way, because human beings are built in the way they are, very few people are able to achieve the fullest human relationship, the 'allerinnigster Verein'; most of us are simply not equipped to do it. What prevents the common run of people from jumping so high is a gravitational pull which is stronger than they are and which returns them to the most natural and characteristic human position, that is, on the ground. In the same way, what prevents the common run of people from achieving such a relationship is a gravitational pull which is stronger than they are and which returns them to the most natural and characteristic human situation, that is, solitude, the opposite of relationship. The only difference is that men seem able to live perfectly satisfactory lives without the ability to jump seven feet, whereas the inability to achieve a relationship is life-denying. Otherwise, the analogy holds; to cross the wall, and to cross the barrier between 'Ich' and 'Du', requires a leap, a defiance of basic forces, which is beyond most human beings.

This idea of solitude as a 'gravitational' norm of existence seems to me central to a great deal of Storm's early work; what makes it so original is the fearful dichotomy it involves. Solitude, for Storm, is the *natural* state of equilibrium towards which all human experience tends; it is the most *characteristic* human state. But it is a state in which it is impossible to be *fully* human; the highest aspirations and achievements of men are a leap *away* from it, but the leap is doomed to failure because we are what we are.[29] In the end we shall always return to being alone:

> Du wirst am Ende doch, am Ende
> Nur auf dir selbst gelassen sein.

It is Reinhard's solitude that we see at the beginning and end of *Immensee* — a solitude very like that sketched out in *Marthe und ihre Uhr*. First and foremost, Reinhard is either celibate or indistinguishably near to being so. In the first version of the story, there is a long passage at the close, describing how he marries some years after the break with Elisabeth; a son is born but does not live more than a year; and Reinhard is eventually left a widower. The final version omits all mention of the marriage,[30] and one may conclude from this either that Storm wishes to change the 'facts' and imply that Reinhard never married at all, or, at the least, that he wants to make it that much more difficult for the reader even to consider the possibility that Reinhard might later have attained to a relationship which could mask, let alone cure, the pain of failure with Elisabeth. Either way, it is a 'fact' that Reinhard is unmarried at the time we meet him in 'Der Alte', and it is indisputable that he has remained, as one might say, emotionally celibate all his life; whether he married or not, nothing has ever happened to draw the sting of his unhappy memories or make him feel less alone without Elisabeth.

Other types and indications of solitude are grouped around the central celibacy. What we see of Reinhard in the introduction and conclusion suggests a pattern of life approaching that of a recluse. He takes long walks alone; he seems to have little contact with the present world around him (that is the traditional inference from the details of his old-fashioned dress); he knows few people in his neighbourhood well enough for them even to greet him as he passes by; his only company is his housekeeper Brigitte, with whom he is 'auf Sie und Sie' (it is reasonable to assume that the last person to have called him 'Du' was Elisabeth, whose last words to him were, 'Ich weiß es, lüge nicht; du kommst nie wieder'). (SW I 437)

What are the alternatives or consolations? The total return to the past ('Er war in seiner Jugend') (SW I 409) is commonly put forward as one way in which Reinhard escapes his unhappy isolation (and Storm evades his responsibilities).[31] But how on earth can memories such as these be described as escapes from unhappiness? Every scene passing through Reinhard's mind contains some reference to the breakdown of the relationship between himself and Elisabeth; indeed it is hard to find in these memories a single moment of unalloyed joy. His reminiscence reconstitutes what has been most bitter in his life; the more complete and 'living' the return, the more bitter it is;[32] he would be better advised to escape *out of* it than *into* it. But the escape out of the memory, when the housekeeper brings the lamp, is of course a return to his present loneliness.

Perhaps some comfort, fulfilment and achievement could be derived from his scholarly career; but the space Storm devotes to this possibility is cynically brief — five lines in the chapter 'Immensee', the odd reference in 'Meine Mutter hat's gewollt' (merely as a cue for the singing of the fateful song), and a mention, right at the end of the story, the tone of which is uniquely and astoundingly noncommittal:

> Dann rückte er auch den Stuhl zum Tische, nahm eins der aufgeschlagenen Bücher und vertiefte sich in Studien, an denen er einst die Kraft seiner Jugend geübt hatte. (SW I 438)

What are we to infer from this? Certainly not any idea that Reinhard is fulfilled by his studies.

Reinhard is alone and knows that he is alone. There is no way for him to escape his loneliness, and no way to find peace or fulfilment within it. He takes his place beside Marthe in Storm's portrait gallery of the isolated and the anxious; with Marthe, he quietly treads the wheel of Ixion. That is his punishment for the crime of being human.

3. OTHER STORIES

Marthe und ihre Uhr, then, sketches out the condition, and *Immensee* offers reasons for it. I have suggested that *Immensee* is not the story of two exceptional individuals but the vessel of a more generalised statement: the claim it makes is not, 'This is what Reinhard and Elisabeth are like' but, 'This is what life is like'. In a way, this suggestion has arisen *faute de mieux*; it was the only signpost which did not seem to lead us up a blind alley. The process of elimination is a negative one, because it so happens that, if we approach the story through causal channels, that is the route we have to take. There is another route, a much more positive one, and I shall be talking about it in the next and main part of this study; meanwhile the insight gained from *Immensee* can help us to see a number of the other early stories in a new light. Each of these stories has its own individual shape and colouring, yet each in its way adds a variation to the theme sounded in the two stories I have just discussed: the nature of isolation and the causes of failed relation seen as a general condition, norms of living.

Posthuma is a tiny piece, a mere four pages long.[33] It was first published in 1851, in the collection entitled *Sommergeschichten und Lieder*, but Storm probably wrote it in 1850 (*Immensee* predates it by a matter of months). He thought very highly of it and for some time apparently considered it to be the best of his works[34] — the claim is surprising in view of the story's modest proportions. It deals with the relationship between a young man and a girl, both of them unnamed. He is of a higher class than she, and they must therefore meet secretly; she loves him, he only desires her. But even in life she is given over to death; she dies very young, and it is only after her death that the man's desire fades and is replaced by love. Now (and, it seems, for the rest of his life) he is 'gezwungen, eine Tote zu lieben', tied to the dead and bereft of consolation from the living.

The relation between the young man and the girl is inadequate at every point and doomed to failure from the start — why? Storm casts around (as we saw him doing in *Immensee*) for a possible causality, offering this or that factor as a root or perhaps only a catalyst of failure, never able to commit himself to any motivation as exhaustive, and leaving us finally to conclude that it had to happen this way because this *is* what happens to people in relation. There will always be obstacles, and they will generally be enough to destroy the possibility of loving union.

The social difference between the man and the girl, although nowhere quite directly stated, makes itself strongly felt as a factor drawing them apart. Its centre in the economy of the story is a small incident during the one (presumably representative) meeting we hear about; this incident sends reverberations backwards and forwards over the other scenes and moments, adding the social dimension to a situation that would otherwise have seemed quite individual:

> Ein niedriger Zaun trennte den Fleck, worauf sie standen, von der Straße. Nun hörten sie Schritte in ihre Nähe kommen. Er wollte sie mit sich fortziehen;

aber sie hielt ihn zurück. 'Es ist einerlei', sagte sie.
Er machte sich von ihren Armen los und trat allein zurück . . .
'Du schämst dich!' sagte sie leise, 'Ich weiß es wohl'.
Er antwortete nicht; er hatte sich auf die Bank gesetzt und zog sie schweigend zu sich nieder. Sie ließ es geschehen, sie legte ihre Lippen auf seine schönen vornehmen Hände; sie fürchtete, ihn betrübt zu haben.

The act of physical separation at the sound of other people's footsteps represents in action the social separation which seems inevitable as soon as the relationship moves into the context of a wider community; quickly and surely, Storm has isolated the social thread in the causal skein and held it up for our inspection. But one thread draws up another: as well as the class difference implied in the young man's shame and desire to hide, and in the mention of his 'vornehme Hände', these few lines contain the hint of another tension or weakness, namely the lopsidedness of the relationship in purely personal terms.

Once again, the representation is graphic: she tries to hold him, but he moves out of her arms; she allows him to pull her down onto the seat; she kisses his hands. The gestures are those of permissive, self-abasing love, answered by silent rejection; they are visual restatements of the tension expressed explicitly a few lines earlier:

Sie liebte ihn, sie tat ihm alles . . . Er liebte sie nicht, er begehrte sie nur und nahm achtlos das ängstliche Feuer von ihren Lippen.

She loves him, he does not love her: in its nature, and in the unambiguous directness with which it is portrayed, this situation is a departure from the scheme of *Immensee* — there, the desire for union is (or seems to be) present on both sides, and the final realisation that no relation is possible is as bitter to Elisabeth as it is to Reinhard. There is a further departure also in that the inequality of affection provides a context for a moral judgement and for the postulation of some kind of personal responsibility. That the young man does not love the girl is not his fault; to love or not to love is an alternative beyond the powers of conscience or will to determine. But Storm shows the man to be fairly clearly 'wrong' in exploiting the girl's affection to the end of physical satisfaction and thus denying her human worth. In the quotation above, the word 'achtlos' condemns; and in the sentences which follow that quotation in the text, the tone is one of blame:

'Wenn ich geschwätzig wäre', sagte er, 'so könnte ich morgen erzählen, daß mich das schönste Mädchen in der Stadt geküßt hat'.
Sie glaubte nicht, daß er sie für die Schönste halte, sie glaubte auch nicht, daß er schweigen werde.

And again, a clear moral judgement is implied in the paragraph giving the reasons why the young man does not finally seduce the girl:

Sie war in seiner Gewalt; sie wollte nichts mehr für sich allein. — Er schonte ihrer; nicht weil es ihn ihrer erbarmte oder weil er es als Sünde empfunden hätte, sie ohne Liebe sein zu nennen; aber es war, als wehre ihm jemand, sie ganz zu besitzen. Er wußte nicht, daß das der Tod sei.

The paragraph is interesting because of the unusual construction of the judgement — he does what is morally binding on him, but he does not do it on moral grounds — and also because here, as before, we see one thread drawing up another: death enters the field on the side of the forces of separation.

Death lies right across this piece, from its title, 'Posthuma', to its concluding words, '. . . gezwungen, eine Tote zu lieben'. The opening paragraphs describe a funeral procession, and then the way the seasons pass over the grave in which the narrow coffin rests. The scene of the clandestine meeting (the story is told in retrospect) opens with a notably terse and assertive statement:

> zwei kinderblaue Augen sahen in die seinen.
>   Sie trug den Tod schon in sich; noch aber war sie jung und schön; noch reizte sie und wurde noch begehrt.

and ends with the equally terse reference I quoted before ('er wußte nicht, daß das der Tod sei'). Strikingly, death is seen not as an experience or happening but as a concrete entity, on the one hand a thing carried in the person like a germ or cancer, on the other hand a 'jemand', a personality gaining control of other personalities. The girl is always under sentence: she is hot and feverish in the cold garden where she meets the man, and she is emaciated, almost weightless in his arms. A week after the meeting she must take to her bed, and two months later she is dead. In her death there is an irony that may be a judgement on the young man's turpitude: only after she is dead does he begin to love her, and his love is not enriching, but something to which he is 'compelled', almost condemned.

So the causality is complex; the social difference, the inequality of affection with its moral undertones, and the intervention of death all seem to be working together to frustrate the possibility of loving union. No one cause is sufficient in itself; the disparities of class and affection are shown to be superable in that the man later comes to love the girl, only to be separated from her by her death; her death in turn, while making union impossible, may yet be said to have inspired the man's desire for union, for one cannot think that the same development would have taken place in him had she not died. The factors are intricately interwoven (and it is worth remembering here that Storm has created this complex in a story just over a thousand words long). The composite effect is clear enough: something always gets in the way. The social difference makes the meetings difficult and tense; the two must meet outside, even in the cold season, and it is suggested obliquely that this hastens the girl's death:

> Nachts im kalten Vorfrühling, in ihrem vertragenen Kleidchen kam sie zu ihm in den Garten; er konnte sie nicht anders sehen.

The tensions entailed by the need for clandestine meetings are joined by those inherent in the personal situation: 'Sie liebte ihn . . . er liebte sie nicht'. When the one difficulty is overcome, the other takes its place to put the edge of sadness on the encounter. And by the time real love has grown in the man, eliminating the personal difficulty and presumably invalidating the social one, the object of his love is dead, gone to that nothingness from which there is no recall and in which there is for Storm no reunion.

Something always gets in the way; faced with the mere possibility of an intense relationship, life and circumstance, as if by a law, subject that possibility to a series of assaults which are in sum irresistible. That is one theme. Then there is the possible moral connotation: the man's moral failure being punished by the compulsion to love a dead woman. And there is also room for speculation in psychological terms: how much of the young man's unhappy development is due to an inability to enter into any relationship at all, causing him to reject her while she lives but to love her when she dies — *because* she dies — and to form this posthumous attachment as a defence against the necessity of commitment to others? Such an interpretation would give the young man affinities with Franz Jebe, the central character of a much later story, *Ein Bekenntnis* (1887),[35] though in the small compass of *Posthuma* the problem clearly cannot be worked out in anything like the same detail. Fritz Böttger, in the few lines he devotes to the story, calls it a 'psychologisch merkwürdige kleine Skizze',[36] and, surprisingly for him, omits all reference to the social theme; which is indication enough that the psychological aspect is worthy of attention.

At the end of the skein of cause and effect we find, as might be expected, the situation and condition of loneliness, briefly pointed. The young man is isolated, sleepless in a sleeping world, bound to the dead in a relationship for which there is no fulfilment but which yet excludes him from valid relationship with the living:

> Es war Nacht geworden. In der Stadt waren die Fenster dunkel, es schlief schon alles; nur oben in den hohen Zimmern eines großen Hauses wachte noch ein junger Mann . . .
> Er hing den Rosenkranz über das schwarze Kreuz; dann lehnte er den Kopf daran. — Der Wächter ging draußen vorüber; aber er bemerkte ihn nicht . . .
> Er lebte in einer Stunde, die nicht mehr war, umfangen von zwei Mädchenarmen, die sich längst über einem stillen Herzen geschlossen hatten.
> . . . seit ihrem Tode ist seine Begierde erloschen; er trägt jetzt schon jahrelang ihr frisches Bild mit sich herum und ist gezwungen, eine Tote zu lieben.

The social pressure which makes itself felt in *Posthuma*, as one of several factors which combine to draw the man and the girl apart, comes more clearly to the fore in *Im Sonnenschein* — if anything can be said to come clearly to the fore in this story where all is veiled, all is conjecture. *Im Sonnenschein,* which Storm wrote in 1854, exchanges the psychological oddity for a formal one: it consists of two short scenes separated by a gap in narrated time of no less than sixty years. Paul Heyse, in a letter[37] full of the nervous wit and energy which made him a superb companion but a highly unstable man, accuses Storm of serving up a mouth-watering dish of hors-d'oeuvres, then missing out the main course and asking his literary guests to be content with 'ein wenig Kaltaufgeschnittenem, . . . das immer noch delikat genug ist, aber eine volle Mahlzeit nicht ersetzen kann'. After one or two more mercurial changes of metaphor, Heyse goes on to suggest that the two scenes would be fine as the introductory and concluding chapters of a novel — 'aber wo Teufel bleibt der Roman?' Storm replied with the vague promise to make some changes in the story;[38] in fact, though, he never went back to it. The two scenes, 'durch ahnungsvolle Fäden verknüpft',[39] remain in their original form.

The first scene describes what one imagines to be one of many meetings between a merchant's daughter, Fränzchen, and a young cavalry officer, Konstantin. They meet secretly in the garden of Fränzchen's family home; but here the similarity with *Posthuma* ends. It is not a cold spring night but a warm summer afternoon, and the atmosphere between Fränzchen and Konstantin is loving, happy, and perceptibly, though not heavily, erotic. The second scene is a conversation between a young man called Martin and his grandmother. The old lady, it transpires, is the widow of Fränzchen's brother (who appeared very briefly in the first scene); she recalls moments from her youth, and through her recollections Martin learns (and we learn) that Fränzchen herself never married and died while still young. The story goes, says the grandmother, that Fränzchen did have a lover, who was an officer; but her father forbade the match, and shortly afterwards the officer resigned his commission and went away to live with his sister; he remained unmarried as well. These recollections, called up by the repairs which are being carried out in the family grave, are at length banished by present concerns; for Martin is to be married soon. And with that the story is over.

Two scenes to illuminate a whole destiny in a whole social scheme: Storm seems here to be pushing to its limit the technique we saw him using in *Immensee*, progressions and developments only implied in the way that points on a graph imply a curve.[40] He is usually drawn toward the scenic representation in his early work, avoiding the panoramic sweep; the linking passage between the two scenes is characteristically tense, as though Storm doesn't like the job and is anxious to have done with it:

> Es war eine andere Zeit; wohl über sechzig Jahre später. Aber es war wieder an einem Sommernachmittage, und die Rosen blühten auch wie dazumal. — In dem oberen Zimmer nach dem Garten hinaus saß eine alte Frau. (SW I 463)

The lapse of years stated, the time of day fixed, a Gedankenstrich, and at once we are back with a directly viewed situation. It is in the moment shown as it happens that Storm takes it upon himself to tell his story.

The story is different now from what it was in *Posthuma*. Death casts no threatening shadow over the relation; it does not come till afterwards, when the relation has long been severed; it is there only in the opened grave and in the landscapes viewed by an old woman who remembers. Nor are unequal affections a part of the matter; what there is between Konstantin and Fränzchen flows both ways. The story this time is of the embodiment of 'the way things are' in a social and parental demand.

Konstantin is an officer, Fränzchen is from the Bürgerstand; their desire for union cuts across the eighteenth-century class structure. It is not that the aristocratic officer-class is felt superior to the merchant class;[41] in fact the text indicates the opposite. Almost the first words exchanged by Fränzchen and Konstantin are these:

> 'Rechne ein andermal, Fränzchen!' sagte der junge Mann.
> Sie schüttelte den Kopf. 'Morgen ist Klosterrechnungstag; ich muß das fertigmachen'. Und sie setzte ihre Arbeit fort.
> 'Du bist ein Federheld!'
> 'Ich bin eine Kaufmannstochter!'
> Er lachte.
> 'Lache nicht! Du weißt, wir können die Soldaten eigentlich nicht leiden'.
> 'Wir? Welche wir sind das?'
> 'Nun, Konstantin' — und dabei rückte ihre Feder addierend die Zahlenreihen hinunter —, 'wir, die ganze Firma!'
> 'Du auch, Fränzchen?'
> 'Ach! Ich' — — Und sie ließ die Feder fallen und warf sich an seine Brust, daß sich ein leichtes Puderwölkchen über ihren Köpfen erhob. (SW I 458f.)

And the contentment of the afternoon spent together is qualified by other hints — the obscene and threatening blackness of a slug on a honeysuckle blossom, (SW I 460f.) the joking protest that singing 'taugt für Bürgermädchen nicht', (SW I 462) and above all the sound of a harsh voice coming from an upstairs window. (SW I 459)

The voice is that of Fränzchen's father, talking about the weather in between games of 'Tokadille' with a business associate. The father's role in the scheme is suggested in greater detail in the second, retrospective scene, and it emerges that his exceptionally stern and patriarchal personality is the principal agent in enforcing the unwritten social law that comes between Fränzchen and Konstantin. The old man appears repeatedly in the grandmother's recollections. The first mention of him points to his material success and highly respected position in the community, as 'Klostervorsteher', 'Ratsverwandter' and finally 'zweiter Bürgermeister'; (SW I 466) then the grandmother makes a bald statement of his social prejudice, telling Martin:

> '(Konstantin) war ein Freund deines Großvaters und ein reputierlicher Mensch. Aber er war Offizier und Edelmann; und dein Urgroßvater war immer sehr gegen das Militär'. SW I 466)

A little later she talks of the overwhelming personal domination this man exercised over his children:

> 'was wißt ihr junges Volk auch, wie es dazumalen war. Ihr habt die harte Hand nicht über euch gefühlt; ihr wißt es nicht, wie mäuschenstille wir bei unsern Spielen wurden, wenn wir den Rohrstock unseres Vaters nur von ferne auf den Steinen hörten'. (SW I 466)

And the picture is completed with the most disturbing revelation of all, prefaced with a detail of the man's physical appearance:

> Der Enkel betrachtete das Bild des Urgroßvaters, und seine Augen blieben an den strengen Linien haften, die den starken Mund von den Wangen schieden. 'Es muß ein harter Mann gewesen sein', sagte er.
> Die Großmutter nickte. 'Er hat seine Söhne bis in ihr dreißigstes Jahr erzogen', sagte sie. 'Sie haben darum bis in ihr spätes Alter auch niemals so recht einen eigenen Willen gehabt. Dein Großvater hat es oft genug beklagt. Er wäre am liebsten ein Gelehrter geworden, wie du es bist; aber die Firma verlangte einen Nachfolger. Es waren damals eben andere Zeiten'.(SW I 467)

'Es waren damals eben andere Zeiten' — in those words the two forces, the man and his time, come together and are indissoluble. Only such a father could enforce a code so strictly, but only such a code could produce such a father.

Yet one obscurity remains. The powers ranged against Fränzchen and Konstantin — a social situation linked with the demands of a dominating father — are shown clearly enough; what is not clear is why these powers should prove in the end unconquerable, or at least unconquered on this occasion. The minute indications we are given (minute indications are the currency of this story, as they were of *Immensee*) suggest that the two lovers are strong and ready to fight for their freedom of choice; this is especially true of Fränzchen, who shows herself to be a self-possessed and determined young woman. Her demeanour towards Konstantin is by no means slavish and permissive, like the girl's love in *Posthuma*; on the contrary, she emerges very much as a mature and independent partner in an equal relationship, perhaps by a fraction the dominant partner: she is never at his beck and call (he has to wait while she finishes her accounts, and so on), and is sure enough of herself to be able to laugh at him. A certain quality of firmness and resolve is indicated by this exchange:

> Von der Stadt herüber kam der Schall einer Militärmusik. Die Augen des jungen Kapitäns leuchteten. 'Das ist mein Regiment!' sagte er und hielt das Mädchen mit beiden Armen fest.
> Sie bog sich lächelnd mit dem Oberkörper von ihm ab. 'Es hilft dir aber alles nicht!'.
> 'Was soll denn daraus werden? '
> Sie hob sich auf den Fußspitzen zu ihm heran und sagte: 'Eine Hochzeit!'
> 'Aber die Firma, Fränzchen!'
> 'Ich bin meines Vaters Tochter'. Und sie sah ihn mit ihren klugen Augen an. (SW I 459)

The import of this passage is not clear; we are being asked, I think, to look behind the words and guess at the associations they have for the lovers, who are alluding in their private language to something they are well aware of and have presumably discussed before. Is Konstantin suggesting a relationship outside marriage, hoping that the sound of the military band, a reminder of his virile status as a soldier, will somehow help to win Fränzchen over? Is she warning him that she will not countenance anything apart from marriage, or reassuring him that she will not let her family stand in the way of her marrying him? If she is speaking reassuringly, then her subsequent words become meaningful: her claim that she is 'her father's daughter' will then mean that she feels herself to be as strong-willed as her father and quite able to stand up to him. This would be confirmed again by what she says a moment later, after hearing the voice from the upstairs window; she talks in an amused, almost a condescending tone about her father's habits and mannerisms, (SW I 459) and one has the feeling that she does not find him by any means perfect or awe-inspiring.

However that may be, Fränzchen is strong in her love for Konstantin and ready to resist her father if necessary. This part of her character is taken up again in the second scene; the old lady remembers:

> 'Unsere alte Anne konnte nicht genug davon erzählen, wie lustig und umgänglich ihre Mamsell in jüngeren Jahren gewesen sei; auch war sie die einzige von den Kindern, die bei Gelegenheit mit dem Vater ein Wort zu reden wagte ...'

But then — and here is the obscurity — the grandmother continues:

> '... zu reden wagte. — Solange ich sie gekannt, ist sie immer still und für sich gewesen; zumal wenn der Vater im Zimmer war, sprach sie nur das Notwendige und wenn sie just gefragt wurde'. (SW I 467)

Why the change? Why did this strong young woman, stronger even than her brothers, finally give in and allow her father to override her claim to independent fulfilment? What paralysed her will to live according to her own wishes, or indeed her will to live at all? There is no answer now, and if there ever was one, it is buried with the dead:

> 'Was da passiert sein mag; — dein Großvater hat nie davon gesprochen. Nun sind sie alle längst begraben'. (SW I 467)

So ultimately we do not know the 'real' reason. We can see the confrontation between the two opposing forces — love and free choice against class and paternal domination — but we cannot see why the battle goes one way when the signs were that it would go the other.[42] I suggest that to find the reason we have to come back to Storm's peculiar fatalism, the feeling that the attempt at a real loving union is doomed to failure from the start, just because such a union is more than a human goal. Storm writes and thinks in images, so we must be content with an image[43] as an answer beyond words: the two heads close together, the woman's hair powdered but the man's sleek and black, and the little cloud of powder that rises as she comes against him.

The incompleteness of *Im Sonnenschein,* the suggested but not quite adequate cause, also characterises *Drüben am Markt* (1860-1), though here the situation is slightly different: it is not the joint wishes of man and woman that are thwarted, but the man's suit that is rejected by the woman. One of the last scenes of *Drüben am Markt* is a conversation between the little Doktor and his friend the Justizrat.[44] It becomes clear from the context that the doctor has sent his friend to the burghermaster's daughter, Mamsell Sophie, to make to her on his behalf something like a proposal of marriage; and the Justizrat has just returned with her refusal. All she said, he reports, was 'Ich kann es nicht', several times over. The doctor asks if she said why, the Justizrat replies that she did not. The doctor gets up and walks over to the mirror, to gaze moodily at his own rather ugly face and figure:

> Der Freund sah gespannt zu ihm hinüber. Jetzt, jetzt mußte er selbst die Antwort auf seine Frage finden. — Aber er fand sie nicht; er wandte sich und begann zu sprechen. 'Eduard', sagte er leise, und es war, als blieben ihm die Worte in der Kehle hängen, 'Ich denke wohl kaum, daß es wegen meiner alten Mutter ist'.
> Der Justizrat richtete sich fast wie erschrocken in die Höhe; über seine regelmäßigen und sonst wohl kalten Züge zuckte es wie etwas, das er nicht bekämpfen könne. (SW I 560)

What is this answer? At first it seems obvious: the Justizrat thinks the doctor will find it himself as he looks in the mirror, the answer therefore being that he is simply unattractive, even physically repellent. But when the doctor obliquely gives that answer (for I take it that when he says 'I hardly think it's because of my mother' he means 'it must be because of me personally'), his friend seems startled — this is not the answer *he* was expecting, evidently, and an indecipherable emotion passes across his face. It seems that we must look further; and as we look, complications begin to arise, just as they arose when we looked further in *Immensee.*

So far as I can see, the text suggests five possible reasons (apart from the strange and immediately dismissed one about his mother) why Sophie should reject the doctor; and equally, the text itself questions each one. Here again, it is not a matter of explicit statements made, and subsequently contradicted by events or other explicit statements; the material we have consists of small signs pointing in one direction and then more small signs pointing in the other. We *have* to give what at first seems undue weight to these things — there is nothing else to go on. The first possibility is the one seemingly considered and discarded in the scene I have just discussed: the possibility that Sophie is simply repelled by the little doctor's ill-favoured features and generally unkempt appearance. A good deal is made of the way the doctor looks and dresses, particularly in contrast to Sophie's neat prettiness, and there is one passage where her dislike of his untidiness seems to become clear:

> Das Mädchen, deren Hände auf ihrem sauberen Morgenkleide ruhten, musterte währenddessen die kleine untersetzte Gestalt des ihr gegenübersitzenden Mannes. Es entging ihr nichts; weder die Bänder des bescheidenen Vorhemdchens, die über den Rockkragen hervorsahen, noch der ungepflegte Zustand des Haupthaares, von dem unzählige Spitzen wie Flammen in die Höhe ragten. Zuletzt blieben ihre Augen an zwei kleinen Daunen haften, die, je nachdem der Doktor den Kopf bewegte, entweder wie aufstrebende Räupchen in der Luft gaukelten oder in das allgemeine Wirrsal wieder hinabtauchten. Mamsell Sophie strich sich unwillkürlich mit den Fingern über ihren seidenen Scheitel, und in ihrem Gesichtchen zuckte es wieder wie vorhin, da sie vor dem Branntweinfäßchen kniete. (SW I 549)

This last reference is to an incident a little earlier: Sophie had been helping in a shop and had had to fill a bottle with brandy; she had done so with a slight grimace and a shake of the head, 'als widre sie der Dunst des Alkohols'. (SW I 547) The inference is that she finds the doctor as unpleasant as the alcohol.[45] But a second later, this fleeting expression gives way to a deep blush, and then to silent laughter; it seems, then, that Mamsell Sophie is assailed with a mixture of emotions. And elsewhere there are other indications that she is not at all repelled by the doctor.[46]

Could it be, then, (and this is the second possibility), that she is not actively repelled but merely indifferent in a friendly way and ignorant of the doctor's feelings, so that his belief that she is fond of him is just an unfortunate mistake?[47] Looked at *in vacuo*, Sophie's words and actions can nowhere be said to signify definitely that she is positively attracted to the doctor, so strictly speaking it might be possible to claim that he does misinterpret what he sees. But there are several objections to that. In this story, as in *Immensee,* Storm is clearly representing certain patterns of experience which seem to him important in governing the way men live and what happens to them — he is conveying his particular 'truths about life'. Here, as there, he is tracing the pattern of reticence, the 'truth' that people are not generally very loquacious about the emotions and desires.[48] We cannot expect Sophie (particularly her, but also the doctor) to make outright declarations of undying love from the start; for Storm, that would be not only a minor lapse of naturalistic verisimilitude but also a major offence against the truth of human experience. We have to 'read the signs' in life, and so Storm in his story gives us only the signs to read. That is why I feel justified in talking, for example, of what Sophie's words and actions suggest, rather than of what they say or mean. And the suggestion is usually in the direction of interest, attraction, fondness and potential love — she has moments of coquetry, she remembers with amused pleasure two dances with the doctor, some time later she asks him for another and is hurt by his refusal, and so the feeling is built up. And her answer to the proposal of marriage, too, is couched in words which seem not to indicate indifference. If she felt nothing for him and had no awareness, let alone intention, of encouraging his affection and hopes, surely her tone would have been one of surprise, a protest that she had no idea he felt this way? But the oft-repeated 'Ich kann es nicht', the hand tracing invisible letters on the marble table-top,[49] does not suggest surprise but something else, the sense of a possibility seriously considered, and ultimately rejected, before the proposal is ever made. 'Ich kann es nicht' — Sophie seems to have expected the question; her answer is ready, and she will say no more.

So the third possibility arises: it may be that Sophie does care for the doctor at first, but that she becomes impatient with his lack of energy in courting her and alienated by his occasional perverse rejections when she tries to approach him. The doctor is undoubtedly an odd little man, shy and gauche and resentfully aware of his plebeian origins; there is a charm about him, certainly, which resides in his kind and cheerful nature, his fine eyes and 'sein volles herzliches Lachen, dem weder seine Mutter noch einer seiner Freunde widerstehen konnte'; (SW I 551) but he is without grace and social skill, and his acute consciousness of this leads him to act hurtfully and even against his own desire. He stays away from a soirée at the Justizrat's family home, knowing that Sophie will be there, (SW I 553f.) and then later he refuses to dance with her, in a scene which is clearly meant to be significant:

> 'Wir sind beim Pfänderspiel', rief sie und streckte ihm lächelnd die Hand entgegen. 'Sie sollen Zweitritt mit mir tanzen!'
> Er blickte auf. Ihr Antlitz war gerötet vom Spiel und von der Sommerluft, ihre Augen glänzten; der weiße Florschal hatte sich verschoben und hing über die Schulter hinab. — Der Doktor schwieg noch eine Weile. 'Sie dürfen es mir nicht übel deuten, Mamsell Sophie', sagte er dann, ohne die dargebotene kleine Hand zu nehmen, 'ich tanzte lieber nicht'.
> 'Also ein Korb, Herr Doktor?'
> Der Justizrat legte beide Hände auf die Schultern seines Freundes. 'Doktor', sagte er, indem er langsam den Kopf schüttelte, 'ich glaube fast, die Luft in deinem Prunksaal hat dich krank gemacht!'
> Der Doktor fühlte, wie ihm die Röte ins Gesicht stieg, und er neigte den Kopf, um es zu verbergen. (SW I 559)

It appears that the doctor, caught in his little vortex of self-hatred, is deliberately provoking the reaction he desires least of all: he is embarrassing and alienating Sophie. If that were all, then the cause would be found; but it is not all. Sophie refuses to be alienated; with her considerable personal strength and (one guesses) her understanding of the doctor's particular anxieties, she rides out the squall, refuses to be angry, and keeps the future open:

> Als er wieder aufblickte, waren die Augen des Mädchens mit einem Ausdruck von Güte auf ihn gerichtet ...

> Dann ging sie, aber im Fortgehen wandte sie noch einmal den Kopf
> zurück. 'Ich habe warten gelernt', rief sie, 'wir tanzen doch noch miteinander!'
> (SW I 559)

That, in the symbolic shorthand of Storm's early work, seems to me to mean that
she does not blame him for his difficulties and is content to wait until he has
resolved them.

But still, in the end, she refuses him, and there is no clear reason yet. The
fourth possibility takes us outside the purely personal problems of the attachment:
could 'Ich kann es nicht' mean 'Ich darf es nicht'? The doctor is from a humble
background, and Sophie is the daughter of the burghermaster; the social difference
is larger than it might seem, and a good deal of attention is accorded it in the text.
The doctor's allegiance to the social group into which he was born is never shaken;
he makes determined attempts to resist the cutting loose which could have resulted
from his studies and subsequent entry into the medical profession. He goes back to
live with his mother; he gives, and makes sure to be seen to give, preferential
treatment to his poorer patients, with the half-desired effect that his practice does
not attract the genteel; (SW I 541, 543) he is more at ease in a tavern by the
harbour drinking grog than in the drawing-rooms of polite society; (SW I 553, 563)
he is inclined to lash out irritably at the manners of 'die feinen Leute'. (SW I 541, 559)
All in all, the doctor is a fairly militant representative of his class; and over
against him, Sophie's father the burghermaster is just as jealous of *his*. We witness
one encounter between the two men, and the tension is evident enough:

> Vor dem Rathause begegnete ihm der Herr Bürgermeister, der mit seinem
> Portefeuille unter dem Arm soeben aus der Ratssitzung kam. Es war eine
> stattliche Gestalt; er trug den starken Kopf aufrecht und trat so fest einher,
> daß ihm bei jedem Schritt die wohlgenährten Wangen schütterten. – Nachdem
> er den jungen Arzt nicht ohne eine gewisse Herablassung gegrüßt hatte,
> erkundigte er sich eingehend nach dem Befinden seines alten Handlungsdieners,
> und so schritten beide im Gespräche miteinander über den Markt. Der Doktor
> aber wußte nicht, weshalb es ihm heute unbehaglich war, sich diesen huldreich
> zu ihm redenden Herrn als den Vater jenes hübschen Mädchens zu denken;
> immer wieder, bis vor der Tür des großen Giebelhauses, zu der er ihn zurück-
> begleitete, stand es vor seiner Seele, wie unbequem es sein müsse, diesem
> gewichtigen Mann eine Bitte vorzutragen oder im geheimen Zwiegespräch
> gegenüberzustehen. (SW I 550f.)

A decided social disparity, then: is it *these* considerations (perhaps reinforced
by a fatherly directive) that ultimately stand in the way of a match between the
gently-reared Sophie and the lower-born and less polished doctor?[50] But this
possibility falls down for lack of further evidence (even Storm's minimal sort of
evidence) to support it. All the other indications suggest that it is the doctor's
anxieties and prejudices that have to be overcome, not Sophie's (or her father's);
and presumably the fact that he eventually makes a proposal means that he *has*
overcome his doubts. And even if Sophie were indeed under pressure from her

family, we should be faced with the situation we saw in *Im Sonnenschein*: the motiveless acquiescence of a young woman who is deliberately represented as being self-possessed and determined to live her own life according to her principles and desires. That she is a young woman in command of her destiny is an impression that arises from the text clearly yet in ways so subtle that I find it difficult to pinpoint them. Nonetheless, one only has to place her in one's mind beside a woman like Elisabeth of *Immensee* for her individual qualities of strength and independence to become obvious. There is in fact one definite clue to this side of her character. It comes from the lips of Friedeberg, the old man who runs a shop on the mayoral premises (it is through treating Friedeberg that the doctor is first brought into close contact with Sophie). Sophie is looking after the shop and serving behind the counter while the old man is unwell; he is grateful for her help, but says:

> 'aber es schickt sich nicht so recht, und der Herr Bürgermeister sehen es auch nicht gern'. (SW I 548)

Sophie is following her conscience and helping someone who needs help, in spite of her father's disapproval (I draw this general inference from those few words because, as I said, that is what the narrative method of this story demands of its reader). That makes it all the less likely that she will give in to family pressure on the matter of whom she should have for a husband. To motivate such a surrender, there would have to be similar particular incidents, other chance words, indicating that she *is* in the end subservient to her father's wishes. But there are none; wherever we look we find signs pointing in the opposite direction. So the social causality does not work properly either.

The fifth possible reason – one which is rarely considered, though it seems to me no less plausible (or no more implausible) than the others – is that Sophie prefers the Justizrat to the doctor. She does, after all, eventually marry the Justizrat, who is clearly represented as the better match in terms of birth, upbringing, professional status, and personal charm and accomplishment. The fact of this marriage makes meaningful in retrospect two very obscure places in the account of the doctor's hesitant courtship. The first comes after the doctor refuses Sophie's request for a dance.[51]

> Die beiden Freunde blieben noch lange im geheimen Zwiegespräch in der Laube sitzen. Einige Tage später aber ging auch der Justizrat in auffallender Nachdenklichkeit umher; sein indisches Schnupftuch hing ihm ungewöhnlich lang aus der Tasche, und mehr als sonst schob er die goldene Brille auf die Stirn und rieb sich kopfschüttelnd mit der Hand die Augen. (SW I 559)

And the second is the description of the Justizrat's curious reaction (which I quoted earlier)[52] when the doctor hazards his guess at why Sophie has rejected the proposal. So it could be just a question of rivalry between friends – one of them unconscious of the rivalry – with the better man winning. But during the time when the actual events of the story take place (they are in fact recounted as memories in the doctor's mind many years later), there is no hint at all that Sophie looks kindly on the Justizrat, nor that the latter has any intention of conducting a courtship on his own account. Moreover, it seems unlikely that a man would consent to present his friend's proposal of marriage to a woman he already wanted to marry himself. I cannot think that a massive irony is intended here; it would be out of character with the rest of the story, and anyway, apart from the two references I have mentioned, there is not a single word that could be seen in any way as exploiting such an irony. In the closing paragraphs the doctor, returned from his memories to the present, looks out of his window at the house across the market square:

> Dort wohnte sie noch jetzt, wie sie es einst getan; sie wohnte dort mit dem Justizrat, den sie im Lauf der Jahre geheiratet hatte, noch jetzt im Alter heiter und geliebt, wie sie es einst in ihrer Jugend gewesen war. (SW I 562)

'Im Lauf der Jahre' — that suggests a firm separation from the time of the doctor's courtship; it suggests also a marriage calmly entered upon, a match agreed by all parties to be a respectable and favourable one; something altogether less dramatic than a choice between rivals.

A multitude of causes, then, and yet no cause; reasons seemingly considered only to be discarded; no one interpretation fitting all the facts and all the indications which here do service for facts — it is all very much like *Immensee*. And we are led by default to much the same vague conclusion: that the doctor is denied his fulfilment somehow 'because' he seeks it at all, that in loving and wanting his love returned he is trying to break away from the gravitational pull of that condition which is the human norm, the condition of being alone. In the world that Storm sees and talks of, something will always get in the way.

The notion of failure not wholly motivated is one which in these early stories seems to emerge behind a veil of apparent motivation. We try each reason and find it wanting, and in the end we arrive at a point where we cannot push any further back; our explanation is there because it is all we are left with. There are a couple of stories, though, in which the veil is drawn aside: reasons are clearly given and then just as clearly set aside as inadequate, and we are brought face to face with 'the way things are', the absolute condition of things, in a way which so purely defies logic and expectation that it comes disquietingly close to the absurd.

The first of these stories is *Angelika* (1855). It is the simple line of the action here that traces out the perverse movement of experience and leads to the conviction that whatever happens, whatever changes are brought about, whatever efforts are made, something will always get in the way. Ehrhard and Angelika, friends since childhood, come to love each other with a strength which brings them to full physical union. But they cannot marry; Ehrhard's profession, we are told (though we do not know what it is),[53] makes it completely impossible for him to take a wife. Their meetings have to be secret, and this, together with the fact that no future is possible for them together, imposes a strain which becomes less and less tolerable, particularly for Angelika. Gradually, though with frequent reconciliations, she grows away from him; he begins to see her frequently in the company of another man, a doctor — with whom she admittedly does not seem very happy. Ehrhard moves away, and for a while the contact is severed; but after a year, sudden (unspecified) changes in the political situation improve his position so much that his (unspecified) profession no longer debars him from marrying. He rushes home to see Angelika and tell her the good news, but on his arrival he is told that she has become engaged to the doctor; so he goes away again despairing. But then, some time later, he hears by letter that Angelika is suddenly free, and ready, to marry him; her fiancé has died before the wedding could take place. Convinced of her love now, he is overwhelmed with memories of her; alone in his room, in passionate longing and expectancy, he calls out her name — and then comes the second and final volte-face:

> Aber sie kam nicht, die er rief, sie konnte nicht mehr kommen; der Zauber ihres Wesens, wie er noch einmal vom Abendschein erinnernder Liebe angestrahlt schien, war in der ganzen Welt nur noch in seiner Brust zu finden . . .
> Und als er endlich seiner Sinne und seiner Seele wieder Herr geworden war, da wußte er auch, daß er erst jetzt Angelika verloren und daß sein Verhältnis zu ihr erst jetzt für immer abgeschlossen und zu Ende sei. (SW I 490)

Ehrhard realises that his real feeling for the real Angelika is quite dead: he has been sustained only by an image of his own making, painfully in love with a figure of fantasy. The Angelika to whom he would now have to make a living commitment is someone quite different and unknown and irrelevant to his life.

Here is the perversity, the approach to the absurd, of which I spoke. Mutual love is first denied its fulfilment by a force hanging over them both, Ehrhard's profession. That force is removed, only to be replaced by another.— Angelika has stopped waiting for Ehrhard and is engaged to someone else. When *that* force in its turn is removed, yet another appears and finally destroys the former love — Ehrhard discovers that his desire to marry Angelika has gone from him entirely. And I suggest the feeling grows in us that the whole enterprise was doomed from the start, simply because it was that kind of enterprise. Something always gets in the way, and this time things get in the way with a symmetrical, chilling precision; there is the sense of circumstances deliberately arranging themselves (even working through emotional structures) to make the love between Ehrhard and Angelika impossible, for no other reason than that it tries to exist at all.

The other story is *In St Jürgen,* which was written in 1867 but feels a good deal earlier.[54] Here again, it is the action itself, rather than the mood or characterisation, that holds the clue. The story of Agnes Hansen and Harre Jensen is pieced together from the account each gives on separate occasions to the grandson of Agnes' former mistress. Agnes tells the first half, Harre overlaps slightly and then gives the second; and the conclusion is witnessed by the story-teller himself.

Agnes and Harre become betrothed after knowing each other throughout childhood; Harre is an orphan, and Agnes' father acts as trustee for his small inheritance. Harre is close to the completion of his apprenticeship to a master-carpenter, and almost in a position to marry Agnes, when her father goes bankrupt, his downfall hastened by an unscrupulous 'Goldmacher' who exploits his superstitious hopes of finding the treasure which local legend says is hidden at the bottom of a well in his garden. In his desperation, Agnes' father throws Harre's inheritance, as well as his own money, into the crackpot scheme, and everything is lost. Harre, rather than subject the old man to the humiliation of being confronted with the person whose trust he has betrayed, decides he must go away and find work elsewhere (he says he can now no longer hope to become a master-craftsman anyway), and return only when he has enough to support a wife and when everything has been forgotten. He will not write, he says, but will return as soon as the time comes. There is one last meeting in the church-tower, up among the circling swallows, then Harre takes his leave. The years pass, but he does not return, and no word is heard from him. Agnes' father dies: she goes into domestic service (with the story-teller's grandmother) and eventually retires, being given a place in the town's home for old people, the 'St Jürgenstift' (hence the title of the story). During her years of work, she has managed to save out of her earnings a sum equivalent to Harre's lost inheritance; it will be there for him when he comes back, as she is sure he will — even though nearly forty years have passed and she has never heard a word from him.

That is Agnes' part of the tale. Harre's account takes it up at their parting; with the delicacy of the good man he obviously is, he makes no mention of the reasons why he had to go, saying only that he lost his property 'durch einen unerwarteten Zufall'. (SW II 227) Harre travels south, first to Vienna and then to Württemberg, where he works for a young master-piano-maker. He is happy there and becomes more or less one of the family. But the business is not financially sound, and the strain and worry tell on the Meister; he falls fatally ill, and his last hours are filled with anguish at the thought of leaving his wife and children destitute. Harre makes a deathbed vow never to leave the family until they are freed from the threat of poverty. The climb back to a measure of prosperity takes a good many years; and by the time Harre has fulfilled his promise, the widow and her children are so dependent on him that they cannot bear to see him go. Finally, urged by the children, he marries the widow. But every spring, when the swallows come, he thinks of the swallows in the town of his birth and is tormented by the memory of Agnes and the promise he has broken. Later, at a moment of extreme tension,[55] he reveals everything to his wife, who had known nothing about Agnes before; this gives him some release. Many years pass; and every spring brings swallows and with them the undiminished memory of Agnes. In the end, his wife tells him that he must go home and make his peace with Agnes before he dies. So, an old man now, he embarks on the long journey back (it is on this journey that he meets the narrator and tells him the story). He arrives and goes to the St Jürgenstift, only to find that Agnes has died that very morning. There can be no explanations and no reconciliation now. As the story ends we see him pulling up the shroud which he had drawn back to take a last look at her face.

After fifty years, Harre comes half a day too late, and Agnes has died not knowing. And the reasons, though stated with perfect clarity, are so terribly inadequate. It happened because Harre had to go away, said he would not write, and married someone else. But why does Harre have to go away in the first place? There must be some less drastic way of salvaging the last shreds of self-respect in Agnes' father; and there is no obvious reason why he should be unable to finish his apprenticeship, in his hometown or elsewhere. Why does he say he will not write to Agnes while he is away? Surely it is vital that they should be sustained by each other in their separation, and (on a more practical level) that Agnes should know exactly how Harre's fortunes are progressing? And even if it were reasonable not to write at first, why does Harre not break his silence when it becomes evident that things are turning out very differently from what he had originally planned? She has a right to know, surely, that he is being kept away much longer than he intended, and later (above all) that he has married? He knows he has broken his vow to remain faithful and to return; could he not break the more trivial vow of silence? His deathbed promise to his master does put him in an ethical predicament; he says himself:

'Ich habe mein gegebenes Wort gehalten . . . aber da ich es gab, brach ich ein anderes; denn ich habe nun nicht fortgekonnt'. (SW II 233f.)

But the predicament is nowhere near fully worked out, nor is it really forceful; there must be many ways of arranging things so that the two promises do *not* clash. And why does he allow himself to be coaxed into marrying his master's widow? He does, admittedly, give a reasonably convincing justification for staying with them longer than he wishes:

> An einem solchen Morgen erklärte ich einmal, daß ich nun fort müsse,
> daß es jetzt endlich Zeit sei, auch an mein eignes Leben zu denken. Aber die
> beiden Knaben brachen in laute Wehklagen aus, und die Mutter setzte, ohne
> ein Wort zu sagen, ihr Töchterchen auf meinen Schoß, das sogleich die kleinen
> Arme fest um meinen Hals schlang. — Mein Herz hing an den Kindern, lieber
> Herr; ich konnte die Kinder nicht verlassen. Ich dachte: 'Bleib denn noch ein
> Jahr'. Der Abgrund zwischen mir und meiner Jugend wurde immer tiefer;
> zuletzt lag alles wie unerreichbar hinter mir, wie Träume, an die ich nicht
> mehr denken dürfe . . .

But the reasons he gives for going so far as marrying the widow are ludicrously
lacking in force:

> . . . nicht mehr denken dürfe. — Ich war schon über die Vierzig hinaus, da
> schloß ich *auf den Wunsch der schon herangewachsenen Kinder* das Ehebündnis
> mit der Frau, *deren einzige Stütze ich so lange gewesen war.* (SW II 235)

When Harre at last overcomes these difficulties which are patently, almost grossly,
not difficulties, when he in fact fulfils to the letter his promise to Agnes, he arrives
a few hours after she has been lost to him beyond reach. If he had set out on his
journey the year before — the *day* before — he could have made his peace with
Agnes, and she could have died, if not happy, then at least with her mind set at
rest. As it is, her fifty years of waiting (and I shall talk more of them later) have
been made totally meaningless by the accident of half a day.

It is all implausible. The fact that Harre is kept away from Agnes by such
inadequate considerations is entirely out of tune with the character of the deeply
virtuous and honourable man that Storm clearly intends him to be; and the 'timing'
— a few hours late after fifty years — bears no resemblance to the undramatic
untidiness of life as we know it. These objections are forcibly made by Wolfgang
Kayser (the 'Vorlage' he refers to here is the story called *Das Heimweh* which
Storm took as his model for *In St Jürgen*):

> Der zweite Teil der Novelle gehört dem Alten, der seinen Lebensweg
> wie in der Vorlage selber erzählt. Storm schließt sich gelegentlich wörtlich
> an und übernimmt den Inhalt im ganzen. Aber er bringt nun doch ein Neues
> hinein und das ist die lückenlose psychologische Motivation; daß seine Liebe
> zu weit und abgeblaßt hinter ihm lag, daß das 'rein menschliche Bedürfnis
> nach einer festeren Heimstätte', wie Storm es später formulierte, in ihm
> mächtig war, daß seine Umgebung ihm die Erfüllung bot und ihn dahin
> drängte. Diese ganze Motivation kann man nur bedingt gelten lassen, nämlich
> nur unter der Voraussetzung, daß der Mann ein Schwächling ist . . . Freilich
> paßt die Schwäche, die an dem Heiligsten sündigt, nicht zu dem Bild, das
> sonst von diesem Mann gezeichnet wird . . .
> Völlig unecht wirkt bei Storm der Schluß. In der Vorlage erfährt der Mann
> in der Heimat, daß die Geliebte schon vierzig Jahre tot ist, hier ist sie an dem
> Morgen seiner Ankunft gestorben. Übelste Sentimentalität führt aus aller
> glaubhaften Realität heraus.[56]

I think Kayser is quite right about the weakness of motivation and inconsistent characterisation of Harre on the one hand, and about the desertion of 'glaubhafte Realität' in the conclusion on the other. But supposing these things did *not* just imply a badly wrought piece of work, and supposing the end were *not* just sickly sentimentality?

Storm himself was well aware of the first objection (though not, so far as one can see, of the second); in one letter he writes:

> Mit meinem 'St Jürgen' hast Du recht. Es liegt eine einfache Mitteilung aus einem unserer alten Volksbücher zugrunde; da aber wird der Mann wirklich untreu; und dabei hätte auch ich es lassen sollen, eine reelle Schuld wäre besser als diese Schwäche. Nun aber weiß ich nicht, ob sich's noch umschreiben läßt; und 'St Jürgen' muß sich vielleicht so durchschlagen.[57]

And in another he says this:

> Bei 'St Jürgen' hast Du wohl freundlich verschwiegen, was Dir nicht gefallen; jetzt, wo es alle Leute mir ins Ohr schreien − die meisten klammern sich freilich an die äußerliche Heirat −, sehe ich's freilich wohl, daß ich den Harre lieber mit einer Schuld der Leidenschaft als mit einer gutmütigen Schwäche hätte belasten sollen. Aber in dem Interesse an dem Problem, wie ich es jetzt behandelt, schrieb ich mit Scheuklappen an den Augen weiter und dachte nicht daran, daß ich meinen Helden damit um das Interesse der Leser brachte. Nun, trotz dessen ist wohl noch so viel daran, daß es auf den paar Bogen, die es einnimmt, existieren darf.[58]

What is most interesting about these quotations is the last sentence of each. The regretful statement of unwillingness to go through the business of recasting very probably implies a firm refusal to change, a more or less complete satisfaction with the story in its present form. For the tone of Storm's letters tends to be uncontentious and compliant; he seems almost excessively anxious not to tread on his correspondent's toes or open the way to acrimony; Kayser points out, 'daß Storm in seinen Briefen sich vielfach bis zur Selbstverleugnung auf die Meinung des Empfängers einstellt.'[59] It is arguable, then, that Storm liked the story as it was; he felt he had got it right, and his reflections about his writing never went much beyond that stage.[60]

We can draw the same conclusion, I think, about the ending, though for a different reason. One of the major changes which Storm makes in the purely factual skeleton he takes from *Das Heimweh* is the timing of Agnes' death. In the original story, by the time the man comes back the woman has been dead for forty years; Storm brings Agnes' death right up to the very day of Harre's arrival. A change as striking as that can hardly be fortuitous; Storm must have made it deliberately, wanting to achieve some effect. So we may be fairly sure that, in having made a decision of this kind, he has followed his own wishes, done what he wanted to do, and thus, in his own eyes, 'got it right'.

If this is so, then we have come back to what I said about *Immensee* − that the effect is in some sense intentional, that the cul-de-sacs are meant.[61] Only here the position is much more extreme: the cul-de-sacs never look like anything *but* cul-de-sacs; we are hardly deceived for a moment into thinking that they will lead anywhere. Harre's motivations are completely inadequate, Agnes' death is utterly contrived — *absurdly* inadequate, *absurdly* contrived.

That seems to me to be the key to *In St Jürgen.* A basic force of existence ('the way things are', the pull to solitude) decrees that these two people shall be drawn apart, because they seek a union in love. Axiomatically, that force will prevail, and the new statement this story makes is that, in prevailing, the force will override sense and circumstance and human will if necessary. In the other stories it has been hidden behind, or has shown itself through, a 'veil of apparent motivation'; the combination of real and discoverable reasons has played its part in bringing about the separation of those who want to be together. But in this story the force is naked; it needs no help from reasonable circumstance. The 'causes' are made deliberately derisory, so that no-one may be in any doubt but that we are presented, not with rational cause and effect, but with the irrational, absolute, absurd condition of things. And the absurdity is heightened by the tiny fraction of time which comes finally and irrevocably between Agnes and Harre. One feels that whatever day Harre had chosen to come back, Agnes would have died just before. The maximum of pain is exacted: as if in punishment for bearing a love that has tried to exist, Agnes is made to hope (and here that is to suffer) fruitlessly until the last possible moment, and then to die with no meaning given to her suffering. The game is played through to the very end; and in thinking of Agnes as a plaything we have come close to that terrible phrase at the end of Thomas Hardy's *Tess of the D'Urbervilles*: 'The President of the Immortals (in Aeschylean phrase) had ended his sport with Tess'. And *In St Jürgen,* this story that draws aside the veil and exposes Storm's early vision for what it is, leaves us with a true and lasting image, the image of an old man who draws back the shroud from a dead face, gazes for a while across it at a blank wall, and then draws the shroud gently up again.

Beneath the serene surface, then, these stories record the well-nigh inevitable failure of the loving enterprise. And with failure comes the return to the human norm, the norm of isolation. Marthe with her deceiving furniture and unhappy memories, and Reinhard with his old-fashioned clothes and distant greetings and studies that do not console, are joined by the young man alone by a grave at night, leaning his head on the wreathed cross, deaf to present sounds and lost to present relationships, faced always with the image of a dead love; and by Fränzchen, speaking little and apportioning no blame, visiting her brother now and then, wasting slowly away and in her sickness falling asleep over her columns of figures, dying young; and by the doctor, fishing on the dyke, approached by a woman who needs nothing from him but advice, stroking his dog 'mit jener hastigen Innigkeit, womit in Gegenwart anderer einsame Menschen den an sie gewöhnten Tieren zu begegnen pflegen', (SW I 540) sitting in his upstairs room which has been lavishly decorated to no purpose and unchanged over the years, looking through the window at a house whose lights remind him continually of his loss, seeking release in surface resentment and a glass of grog and rougher friends in a tavern; and by Ehrhard, waiting in the dark for a carriage to come by, pleading for a word with Angelika and being rejected, (SW I 478) asking questions and receiving no answers, (SW I 479f, 484) standing at a front door and hearing his hopes dashed, not in an honest though searing encounter with the woman he loves, but humiliatingly, in the unconcerned words of an inquisitive housemaid, (SW I 487) and in the end sitting alone and knowing that he has been viciously deceived by his own fantasy. (SW I 489f.) And the gallery[62] is completed by the portrait of Agnes Hansen, about whose sentence I would say a little more.

It is easy to forget (or rather, not to perceive) the full extent of what Agnes is made to suffer. Little is made of it in any specific way in the text — a consequence, I think, of the narrative standpoints the story adopts. Agnes, who tells the first part, is patently not the kind of person to dramatise her own troubles; Harre, who tells the second part, knows nothing about them; and the young man who brings the two halves together adds little personal comment, partly because he is content to reproduce without much embellishment what he hears from his interlocutors, and partly because of his own character as it emerges in what he writes — his tone contains a tiny element of self-congratulatory priggishness, as though he were rather pleased with himself at taking such a kindly interest in the humble destinies of these 'simple folk'. One has the impression that he does not ultimately make any real imaginative entry into their predicament, treating their story rather as an interesting case of love among the lower classes. The element *is* very slight, but it is there, and we have to remember that he is as much a character in the tale as they are, with a personality and possibly failings; to contemplate the facts we must look beneath *his* account as well, and not treat him as the final and governing authority.[63]

The first hint of Agnes' suffering comes when the story-teller recounts the memory of a childhood hour spent in her company. She taught him about the ways of swallows, he remembers, and then:

> 'Vom Turm aus', sagte Hansen, 'solltest du sie fliegen sehen; das heißt von dem Turm der alten Kirche, der noch ein Turm zu nennen war'.
>   Dann, mit einem Seufzer meine Wangen streichelnd, ging sie ins Haus zurück an die gewohnte Arbeit. 'Weshalb seufzt denn Hansen so?' dachte ich. (SW II 205f.)

Later he learns the reason for that sigh, as she tells him of her life. After describing how Harre came to her to say that he must leave, she goes on:

'Nach diesen Worten trennten wir uns; das Herz war wohl zu voll, als daß wir Weiteres hätten sprechen können'. —
Die Erzählerin schwieg eine Weile. Dann sagte sie: 'Am andern Morgen sah ich ihn noch einmal, und dann nicht mehr; das ganze lange Leben niemals mehr'.
Sie ließ den Kopf auf ihre Brust sinken; die Hände, die auf ihrem Schoß geruht hatten, wand sie leise umeinander, als müsse sie damit das Weh beschwichtigen, das, wie einst das Herz des jungen blonden Mädchens, so noch jetzt den gebrechlichen Leib der Greisin zittern machte. (SW II 219f.)

The sentence is passed; Agnes promises to wait, (SW II 230) and she keeps her promise, waiting in vain and without knowing it is in vain, not for a month or a year or two, but for fifty years. The idea is terrifying. Fifty years of her life are spent half-living, simply holding on to a provisional existence in preparation for the time when real living will start again. Keeping her promise is not a moral act but an act of necessity; she can do nothing else. This becomes clear when we think of her situation: she loves and trusts Harre and knows, with the knowledge of love, that he will come back as soon as he can; but she has no idea when, and this means (after perhaps the first few months) that he may return at literally any moment on any day. Every single moment throughout those fifty years *might* see him walking through her door; he does not come, but there is the next moment, and the next, which might bring him, and so she must see those moments out too. Her awareness of her plight hardly diminishes in intensity over this vast tract of time, as one might have expected it to; that we can deduce from what the story-teller says in my last quotation (especially the connection 'wie einst . . . noch jetzt'), and from the 'present' vividness and emotional involvement with which she recalls and recounts the events of her youth.[64]

Her life is solitary, but she can make no extensive plans to counteract her solitude, because always, at every minute, Harre might arrive and make those plans meaningless. She can never take her life into her own hands again and, for instance, marry someone she loves less, for Harre could come back an hour after the wedding, and she would have the rest of her life to reproach herself for throwing away her fulfilment and breaking her faith, through not waiting for just one more day. At what point in those fifty years is she to stop waiting and tell herself that he will never come back now? He might appear the moment after she has convinced herself. The objection that she ought at some stage to have become reconciled to his never returning is made senseless by the fact that he *does* return, be it ever so belatedly. Her faith in him and her waiting *are* justified in the end; but by the time he comes, death has ended her vigil for her. It is only others who can see that she is finally justified; she herself has not even that satisfaction to take with her to the grave. Fifty years of faith kept though never proved right: that sounds like the citation of a human spirit's act of immense fortitude and worth. But it is not; it is the record of a *noblesse oblige,* a life-sentence of worthless deprivation. There can be few tortures more exquisite than the one to which Agnes is subjected: waiting for something that could happen at any moment but does not happen, chained to a hope from which there is no release and which, when it asks for assurance, is answered not with a 'yes' nor even a 'no', but with half a century of absolute, deathly silence.

It is in its sheer bleakness that the picture I have tried to draw in discussing these stories differs most clearly from more conventional judgements about the nature of the world portrayed in Storm's early work. These judgements do indeed point to things that are present in the stories, but they seem to me to be judgements which stop short of the heart of the matter. The critics do *not* say the last word or uncover the central effect when they talk of sentimental 'Stimmungsnovellen' exuding elegaic melancholy;[65] or of 'Erinnerungsnovellen' which seek to mask the pain of the actual events by the sweetness of memory;[66] or of 'Situationsnovellen' which present the action as a series of scenic idylls;[67] or of 'Entsagungsnovellen', which resolve their conflicts by the easy resort of resignation;[68] or when they refer to the 'biedermeierlich' quality of these stories,[69] their tendency to be havens of 'Bürgerlichkeit',[70] the passivity of their heroes,[71] or their lyricising element and 'romantisierende Verklärung'.[72] These perceptions are incomplete, as are the value-judgements they imply; they leave out of account the major artistic achievement, which is the fruitful tension created between the surface and the issues just below the surface — on the one hand, unexceptional settings, a restrained mood, a narrow range of conventions and values, a lack of violence or posturing or dramatic confrontation, a dearth of physical action even; and on the other hand, a stark and disturbing fatalism, the vision of a general condition, the spectacle of a force in living which will prevail, usually with the help of circumstance but sometimes, to show its strength, despite it (that is, 'absurdly'). We may in the end reject such a fatalism, but in doing so we may yet recognize the subtle compulsion with which it is enacted in these works.

The picture, then, is of men alone and knowing that they are alone; men not by nature passive, but forced into passivity because they are given nothing clear to act upon, no defined obstacle to overcome and no specific enemy to fight; men drawn inexorably away from relationship and back to solitude and anguished self-communion; men cut off from each other's hearts and minds; men with an unhappy past, an unfulfilled present and an empty future; men connected to the lives around them only by the most fragile links. In Storm's world, they are thus because they are human.

But there is more to be said. The picture here is part of a larger and more encompassing vision, which I think informs Storm's work from first to last. His writing is conditioned, beyond choice or consciousness, by a view of the world in which the uncertainty of men's relations with each other is extended to their relations with all the reality outside them. The view is enshrined in phenomena which seem at first purely technical, purely a matter of craft; but as we move among the techniques and devices and mannerisms which mould a phrase, a paragraph or a whole fictional scheme, we find ourselves led into strange areas and begin to be aware of a narrative voice whose tone is one of radical doubt. It is to these matters of craft, and to their disquieting implications, that I turn now.

II TECHNIQUES OF SOLIPSISM

1. NARRATORS

As one reads Storm's stories, one becomes increasingly aware of certain distinctive and fairly consistent qualities of style and narrative technique; one comes to accept and expect these qualities, and in the end they are indissolubly linked with the image of Storm which one retains. The fact that they are *Storm's* techniques is, of course, one thing that draws them together and makes them of a piece in the mind; but there is the sense of another denominator between them, a unity of function which is not immediately clear. They *seem* to complement each other and to serve some common end, but one isn't quite sure how they do it or what the end is. External evidence is not much help: there is no specific discussion of the problem in the correspondence or theoretical writings, and Storm's critics have not, to the best of my knowledge, arrived at any satisfactory explanation.

The most obvious distinguishing feature of the stories as a whole is the enormous preponderance of Rahmenerzählungen. Of the total of forty-six completed 'Novellen' (in Goldammer's grouping),[73] no less than thirty have a Rahmen in varying degrees of elaboration. Of the sixteen that do not, a dozen seem to me to be uncharacteristic in other ways as well. Several have unreservedly happy solutions, some are comic in tone; there are a couple of political idylls, one story *(Veronika)* with a specifically religious theme, one *(Psyche)* which is a combination of 'klassisches Moment' and 'Künstlernovelle', and so forth. There are only four stories without a Rahmen which I would yet consider to be 'in the mainstream' of Storm's narrative development: *Waldwinkel, Carsten Curator, Zur 'Wald– und Wasserfreude'* and *Hans und Heinz Kirch.* As a general rule, then, and a rule with less exceptions than many literary generalisations, the Rahmen is a 'characteristic' feature of Storm's 'characteristic' stories. It takes many forms, and will make its presence felt often in what follows.

Another recurrent narrative phenomenon, in part a consequence of the Rahmen technique but not wholly explained by it, is the way in which Storm constructs many of his stories entirely without recourse to one of the mainstays of the novelistic art, the 'fictional, omniscient narrator'. The clearest way to elucidate this is by example; I will start from the opposite of what I mean. The novels of Charles Dickens are splendid repositories of omniscience: the narrator (which is not quite the same as saying Dickens) is in constant control of all his characters, knows what is going on in all their minds (though sometimes he chooses not to tell *us*), can flit back and forth from place to place in literally no time at all – indeed, he can hold up time when he wants to tell us in succession of two events that are happening at the same moment in two quite different places. In his persona as 'humble author' he is all-powerful; he is perfectly well aware of this, and doesn't care if we become aware of it as well; the convention of a special, 'fictional' relationship between author, reader, characters and events is highly conscious throughout. A section taken more or less at random from *Oliver Twist* will serve to illustrate these points: the chapters concerned are 23-7. Chapter 23 deals with the interrupted courtship of Mrs Corney by Beadle Bumble; Dickens makes quite sure that we are clear about the motives and feelings of the protagonists, by the simple process of asserting them to be the exact opposite of what they really are. The interlude is disturbed when Mrs Corney is called away to the deathbed of one of the workhouse women, leaving Mr Bumble warming his back at the fire. Chapter 24 describes the death of the woman; it treats, says the heading, 'of a very poor subject. But it is a short one, and may be found of importance in this history'. Dickens, that is, will explain when he is ready. Chapter 25, 'Wherein this history reverts to Mr Fagin and company' (the heading again), begins:

> While these things were passing in the country workhouse, Mr Fagin sat in the old den — the same from which Oliver had been removed by the girl — brooding over a dull, smoky fire.

This chapter and the next are devoted to Mr Fagin and company, and recount the events of some hours. But then we are returned to the beadle, at the precise moment and place at which we left him. Chapter 27 (says the heading) 'Atones for the unpoliteness of a former chapter; which deserted a lady, most unceremoniously', and begins:

> As it would be, by no means, seemly in a humble author to keep so mighty a personage as a beadle waiting, with his back to the fire, and the skirts of his coat gathered up under his arms, until such time as it might suit his pleasure to relieve him; and as it would still less become his station, or his gallantry to involve in the same neglect a lady on whom the beadle had looked with an eye of tenderness and affection, . . . the historian whose pen traces these words — trusting that he knows his place, and that he entertains a becoming reverence for those upon earth to whom high and important authority is delegated — hastens to pay them that respect which their position demands, and to treat them with all that duteous ceremony which their exalted rank, and (by consequence) great virtues, imperatively claim at his hands. Towards this end, indeed, he had purposed to introduce, in this place, a dissertation touching the divine right of beadles, and elucidative of the position, that a beadle can do no wrong: which could not fail to have been both pleasurable and profitable to the right-minded reader, but which he is unfortunately compelled, by want of time and space, to postpone to some more convenient and fitting opportunity . . .

This passage is funny; but it derives its humour from *two* sources. One is the grotesque parody of sycophantic grovelling before these two coarsegrained and money-grabbing petty tyrants, the beadle and the workhouse-keeper (the chapter continues hilariously in this vein); the other, in which I am more interested here, is the exploitation, rising to parody, of the extremes involved in the position of the omniscient narrator. Dickens is *playing* with his powers, using, to the point of abuse, his privilege of intruding upon the action without being conditioned or limited by it, without giving himself a name or a real, human identity and position, and thus without subjecting himself to the limitations which such an identity and such a position would impose. He can do what no *man* could ever do: be in two places at once, reveal the essences of many personalities and events, know the future without necessary recourse to ideas of causality — indeed, keep Mr Bumble waiting and roasting his back at the fire for as long as he likes, and then abolish the period of waiting by jumping back hours in time with a few strokes of the pen. He wields the authority of a puppeteer[74] over his characters, but wields it here in a manner very like that of a private secretary, politely shooing his employer (or employers) about and discreetly telling them where to be and what to do next. And that is where the two streams of humour in this passage flow together: in the incongruity between his absolute power over his creations and his ironically servile posturing towards them.

I have chosen Dickens as an example because he adopts the omniscient (or omnipotent) attitude so clearly, consciously and obtrusively. This very consciousness and obtrusiveness, and, just as important, the comedy which he finds in and draws from the attitude, suggest the possibility that at the time he is writing *(Oliver Twist* was published in 1838), he might feel this whole narrative convention to be in decline or at least to have become problematic. The phenomenon of a writer displaying acute and conscious awareness of the tradition in which he is writing may be taken as a possible indication of the decline of that tradition; Thomas Mann, of whom I shall be talking in a moment, is arguably a case in point. In addition, while an evident function of parody is to call into question the value and validity of the things parodied, it seems to me also reasonable to infer from the fact of the parody that it may be the symptom or product of a climate where its particular targets are *already* being called into question. Be that as it may, the convention of narrative omniscience dies hard: in this century, E.M. Forster has stated it to be one of the essential tools of the novelist's craft,[75] and for Thomas Mann it has been an issue live enough to be worth examining again in *Der Erwählte*. At the beginning of this novel, it is asserted that all the bells of Rome are ringing; then this follows:

> Wer läutet die Glocken? . . . Der Geist der Erzählung — Kann denn der überall sein, hic et ubique, zum Beispiel zugleich auf dem Turme von Sankt Georg . . . und droben in Santa Sabina . . . An hundert weihlichen Orten auf einmal? — Allerdings, das vermag er. Er ist luftig, körperlos, allgegenwärtig, nicht unterworfen dem Unterschiede von Hier und Dort. Er ist es, der spricht: 'Alle Glocken läuteten', und folglich ist er's, der sie läutet. So geistig ist dieser Geist und so abstrakt, daß grammatisch nur in der dritten Person von ihm die

Rede sein und es lediglich heißen kann: 'Er ist's'. Und doch kann er sich auch zusammenziehen zur Person . . . und sich verkörpern in jemandem, der in dieser spricht und spricht: 'Ich bin es. Ich bin der Geist der Erzählung, der . . . diese Geschichte erzählt'.[76]

But from 1847, ten years after *Oliver Twist* and half a century before Mann and Forster, Storm is writing prose fiction which is, as often as not, entirely *outside* this convention. Just over half his stories (twenty-four out of forty-six)[77] lay no claim whatever to 'fictional' omniscience or a privileged narrative position of any kind, even in their Rahmen; they are narrated by people who have a perfectly definite place within the economy of the story, 'real' characters with names, jobs, relationships and (most important) the limitations of 'real-life' human beings: they can recount only what they themselves have seen, heard, experienced, read or been told by somebody else. A certain amount of pedantry is sometimes needed to define their identities, but in these stories it can always be done. *Marthe und ihre Uhr*, for instance, is 'told' by one of Marthe's tenants, a 'Primaner' who lodged with her during his last years at school; *Auf dem Staatshof* by Marx, the middle-class suitor of the aristocratic heroine Anne Lene; *Auf der Universität* by Philipp, a student at the university of Kiel and an admirer (exercised by his higher social standing) of the tailor's daughter Lenore Beauregard; *In St Jürgen* by the grandson of Agnes Hansen's former mistress; *Draußen im Heidedorf* by the Amtsvogt who has to conduct an enquiry into the disappearance of the central figure, Hinrich Fehse; *Aquis submersus* by a young man who as a boy had loved climbing trees with his friend the pastor's son, was fascinated by a particular church and by the mysterious pictures in it, and some years later discovers by chance a manuscript which yields their secret; '*Es waren zwei Königskinder*' by the cousin of Fritz, a music student at Stuttgart and one of a group of friends which contains the doomed hero Marx; *Ein Bekenntnis* by Hans, a lawyer and former fellow-student of Franz Jebe, who later meets Franz again (at Bad Reichenhall in June 1856!) and hears his 'confession';[78] and so on. In every case, the narrator is 'part of the story'; at least some of the other characters *know* he exists (whereas of course they are entirely unaware of Mann's 'Geist der Erzählung'), and are affected by his interest; he is a person among persons, and we are often as vitally concerned with *his* qualities as with those of the people he is talking about, for insofar as he is involved in the action he is talking about himself as well; all his judgements about people and events which go beyond mere reporting (and even some which apparently do not) are valid objects of critical examination by the reader, in just the same way as judgements made (that is, practically, things said) by the other characters may be examined with a view to achieving some idea of *their* natures.[79] Storm the omniscient narrator simply does not enter the scheme; and if it be protested that he must do so, since he is after all writing the story, then I can only define his entry as Storm the *man* assuming a complete identity which is strictly quite separate from his own (Marx, Philipp, the Amtsvogt, Hans), 'acting the part of' one of the characters and controlling the narrative in that way. But such a definition does not affect my argument, for it indicates a very different convention; the 'Geist der Erzählung', the fictional middleman, has been bypassed.

There is obviously a difficulty here. In the passage from *Der Erwählte,* Thomas Mann specifically allows for the possibility of the 'spirit of story-telling' moving from the third to the first person and becoming embodied in an 'Ich', while yet remaining omniscient, omnipresent and so on. Does this proviso not cover the cases I have mentioned and make valid again the claim that narrative omniscience is a necessary condition of story-telling and not merely an optional aid or convention? C.A. Bernd, in his book *Theodor Storm's Craft of Fiction, The Torment of a Narrator,*[80] clearly thinks it does. He quotes that same passage[81] from *Der Erwählte* in support of his contention that there *is* a fictional, omniscient narrator in all (thus in all of Storm's) stories, and that in the case of Storm this narrator is

> a tormented intelligence, ever oscillating between the two conflicting thoughts by which he is obsessed: his fear of the all-consuming maw of passing time on the one hand, and the soothing knowledge of his ability to overcome his phobia on the other.[82]

Bernd's book is devoted to the 'concrete form-analysis'[83] of two stories *(Aquis submersus* and *In St Jürgen),* sketching out the tortures supposedly suffered by the fictional intelligence which narrates them. But these are two of the stories in which, as I said, there is clearly no such intelligence at work. Where does the confusion lie?

Bernd makes the mistake of concluding from the one section he quotes from *Der Erwählte* that all Ich-Erzählungen are essentially of one kind, namely the kind that Mann describes. The stories of Storm that I have been talking about show well enough that this is not so. Here, the narrating 'Ich' is a fully-embodied person, specifically caught up in the action, a character among characters, relating with all or some of them, and possessed only of such knowledge as is consistent with individual human limitation. As one reads further[84] into *Der Erwählte,* on the other hand, it becomes clear that Mann is concerned with quite a different *kind* of first-person narrator and is leaving out of account (whether consciously or not, one doesn't know) the kind we have met in Storm. Mann's 'Ich' is a highly specialised entity: its sole and absolute function in the narrative scheme is to tell the tale, by extension to create the people and events, to 'ring the bells'. Its relation to the things and people it describes is that of the craftsman to his work; telling stories is its *job* — there is a 'professional' ring about sentences like this:

> In meiner so viel bescheideneren Eigenschaft als Inkarnation des Geists der Erzählung habe ich alles Interesse daran, daß man mit mir die Berufung zur Sella gestatoria als der Erwählungen höchste und gnadenvollste betrachte.[85]

The entity does become a person, certainly, even a person with a name and characteristics in this case; the teller of the tale is Clemens, born Morhold, an Irish monk. But he is a person totally divorced from the action in any experiential way, uninvolved in it except in his capacity as narrator (inventor, creator) of it.

He has no 'real-life' contact with the characters: he does not know them, hear their stories from their lips (as does the narrator of *In St Jürgen*), or even find their written account of their lives (as does the narrator of *Aquis submersus*); to all intents and purposes, he has produced them out of thin air. What is more, far from being a 'real' person 'really' involved, he will not admit to being unambiguously a person at all. He does all he can to play *down* his definitely human qualities, and encourages us all the time to think of him as a disembodied voice or, more appropriately, as a walking quill-pen (which makes the whole introduction a bit pointless, since if Clemens hadn't announced himself in the first place we should probably not have thought of him as anything else). He is a monk; and that gives him a chance to further his ends by exploiting the principal connotation of the monkish calling — abjuration of the flesh:

> Ja, es ist der Fleischesleib gar nicht mehr, der im Wams jenes Morhold herumlief, sondern ein geistlicher Leib ist es, den das Cingulum umwindet, — *ein Körper demnach nicht in dem Grade, daß mein früheres Wort, es 'verkörpere' sich etwas in mir, nämlich der Geist der Erzählung, ganz billigenswert gewesen wäre.* Ich liebe dies Wort 'Verkörperung' gar nicht sehr, da es sich ja vom Körper und vom Fleischesleibe herleitet, den ich zusammen mit dem Namen Morhold ausgezogen habe . . .[86]

Then this not-quite-fleshly being goes on to blur yet other contours which would mark him out as a concrete personality:

> Nein, indem der Geist der Erzählung sich zu meiner mönchischen Person, genannt Clemens der Ire, zusammenzog, *hat er sich viel von jener Abstraktheit bewahrt,* die ihn befähigt, von allen Titular-Basiliken der Stadt zugleich zu läuten, und ich werde dafür sogleich zwei Merkmale anführen.[87]

The first of these 'Merkmale' is the refusal to set himself (not his story) in any particular place or time. He has, admittedly, revealed that he is writing his story at Notker's desk in the monastery of Sankt Gallen, but that, he says, is useless information — 'Da gibt es überhaupt nichts zu wissen'. And as for time, we cannot pin him down: he will give us no means of knowing

> zu welcher Zeitenstunde, in dem wievielten Jahre und Jahrhundert nach unseres Retters Geburt ich hier sitze und das Pergament mit meiner kleinen und feinen, gelehrten und schmuckhaften Schrift bedecke. Dafür gibt es keinen festen Anhaltspunkt, und auch der Name Gozbert unseres Abtes hier ist kein solcher. Er wiederholt sich allzuoft in der Zeit und verwandelt sich, wenn man nach ihm greift, auch gar leicht in Fridolin oder Hartmut.[88]

The second 'Merkmal', interestingly, is the concealment of the language in which Clemens is writing. It might be any one of a dozen, he says, perhaps even several languages at once, flowing into each other to form one substance — 'Sprache':

> Denn so verhält es sich, daß der Geist der Erzählung *ein bis zur Abstraktheit ungebundener Geist* ist, dessen Mittel die Sprache an sich und als solche, die Sprache selbst ist, welche sich als absolut setzt und nicht viel nach Idiomen und sprachlichen Landesgöttern fragt. Das wäre ja auch polytheistisch und heidnisch. Gott ist Geist, und über den Sprachen ist die Sprache.[89]

On the whole, no ordinary cleric. All he *will* say is that he is writing in prose, not in verse. The whole figure of Clemens is a masterly and utterly characteristic amalgam of ambiguities, evasions and tricky logic.

All that, of course, is totally different from the situation we saw in Storm's work. Can an Amtsvogt be 'luftig, körperlos'? Can a lawyer at Reichenhall in June 1856 be 'allgegenwärtig, nicht unterworfen dem Unterschiede von Hier und Dort'? Can a Stuttgart music student be 'geistig, abstrakt'? Clearly not. Thomas Mann is simply not talking about the same phenomenon.

2. BEGINNINGS

In half of Storm's prose fiction, then, one finds no ringer of the bells, no creating figure beyond the relationships within the tale. In the other half there *is,* in order to be true to the technical structure, the necessity to postulate some kind of external narrator who takes no part in the action and is unknown to any other characters, and who may be endowed with gifts of perception beyond the normal human possibility. But this adherence to the convention of a 'fictional intelligence' is very often ambiguous and hedged about with reservations. The first of these reservations I want to talk about is concerned with the question of names.

It is obvious enough that in most works of prose fiction people have names — or titles or distinguishing appellations serving the same function as names.[90] It is also obvious that in most traditional works of fiction (by 'traditional' I mean in this context works that employ the omniscient convention) the writer gives names to his characters and then tells us (in his persona as narrator) what their names are. This is part of the information service which the omniscient narrator provides and which covers other facts, physical and mental characteristics and so on, created by the author in the same way as the names are created. And so: 'Once upon a time there was a little girl called Little Red Riding Hood' or 'Mister Anstruther, a red-faced lawyer in his early fifties, was sitting . . .'

We accept that kind of opening (and it is far and away the commonest) so readily as to be quite unconscious of any claim it makes on imagination, credulity, receptiveness or willingness to abide by the rules of the novelistic game. But a claim is made; and though it would normally be trivial and cavilling to examine it in any detail, it seems to me necessary, in view of the problems we are looking at here, to make it clear that such an opening does entail a number of suspensions of disbelief. For the sake of the story, the reader must be willing to enter into a kind of pact with the writer; he is more interested in other (psychological, ex-periential) truths which the writer may offer through his characters, and therefore 'agrees to make no objection' if the first encounter with these characters is arranged in a way that is less than 'true to life' — that is, if certain facts are given and not discovered. Let me single out that part of the scheme which establishes the name. 'In life' we find out people's names in various ways, sometimes devious and difficult ways: by being introduced to them formally (though so often this does not work — the name is mumbled, and we have to think up subterfuges to discover it later); by receiving a letter with their name at the bottom, perhaps with a photograph to enable us to put name to face, or with an elaborate arrangement to aid recognition at the first face-to-face meeting (a carnation in the button-hole, perhaps); by door-plate, letter-head or coat-of-arms; above all by hearing a third party address by name the person in whom we are interested. But 'in the story' it is quite different: the girl's name is Little Red Riding Hood, the man is a lawyer called Anstruther. Who says so? The author-narrator, and that is all well and good, because after all they are *his* creations. The painter says: 'This is the painting I have created; I have made it a landscape and called it "Impression: soleil levant" '. The writer says: 'This is the person I have created; I have made him a lawyer and called him Anstruther'. We take what we are given; nobody minds; it has to be that way, because this kind of 'giving' is inherent in the peculiar activity of reading and writing prose fiction.

But *is* it inherent? I think there is a case for saying that it is not; that 'giving us people's names' in this way (and of course I am arguing this all the time about narrative omniscience as a whole) is *not* an absolute and inescapable condition of the art of story-telling, but a convention, a piece of equipment which the author may use or leave unused as he wishes; in sum, that if he doesn't use it, we can still define what he is doing as 'telling a story'.

Half of Storm's work shows quite unquestionably that the device of omniscient name-giving can be done away with; for we have already seen that, in twenty-four of his stories, he has eliminated the fictional, omniscient narrative entity altogether, replacing it with a perfectly definite and normal human being with 'real-life' human characteristics and limitations, who tells the tale in the first person. It is an automatic inference that this human being must have discovered the names of the people he describes in a normal human way, that is, at the beginning or in the course of his definite relationship with them. When we enter the scheme as readers, nothing is changed or made more 'fictional'; the situation remains, in its way, absolutely 'true to life'; here is a man telling us the names of people he knows.[91]

In the other stories, where, as I have said, the fictional entity has to be posited, the situation is naturally different — but the notable thing is that in many cases it still does not wholly conform to the conventional situation I have been describing. What we see is Storm employing the fictional entity but denying it many of its commonest functions, among them the function of 'giving us people's names'.

'Above all, by hearing a third party address by name the person in whom we are interested'. This, I have said, is the way we most frequently find out names in life, and this is the way, again and again, that the information is conveyed to us in Storm's works. No inkling is given in the first encounter with the character or characters — they are described as a stranger might see them, and a stranger would not know their names. We have to wait for a piece of dialogue before we are allowed to *overhear* names as people address each other. Some examples:

Drüben am Markt opens with the picture of a little old man in a blue coat sitting on a dyke with his dog and fishing. The scene is carefully and evocatively sketched in the first paragraph, but no more information is given about the little man. In the second paragraph, an old woman comes towards him crying and talking; then this conversation follows:

> 'Schrei Sie nicht so, alte Person!' sagte er und bückte sich nach seiner Angel. 'Hat denn die Mixtur von gestern noch nicht angeschlagen?'
> Das Weib schwieg plötzlich und strich sich verlegen mit der Hand über ihre Schürze.
> 'Ja so', sagte er, 'ich kann's mir denken; Ihr habt wieder einmal selbst gedoktert! — Da habt Ihr mir nun auch den Fisch verjagt!'
> Indem hatte er sich aufgerichtet; und in seine kleinen Augen trat ein Ausdruck von Schelmerei, der vorzeiten diesem unschönen Antlitz eine vorübergehende Anmut mochte verliehen haben. 'Kleine Frau', sagte er, 'kennt ihr das Gebet der Ärzte?'
> Die Frau sah ihn verdutzt an. 'Nur das Vaterunser, Herr Doktor, und die hinterm Gesangbuch'.
> 'Nun, so will ich es Euch sagen: Gott behüte uns vor den alten Weibern!'
> Die Alte lächelte. 'Herr Doktor sind allzeit so spaßig'.
> 'Und nun', fuhr der Doktor fort, indem er seinen alten Hut aus dem Grase aufsammelte, 'nun bleib Sie hier und paß Sie mir auf meine Fischerei!' — Der kleine Hund sprang gegen ihn empor. 'Leg dich, Pankraz!' sagte er und bückte sich, um ihn zu streicheln ... (SW I 539f.)

The doctor is called 'der Doktor' throughout the story; that is his title, and it serves adequately as a name — even his mother calls him 'Doktor'![92] But his name and profession (which happen to be the same thing) only emerge in his conversation with the old woman; and she has to say it twice, it seems, before the narrator can pluck up courage to use it *outside* the dialogue! One further point: even the dog has to be addressed in order to be accorded a name. The same thing happens later on with Sophie, the central female figure: we only find out what she is called when the doctor addresses her as 'Mamsell Sophie', (SW I 544) and this right at the end of the section in which she first makes her appearance.

Im Schloß goes for seven large pages without mentioning any names at all, while somehow managing to convey a fairly detailed history of what has been going on at the Schloß for a number of years, and giving a close physical description of the young woman who turns out to be the central character in the story. We discover the names in the following passage (strangely enough there is another dog here, and we hear his name even before those of the human characters):

> Aber unten neben dem auf dem Boden liegenden Sommerhut stand der Hund, die Schnauze gegen den Baum gedrückt, mit den braunen Augen zu seiner Herrin emporsehend. Jetzt kratzte er mit der Pfote an den Stamm. 'Ich komme, Türk, ich komme!' rief sie hinab; und bald war sie unten und ging mit ihrem stummen Begleiter den hinteren Buchengang hinab, der von dem

Rondell aus nach der breiten Lindenallee fuhr.

Als sie in diese eintrat, kam ihr ein junger, kaum mehr als zwanzigjähriger Mann entgegen, in dessen gebräuntem Antlitz mit der feinen vorspringenden Nase eine Familienähnlichkeit mit ihr nicht zu verkennen war. 'Ich suchte dich, Anna!' sagte er, indem er der schönen Frau die Hand küßte.

Ihre Augen ruhten mit dem Ausdruck einer kleinen mütterlichen Über-legenheit auf ihm, als sie ihn fragte: 'Was hast du, Vetter Rudolf?' (SW II 13)

And finally, *Waldwinkel* (1874) opens with the description of a burghermaster working in his office in the town hall. He is interrupted by the entry of 'ein brauner stattlicher Mann':

Der Bürgermeister erhob das rote behagliche Gesicht aus seinen Akten, warf einen flüchtigen Blick auf den Eintretenden und sagte, als er die feinere Kleidung desselben bemerkt hatte, mit einer runden Handbewegung: 'Wollen Sie gefälligst Platz nehmen; ich werde gleich zu Ihren Diensten sein'.

Der andere aber war einen Schritt näher getreten. 'Bist du jetzt immer so fleißig, Fritz?' sagte er. 'Du littest ehemals nicht an dieser Krankheit'.

Der Bürgermeister fuhr empor, hakte die Brille von der Nase und starrte den Sprecher aus seinen kleinen gutmütigen Augen an. 'Richard, du bist es!' rief er. (SW II 438)

It is only towards the end of the long ensuing conversation that the narrator first calls Richard by name *outside* dialogue; till then he remains 'der andere' or 'der Gast'.

The statistics of this device are remarkable. When we look at the twenty-one stories which use a fictional narrator,[93] we find that nearly two-thirds of them (thirteen to be exact) follow the pattern of the stories quoted above. Moreover, the chronological division is astonishingly neat. With two minor exceptions, the position is this: before 1877, every single story in the group takes the giving of names *out of* the hands of the narrator;[94] and from 1877 onwards, every single story leaves this function *with* the narrator.[95]

I have expended a great many words over a technicality; but I would claim that it is not a technicality *in vacuo* — it has implications. What it does ultimately is to cast doubt on the omniscience of the 'fictional narrative intelligence'. We do not discover names directly from the intelligence itself, but 'overhear' them in the dialogues it reports. This certainly doesn't speak *for* the conclusion that the intelligence knows the names in question; indeed, taken together with other indica-tions that the intelligence is reporting from the standpoint of a stranger (I have touched on this already and shall return to it in a moment), it tends rather to speak *against* such a conclusion. It seems to me, then, to be an honest inference to suggest that the presence of this technicality offers considerable grounds for doubt that the narrator knows everything. And Storm, for a period of twenty-six years (1849-1875), rather more than half his creative life, makes use of this technicality every single time he sits down to write a story with a fictional narrator.

If names are the clearest symptom of 'reserved' or 'questioned' omniscience, there are other symptoms which are probably more significant. I have held back discussion of them so far because they are not quite so susceptible to mechanical reasoning; my arguments about them must be more impressionistic and speculative.

When Storm employs the convention of a fictional narrative entity, it is frequently possible to discuss meaningfully the standpoint which this entity adopts, and thence to delimit its nature or *describe* certain of its qualities. Very often, for example, we are made to feel that we are seeing people and events through the eyes (from the standpoint) of a stranger – someone quite perceptive, intelligent and imaginative, but nonetheless a stranger – who can tell us only what he sees done and hears said by people whom he seems to know no better than we do at first. He may sometimes suggest other, less superficial things about the people he is describing – what is passing through their minds, how they are related to one another, and so on – but if he does this, he is generally at pains to make it clear that these suggestions are nothing more than guesses, or rather *deductions* from what he is seeing and hearing now, inferences which any fairly intelligent person could draw from the present available data. We have seen how, in many stories, the use of names is consistent with the position of a listening stranger, who only discovers what people are called when they address each other in dialogue, and sometimes even seems to want the names repeated before he will venture to use them himself. In the same way, other information is frequently conveyed in a manner consistent with that of a detached and ignorant observer. Here is the introduction to a short early story; I have omitted some passages purely for the sake of brevity (if included, they would not, I think, weaken my argument in any way – if anything they would strengthen it). The story is *Im Sonnenschein:*

> In den höchsten Zweigen des Ahornbaums, der an der Gartenseite des Hauses stand, trieben die Stare ihr Wesen. Sonst war es still; denn es war Sommernachmittag zwischen eins und zwei.
>
> Aus der Gartentür trat ein junger Reiteroffizier in weißer festtäglicher Uniform . . . und sah nach allen Seiten in die Gänge des Gartens hinab; dann . . . horchte er nach einem offenstehenden Fenster im oberen Stockwerke hinauf, aus welchem sich in kleinen Pausen das Klirren holländischer Kaffeeschälchen und die Stimmen zweier alter Herren deutlich vernehmen ließen . . Der junge Mann lächelte, wie jemand, dem was Liebes widerfahren soll, indem er langsam die kleine Gartentreppe hinunterstieg. Die Muscheln, mit denen der breite Steig bestreut war, knirschten an seinen breiten Sporen; bald aber trat er behutsam auf, als wolle er nicht bemerkt sein. – Gleichwohl schien es ihn nicht zu stören, als ihm aus einem Seitengange ein junger Mann in bürgerlicher Kleidung mit sauber gepuderter Frisur entgegenkam. Ein Ausdruck brüderlichen, fast zärtlichen Vertrauens zeigte sich in beider Antlitz, als sie sich schweigend die Hände reichten . . . (the two young men talk briefly, then separate; the officer walks towards a summerhouse).
>
> Die eine Flügeltür stand offen; er trat vorsichtig auf die Schwelle. Aber die Jalousien schienen von allen Seiten geschlossen; es war so dämmerig drinnen, daß seine noch eben des vollen Sonnenlichts gewöhnten Augen erst nach einer ganzen Weile die jugendliche Gestalt eines Mädchens aufzufassen

vermochten . . . Dann, als einige Zeit vorübergegangen, zog er seinen Degen eine Handbreit aus der Scheide und ließ ihn mit einem Stoß zurückfallen, daß es einen leichten Klang gab. Ein Lächeln trat um den Mund des Mädchens, und die dunklen Augenwimpern hoben sich ein weniges von den Wangen empor; dann aber, als hätte sie sich besonnen, streifte sie nur den Ärmel der amarantfarbenen Kontusche zurück und tauchte aufs neue die Feder ein.

Der Offizier, da sie immer nicht aufblickte, tat einen Schritt ins Zimmer und zog ihr schweigend die Feder durch die Finger, daß die Dinte auf den Nägeln blieb.

'Herr Kapitän!' rief sie und streckte ihm die Hand entgegen. Sie hatte den Kopf zurückgeworfen; ein Paar tiefgraue Augen waren mit dem Ausdruck nicht allzu ernsthaften Zürnens auf ihn gerichtet. (SW I 457f.)

The emphasis here is always on the visible and audible (described, it is true, with superb evocativeness — the two moments of play with the Offiziersdegen and the pen, for instance, stand before the eye in brilliant clarity, and their erotic symbolism is striking and forceful). Indeed, a great deal of attention is paid to the actual process of seeing and hearing things: the young officer *looks* down the garden paths, *listens* up at a window, seems not to want to be *noticed*, has to wait till his eyes become used to the darkness before he can make out the figure of the girl in the summerhouse, the girl's eyelashes rise and then drop; at first she doesn't look up, but then she throws back her head so that we can see her eyes. The narrator, too, is looking and listening; he 'gives' us only what he sees and hears; everything else is the result of deductions from his sense-impressions. The young man is a cavalry officer: how does the narrator know? not necessarily because he knows everything, but because the young man is in uniform. Two old men are upstairs drinking coffee — but the narrator does not actually assert this to be so; he merely tells us that the voices of two old men and the clink of coffee-cups can be clearly heard from an upstairs window.[96] The young man smiles, not *because* he is looking forward to a pleasant experience, but *in the way that* someone would who was thus looking forward. The narrator is confused about whether or not the officer wants his presence known: he treads carefully, *as if* he didn't want to be noticed, and yet he *seems* not to be disturbed at the approach of another young man. The suggestion is made that there is a tender, brotherly relationship between these two men — but this is not a 'given' fact but a deduction from the expression on both their faces. The first we are told about the girl is not that she *is* indisputably there in the summerhouse, but that the officer's eyes eventually make out a figure in the semi-darkness. The girl hears and reacts to the sound of the dagger being dropped into its sheath: but again, that is not a fact but a deduction from appearances, the smile playing round her lips and the movement of her eyelashes. Then she collects herself — but no, all we are told is that she pushes back her sleeve *'als hätte* sie sich besonnen'. When the officer draws the pen through her fingers, we are told not that she feigns anger, but that her eyes have in them the *expression* of feigned anger.

All this, together with the fact (it hardly needs saying) that we have to look at the dialogue to discover the names of the three characters thus far introduced, leaves the strong impression that we are reading the account of someone to whom these characters are strangers; so we get an idea of the quality of his relationship with them (for we can say of it that it is as limited as *our* acquaintance). In addition, there is room and opportunity for us to speculate about his *physical* relation to them in space. The narrator seems first of all to be somewhere in the garden, in a position where he can see the gate through which the young man enters. He must be some way away from the gate; for though he can recognize immediately that the young man is in the dress uniform of a cavalry officer, he is not close enough to make out the rank — it is left to the girl later to establish that he is a captain. Then the narrator comes closer to the officer, seeing him smile, hearing the crunch of his spurs on the path, noting the expression on his face as he shakes hands with the young man who has just approached. As the officer walks to the summerhouse and stops in the doorway, the narrator seems to be following close behind him and to be looking over his shoulder into the semi-darkness of the interior. It is from the darkness that the narrator concludes that the shutters *seem* to be closed — he cannot actually *see* them from where he is. As the officer unsheaths and then sharply sheaths his dagger, it is as though the narrator has ducked in past him and got close to the girl in order to watch her reactions; *he* sees the movement of her eyelashes, whereas the officer probably doesn't.

I would feel considerable sympathy for anyone who found these remarks utterly fantastic, absurdly pedantic, or both. My only defence for them is that they do have an end in view and are not just reports on an act of gratuitous text-shredding. Their function is this: the fact that observations like these *can* be made and verified from the text is a further indication that in many cases Storm's narrator simply does not conform to conventional ideas of the 'fictional intelligence'. In such cases we are enabled to discuss various characteristics of the narrator: we can say 'He knows this but not that; he can hear this but not see it; he assumes this to be so on the evidence of his eyes and ears; he is here, but after a while he moves over there; he is here now, but a few minutes ago he was somewhere else and did not see what happened here' and so on. The common ground between these statements is that they define limitations (limitations of knowledge, perception, movement), and it is evident that the limitations thus defined are the very ones imposed by nature on that constant apparition in these pages, the 'real-life' human being. We are a long way from Dickens' puppeteer/secretary figure, and from Thomas Mann's 'Geist der Erzählung'. In story after story we seem to be faced with an entity to which we cannot apply with any certainty words like 'omniscient', 'controlling', 'privileged', 'allgegenwärtig, nicht unterworfen dem Unterschiede von Hier und Dort' — an entity which we are, on the contrary, much more apt to think of as a person ('He', not 'it'), with eyes and ears and a good interpretative intelligence to go with them, and with the ability to move about as far and as fast, and in the same ways, as ordinary men. Indeed, the only thing marking him out from ordinary men (and one wonders, in this context, whether it is such a radical one) is that he is imperceptible to the people amongst whom he is moving. His feet make no noise on the path. That is the extent to which Storm has pared away the resources of the conventional narrator.

I noted earlier[97] the remarkable neatness in the chronology of 'omniscient name-giving' — how in every relevant story before 1877 this particular device is eschewed, and how in every relevant story after 1877 it is used in the traditional way. As might be expected, the same chronology applies (not so neatly, but then the phenomena are not so neat) to these other questions of narrative standpoint I have talked about since. This is natural enough: the discovery, rather than the giving, of names is implied in the position of the non-omniscient stranger. The stories after 1877, then, tend to employ the fictional, omniscient narrator more conventionally.[98] I want briefly to look at these stories, drawing examples from them to indicate the conventional usage; these should throw into relief the departures from convention which have been my main concern so far. The seven works involved are *Carsten Curator, Zur 'Wald- und Wasserfreude', Eekenhof, Die Söhne des Senators, Hans und Heinz Kirch, Schweigen*, and *Ein Fest auf Haderslevhuus.*

A glance at two stories from this group, those which examine the relationship between father and son, will show narrative omniscience at work; again, it is the openings which give the clearest indications. *Carsten Curator* (1877) begins like this:

> Eigentlich hieß er Carsten Carstens und war der Sohn eines Kleinbürgers, von dem er ein schon vom Großvater erbautes Haus an der Twiete des Hafen-platzes ererbt hatte und außerdem einen Handel mit gestrickten Wollwaren und solchen Kleidungsstücken, wie deren die Schiffer von den umliegenden Inseln auf ihren Seefahrten zu gebrauchen pflegten. Da er indes von etwas grübelnder Gemütsart und ihm, wie manchem Nordfriesen, eine Neigung zur Gedankenarbeit angeboren war, so hatte er sich von jung auf mit allerlei Büchern und Schriftwerk beschäftigt und war allmählich unter seinesgleichen in den Ruf gekommen, daß er ein Mann sei, bei dem man sich in zweifelhaften Fällen sicheren Rat erholen möge.[99]

There are no doubts here. The first word is an uncompromising 'eigentlich' — the name is established at once beyond any doubt. In the same way, the narrator goes on, in the space of a few lines, to 'give' Carsten all his contours: a social class, a father and grandfather, a place to live, a trade, certain intellectual characteristics, a racial provenance, a childhood and a reputation (and this stock of attributes is prodigally supplemented as the story continues). If there is any reservation to be made, it is that something in the tone of this passage seems to tell us a little about the narrator as well as a lot about Carsten: words like 'eine Neigung zur Gedanken-arbeit' and 'allerlei Büchern und Schriftwerk' suggest that the narrative is being very slightly coloured with the attitudes of people in Carsten's milieu, a firm practicality and an unease in face of 'things of the mind'. But the colouring *is* slight and hardly affects the dominant impression of *données* rather than deductions, given facts rather than opinions.

In *Hans und Heinz Kirch* (1881-2), Storm adopts a different introductory technique, but the omniscience is no less apparent. The first few paragraphs contain a physical description of the setting, 'eine kleine Stadt auf einer Uferhöhe der Ostsee', and a sketch of the town's social structure, with particular reference to the honour in which its seamen are held. We are given details of the stages in the mariner's career, which is stated to be the proudest ambition of the town's youth; the ultimate distinction is the right to sit in the 'Schifferstuhl' in the church — a pew reserved for those who have passed the 'Steuermannsexamen' and own their own ship — and many a seaman aspires exclusively to this end. The passage continues:

> Zu diesen strebsamen Leuten gehörte Hans Adam Kirch. Mit unermüdlichem Tun und Sparen hatte er sich vom Setzschiffer zum Schiffseigentümer hinaufgearbeitet; freilich war es nur eine kleine Jacht, zu der seine Mittel gereicht hatten, aber rastlos und in den Winter hinein, wenn schon alle andern Schiffer daheim hinter ihrem Ofen saßen, befuhr er mit seiner Jacht die Ostsee, und nicht nur Frachtgüter für andre, bald auch für eigne Rechnung brachte er die Erzeugnisse der Umgegend, Korn und Mehl, nach den größeren und kleineren Küstenplätzen; erst wenn bereits außen vor den Buchten das Wasser fest zu werden drohte, band auch er sein Schiff an den Pfahl und saß beim Sonntagsgottesdienste droben im Schifferstuhl unter den Honoratioren seiner Vaterstadt. (SW III 341f.)

Again, everything is given: physical and social setting, name, characteristics, previous history. And again, the story goes on in this mode, with 'characterising' passages like this one:

> Trotz dieser dem Geize recht nahe verwandten Genauigkeit war und blieb der Kapitän ein zuverlässiger Geschäftsmann, der jeden ungeziemenden Vorteil von sich wies; nicht nur infolge einer angeborenen Rechtschaffenheit, sondern ebensosehr seines Ehrgeizes. (SW III 343)

No inferences are necessary; the elements are pieced together for us; the figure is *created*.

Two of these seven late stories contain the only examples I can discover in Storm's work of that 'Ich' to which I think Thomas Mann is referring when he talks of the way the 'Geist der Erzählung' can be embodied in an 'Ich'.[100] The stories are *Eekenhof* (1879) and *Ein Fest auf Haderslevhuus* (1885); I want to single out the latter of these two for mention, since it shows the phenomenon with striking clarity. The opening sets the scene in 14th-century Schleswig and tells how the Ritter Klaus Lembeck frustrated the murderous designs of the Danish king Atterdag by escaping to the island of Föhr and leaving his knightly fortress, Schloß Dorning, in the hands of his eldest son. The relevant passage runs:

> (Der älteste Sohn) aber war nicht, wie ein Chronist nach dem anderen es nachgeschrieben hat, der Henneke Lembeck, welcher späterhin die Keiler in Not brachte, weil sie einigen seiner straßenräuberischen Burgleute den Kopf

hatten vor die Füße legen lassen; es stand noch einer zwischen ihnen, von dem jede Kunde fast verschollen scheint: der älteste Sohn des viel berufenen Ritters war Rolf Lembeck und saß, wenn auch nur wenig Monde, auf Schloß Dorning. Er war nur halb vom Eisenstoffe seines Geschlechtes, und lieber als im Harnisch ging er auf leichten Sohlen und in zierlichen Gewändern von Sammet oder Seiden; von ihm war nur ein jäh zerrissenes Minneabenteuer zu berichten, das wie Mondlicht in die Wirrnis dieser finsteren Zeiten fällt; doch damit hatten die Chronisten nichts zu schaffen. Und obschon sein Leben ein Vierteljahrhundert kaum erreichte, so war er doch ein deutscher Ritter, blauäugig und mit blondem Haupthaar, von froher, leichter Jugend und von heißer Lebenslust.

Ich aber weiß von ihm; und was ich weiß, das drängt mich heut, es zu erzählen. (SW IV 61f.)

The narrator knows all about Rolf Lembeck. There is no suggestion that he has found out about him through a manuscript or through oral tradition or in any other way that a 'real' person might; he merely *knows*. There is no question of his being a participant in the events and relationships he is about to describe, for he is writing five hundred years after they happened. He knows all about the story he is telling because his sole and total function is that of story-teller; it is his story, and thus he is the creator of the world he reports — 'Er ist es, der spricht: 'Alle Glocken läuteten', und folglich ist er's, der sie läutet'. And he speaks of himself in the first person.

The situation here is a little confused by the sense of 'historicity', the confrontation between narrator and chroniclers; but it is essentially the same as the more simply-drawn situation in, say, Stifter's *Abdias,* where the famous introductory plaiting of the 'heitere Blumenkette' of causality and responsibility is followed by:

Es ist der Jude Abdias, von dem ich erzählen will.

It seems to me undeniable that the 'Ich' of *Ein Fest auf Haderslevhuus* (and of *Abdias*) is different *in kind* from the 'Ich' we have encountered in so many of Storm's other stories.[101] It can be described comprehensively in the words Mann uses: it is 'luftig, körperlos, allgegenwärtig, nicht unterworfen dem Unterschiede von Hier und Dort . . . geistig . . . abstrakt'; while remaining all these things, it becomes embodied in somebody who says 'Ich' and thereby identifies himself, *not* as a character in the tale, but wholly as the teller of it, the omniscient creator of its contours, the 'spirit of story-telling'.

What I have said so far has been almost exclusively concerned with the way Storm's stories begin. It can be argued that one is not justified in drawing conclusions of a general kind about Storm and narrative omniscience merely from an examination of openings — that the way stories start is not necessarily a guide to the way they will continue, since a writer may, in order to catch his reader's interest and desire to read on, fashion his opening with tools he takes up for this purpose alone and later abandons — that beginnings are the most fictional part of fiction (after all, nobody knows what it is like to begin, or end, life) and thus liable to be contrived and to some extent capricious, a mechanical problem to be dealt with somehow before the writer gets into his own narrative stride — in sum, that the techniques and mannerisms of an opening might be anybody's and not reliably peculiar to the writer who is using them. It seems to me that such an objection does not apply to our particular concern, for two reasons. First, it is precisely in beginnings that narrative omniscience emerges most clearly and performs its most useful functions, especially in short works of fiction where space is at a premium. Basic prerequisites of the story — names, personalities, places, facts, relationships — have to be established, and the omniscient assertion is the quickest, most direct and common way, at first sight the only way, of establishing them. When that kind of assertion is not (or not unambiguously) made, it follows that the effect may justly be called striking and unusual (particularly, again, in the short work), and that the situation is one from which inferences may be drawn: omniscience is being wholly or partly dispensed with at the very point where it would seem indispensable — at the outset of the narration. Secondly, the general impression we get of Storm's openings is one of consistency, not of caprice. If it were just the odd isolated case we were dealing with, we could say that the air of mystery surrounding the opening (with people appearing about whom we know nothing, and things happening which we cannot fathom) is simply a device Storm happens to have picked on in order to arouse the reader's curiosity and make him involved and receptive. But we are not dealing with isolated cases; story after story begins in the same way. The device occurs with such frequency and regularity that we can no longer describe it adequately as 'simply a device'; it has become part of Storm's stock-in-trade (which is another way of saying part of his way of looking at the world); and we can claim to recognize it, when it appears, as something characteristic of *him*, peculiar to *his* manners of composition and bound up with *his* creative act.

3. IMPRESSIONS

Moving further into Storm's stories, we often encounter a curious indirectness in the description of events: broadly speaking, we tend to be told, not that things happen, but rather that they are experienced in the sensibility of whoever is there at the time. This diverting of attention, away from the actual absolute event and onto the impression (especially the sense-impression) it creates, may be encompassed by something so small as the turn of a phrase or the use of a word, or, at the other extreme, it may extend over pages. It is contained, for example, in a sentence from *Hinzelmeier,* a somewhat dark fairy-tale written in 1850; the sentence occurs during the first encounter between Hinzelmeier and his Rosenmädchen, a supernatural figure with whom he is destined to seek union but doomed never to achieve it. The two talk in a kitchen, then:

> Dann schwiegen beide eine Weile, und man hörte nur das Zischen der Pfanne und das Prasseln der Eierkuchen. (SW I 282)

One of Storm's most admirable characteristics is the ability to take a moment like this and make it suddenly come alive; the words on the page cease to be words and become sounds, sights and smells. At such a moment, the reader responds and appreciates and passes on very quickly; an effect so fragile and transient is hard to analyse, and anyway this is the sort of case where analysis is likely to defeat its own ends and destroy the achievement it seeks to understand. But the fact remains that with absolute economy of means (there are few words and no very exotic ones), Storm does manage to charge the moment with plastic value and make it speak plangently to the senses. Clearly the effect is helped by the onomatopoeic 'Zischen' and 'Prasseln', but beyond that one can say little; ultimately the sentence has to stand on its own and be felt or not felt. There is, though, another element in it which gives it greater life and body: this is the fact that the sounds are not conveyed as sounds in isolation, but explicitly as sounds *heard* by someone – not 'Die Pfanne zischte und die Eierkuchen prasselten' but 'Man hörte nur . . .' An essential part of the scene is the idea of people standing in silence, listening; the sounds are made indivisible from the hearers. This is the indirectness of which I spoke; the bald phenomena of sound come to us 'wrapped up' as sense-impressions.

Such moments are not uncommon; and there are a largish number of more extended passages where sensual phenomena tend in the same way to coalesce with the impression they make on the person experiencing them, so that we cannot separate the one element from the other. This seems to occur fairly regularly at moments of crisis in stories; when events take a decisive turn, one almost has the feeling that Storm is reacting to this decisiveness precisely by moving into a subjectivised descriptive mode, in the awareness that the situation is too critical to be conveyed lightly or loosely. There are a couple of passages like this in *In St Jürgen.* The first of them forms part of the account Agnes Hansen gives of her early life. One evening she returns home unexpectedly from a visit to relatives and before going to bed looks out of her window into the garden, in which there is a deep well:

> Da, wie ich eben in das Zimmer zurücktreten wollte, *sah ich* plötzlich aus der Röhre des Brunnens, welcher dort im Schatten lag, eine rote Glut emporlodern; *ich sah* die am Rande wuchernden Grasbüschel und dann darüberher die Zweige des Gebüsches wie in goldenem Feuer schimmern. Mich überfiel eine abergläubige Furcht; denn ich dachte an die Kerze des grauen Männleins, das drunten auf dem Grunde hocken sollte. Als ich aber

schärfer hinblickte, bemerkte ich eine Leiter an der Brunnenwand, von der jedoch nur das oberste Ende *von hier aus sichtbar* war. Im selben Augenblicke *hörte ich* einen Schrei aus der Tiefe; dann ein Gepolter; und ein dumpfes Getöse von Menschenstimmen scholl herauf. Mit einem Male erlosch die Helligkeit; und ich *hörte deutlich,* wie es sprossenweise an der Leiter emporklomm. (SW II 214f; my italics.)

Agnes soon discovers that it was her father whom she had heard; against his better nature, and in the hope of finding enough wealth to save his failing business, he has been persuaded by an evil little man called the Goldmacher to seek for the treasure which local superstition says is hidden at the bottom of the well. The Goldmacher has tricked him into handing over what little money he had, claiming that it was needed to finance the search; so Hansen is now ruined and humiliated. Worse than this, he has given the Goldmacher money entrusted to him by Agnes' fiancé, Harre; Harre, when he finds out, leaves the town in order to spare Hansen the indignity of meeting him face to face; so Agnes' chance of happiness is lost, for Harre never returns in her lifetime. A crisis indeed; and the scene is so constructed that almost every piece of information contained in it is conveyed to us as impressions reaching Agnes' eyes and ears, and as her response to these impressions. Our knowledge of what is going on at any point is delimited by Agnes' imperfect knowledge; that is inherent in her dual role of story-teller and protagonist. In turn, what she knows is limited to what she can perceive; that is verified and reinforced by the anxious accumulation of words of seeing and hearing. The red glow from the well, the golden fire on the grass and in the bushes, the ladder, the cry and clatter and the sound of climbing — all these things enter the narrative, not by virtue of actually existing or occurring, but 'because' Agnes sees and hears them. And even they are not the event itself but only the outward signs of it; what really happened only emerges afterwards, in the father's confession to his daughter; so there, already, is a second indirectness.

The other passage is contained in Harre's account of his experience after leaving Agnes and his birthplace. A deathbed promise obliges him to marry a widow in southern Germany; as the years go by, he is increasingly beset by feelings of guilt at having abandoned Agnes, and by the desire to free himself and go back home to his former life and love. One day, he and his wife are walking along the top of a sheer and crumbling rock-face; she goes ahead to pick flowers:

Ich folgte langsam und war bald in meine alten Träumereien versunken. Wie die verlorene Seligkeit lag die Heimat vor meinen Sinnen, und grübelnd, aber vergebens suchte ich nach einem Weg dahin. Nur wie durch einen Schleier sah ich, daß es nach dem Bruche zu ganz blau von Gentianen wurde und daß meine Frau sich einmal um das andere nach diesen Blumen bückte. Was kümmerte mich das alles! — Da hör ich plötzlich einen Schrei und sehe, wie sie mit den Händen in die Luft greift; ich sehe auch schon, wie unter ihren Füßen das Geröll sich löst und zwischen den Klippen fortpoltert, und zehn Schritt weiter abwärts steht der Fels lotrecht über dem Abgrund.

> Ich stand wie gelähmt. Es brauste mir in den Ohren: 'Bleib; laß sie stürzen;
> du bist frei!' Aber Gott half mir. (SW II 236)

Harre saves his wife; his tension and secretiveness are dissolved, and he reveals his
predicament to her (she knew nothing about Agnes before); later, she tells him
that for his peace of mind he must return and see Agnes again, and he embarks on
the longed-for but finally abortive journey. Another turning-point — but again,
it does not come to us as incidents in an objective setting, but purely as movements
on the canvas of Harre's mind. He sees the things around him 'nur wie durch einen
Schleier'; the crisis becomes a crisis only when his sense-impressions are brought up
against his 'alte Träumereien'; and each element of the whole is insistently prefaced
by the reminder that Harre has seen or heard it. And the atmosphere of subjectivity
is further intensified by the fact that two of Harre's most vivid impressions, that
of his homeland 'vor seinen Sinnen' and that of a voice roaring in his ears, are no
ordinary sense-impressions at all (even though they are described in totally sensual
terms and put on a par with his other perceptions), but projections of his own
imagination, visible and audible to no-one but himself.

Of a kind with the examples I have mentioned — and illustrating the extreme
to which they tend – is what seems to me a very remarkable passage in *Ein stiller
Musikant* (1875). The musician, who tells his own story, has suffered since early
youth from a lack of concentration which invalidates his other musical talents.
He recalls one occasion when he was accompanying his father in a four-handed
piano sonata by Clementi. He tripped up in the rondo section, and his father
became agitated; they began the section again, but he became lost in the same
place:

> Da sprang (mein Vater) auf und warf seinen Stuhl zurück. — — Ich weiß
> nicht, wie es in anderen Familien zugeht — bei all seiner Heftigkeit, ich hatte
> nie von meinem Vater einen Schlag erhalten. Es mag ihm wohl sonst noch
> etwas im Gemüt gelegen haben; denn jetzt, da ich schon fast kein Knabe
> mehr war, wurde er so von seinem Zorne hingerissen.
> Die Noten waren vom Pulpet herab auf den Fußboden gefallen; ich hob
> sie schweigend auf; meine Wange brannte, und in der Brust quoll es mir auf,
> als solle das Blut über meine Lippen stürzen; aber ich setzte mich wieder
> zurecht und legte meine zitternden Hände auf die Tasten. Auch mein Vater
> saß wieder neben mir. (SW II 499)

The actual event described here is a slap in the face; but that one straightforward
fact is never given. What we have is an extraordinarily impressionistic account of
what it *felt* like to be slapped in the face. The passage is an absolutely faithful
record of the boy's sensations (and the man's attempt in later life to encompass
and justify the experience). The blow itself is not reported. We see it coming, and
realise afterwards that it has fallen, but the actual moment is a blank — and that is
a peculiarly powerful and suggestive representation of the way the boy is momentarily stunned (for a blow itself is very commonly the least of our sensations: what
we really feel is the fear before and the pain after); he can only reproduce the

evidence registered by his bewildered senses after he has regained consciousness. By this time the music is already on the floor (we do not see it fall, the tense is pluperfect); the welling-up of feeling or tears inside him must, he feels, be blood ready to spurt from his lips; his hands are trembling. Of a sudden, he realises that his father *is sitting* beside him (the intransitive, positional 'sitzen', not the reflexive, motional 'sich setzen'); there is a dreamlike quality in this abrupt apparition, this breach of continuity; the father is simply there, and the way he got there is unseen and unexplained. In this passage, more strikingly than ever, we are at one remove from the world of exterior events; our knowledge of 'what happened' is conditioned by the fragmentary perceptions of a reeling consciousness.

To round off this series of examples, I want to look at the best-known portrayal of crisis in Storm's work. More accurately it is a climax: the hard and brilliant account of Hauke Haien's last ride over the dykes in *Der Schimmelreiter*. The sequence is too long to reproduce in full; I will just quote the relevant extracts:

> Da klang es wie ein Todesschrei unter den Hufen seines Rosses. Er riß den Zügel zurück; er sah sich um: ihm zur Seite dicht über dem Boden, halb fliegend, halb vom Sturme geschleudert, zog eine Schar von weißen Möwen, ein höhnisches Gegacker ausstoßend; sie suchten Schutz im Lande. Eine von ihnen — der Mond schien flüchtig durch die Wolken — lag am Weg zertreten: dem Reiter war's, als flattere ein rotes Band an ihrem Halse. 'Klaus!' rief er. 'Armer Klaus!'
>
> War es der Vogel seines Kindes? Hatte er Roß und Reiter erkannt und sich bei ihnen bergen wollen? — Der Reiter wußte es nicht ...
>
> Eine furchtbare Böe kam brüllend vom Meer herüber, und ihr entgegen stürmten Roß und Reiter den schmalen Akt zum Deich hinan. Als sie oben waren, stoppte Hauke mit Gewalt sein Pferd. Aber wo war das Meer? Wo Jeverssand? Wo blieb das Ufer drüben? — — Nur Berge von Wasser sah er vor sich, die dräuend gegen den nächtlichen Himmel stiegen ...
>
> ... den Reiter aber wollte es überfallen, als sei hier alle Menschenmacht zu Ende; als müsse jetzt die Nacht, der Tod, das Nichts hereinbrechen ...
>
> Aber — was war das? — Er hielt an dem Winkel zwischen beiden Deichen; wo waren die Leute, die er hieher gestellt, die hier die Wacht zu halten hatten? — Er blickte nach Norden den alten Deich hinauf, denn auch dorthin hatte er einzelne beordert. Weder hier noch dort vermochte er einen Menschen zu erblicken; er ritt ein Stück hinaus, aber er blieb allein; nur das Wehen des Sturmes und das Brausen des Meeres bis aus unermessener Ferne schlug betäubend an sein Ohr. Er wandte das Pferd zurück: er kam wieder zu der verlassenen Ecke und ließ seine Augen längs der Linie des neuen Deichs gleiten; er erkannte deutlich: langsamer, weniger gewaltig rollten hier die Wellen heran; fast schien's, als wäre dort ein ander Wasser. 'Der soll schon stehen!' murmelte er, und wie ein Lachen stieg es in ihm herauf.
>
> Aber das Lachen verging ihm, als seine Blicke weiter an der Linie seines Deiches entlangglitten: an der Nordwestecke — was war das dort? Ein dunkler Haufen wimmelte durcheinander; er sah, wie es sich emsig rührte und drängte — kein Zweifel, es waren Menschen! Was wollten, was arbeiteten die jetzt an seinem Deich? — ...
>
> Schon gewahrte Hauke, daß wohl ein paar Dutzend Menschen in eifriger

Arbeit dort beisammen seien, und schon sah er deutlich, daß eine Rinne quer durch den neuen Deich gegraben war ...

Sie hatten in Schreck die Spaten ruhen lassen, als sie auf einmal den Deichgraf unter sich gewahrten; seine Worte hatte der Sturm ihnen zugetragen, und er sah wohl, daß mehrere ihm zu antworten strebten; aber er gewahrte nur ihre heftigen Gebärden, denn sie standen alle ihm zur Linken, und was sie sprachen, nahm der Sturm hinweg, der hier draußen jetzt die Menschen mitunter wie im Taumel gegeneinanderwarf, so daß sie sich dicht zusammen- scharten. Hauke maß mit seinen raschen Augen die gegrabene Rinne und den Stand des Wassers, das, trotz des neuen Profiles, fast an die Höhe des Deiches hinaufklatschte und Roß und Reiter überspritzte. Nur noch zehn Minuten Arbeit — er sah es wohl —, dann brach die Hochflut durch die Rinne, und der Hauke-Haien-Koog wurde vom Meer begraben! ...

Ein donnerartiges Rauschen zu seinen Füßen weckte ihn aus diesen Träumen; der Schimmel wollte nicht mehr vorwärts. Was war das? — Das Pferd sprang zurück, und er fühlte es, ein Deichstück stürzte vor ihm in die Tiefe ...

Wie sinnlos starrte Hauke darauf hin; eine Sündflut war's, um Tier und Menschen zu verschlingen. Da blickte wieder ihm der Lichtschein in die Augen; es war derselbe, den er vorhin gewahrt hatte; noch immer brannte der auf seiner Werfte; und als er jetzt ermutigt in den Koog hinabsah, gewahrte er wohl, daß hinter dem sinnverwirrenden Strudel, der tosend vor ihm hinabstürzte, nur noch eine Breite von etwa hundert Schritten überflutet war; dahinter konnte er deutlich den Weg erkennen, der vom Koog heran- führte. Er sah noch mehr: ein Wagen, nein, eine zweirädrige Karriole kam wie toll gegen den Deich herangefahren; ein Weib, ja auch ein Kind saßen darin. Und jetzt — war das nicht das kreischende Gebell eines kleinen Hundes, das im Sturm vorüberflog? Allmächtiger Gott! Sein Weib, sein Kind waren es; schon kamen sie dicht heran, und die schäumende Wassermasse drängte auf sie zu ...

Da sah er, daß das Weib wie gegen ihn hinauf die Arme streckte: Hatte sie ihn erkannt? Hatte die Sehnsucht, die Todesangst um ihn sie aus dem sicheren Hause getrieben? Und jetzt — rief sie ein letztes Wort ihm zu? — ...

... noch einmal sah er drunten den Kopf des Pferdes, die Räder des Gefährtes aus dem wüsten Greuel emportauchen und dann quirlend darin untergehen. Die starren Augen des Reiters, der so einsam auf dem Deiche hielt, sahen weiter nichts ...

... noch immer sah er das Licht von seinem Hause schimmern; es war ihm wie entseelt. (SW IV 395ff.)

Clearly, we are seeing things 'from inside' Hauke in these passages; what is given is what his eyes and ears can imperfectly make out in the howling gale. The true setting for the events is not the outside world but Hauke's mental landscape, his processes of thought, feeling and perception. The narrative is punctuated throughout by his anguished questions: has he crushed his daughter's pet gull? where is the sea, Jeverssand, the opposite shore? where are the men he put on watch? what is making his horse baulk? is that the cry of a dog? does his wife recognize him this last time and call out to him? The narrative is carried forward, or in effect held back, by these questions, of which some are answered incompletely and others not at all; it is partly because of them that we know, or do not know, what is happening.

And of course, here as in the other stories I have talked about, incident is conveyed repeatedly and explicitly as sense-impression: not 'this or that happened' but 'he saw this, he heard that' — even, at one point, 'er *fühlte* es, ein Deichstück stürzte vor ihm in die Tiefe'. The dice are somewhat loaded here, certainly; in the search for 'relevant extracts' I have cut the scene down to about a third of its length. But the fact that even a third of this climactic sequence is so insistently couched in the terms I have described seems to me sufficient to justify its inclusion as evidence for my argument, which in summary is this: Storm has recourse to this highly specialised narrative mode frequently enough for us to talk of it as characteristic of him; moreover, he tends to move into it particularly when he is dealing with critical situations, points in a story where, more than elsewhere, we may expect a writer to be exerting his powers to the utmost in order to show incidents at what seems to him to be their most vivid and penetrating, their most immediate and authentic and experientially 'real'.

4. COMMUNICATION

One of the conundra of literary enquiry is the distinction between theme and technique. Ultimately, I think, the line is nowhere certainly to be drawn, because it does not seem to be possible to divorce the nature of a thought from the way in which it is expressed, the act of thinking being in itself an act of formulation and expression. The *raison d'être* of this study is after all the principle that in literary creation the manner *is* the matter, that a specific and valid guide to what a writer says about the world is the way he says it. If the writer's preoccupations are inseparable from the devices, general and particular, which he uses to formulate them, then theme is technique and technique theme: the discussion of the one involves immediate encounter with the other. I hope this argues for the appropriateness to my concern of the phenomenon I want to talk about next, which at first sight appears to be 'thematic' rather than 'technical', or at least to have a foot in both camps. The phenomenon in question is Storm's handling of the problem of communication.

To call it a problem is justified, for it is frequently a major factor in the plot of Storm's stories; and even when it plays only a minor or transitory role, it tends to be the object of anxious attention and close description. A man tells another what he feels, thinks or wants, and the other understands and answers him — this everyday occurrence is elevated by Storm into a 'problematic' event, which has to be treated with elaborate, almost exaggerated, care and circumspection. Acts of communication are rarely shown to be easy or straightforward; very often they are unsuccessful. At the simplest level, as in this moment from *Veronika* (1861), the situation is simply one of words calling forth no reply:

> Er schwieg eine Weile. 'Haben Sie denn', fragte er zögernd, 'das kluge Auge des alten Mannes nicht bemerkt, der Ihnen gegenüberstand?'

Sie wandte den Kopf und blickte flüchtig zu ihm auf.

'Ich mußte es selber tun, Veronika – verzeihen Sie mir! – Ich kann Sie nicht vor andern tadeln hören'.

Es zog sich wie ein Schleier über ihre Augen, und die langen schwarzen Wimpern senkten sich tief auf ihre Wangen; aber sie erwiderte nichts. – – (SW I 566)

A little later in this story of a woman who is nearly enticed into an affair with her husband's cousin, the veil is briefly drawn aside, and there is a response and an understanding; but it is of the strangest kind. Veronika and Rudolf, the cousin, are at a water-mill:

Veronika war gegenüber in die Tür getreten, die zu dem Gerinne hinaus-führte, und blickte unter sich in die tosenden Räder, auf denen das Wasser in der Abendsonne blitzte. Rudolf folgte ihr nicht; er stand drinnen neben dem großen Kammrade, die Augen düster und unablässig auf sie gerichtet. – Endlich wandte sie den Kopf. Sie sprach, er sah, wie ihre Lippen sich bewegten; aber er vernahm keine Worte.

'Ich verstehe nicht!' sagte er und schüttelte den Kopf.

Als er zu ihr gehen wollte, war sie schon in den innern Raum zurückgetreten. Im Vorübergehen kam sie dem Rade, neben welchem er stand, so nahe, daß die Zacken fast ihr Haar berührten. Sie sah es nicht, denn sie war noch geblendet von der Abendsonne; aber sie fühlte ihre Hände ergriffen und sich rasch zur Seite gezogen. Als sie aufsah, blickten ihre Augen in die seinen. Sie schwiegen beide; ein plötzliches Vergessen fiel wie ein Schatten über sie. Zu ihren Häupten tosten die Mühlwerke; von draußen klang das eintönige Rauschen des Wassers, das über die Räder in die Tiefe stürzte. – Allmählich aber begannen die Lippen des jungen Mannes sich zu regen, und unter dem Schutze des betäubenden Schalles, in dem der Laut seiner Stimme wesenlos verschwand, flüsterte er trunkene, betörende Worte. Ihr Ohr vernahm sie nicht, aber sie las ihren Sinn aus der Bewegung seines Mundes, aus der leidenschaftlichen Blässe seines Angesichts. Sie legte den Kopf zurück und schloß die Augen; nur ihr Mund lächelte und gab von ihrem Leben Kunde. So stand sie wie in Scham gebannt, das Antlitz hülflos ihm entgegenhaltend, die Hände wie vergessen in den seinen. (SW I 567)

Then the mill-wheel stops, the spell is broken, and the affair is already over. This is the nearest these two people ever come to any union of feeling, the nearest each comes to being illumined for the other; yet the violent racket of the wheel, which contributes more than anything else to the erotic intensity of the moment, is the very thing in which all attempts at specific verbal communication are drowned out. He does not understand her words, she does not understand his: we are told as much. It is the undefined movements of his lips and the paleness of his face that convey to her the import of what he tries to say; he must read her response, even assure himself that she is alive, from the smile on her mouth and her hands in his. And at the beginning and end stand the twin images of 'forgetfulness' – forgetfulness, perhaps, of the commitment which such a moment, with more definite understanding, might normally bring.

An earlier story, *Angelika,* is a series of episodes which trace the gradual drawing apart of Angelika and Ehrhard, whom she loves but who cannot at first marry her because of the demands of his (unspecified) profession. By the time he is free to make her his wife, she has become engaged to someone else; then, before the wedding, her fiancé dies, but Ehrhard finds that by now his feelings for her have faded and disappeared beyond recall in the anguish of renunciation. The major indication of this progressive (and, it seems, inevitable) estrangement is an ever clearer failure on the part of Ehrhard and Angelika to communicate their feelings and fears directly and unambiguously to each other. This incident, for instance, occurs about half-way through; the two are sitting outside an inn beside a lake, and Ehrhard tries to ask Angelika what a particularly disturbing scene between them the day before had meant:

> Der Abendwind erhob sich; und Musik, von der Luft getragen, vom Wasser her, ganz aus der Ferne, kam herangeweht. Er legte die Arme weit vor sich auf den Tisch; seine Augen glänzten. 'Musik!' sagte er, 'törichtes Entzücken befällt mich; — mir ist, als müsse nun noch einmal alles wiederkommen'.
>
> Sie sah in seine Augen, sie konnte nicht anders; aber während er die Hand nach der ihrigen ausstreckte, die ohne Handschuh auf dem Tische lag, stand sie auf und ging über den kurzen Rasen nach dem See hinab. Er gesellte sich zu ihr. Sie sprachen nicht, sie sahen vor sich hinaus auf das Wasser; es war so still, daß sie die Ruderschläge der fernsten Kähne hörten. Er pflückte einen Immortellenstengel, wie deren viele auf dem Rasen waren, und gab ihr den. Sie nahm ihn, ohne hinzusehen, und drehte ihn langsam zwischen den Fingern. So gingen sie nebeneinander her, vom Rasen auf die Kiesel und auf den Sand hinunter, und standen erst still, als schon das Wasser ihre Schuh' benetzte.
>
> Da sie so weit gekommen waren, sagte Ehrhard, und sie mußte es fühlen, wie mühsam er es sagte: 'Angelika, war das ein Abschied gestern?'
>
> Sie antwortete nicht; sie sah ins Wasser zu ihren Füßen und bohrte mit der Spitze ihres Sonnenschirmes in dem feuchten Sande.
>
> 'Antworte mir, Angelika!'
>
> Sie öffnete, ohne aufzusehen, ihre Hand und ließ die Blume, die er ihr gegeben, in den See fallen.
>
> Er fühlte einen Schrei in seiner Brust aufsteigen; aber er biß die Zähne zusammen und erstickte ihn. (SW I 479f.)

Ehrhard seems to be banging his head against a brick wall in trying to coax some response, *any* response, from Angelika. He tries to dissolve the tension by somewhat synthetically cheerful references to the gaiety of the music, but without success. She gets up from the table when he reaches for her hand. They stand by the water and say nothing. He gives her a flower, and she twists the stem between her fingers without looking at it. He asks her a question with obvious strain in his voice, but there is no reply. He insists on an answer, but still no words come; she merely drops the flower into the water. This nightmarish, impassive silence begins to infect him too, numbing what small stock of effective or affecting expression he has left:

when a cry wells up in him, he stifles it. The whole interlude has been abortive; he has no answer to his question, and no clue even to her state of mind. And in case it should be thought that the hints are pretty obvious and that he must be a very obtuse and lovesick young man not to recognize her complete indifference, I should add that five minutes later she has thrown herself into his arms, breathless and stammering (inevitably, no actual *words* come out) and it is he who now seems in danger of being closed off from her:

> 'Sei ruhig', sagte er, 'sei ruhig!' und strich ihr mit zitternder Hand über das heiße Haar. Aber derselbe Augenblick, in welchem sie die Kränkung der letzten Tage von ihm nahm, legte mit einem Male all ihren Zwiespalt und ihre Unruhe wie eine Last auf seine Seele, so daß er nur mit Zagen die in seinen Armen hielt, die jetzt mit vollem ungestümem Herzen zu ihm drängte. (SW I 480)

'A man tells another what he thinks, feels or wants, and the other understands and answers him' — what a remote possibility that seems in the face of Ehrhard's predicament.

Situations like this crop up time and again, with variations, in Storm's writing. Whenever two people are together, the odds are that one will be unwilling or unable to convey his state of mind to the other, and the other will thus be forced to glean what he can from odd outward signs and indications, sometimes successfully, sometimes not, but always with much effort. A moment of partial success is to be found in *Auf dem Staatshof* (1856-8). Marx, who tells the story, is an admirer of Anne Lene, the last surviving member of a formerly wealthy and brilliant family. She becomes engaged to a Kammerjunker of unprepossessing character; then:

> Einige Tage darauf vermißten wir Anne Lene bei der Mittagstafel, was sonst niemals zu geschehen pflegte. — Als ich, um sie zu suchen, in den Garten trat, begegnete mir der Kammerjunker, der wie gewöhnlich mit einem halben Kopfnicken an mir vorbeipassierte. Da ich Anne Lene nicht gewahrte, so ging ich in den untern Teil des Gartens, in welchem mein Vater eine kleine Baumschule angelegt hatte. Hier stand sie mit dem Rücken an einen jungen Apfelbaum gelehnt. Sie schien ganz einem innern Erlebnis zugewendet; denn ihre Augen starrten unbeweglich vor sich hin, und ihre kleinen Hände lagen fest geschlossen auf der Brust. Ich fragte sie: 'Was ist denn dir begegnet, Anne Lene?' Aber sie sah nicht auf; sie ließ die Arme sinken und sagte: 'Nichts, Marx; was sollte mir denn begegnet sein?' Zufällig aber hatte ich bemerkt, daß die Krone des kleinen Baums wie von einem Pulsschlage in gleichmäßigen Pausen erschüttert wurde, und es überkam mich eine Ahnung dessen, was hier geschehen sein könne; zugleich einen Reiz, Anne Lene fühlen zu lassen, daß sie mich nicht zu täuschen vermöge. Ich zeigte mit dem Finger in den Baum und sagte: 'Sieh nur, wie dir das Herz klopft!' (SW I 513)

Anne Lene's emotion is translated into heartbeats, which in their turn shake the tree and provide something that Marx can *see*. He relates this to his encounter with the Kammerjunker; and so he discovers that Anne Lene is upset, and dimly divines the reason for her state — how modest the accomplishment, yet how elaborate and oblique the means, and how great the sense of pride and success!

In Storm, one of the major unhappinesses of unhappy love is the presence of this barrier to direct communication; the more intense the feeling, the less easy it seems to formulate it, even to oneself; the greater the desire to understand, the denser the mists of incomprehension surrounding the attempt; the sense of impotent frustration is everywhere apparent. Take this unsatisfactory conversation from *Auf der Universität* (1862); Philipp, the pupil at the 'Lateinische Schule', and Lore, the tailor's daughter, talk to each other in the darkness:

> Sie wandte sich um und blieb ruhig vor mir stehen. Ich hörte, wie sie mit den Händen über ihr Haar strich, wie sie ihr Tüchelchen fester um den Hals knüpfte; aber ich suchte lange vergebens des Gedankens habhaft zu werden, der wie ein dunkler Nebel vor meinen Augen schwamm. 'Lore', sagte ich endlich, 'bist du noch bös mit mir?'
>
> Sie blickte zu Boden und schüttelte den Kopf.
>
> 'Willst du morgen wieder hier sein?'
>
> Sie zögerte einen Augenblick. 'Ich darf des Abends sonst nicht ausgehen', sagte sie dann.
>
> 'Lore, du lügst; das ist es nicht, sag mir die Wahrheit!'
>
> Ich hatte ihre Hand gefaßt; aber sie entzog sie mir wieder.
>
> 'So sprich doch, Lore! — Willst du nicht sprechen?'
>
> Noch eine Weile stand sie schweigend vor mir; dann schlug sie die Augen auf und sah mich an. 'Ich weiß es wohl', sagte sie leise, 'du heiratest doch einmal nur eine von den feinen Damen'.
>
> Ich verstummte. Auf diesen Einwurf war ich gar nicht gefaßt; an so ungeheuere Dinge hatte ich nie gedacht und wußte nichts darauf zu antworten.
>
> Und ehe ich mich dessen versah, hörte ich ein leises 'Gute Nacht' des Mädchens; und bald sah ich sie drüben in dem Schatten der Häuser verschwinden. Ich vernahm noch das vorsichtige Aufdrücken einer Haustür, das leise Anschlagen der Türschelle; dann wandte ich mich und ging . . . (SW II 80f.)

Philipp is not clear about his own attitude, Lore's is a mystery to him. His first question is answered in dumb show, the second is evaded with an excuse, the demand for truth elicits no response but the withdrawing of her hand; the answer, when he finally wrests one from her, is startling and at cross-purposes, consonant with none of his preoccupations and seemingly irrelevant to his predicament. Her words are hardly more communicative than the other scraps of sound which reach him; he is reduced to recording how he hears her hand passing over her hair and the knotting of her kerchief (could any sounds be more nearly inaudible than these?), and finally the noise of the door and the bell — almost as though these things might tell him (and us) something. Lore goes in, and Philipp is left with a few ill-fitting fragments of information which he must somehow piece together into a judgement of what is happening to her and to him. The chances of illumination cannot be very great.

Storm seems fascinated by the complexity and obliqueness of it all, preoccupied with the circuitous conventions and tentative devices by which his human beings try to make known to one another what they feel; the conventions and devices, indeed, rival the feelings as the centre of interest. Edde Brunken, the ugly little hunchbacked painter of *Eine Malerarbeit* (1867) becomes infatuated with a young and beautiful girl, Gertrud (Gertrud's cousin Arnold, who tells the story, is a friend of Brunken's). Gertrud is at first quite unaware of the affection she has inspired in Brunken, and when he eventually declares himself she is shocked and repelled.[102] A straight-forward and predictable situation; but the *manner* of the declaration and its rejection is elliptical in the extreme. The occasion Brunken seizes upon is a 'Wald- und Bergpartie'. At one point the children on the excursion, who are under Gertrud's care, clamour to be told the story of Beauty and the Beast. Gertrud does not know it, so Brunken steps in and tells it himself. As the tale progresses, Beauty assumes ever more clearly the features of Gertrud, and the Beast those of Brunken — Brunken is in fact weaving his declaration into the fabric of a fairy-tale. After a while Gertrud leaves the children and walks away through the trees. Arnold follows her, and after much persuasion she sobs out her realisation of Brunken's love for her, the revulsion she feels at it, and her sense of guilt at having unintentionally en-couraged him. Arnold calms her as best he can, then leaves her, hoping to find Brunken and get him away before he can see Gertrud and realise what he has done. But after only a few steps he finds Brunken leaning against a tree:

> 'Brunken', rief ich, 'was machst du hier?'
> 'Nicht eben viel', erwiderte er, 'die Kleine da hat mir das Ende meiner Ungeheuergeschichte erzählt; eigentlich freilich hat sie es wohl nur dir erzählen wollen, aber ich habe scharfe Ohren'. (SW II 252)

Gertrud only becomes aware of Brunken's feelings by discerning them through the veil of a fairy-story; Brunken must eavesdrop on her conversation with someone else in order to discover her reaction. For a while, at least, it is this tortuous process of clarification which absorbs our interest — this is the necessary and significant prelude to the ensuing examination of Brunken's self-hatred, contemplated suicide and final regeneration.

To commit the expression of one's love to the vessel of a fairy-tale; that is one kind of innuendo. Here is another, from *Eine Halligfahrt* (1871). The event described is basically the same — an indirect challenge indirectly refused — but the ingredients are different. Here both characters seem tacitly agreed on the convention they will use; they exploit the same external or neutral situation to convey their feelings to each other (rather as if Gertrud had given Brunken her answer in another fairy-tale told to the children). The story-teller finds a new boat in a shed; he sits in the boat and muses for a while; then he realises that he has been followed into the shed by Susanne, the girl to whom he is attracted. They exchange a few words, and then:

> 'So gehen Sie bei mir an Bord!' erwiderte ich, auf meiner Ruderbank zur Seite rückend, 'es ist ein neues sicheres Fahrzeug'.
> 'In diese Boot soll ich steigen? Weshalb? Es ist so düster hier'.
> 'Hören Sie nur, wie die zarten Geister musizieren!'
> Sie horchte einen Augenblick, dann kam sie näher und hatte schon ihr

Füßchen auf den Rand des Bootes gesetzt.

'Nun, was zögern Sie, Susanne? Haben Sie kein Vertrauen zu meiner Steuerkunst?'

Sie sah mich an; es war etwas von dem blauen Strahl eines Edelsteins in diesem Blick, und es überfiel mich, ob mir nicht doch von diesen Augen Leids geschehen könne. Ich mag sie dabei wohl seltsam angestarrt haben; denn, als wandle eine Furcht sie an, zog sie langsam ihren Fuß zurück.

'Wir wollen lieber an den Strand hinab!' sagte sie leise . . . (SW II 283f.)

It could be said that this passage, like many others, is an example of Storm's gratuitously and annoyingly roundabout way of giving us information that is essentially simple: all he need have said is that the man is fonder of the girl than she of him. But the situation is not simple. The girl's attitude remains enigmatic throughout — minutes later on the beach she flies into his arms, from motives which are never made clear (we saw the same thing happen in *Angelika*),[103] and yet almost immediately the spell is broken by the man's clumsiness, and the two are at a distance again; nothing unambiguous emerges. Moreover, I would question whether Storm's principal concern here is to tell *us* anything about the nature of the man's and the girl's feelings. The first function of the scene (the more so since it is in dialogue) is to explore and show the way in which the characters try to reveal themselves *to each other.* In the fictional scheme, the ellipsis is theirs, not Storm's; what we observe is the manner they choose to enlighten each other, not the manner Storm chooses to enlighten us.

Examples multiply, each with its individual colouring, yet each contributing to a composite effect — communication examined so attentively that it rises to the level of a problem. The passages I have looked at so far have been drawn in the main from stories where the thematic context is one of young love, attachments formed before maturity (though none the less intense or absorbing for that); and this is the context, it is true, in which we become most frequently and sharply aware of the problem. The concern does, though, make itself felt in other areas too, less often but just as clearly: different and maturer relationships can contain (and be bedevilled by) the sense of how difficult it is to make one's words and actions a true mirror for one's thoughts and feelings, how difficult it is, by extension, to find a means of understanding what another thinks or feels. *Hans und Heinz Kirch* (1881-2) is first and foremost the enactment of a basic incomprehension between father and son. Hans Kirch's absorbed and anxious love for his son Heinz undermines and finally destroys the relationship, instead of enriching it, because Hans is unable to demonstrate his affection directly for what it is. When he tries to express himself, the words come out wrong, coloured so highly with what is severe and irascible in his temperament that only the severity and irascibility are conveyed and the love is hidden beyond finding. An early incident is indicative. While Heinz is still a boy, Hans takes him out on a short voyage in his ship. Heinz, six years old and adventurous, climbs out onto the bowsprit and thus unwittingly exposes himself to the grave risk of being knocked overboard by the flapping sail and drowned.

Eventually, while Hans looks on in an agony of suspense, he climbs back onto the deck, still quite unaware of the danger he has so narrowly escaped:

> Im selben Augenblicke war der Knabe fröhlich aufs Verdeck gesprungen; nun lief er mit ausgebreiteten Armen auf den Vater zu. Die Zähne des gefahrgewohnten Mannes schlugen noch aneinander: 'Heinz, Heinz, das tust du mir nicht wieder!' Krampfhaft preßte er den Knaben an sich; aber schon begann die überstandene Angst dem Zorne gegen ihren Urheber Platz zu machen. 'Das tust du mir nicht wieder!' Noch einmal sagte er es; aber ein dumpfes Grollen klang jetzt in seiner Stimme; seine Hand hob sich, als wolle er sie auf den Knaben fallen lassen, der erstaunt und furchtsam zu ihm aufblickte. (SW III 344f.)

Relief gives way to anger, love is veiled beneath bitter reproach; and Heinz's response can be nothing other than fear and, later, rebellion. The strain engendered here is never dispelled; Hans finds little difficulty in revealing to others his continuing fatherly pride in Heinz's intelligence and unbounded, often mischievous energy; (Cf. SW III 349) but when he is face to face with his son, this capacity for direct communication fails him, and his affection only appears in its distorted images of irritation and censure. The day before Heinz is due to leave home, Hans tries desperately to banish the distortion and simply 'say what he feels'; the attempt is described in this beautifully wrought and moving passage:

> Die Mutter hatte diesmal nicht ohne Tränen ihres Sohnes Kiste gepackt, und nach der Rückkehr aus der Kirche legte sie noch ihr eigenes Gesangbuch obenauf. Der Vater hatte auch in den letzten Tagen außer dem Notwendigen nicht viel mit seinem Sohne gesprochen; nur an diesem Abend, als er auf dem dunklen Hausflur ihm begegnete, griff er nach seiner Hand und schüttelte sie heftig: 'Ich sitze hier nicht still, Heinz; für dich, nur für dich! Und komm auch glücklich wieder!' Hastig hatte er es vorgestoßen; dann ließ er die Hand seines Sohnes fahren und trabte eilig nach dem Hof hinaus.
>
> Überrascht blickte ihm Heinz eine Weile nach; aber seine Gedanken waren anderswo . . . (SW III 350f.)

The struggle and embarrassment speak from each word; to make this apparently modest demonstration the father has been extended to the utmost, because it is full of the directness which background and temperament have conditioned him not to achieve. But the effort has come too late; its failure is measured by the son's reaction, and sealed only a few hours later by a last raging quarrel; Heinz departs in a mood of animosity as bitter as there has ever been between the two. Hans never finds his son again; some years later he turns back a letter from him because it is unfranked (the unread letter — a perfect figure of failed communication); and when Heinz, if it *is* Heinz,[104] finally returns, the alienation is so complete that his father cannot even be sure that it is he.

What is there to set against all this sum of incomprehension? *Der Schimmelreiter*, I think, contains an alternative and a hope. It is something of a departure because it sets the personal relation at one side; the real centre of the story is in Hauke Haien's encounter with wider entities, a social order and a pattern of nature. The marriage of Hauke and Elke is more a given factor, and less a 'problem', than most other relationships or marriages we find in Storm's work. Its firmness and resilience are never in doubt, and the interest is in what it *provides* – constant companionship and mutual comfort, an area of assurance in Hauke's explosively uncertain world. Hauke never has to be too worried about what it *is* or *needs*; that comes of itself. The 'given' quality of the marriage certainly doesn't exclude its having human verisimilitude and individual colour (in this regard I would contrast it with that other 'given' marriage, the blissful blank hidden somewhere between the second and third acts of Hebbel's *Agnes Bernauer*), and there are elements which show it as less than a perfect union. There is above all a reticence, which at first sight looks very like that which we have seen in the other stories: the courtship is conducted in a characteristically oblique way,[105] and even after many years of marriage Hauke is always loath, beyond a certain point, to reveal the extent of his worries to his wife, so that we frequently read things like: Er machte sich los, um weiteren Fragen des geliebten Weibes auszuweichen'.[106] But the reticence is one of choice and born of a kind of consideration; it does not undermine the basic love and trust but is indeed part of it. There is only one 'problem' by which the marriage seems really threatened: this is Elke's fear of having failed Hauke by remaining childless for so long and then by bearing him a child which turns out to be feeble-minded. The fear is finally dispelled by being expressed (and this is enough, because it is the fear, not the facts it centres on, that is the danger). I quote the scene because it embodies something rare in Storm, a direct and explicit and redeeming act of communication, and because it is superbly written, a model of delicacy and insight:

'Nein, Hauke, laß mich sprechen: das Kind, das ich nach Jahren dir geboren habe, es wird für immer ein Kind bleiben. O lieber Gott! Es ist schwachsinnig; ich muß es einmal vor dir sagen'.

'Ich wußte es längst', sagte Hauke und hielt die Hand seines Weibes fest, die sie ihm entziehen wollte.

'So sind wir denn doch allein geblieben', sprach sie wieder.

Aber Hauke schüttelte den Kopf: 'Ich hab sie lieb, und sie schlägt ihre Ärmchen um mich und drückt sich fest an meine Brust; um alle Schätze wollte ich das nicht missen!'

Die Frau sah finster vor sich hin: 'Aber warum?' sprach sie; 'was hab ich arme Mutter denn verschuldet?'

– 'Ja, Elke, das hab ich freilich auch gefragt, den, der allein es wissen kann; aber du weißt ja auch, der Allmächtige gibt den Menschen keine Antwort – vielleicht, weil wir sie nicht begreifen würden'.

Er hatte die andere Hand seines Weibes gefaßt und zog sie sanft zu sich heran: 'Laß dich nicht irren, dein Kind, wie du es tust, zu lieben; sei sicher, das versteht es!'

Da warf sich Elke an ihres Mannes Brust und weinte sich satt und war mit ihrem Leid nicht mehr allein. Dann plötzlich lächelte sie ihn an; nach einem heftigen Händedruck lief sie hinaus und holte sich ihr Kind aus der Kammer der alten Trin' Jans, und nahm es auf ihren Schoß und hätschelte und küßte

es, bis es stammelnd sagte: 'Mutter, mein liebe Mutter!'
So lebten die Menschen auf dem Deichgrafshofe still beisammen; wäre das
Kind nicht dagewesen, es hätte viel gefehlt. (SW IV 380f.)

Once at least, then, it can be done. But it *is* rare, and over against Hauke and
Elke there is a long line of Storm's people who are beset by the difficulty of telling
their mind to others and reading and understanding the oblique messages which
may open the minds of others to them. Let the hunchback Edde Brunken speak
for them all. Thinking about suicide himself, he finds a shoe at the edge of a well
and wonders whether someone else might have carried out the same design; his wry
reflection reverberates across so many other situations:

> Unter mir in den Binsen saß freilich ein großer Frosch mit seiner ganzen
> Gesellschaft und suchte mir die Geschichte vorzusingen. Ich merkte wohl,
> daß sie von allem Bescheid wußten. Aber du weißt, ich bin immer ein
> schlechter Linguiste gewesen; ich verstand die Kerle nicht. (SW II 258)

5. FACTS

If Storm's characters have difficulty in divining what is actually going on in each
other's minds and lives, his readers can often be said to be in no better case. It is
common for us to be mystified about what makes these people behave as they do,
or where the responsibility lies for their downfall or (Storm's habitual and less
sensational equivalent) the frustration of their desires. In an earlier chapter I tried
to describe the proliferation of false starts, contradictions and cul-de-sacs with which
we are faced in a number of the early stories when we begin to move around inside
them in a real attempt to discover their causal centre. What draws Reinhard and
Elisabeth apart with such curious inevitability, crossing their aspirations and numbing
their energy? What, if anything, is the underlying motivation of the catalogue of bad
luck, perverse timing and incommunication which attends the relationship of Ehrhard
and Angelika, eventually destroying the hope of union? Why does Mamsell Sophie
reject the Doktor? Why are Agnes Hansen and Harre lost to each other in the way
which produces the maximum of suffering and through a concatenation of events
which approaches the absurd? I suggested that the answer to these questions does
not lie on the surface: any immediate cause we fasten on is soon surrounded with
reservations, and has as much speaking against it as for it; and we are compelled to
push further and further back until we arrive at a kind of explanation in terms of a
general human predicament or, more mundanely, 'the way things are'. And later on
I shall be discussing a related problem in the last two stories, namely the complications that arise when we come (and the reference of these stories is such that
we *must* come) to apportion blame, that is, to perceive causality in a moral light.
Patterns of guilt which at first seemed clear enough break up as soon as we examine
them more closely, and we are left in the end with a very different picture. Is Franz
Jebe's penance 'necessary and just', and if so, what is the nature of his crime?[107]

Who bears the responsibility for the destruction of Hauke Haien and his family? If we consider Hauke even partly to blame, what precisely do we charge him with?[108] I shall suggest that here too the immediate answer is not the ultimately satisfactory one, that the two stories are rooted in ambiguity, and that there is a conflict between what Storm seems to have intended and what actually emerges from the text.

This misting over of causality (or of responsibility, its ethical counterpart) is present in other works as well. We must search long and hard to discover what pushes the heroines of *Auf dem Staatshof* and *Auf der Universität* onto the edge of a precipice and finally topples them over into the void; or exactly why and how the intense attachments of *Eine Halligfahrt, Waldwinkel* and *'Es waren zwei Königskinder'* come to nothing, leaving only desolation and, commonly, death in their wake; or which of a handful of factors (an inadequate wife and foolish mother, the demon drink, a thoughtless friend, heredity, a preying aristocrat) preponderates in the death of a seaman and the corruption and suicide of his daughter in *John Riew'*.[109] But it is not only the causality which is misted over. Very often, we are denied direct access to the very facts on which we could base our assessment of 'why it all happened'. Indeed, we may simply be denied *any* access. A precondition of the conflicts of *Angelika,* for instance, is the nature of Ehrhard's profession, which at first prevents him contemplating marriage to Angelika in the foreseeable future, and effectively makes him ineligible in the eyes of her family. What profession is this, whose demands cast such a shadow? Ehrhard has loved Angelika for years; what vocation could have been insistent enough for him to obey it even though it meant relinquishing his hope of marrying her? We need to know these things fairly precisely before we can judge just *how* irreconcilable the two conflicting claims on Ehrhard are, and thus before we can come to any proper conclusion about his initiative, integrity of feeling and strength of purpose; and this we must do, since the accusation most easily levelled at Ehrhard and other of Storm's early characters is that they are merely vacillating and pusillanimous, lacking the courage, energy or imagination to question and resist the pressures which are brought to bear on them by their narrow social situation. But we never find out what Ehrhard does for a living. The story opens like this:

> Seit Jahren hatten im stillen seine Augen an ihren feinen Zügen gehangen; denn sie war aufgewachsen, während er, wie auch noch jetzt, fast täglich in ihrem mütterlichen Hause verkehrte. Aber er war in einer erst in spätester Jugend eingeschlagenen Laufbahn, welche ihm die Aussicht auf Begründung einer Familie für immer oder wenigstens innerhalb der Jahre zu verwehren schien, in welchen Sitte und Gefühl dies gestatten. Noch jetzt nach fast geschlossener Jugend ein anderes zu versuchen, vergönnte ihm der Umfang seiner Bildung und seiner äußern Mittel nicht ...

The two claims are stated in what appears to be naked and diametric contrast, pivoting on the 'Aber'; yet the first avoids the word 'Liebe' and its cognates (in the same way as they are completely excluded from *Immensee*),[110] and the second is really quite a detailed gloss on the one word which is not there — 'dustman' or 'postman' or whatever Ehrhard's job is. The passage goes on to describe Ehrhard's unsuccessful efforts to resolve the conflict:

> . . . seiner äußern Mittel nicht. — Alles dessen war er sich bewußt; oft und vergeblich hatte er auf Mittel gedacht, wie er die Geliebte, wenn sie ja sonst die Seine würde, vor der geistigen und körperlichen Verkümmerung zu bewahren vermochte, welche in dem Staate, dem seine Heimat angehörte, das gewöhnliche Los der Frauen seines Standes war. So gelangte er endlich dahin, in allen Gedanken an die Zukunft sein Leben von dem ihrigen zu trennen. (SW I 470)

'Geliebte' — that claim is now in the open, but the other is still obscured. The gloss is extended, but the obscurity is, if anything, deepened. The extra indications which subsequently appear (" 'das weißt du, unter welche Zahl ich gehöre . . .' " or 'die Ungunst seiner vergangenen Jahre sowie die Öde und Kargheit seiner Zukunft . . .') (SW I 471) do little to help. We are asked to take on trust the assertion that this unspecified calling makes union impossible. But even that is later thrown into the melting-pot when we read:

> In dem Jahre, welches diesen Vorgängen folgte, war in den öffentlichen Dingen eine Sturm- und Drangperiode eingetreten, welche jede bisherige Berechnung in den Verhältnissen der einzelnen über den Haufen warf . . . (Ehrhard) sah sich plötzlich in einer äußern Lage, welche seine früheren Wünsche . . . bei weitem übertraf. (SW I 486)

So all has changed: the circumstance (we know not what) which previously forbade Ehrhard's aspirations is transformed (into we know not what), and he can now think in terms of making Angelika his wife. By this time, though, it is too late; she is engaged to someone else, and the misery continues. However that may be, we are left in the dark: our involvement with the predicament of these two is hampered by our ignorance (in all but the vaguest reference) of a fact which is central to it.

Such an extreme of reticence is rare; I begin with it, not for its typicality, but because it *is* an extreme and shows up in a strong light what I have to say. When an obscurity occurs in these stories, it is more commonly possible to work out the fact concerned by inference from other indications; but the important thing is that we are called upon to do the inferring and the working out, not to accept a fact directly given. And as words like 'inferring' and 'given' suggest, the situation is often an extension of the one present in the openings[111] of various stories: narrative omniscience and its privileges almost entirely renounced, and the events described from the viewpoint of an observer who is humanly limited and something of a stranger. I have said[112] that it is striking to see this viewpoint adopted at the outset of stories, since that is where omniscience seems most useful and necessary and its renunciation most difficult; similarly, I think we can be surprised to find the same thing happening *in medias res,* at points where (or perhaps for the reason that) the particular fact to be established may be basic to our understanding of the action's elementary shape, to say nothing of its deeper import.

Here is a passage from *Drüben am Markt*. It opens the final section of the tale and is not prefaced by any introductory or explanatory remarks:

> Die Zeit verging; die Linde unter dem Fenster der neuen Stube stand schon in dunklen Blättern. Dann war es eines Sonntages, früh noch am Vormittag; durch das offene Fenster kam der Klang des Orgelspiels aus der nahen Kirche. Auf einem Stuhle in der Mitte des Zimmers saß der Doktor und hörte auf einen Bericht seines Freundes, des Justizrats, der mit untergeschlagenen Armen vor ihm stand. Es mußte aber nichts Frohes gewesen sein, das er erfahren hatte; denn er blieb, als der Justizrat seine Mitteilung beendete, stumm und mit zitternden Lippen sitzen; nur zuweilen hob er die Hand und trocknete mit seinem Schnupftuch sich den Schweiß von den Wangen. Und es war doch kühl genug im Zimmer; die Sonne streifte eben den erst die Fensterstäbe. − 'Und weiter', fragte er endlich, 'weiter sagte sie nichts, Justizrat? Weiter nichts als nur: Ich kann es nicht?'
>
> 'Nein, Doktor, sie hatte auf alle meine Reden nur diese Antwort; aber mißverstehen konnte ich sie nicht; denn sie hat es oft genug gesprochen'.
>
> 'Und weshalb', fuhr der Doktor zaghaft fort, 'weshalb − das hat sie nicht gesagt?'
>
> Der Justizrat schüttelte den Kopf. 'Es war in unserem Garten, hinten an dem Steintischchen', sagte er; 'was die kleine Hand in der weißen Manschette dort auf die Marmorplatte mag geschrieben haben, das hab ich freilich nicht entziffern können; aber gesprochen hat sie nichts hierüber'.
>
> Der Doktor war aufgestanden. Ihm gegenüber in dem großen Spiegel stand noch einmal dieselbe unscheinbare, vernachlässigte Gestalt; das wirre Haar, das runde ausdruckslose Gesicht, aus dem die kleinen Augen jetzt trübselig auf den draußenstehenden Doppelgänger hinausstarrten. Der Freund sah gespannt zu ihm hinüber. Jetzt, jetzt mußte er selbst die Antwort auf seine Frage finden. − − Aber er fand sie nicht; er wandte sich und begann zu sprechen. 'Eduard', sagte er leise, und es war, als blieben ihm die Worte in der Kehle hängen, 'ich denke wohl kaum, daß es wegen meiner alten Mutter ist'.
>
> Der Justizrat richtete sich fast wie erschrocken in die Höhe; über seine regelmäßigen und sonst wohl kalten Züge zuckte es wie etwas, das er nicht bekämpfen könne. (SW I 559f.)

About what and whom are the two friends speaking? This is obviously a significant and highly-charged moment; the doctor is showing signs of an emotion stronger and more painful than we have detected in him before − we have seen him pre-occupied, but never very far from laughter at his own preoccupation − and the Justizrat is looking on with tense sympathy. But what has given rise to all this? Who is the 'sie' whose 'Ich kann es nicht' changes so much? It soon becomes evident that the 'sie' in question is Sophie; and from various signs and symptoms recalled from earlier in the story (the special, tense awareness in the relations between the doctor and Sophie, the redecoration of the doctor's room, the doctor's reliance on the Justizrat in matters of taste and polite convention) we can conclude without much difficulty that the doctor has sent the Justizrat to Sophie on a commission of love, presumably either to make a formal proposal of marriage to her on his behalf or to sound out informally how she would react if the doctor were to come to her himself with a proposal. And the passage itself makes it clear that the approach has been unfavourably received. We reach these conclusions easily and rapidly; to set down by hindsight all the elements in the deductive process would be a distortion, giving a laborious air to what is after all worked through very quickly in the mind as one reads the story. But this does not detract from the point I want to make: that the process, no matter how rapid, *is* a deductive one, that we are not *given* the fact but are called upon to *discover* it for ourselves, by inference and guesswork based on bits and pieces of information about people's behaviour and utterances, with no seal of authoritative truth from any source. That this is so is a product of the narrative standpoint adopted; we are reading the account of an invisible but otherwise humanly limited stranger, who to all intents and purposes is eavesdropping on a conversation and telling us what he sees and hears. We can be tempted into conjecture about him: he knows who the two men are, because he has told us about previous meetings he has witnessed between them; but he seems to have been absent from the all-important encounter when the doctor must have asked the Justizrat to go to Sophie, and seems moreover to have stumbled unexpectedly (an impression reinforced by the peculiar jerkiness of 'Dann war es eines Sonntags . . .') on the present conversation at the end of the Justizrat's 'Bericht'. His late arrival has prevented his knowing what the report is about; he *deduces* from the doctor's silence and trembling lips that it cannot have contained good news. Odd, he thinks, that the little man should be perspiring when the room is so cool — and again there is the strange feeling that the narrator is *there,* sensitive to the temperature of the room, feeling quite cool himself. Then he is content to retail faithfully the words he hears spoken and the gestures and expressions that accompany them, apparently knowing their purport little more than we do. He sees the doctor stand up and look at himself in the mirror — and suddenly there is the highly imaginative and disturbing perception of *two* identical figures, the doctor outside himself, seeing a Doppelgänger more real than a mere reflection. Then follows an inconsistency in the point of view; the narrator moves inside the Justizrat and exposes his thought: 'Jetzt, jetzt mußte (der Doktor) selbst die Antwort auf seine Frage finden'; and 'Aber er fand sie nicht' extends and completes the same thought. But immediately afterwards we are where we were, outside the two men: the doctor speaks *as though* the words were sticking in his throat, and the Justizrat rises '*fast wie* erschrocken' —'über seine . . . Züge zuckte es *wie etwas,* das er nicht bekämpfen könne'.

The narrative standpoint causes much to be left obscure; there are a number of discoveries which we have to make for ourselves, piecing scraps of evidence together into some sort of picture. What are Sophie's reasons for refusing the doctor? We are never properly told, and Sophie cannot express them herself; the image of the hand on the marble table-top, and the anxiously pressed point about the Justizrat's having properly heard the one thing she did say, are perfect emblems of what I have talked about before,[113] communication made into a 'problem'. What does it all mean to the doctor? We get little definite help on that. How, at a tentative assessment, are the Justizrat's own feelings involved? Before the scene described in the passage there have been slight indications that he is himself fond of Sophie; the passage itself contains the suggestion of some emotion that he cannot control; and afterwards we learn that he in fact marries Sophie some years later; so his motives throughout are not likely to have been quite straightforward. But (and this is my point) before we can even begin to make inferences and conjectures about the deeper motivations at work in the characters, we are compelled to take the same circuitous course towards establishing the simple fact around which these motivations are grouped — the fact of a rejected proposal. And at no point in the story is there any authoritative statement confirming that the fact we have deduced is the correct one.

Psyche (1875) has the same kind of factual obscurity at its centre. A young sculptor saves a girl from drowning, and for months afterwards is obsessed by the memory of her. He produces a sculpture portraying the rescue of Psyche; the features of the god are very like his own, those of Psyche very like the girl's. It is, predictably, his finest work. Meanwhile the girl (only fourteen or fifteen years old and one of a series of Lolita-esque nymphet figures — she is described as a 'Mädchenknospe' — that appear in Storm's work) has reacted violently to the incident and is filled with a hysterical sense of shame. Her awakening love for her rescuer is overlaid with terror at the prospect of encountering him again; she is also frightened of anyone finding out what happened (beyond the young man's friend and an old Badefrau, who actually witnessed the scene), and she withdraws almost completely from a previously vivid social life. After some months she sees the sculptor's work in an exhibition; he is there, the Psyche sculpture performs some kind of exorcism, and the two are reunited in love. In its own compass this story does not, so far as I can see, lend any conviction to the naive and provocative claims it makes about the sources and powers of art; nor does it succeed in giving life or credibility to the girl's violent psychological reversals from tomboyish extroversion to obsessive shame to final released passion — such a development is no doubt possible, only the story does not *make* us see it as real. But the situation of *Drüben am Markt*[114] faces us again here: before we can arrive at this kind of judgement about the quality and coherence of the story and the preoccupations of its characters, we have to do our own factual groundwork to find out the crucial aspect of the event which is the mainspring of the action. What happened during the rescue to bring about such overwhelming shame and grief in the girl? No authoritative statement is ever made; once again, it is left to us to infer what we can.

The inference most in accordance (or least at variance) with the information we have is that the girl must have been naked when she was rescued. But we have to go outside the story for any specific confirmation of this; in a letter to Julius Rodenberg,[115] Storm writes:

Ich las vor einiger Zeit in der Zeitung, daß ein Sekundaner die Rettungsmedaille gewonnen, weil er ein Mädchen *(vermutlich indes anständig bekleidet)* aus dem Wasser geholt. Daraus entsprang die Novelle.

The words I have italicised are evidently an indication (in reverse, as it were) that the girl in the story is unclothed; but they are the clearest indication we have. The subject crops up again in an exchange of letters between Storm and Paul Heyse. Interestingly, Heyse seems *not* to have been quite certain about the girl's nakedness, while on the other hand having no doubts about Storm's reasons for not making the matter more obvious in the text; he writes:

> Sie haben sich bemüht, äußerst dezent zu bleiben; um so aufgeregter arbeitet die Phantasie des Lesers mit. Baden denn Mädchen splitterfasernackt? Und wenn nicht, wie kann ein im Strandkostüm ohnmächtig den Wellen entrissenes junges Ding gerade eine Bildhauerseele so mächtig entzünden, die je mit *ganzer* Nacktheit vertraut ist?[116]

Storm replies:

> Im übrigen können Sie unbesorgt sein, unsere eingeborenen Damen von der Nordsee gehen ohne jegliche Hose in die Wellen; so was wär mir auch nicht einmal im Traum eingefallen. Da müßte man wohl für die durch 'Bäder' Entarteten auch eine Nota unter den Text setzen! In *einem* irren Sie, ich habe mich. nicht *bemüht*, 'dezent' zu sein. Dies — es verdient vielleicht einen besseren Namen — ist die selbstverständliche Folge meiner Auffassung des Stoffes; ich habe in dieser Beziehung nicht das leiseste zu unterdrücken gehabt . . . — Der Konflikt selbst — der jungfräulichen Scham mit der Dankbarkeit und keimenden Liebe zu dem schönen Männerantlitz, das sie über sich gesehen — ist, meine ich, so ziemlich ausgetragen . . .[117]

A couple of things emerge from this. One is that Storm seems perfectly content with the inference (of nakedness) that Heyse draws — it is clear that he had 'intended' it to be drawn from the narrative (though he takes the opportunity of poking fun at Heyse). The other thing is that his aim in being so oblique in the story was *not* primarily to make it 'dezent' — that is, the reticence cannot be wholly explained as the result of a misguided delicacy. After all, Storm cannot be said to take much account of 'the public taste' in his choice of subjects: he has no compunctions about describing 'illicit' affairs,[118] illegitimacy,[119] incestuous love,[120] mental illness,[121] alcoholism[122] or cancer of the womb,[123] or about creating singularly 'distasteful' characters;[124] and his treatment of such subjects is usually far from weak-kneed — he had a number of brushes with his publishers, for instance, on matters of taste.[125] I think we must see his reticence here as springing from a different source; it is of a kind with the obscurity and indirectness which we have seen pervading so many areas of his writing; it is a matter of technique, a way of looking at the world expressed in the putting together of the words — or, as he says, 'die selbstverständliche Folge meiner Auffassung des Stoffes'.

But all that arises from external evidence. In the text itself I can find no unambiguous, 'omniscient' confirmation that the girl is naked when the young man saves her, or that this is the cause of her sense of shame. So far as I can see, the nearest thing to a specific suggestion is this passage:

> Da tauchte die Gestalt des Schwimmers mit der breiten Brust aus den schäumenden Wogen auf, und bald darauf sah man ihn langsam, aber sicher an dem abschüssigen Ufer emporsteigen. In seinen Armen, an seiner Brust ruhte ein junger Körper, gleich weit entfernt von der Fülle des Weibes wie von der Hagerkeit des Kindes; ein Bild der Psyche, wenn es jemals eins gegeben hatte. Aber der kleine Kopf war zurückgesunken; leblos hing der eine Arm herab. – Aus der Mittagshöhe des Himmels fiel der volle Sonnenschein auf die beiden schimmernden Gestalten.
>
> 'Wie in den Tagen der Götter!' murmelte der junge Mann, der atemlos diesem Vorgang zugesehen hatte. (SW II 533)

Seen in isolation and with prior knowledge of what one is looking for, this passage seems quite clear in its implication. But it comes early, and only some time afterwards do we learn of the girl's hysterical reaction; we have to go back and examine the passage again. And how *is* the nakedness of the girl implied? Only in the reference to the Psyche legend, here and elsewhere; no other element gives anything like such a firm clue to the assumption we are apparently asked to make. Some more extended sections are explicable in terms of that assumption, but only by hindsight; we have to make the imaginative leap *before* we can go to these sections and find some sort of sense in them. There are, it is true, several references to 'Jungfräulichkeit', but they serve to remind us of the general area of the experience in question, rather than of its precise nature. The word 'Scham' appears here and there, but its pubic connotations are not exploited. Dialogue is no help, obviously; the people who know are sworn to silence and loath to mention the matter even among themselves; so their reticence joins with that of the narrator to thwart us. Once again, we have been brought to a dark place in the text; our conjectures about what is hidden there are never properly confirmed or refuted by an authoritative, omniscient statement, and above all, that which is hidden is not some subtle motivation or extra layer of significance, but a simple fact, and a fact on which all the actions and reactions of the story are based.

In *Angelika, Drüben am Markt* and *Psyche,* the matter of fact so heavily veiled is a mystery only to the reader, not to the characters immediately concerned. Ehrhard must be only too clear what his profession is; the doctor and the Justizrat know perfectly well what their unhappy conversation is about; the girl and her rescuer are quite aware what has happened to arouse such shame and fear in her; it is we who are left to work out as best we can what is going on. But there are stories in which the characters share our doubt and are themselves obliged to deduce what they can from odd pieces of information, in order to arrive at some knowledge of the facts, knowledge qualified by the lack of any absolutely un-ambiguous confirmation. *They* are left in doubt because circumstances give them no final proof, *we* for want of an 'authoritative' statement from the narrator; and indeed, the narrator, we sometimes feel, is in no position to make such a statement, hampered as he seems to be by certain ('human') limitations and forced to align himself most of the time with the ignorance of the characters whose story he tells — whether he be 'embodied' or 'fictional'. That situation is basic to the problem of communication I have talked about already:[126] the characters have no sure under-standing of what is going on in each other's minds, nor have we, and the narrator doesn't seem to 'know' either (I mean that the effect is one of real uncertainty, not just indulgence in gratuitous mystification). But the doubts raised by difficulties of communication generally relate to comparatively complex issues — what does this or that character truly think, feel or desire? — and I am concerned here with much more elementary points of fact — what are they talking about? what happened? I want to examine now a case where characters, narrator and reader are all exercised by a straight question of identity. The story is *Hans und Heinz Kirch.* Seventeen years after Heinz's angry departure from his father's house, a man returns; is it the true Heinz or an impostor?

The latter half of the tale is devoted to the brief stay of this man (whoever he is) in the Kirch household, his final departure and the bitter suffering of Hans Kirch's declining years under the shadow of this dismally abortive reconciliation. The account takes the form of a skilfully executed dialectical movement between assurance and doubt. At first no-one thinks of questioning the man's identity; then rumours begin to circulate; and thereafter the pendulum swings to and fro, moved by the interpretation of various conflicting clues and in some measure by the operation of diverging individual interests. The people most intimately affected by the problem (apart from the man himself, who presumably knows who he is) are Hans Kirch, his old and malicious sister Jule, his daughter Lina and son-in-law Christian, and Wieb, a woman Heinz had known and loved in his youth. With the significant exception of Wieb, they all veer one way and then the other — is it Heinz or is it not? —, and the action consists in the tracing of these movements. But I want to point to and elucidate a strange effect. The movements, the swings of the pendulum, do not somehow give the impression of taking place against a stable background of truth; when the opinion of one of the characters shifts, the whole narrative structure seems to shift in sympathy; we lose the sense that everything is under control, or that the mystery is a teasing riddle with the answer at the back of the book. The feeling is of real doubt, issues really in the balance. In the end, the evidence points clearly in one direction, fairly clearly at least; but one can say no more than that. The characters themselves, faced with the doubt, are compelled into a deductive process, reading the signs and attempting to weigh the evidence; the conclusion they arrive at may be suspect because of their individual limitation and prejudice. We are in just the same position (*our* prejudices are relevant too, though less obviously so);[127] we are given no essential advantage over the characters; and once again the pivotal factor is that of narrative standpoint.

In the normal fictional scheme, certain facts are sooner or later placed beyond doubt for us by the narrator's assurance that they are true. Whether the people in the story know these facts or not is another question – obviously the interest and tension may depend on what they know – but the facts are irrefutably there. They have a self-contained and logical validity by virtue of being 'given' by an authority which we accept as absolute in its own sphere. The author-narrator can declare 'This happened', and all he need say in justification is, 'because I tell you it happened'. It is his story, he *makes* the facts, and there is an end to the matter. A fact may stick in our throats, but there is nothing we can do about it. To say 'It is highly improbable that a young engineer would go to a sanatorium for a three-week holiday and stay seven years' is a conceivable, if puerile, criticism of *Der Zauberberg;* but to say 'It was not Hans Castorp who went . . .' has no meaning. Thomas Mann says he went, so he went. But in *Hans und Heinz Kirch* we look in vain for this kind of statement about the identity of the man who calls himself Heinz. There is no recourse to either of the two basic ways open to a conventional narrator of stating the fact: the bald assertion (' . . for it was indeed Heinz . . ') or else an entry into the man's mind, the use of the privileges of omniscience to establish for the reader's benefit what only that man knows. Instead, the narrator (whom we have seen unashamedly omniscient in the opening of the story[128] and who in fact exercises his powers quite freely throughout) seems, so far as this question is concerned, to have been edged out of his unique, 'fictional' position and to be at one with his characters in their uncertainty. Cautiously, meekly almost, he hovers when they hover, concludes when they conclude (though he permits himself at times to question their impartiality). The clearest measure of his unstable attitude is the names he gives to the man when called upon to refer to him outside dialogue.

At first no problem exists: there is a report (retailed to Hans by two characters) that Heinz has been seen in Hamburg, at first using a pseudonym, then, when pressed, admitting his identity. The narrator sees no reason to disbelieve this, since the characters are in no doubt, so he is nearly always content to call the man 'Heinz' or accord him blood relationship with the other members of the family. Thus, when Hans goes to Hamburg to bring the man home, we read:

Der Brief, worin der Vater seine und *des Sohnes* Ankunft gemeldet hatte . .[129]

Then, on the arrival of the two in the coach, and at the first meeting with Lina and her husband:

Ebenso nacheinander streckte diesen jetzt *Heinz* die Hand entgegen . . .
(SW III 372)

The greetings over, they go inside:

> Nachdem alle in das Haus getreten waren, geleitete Frau Lina *ihren Bruder* die Treppe hinauf . . . (SW III 372)

There follows a conversation over the evening meal, and the assumption is still quite easily made (" 'Weit genug', erwiderte *Heinz* . .", "*Heinz* hörte ruhig zu . .", "*Heinz* nickte . ."). (SW III 373) It is the same in the description of the next few days:

> *Heinz* erkundigte sich (nicht) nach früheren Bekannten . . . Hans Adam frug sich, ob *der Sohn* das erste Wort von ihm erwarte . . . Aber auch heimisch schien *Heinz* sich nicht zu fühlen . . . Und noch ein zweites war dem Frauenauge nicht entgangen. Wie *der Bruder* einst mit ihr, der so viel jüngeren Schwester, sich herumgeschleppt, ihr erzählt und mit ihr gespielt hatte . . . *Heinz* sah nachdenklich den Knaben an . . . und *Heinz* setzte den Knaben zur Erde . . .
>
> . . . auch *Heinz* hatte sich (zum Kirchgang) bereit erklärt . . . dann aber legte *Heinz* das Gesangbuch, das seine Schwester ihm gegeben hatte, auf das Pult . . . Aber die Schwester ergriff *des Bruders,* dann des Vaters Hände . . . Eine Unterredung zwischen Vater und *Sohn* fand (nicht) statt . . . Am Abend zog Frau Lina *den Bruder* in ihre Schlafkammer . . . *der Bruder,* an den sie sich zu gewöhnen anfing . . . (SW III 373ff.)

So far all seems to be well; in fact, though, the pendulum has begun to swing already. There have been causes for doubt; Heinz seems harder and more withdrawn than his family remember; he is indifferent to his father's concerns and values (like the importance Hans attaches to the Steuermannsexamen and a place in the Schifferstuhl in church); he is not anxious to re-establish the acquaintances of his youth, and is unaffected by the memory of his dead mother; more materially, the tattoo he had etched on his forearm as a boy has disappeared. On the other hand, odd things have arisen to allay the doubt: his love of children and talent for amusing them reminds Lina very strongly of the brother she had known in her childhood; the disappearance of the tattoo is explained by reference to devilish diseases rampant in the New World; the acrimony of the parting seventeen years before, and the grimness of the life Heinz has led in the meantime, are enough to motivate his new hardness and caution in his relations with his family and the other people from the past.

But these considerations are in a sense unreal. It is only in retrospect, *after* we discover that there is uncertainty about the man's identity, that we can meaningfully conduct such an argument. For we are using the various indications as evidence towards the solution of a problem which does not, as yet, exist. In these first few days, the characters are unaware of any need to ask: is it Heinz or not? They are asking a different question: can Heinz overcome the bitterness of years ago, erase the marks engraved upon him by his absence, and work through to some basis for a resumption of life within his family and native community? *That* is their concern; it is in *that* context that they are taking and reading the signs as positive or negative; what worries them is the problem of Heinz's readjustment, not that of his identity.

So it is reasonable that the section should end with a conversation between 'brother' and 'sister', the last exchange of which is this:

> 'Ein halbes Menschenleben — ja rechne, noch mehr als ein halbes Menschenleben kein ehrlich Hausdach überm Kopf; nur wilde See oder wildes Volk oder beides miteinander! Ihr kennt das nicht, sag ich, das Geschrei und das Gefluche, mein eignes mit darunter; ja, ja, Schwester, mein eignes auch, es lärmt mir noch immer in die Ohren; laßt's erst stiller werden, sonst — es geht sonst nicht!'
>
> Die Schwester hing an seinem Halse. 'Gewiß, Heinz, gewiß, wir wollen Geduld haben; o wie gut, daß du nun bei uns bist!' (SW III 377)

And the point of view adopted means that the narrator is content to share the characters' preoccupations. He follows their assumptions (calling the man 'Heinz' and so on) because there is no apparent reason to do otherwise; and he sees and presents the incidents in the light of the question they are asking (readjustment, not identity); he is no more aware than they that there is another question to be resolved. As readers we are absolutely limited by the narrator's limitation, knowing only what he knows or seems to know; his concerns are ours, his perceptions ours. There is equality throughout the scheme: characters, narrator and readers are all placed on the same level and in the same situation. *All* the forces in this act of storytelling are directed to asking the irrelevant question, but as yet there is nothing anywhere to tell us that this is so.

Then it happens:

> Plötzlich, Gott weiß woher, tauchte ein Gerücht auf und wanderte emsig von Tür zu Tür; der Heimgekehrte sei gar nicht Heinz Kirch, es sei der Hasselfritz, ein Knabe aus dem Armenhause, der gleichzeitig mit Heinz zur See gegangen war und gleich diesem seitdem nichts von sich hatte hören lassen. Und jetzt, nachdem es eine kurze Weile darum herumgeschlichen, war es auch in das Kirchsche Haus gedrungen. (SW III 377f.)

The doubt is raised, and the narrative structure shifts. From now on, words and actions and events have a different relevance; they have ceased to be indications for and against the possibility that Heinz will be able to integrate himself again, and have become clues in the search for the true identity of the man who can no longer with any certainty be called Heinz. This places the narrator in a curious predicament. Hitherto he has (together with his characters) made the assumption that the man *is* Heinz; as it turns out, the assumption was rash, so he must now retract as best he can. He has to do this because of his unwillingness, or rather his inability, to claim access to any knowledge beyond what his characters (or a stranger observing them) may possess. He must doubt as they doubt; he, like them, is thrown back on clues. We saw his initial assumption expressed in the names he chose to give 'Heinz';[130] his new uncertainty becomes evident now in just the same manner.

The narrator's procedure is 'almost human'; his reactions seem explicable in quite a normal way. He has got used to calling the man 'Heinz' (or 'der Bruder' and so on), and for a short while after the rumour arises he finds it difficult to break himself of the habit (as the characters do). But as time goes on he becomes more and more infected with the common doubt and resorts increasingly to neutral appellations ('der Gast', 'der Jüngere', or simply 'der Mann'), unable to commit himself either way. He does this within the framework of the conversations and incidents he reports, so that there is the sense of his judgement being constantly conditioned by what he sees and hears. The first reaction we witness is Lina's: she remembers hearing of the similarity between Heinz and Fritz as boys, and begins to think with revulsion of the kisses and embraces she has been giving to this rough man who now might not be her brother:

> Frau Lina vermied es plötzlich, ihn zu berühren; verstohlen aber und desto öfter hafteten ihre Augen auf den rauhen Zügen *ihres Gastes,* während zugleich ihr innerer Blick sich mühte, unter den Schatten der Vergangenheit das Knabenantlitz ihre Bruders zu erkennen.

For a moment, the narrator has yielded to the doubt ('Gast', not 'Bruder'); but he quickly drops back into his earlier assumption:

> . . . zu erkennen. Als dann auch der junge Ehemann zur Vorsicht mahnte, wußte Frau Lina sich auf einmal zu entsinnen, wie gleichgültig ihr der *Bruder* neulich an ihrer Mutter Grab erschienen sei.

and confirms it a few lines later:

> Beiden Eheleuten erschien jetzt auch das ganze Gebaren des *Bruders* noch um vieles ungeschlachter als vordem. (SW III 378)

From Lina (and her husband) the attention moves to Hans Kirch. The narrator is for a time relieved of the necessity to make direct reference himself to 'Heinz', since he confines himself to reporting a conversation between Hans and a third party. Hans goes and talks with the old Pastor, hoping to find some illumination, for the old man has memories (made hazy by age) of Heinz as a boy, and has received a visit from 'Heinz' in the last few days. But there is no reassurance from the Pastor — indeed, he gives more reason for doubt when, in the midst of his errant recollections and in serene ignorance of the rumours that have been circulating, he mentions an incident (the youthful Heinz attacking a boy who had informed on him) and says that 'Heinz' had claimed on his recent visit to have forgotten all about it. (SW III 379) Hans goes away, proud in his remembrance of his son but less sure than ever who 'Heinz' is:

> 'Ja, ja, Herr Pastor; freilich, er war kein Hasenfuß, mein Heinz!'
> Aber der frohe Stolz, womit diese Worte hervorbrachen, verschwand schon wieder; das Bild seines kühnen Knaben verblich vor dem *des Mannes, der jetzt unter seinem Dache hauste.* Hans Kirch nahm kurzen Abschied . . . (SW III 380)

Hans' uncertainty infects the narrator and forces him (while reading Hans' mind) into circumlocution. Then the assumption reasserts itself in the description of preparations for a ball:

> Am Abend war Ball in der Harmonie. *Heinz* wollte zu Hause bleiben, er
> passe nicht dahin; und die jungen Eheleute, die ihm auch nur wie beiläufig
> davon gesprochen hatten, waren damit einverstanden; denn *Heinz,* sie mochten
> darin nicht unrecht haben, war in dieser Gesellschaft für jetzt nicht wohl zu
> präsentieren . . .
> So blieb denn *Heinz* zurück . . . (SW III 380)

But doubt seems to be growing ever stronger, in the narrator's mind as well as
the characters'. A number of scenes follow (SW III 381-93) in which Hans and his
family are driven backwards and forwards by conflicting evidence, and in which,
accordingly, every reference made by the narrator to 'Heinz' is non-committal,[131]
assuming no names or relationships and illustrating the dominant feeling of the
context — the feeling that all is in the balance. 'Heinz', then, stays behind; but after
a while he sees in the sky the glow from a fair being held on one of the offshore
islands, and goes out. The next few moments are seen through the eyes of the
Kirchs' maid:

> Kurze Zeit danach, beim Rüsten der Schlafgemächer für die Nacht, betrat
> die Magd auch die von *ihrem Gaste* vorhin verlassene Kammer.

She goes to the window and, looking out, suddenly sees something on the water:

> Ihre jungen weitreichenden Augen hatten ein Boot erkannt, das von *einem
> einzelnen Manne* durch den sprühenden Gischt der Insel zugetrieben wurde.
> (SW III 381)

The first reference here is a straight substitution, 'ihrem Gaste' for 'Heinz'; the
second belongs more organically to its situation, and indeed the situation could
be said to have been constructed round it, so that the reference could be made in
this form — the narrator is 'with' the maid and relies on her eyes, which at this
distance can only pick out a single male figure in the boat. The maid is left to draw
her conclusions, we to draw ours.

The next paragraph, dealing briefly with the evening spent by the family at the
'Harmonie', bears wholly on the real reason for their going: they had hoped to find
out more about the genesis of the rumour, but had drawn a total blank. The paragraph ends with a comment which reverberates oddly and disquietingly across the
face of the narrative, hinting at more basic uncertainties:

> es war wieder wie kurz zuvor, als ob es niemals einen Heinz Kirch gegeben
> hätte. (SW III 381)

The next morning, 'Heinz' comes home after having spent the whole night out:

> Als dann endlich kurz vor Mittag *der Verschwundene* mit stark gerötetem
> Antlitz heimkehrte, wandte Hans Kirch, den er im Flur traf, ihm den Rücken
> und ging rasch in seine Stube. Frau Lina, der er auf der Treppe begegnete, sah
> ihn vorwurfsvoll und fragend an; sie stand einen Augenblick, als ob sie sprechen
> wolle; aber — *wer war dieser Mann*? — Sie hatte sich besonnen und ging ihm
> stumm vorüber. (SW III 381)

The question, and the separation and alien silence it breeds, are clearly enough expressed; but before that, before the explicit thematic proposition, the narrator already creates his own questioning: matters are so arranged (by accident? or design? or something between the two?) that 'Heinz' appears, not as a man with a perceptible identity, but simply as 'der Verschwundene'.

There follows a conversation between Hans Kirch and 'Heinz'. Its content seems to be tipping the scales in favour of 'Heinz' *not* being an impostor, for he reproaches Hans on two counts: first, for actually *wanting* him to be 'der Hasselfritze aus der Armenkate', so as to have an excuse to throw him out, and second, for the episode of the letter which Hans had received from Heinz some years before but had returned unread because it had not been franked. Surely no-one but the true Heinz could be aware of the existence of this letter and its ultimate fate? But Hans, though impressed by this, is still not convinced; in his bewildered mind, the *other* possibility is reinforced by a less tangible, but for him more intimate and urgent clue – the quality he finds in the voice of 'Heinz':

> Die Stimme, womit diese Worte gesprochen wurden, klang so wüst und fremd, daß Hans Kirch sich unwillkürlich frug: 'Ist das dein Heinz, den der Kantor beim Amensingen immer in die erste Reihe stellte, oder ist es doch der Junge aus der Armenkate, der nur auf deinen Beutel spekuliert?' (SW III 383)

With that doubt sounded, we look back more closely at the preceding dialogue and discover an oddity. In his description of the events that led up to his writing the letter, and of his reactions to its return, 'Heinz' refers to himself almost exclusively in the *third* person – usages like 'einmal hatte er doch geschrieben', or 'als der Sohn . . . seine Hand ausstreckte', or 'der junge Bursche', or 'das Fieber hatte ihn geschüttelt' (SW III 382f.) – a conversational 'conceit' in the first instance, offering no logical evidence either way, yet somehow a device which intensifies Hans' (and the narrator's and our) mood of uncertainty, a reservation right at the core, within the enigmatic figure himself.

And Hans Kirch is quickly justified in his doubts. His sister Jule interrupts the colloquy (causing 'Heinz' rapidly to leave the room) and drops a series of seemingly conclusive bombshells. What first made her suspicious, she says, was the fact that while visiting her a few days before, 'Heinz' had never once called her 'Tante' until she had taxed him about it (a thin point, certainly, but important to *her,* and objectively valuable in that it had caused her to be on the watch for more material signs). She had drawn him to her in order to run her hands over his face (she is nearly blind, and her fingers are correspondingly hypersensitive, doing service for her eyes), and in so doing had discovered that 'Heinz's' nose is of quite a different shape, a different asymmetry, from her nephew's, which she clearly remembers from years ago – 'Nun, Hans, die Nase kann doch nicht von Ost nach West gewachsen sein!' (SW III 384) Hans interjects, mildly and without much conviction, that 'Heinz' has just shown clear knowledge about the business of the letter; but Tante Jule has no trouble in scotching that:

> Die dicke Frau lachte, daß der Stock ihr aus den Händen fiel. 'Die Briefgeschichte, Hans! Ja, die ist seit den vierzehn Tagen reichlich wieder aufgewärmt, davon konnte er für einen Dreiling bei jedem Bettelkinde einen Suppenlöffel voll bekommen!' (SW III 385)

Then, to put everything beyond question, Jule returns to the matter of the tattoo which 'Heinz' claims was deleted by illness in the New World. She calls in the old doctor who had treated the boy Heinz after he had inflicted the tattoo on himself twenty years ago; the doctor is quite certain that a decoration etched on 'nach der alten gründlichen Manier . . . tüchtige Nadelstiche, und dann mit Pulver eingebrannt' (SW III 386) could not possibly disappear without trace, even after twenty years and the ravages of the most virulent and exotic brand of pox – the arm would drop off first.

The family come to their decision. Jule has no doubt that 'Heinz' is a fraud out for an inheritance, she has persuaded Hans with overpowering arguments and with a relish informed by malice, for in memory of old wrongs suffered at Hans' hands she takes any opportunity to wound or humiliate him. Hans and Lina have no choice but to bow to evidence which anyway confirms what they already *feel* to be true. In all this blackness, there is at least a glimmer of good: Lina embodies the anguish in her fear of being left alone in the house 'mit dem fremden Menschen', but Hans answers her with the relief of a father who has been preserved from final disillusion with his son:

'Gott Dank, daß es ein Fremder ist!' (SW III 386)

The narrator seems to have made his decision too, or to be on the way to making it as far as his position will allow. His report of the conversation[132] between Hans and 'Heinz' is the key. He is almost always content, when the occasion demands, to call Hans by name ('Hans Kirch war zurückgetreten . . . Hans Kirch erwiderte nichts . . . Hans Kirch fuhr zusammen . .'), but for 'Heinz' he evades the necessity throughout by recourse to formulae which specify 'Heinz', not through his name or identity, but through the age difference between the two men and through the dialogue situation: so we read, '. . dann richtete *der Jüngere* sich auf . . . *der andre* war aber aufgestanden . . . den trotzigen Blick *des Jungen* . . . da fuhr ein hartes Lachen aus *des Jüngeren* Munde'. (SW III 382f.) And of course, Tante Jule's revelations are made 'in her own voice', and can thus be described without the narrator having to make direct reference to 'Heinz', who leaves as Jule enters. So once again the scheme is erected: the reader bound by the narrator's awareness, the narrator in turn cautiously identifying himself with the shifting attitudes of the people in his story, knowing only what they know. And they know now that 'Heinz' is a fraud.

But the pendulum begins to swing back. The next scene amounts to an act of faith, and in it we are presented, it seems to me, with one of the basic thematic preoccupations of the piece. If there is a reasoning of the heart beyond other reasonings, if there is a devotion which is privileged to look through appearances and deductions and to divine a truth and an essence bathed in its own light, if there is an unconditional knowledge which needs no help from fact because it is born of love — if we can believe that to be so, then we may find our answer here. For 'Heinz' is subjected to the gaze of love, and love's eyes, though no others will, see Heinz.

The confrontation takes place in the ugliest surroundings, the vicious and prurient drunkenness of a disreputable 'Hafenschenke'. 'Heinz' goes in, attracted by the light and noise, and finds himself served by a faded woman who is none other than Wieb, the girl Heinz had loved before he went away. He follows her into the kitchen, and we are offered the moment of recognition in a perfectly achieved and perfectly beautiful passage. At its centre there is one delicate and extraordinary word which stands quite away from the rest, as tremulous and vulnerable, amidst the illusionless grimness of the tone, as this good woman is, amidst the squalor of her background, or as this moment is, amidst the cruel passage of the years:

> Einen Augenblick noch, dann trat er zu ihr; 'Wieb!' rief er, 'Wiebchen, kleines Wiebchen!'
> Es war eine rauhe Männerstimme, die diese Worte rief und jetzt verstummte, als habe sie allen Odem an sie hingegeben.
> Und doch, über das verblühte Antlitz des Weibes flog es wie ein *Rosenschimmer,* und während zugleich die Gläser klirrend auf den Boden fielen, entstieg ein Aufschrei ihrer Brust; wer hätte sagen mögen, ob es Leid, ob Freude war. 'Heinz!' rief sie, 'Heinz, du bist es; oh, sie sagten, du seist es nicht'. (SW III 391)

Suffering or joy? What joy there is soon gives way to bitterness; for the reunion has come too late. Wieb has married a sailor (who staggers into the kitchen at one point and wanders off again, too drunk even to notice that Wieb is not alone), and this tavern belongs to her father-in-law; that is why she serves here. 'Heinz' angrily throws down the ring which Wieb had given him while they were still children and which he has kept on a cord round his neck. Then he goes back into the bar and drinks steadily through the night.

The narrator seems prepared to make the act of faith I spoke of; Wieb's certainty, the certainty of love, is enough for him. Until that moment in the kitchen he preserves his neutrality in the ways we have seen before, making substitutions or taking refuge in the point of view:

> am Bollwerk entlang schlenderte nur *ein einzelner Mann* . . . Ein finsteres Lachen fuhr über das Antlitz *des Mannes . . . der zuletzt erschienene Gast . . .* an den Tisch *des neuen Gastes . . .* ein finsteres Lächeln zuckte um den Mund *des Mannes . . .* (SW III 388ff.)

But then, as soon as Wieb responds, he commits himself, rejecting the evidence that had weighed with him before and giving his trust to Wieb's reaction as the final arbiter:

> Da wurden schlurfende Schritte in dem Gange hörbar, und als *Heinz* sich wandte, stand ein Betrunkener in der Tür . . . *Heinz* sagte nichts darauf; aber seine Hand fuhr nach der behaarten Brust . . . *Heinz* hatte sich auf einen hölzernen Stuhl gesetzt . . . (SW III 392f.)

Throughout the section following this (the setting moves back to the Kirch household), the narrator remains true to his commitment, even though the family do not know the full import of the events of the night before and remain convinced that they have been deceived. In the movements which go to make up the section — Hans Kirch's decision to pack the man off, a last violent quarrel between the two, and the departure of 'Heinz' early in the morning — a name is always accorded:

> In der Kirchschen Familie war es schon kein Geheimnis mehr, in welchem Haus *Heinz* diesmal seine Nacht verbracht hatte . . . Als *Heinz* etwa eine Stunde später . . die Treppe nach dem Oberhaus hinaufging . . . Bald danach trat *Heinz* aus seiner Kammer . . . Am andern Morgen in der Frühe stand *Heinz* vollständig gekleidet droben . . . *Heinz* betrachtete das alles . . . (SW III 393ff.)

But all this *is* a commitment, a placing of faith by a reflective and sentient being, capable of changing his mind, *not* truth-by-definition delivered by an omniscient and all-determining story-teller. In terms of fact, the encounter with Wieb is no more conclusive than any other piece of evidence we have come across so far. There are numerous ways in which 'der Hasselfritze' could have come to know about 'Heinz's', youthful love — a confidence imparted during some meeting in America, perhaps, gossip or information, obtained at a price, from someone during the last few days (Jule's theory about 'Heinz's' knowledge of the letter[133] is perfectly applicable in this context as well) — and the ring could have been stolen or a replica obtained (for it is a cheap thing, purchased at a fair). The scene in the tavern contains no unambiguous suggestion that 'Heinz's' emotions are being seen 'from inside', for it is told almost entirely from the standpoint of a stranger, with the result that even descriptions like this are questionable:

> Er blickte ihr nach, wie sie durch eine Seitentür hinausging . . . es war, als ob er mit allen Sinnen in eine weite Ferne denke . . . Plötzlich . . erhob er sich . . . der hohe kräftige Mann zitterte sichtbar, als er jetzt mit auf dem Tisch gestemmten Händen dastand. (SW III 390)

'als ob er mit allen Sinnen in eine weite Ferne denke' — is this a man whose whole sensibility is directed back to a point in his own youthful experience, or is it a man who is trying desperately to remember, say, the details of a confidence heard (or overheard) far away? '(Er) zitterte sichtbar' — with the violent emotion of a re-awakened lover, or with the nervousness of an impostor facing his sternest test? We may be very clear in our choice of one alternative, rejecting the other as improbable; but the fact remains that we *are* called upon to choose. Both alternatives are real:

we can meaningfully claim 'It is not Heinz' in a way that we cannot claim 'It was not Hans Castorp who went . .'

After 'Heinz' departs, never to return, further points emerge. He has left behind most of the money (a large amount) that Hans gave him to make him go, and this is enough to convince Lina that he was after all the real Heinz. Wieb bursts in, and her passionate certainty stops Hans in his tracks. And some time later, the whole question of the tattoo is reopened by a chance remark from the lips of an old man who had been the poorhouse master:

> 'Ja, ja; ei du mein lieber Herrgott!' fuhr er fort, behaglich in seinem Rede-
> strome fortschwimmend; 'der Hasselfritze und der Heinz, wenn ich an die
> beiden Jungen denke, wie sie sich einmal die großen Anker in die Arme
> brannten! Ihr Heinz, ich hörte wohl, der mußte vor dem Doktor liegen; den
> Hasselfritze aber hab ich selber mit dem Hasselstock kuriert'. (SW III 400)

So Heinz and Fritz both had anchors tattooed on their arms; but what does that prove? That it might have been either of them who returned, or (if we still accept the doctor's verdict that such marks could never disappear) another person entirely. This is no positive pointer; it merely destroys some of the validity of one of the pieces of evidence. But inconclusive as it is, Hans clutches at it in the confusion and guilt of his old age and turns it into a final sign that he has cast out his own son:

> 'Zweimal hab ich meinen Heinz verstoßen, und darum hab ich mit der
> Ewigkeit zu schaffen!' (SW III 405)

Probably everyone will decide that it must have been the true Heinz who came back (I certainly would). We draw this conclusion to a small extent from examination of the factual evidence but it is not that which leads us most (indeed, the factual scale tips very slightly in the direction of its *not* having been Heinz). We are mainly swayed, I think, by that reasoning of the heart;[134] it is Wieb's conviction which accords most with our general hope of a coherence beyond the surface disconnec-tion; we will believe that what she sees with love is seen truly, and she sees Heinz. Is Hans' love of no account, then, or Lina's? Their feeling for Heinz is real enough, yet it has not saved them from basic doubt; what sets it below Wieb's? I suppose that we see the love between a man and a woman as a quality which we must place our greatest faith in; anyway, what the father and the sister feel is shown mostly in its imperfection, and we will readily find blindness among its faults. We will follow Wieb, then, as the other characters eventually do; but we find the narrator following with us, making our kind of judgement and sharing our kind of unveri-fiable faith (or perhaps we are sharing his). We have ceased to expect that he will give us the final, authentic, incontrovertible answer, backed by the authority we may have imagined him to have at his disposal; we have ceased, even, to be sure that such an answer exists for him to give.[135] So, however strong our belief that we have seen the real Heinz, it must remain belief; we shall never *know*, because there is no-one to tell us; that part of the fiction has disappeared. In this sense, the full extent of what we 'know' has to be a proposition which embraces both possibilities (Heinz or not Heinz), while taking into account undoubted changes of relation and attitude — and we find such a proposition there in the text, formulated for us by Hans Kirch:

> 'Mag er geheißen haben, wie er will, der diesmal unter meinem Dach geschlafen hat; mein Heinz hat schon vor siebzehn Jahren mich verlassen'. (SW III 399)

That much, but only that much, is certain.

The process I have tried to show at work in these four stories — *Angelika, Drüben am Markt, Psyche* and *Hans und Heinz Kirch* — is a variation of reserved omniscience which implies a redefinition of 'fictional fact', the paradox which E.M. Forster calls 'a reality of a kind we can never get in daily life'.[136] In these tales, the facts seem to have lost their self-authenticating fictional certainty and to have returned to the inconclusiveness of 'daily life': they are seen or heard or deduced or discovered or tentatively guessed at, but not 'given'. The seal of omniscient authority is never affixed to them; to the last, they remain logically in doubt. Another quality these facts share is their vital importance to an elementary understanding of the story in question; their obscurity looms large precisely because they loom large themselves. As a postscript to this section I want to make three more brief points, drawing in more stories to illustrate phenomena which are slightly different in their aspect but common in their ground.

The first point is really the marking of an isolated oddity which nonetheless seems to me to be germane and worthy of attention. *Ein Doppelgänger* (1886) is one of the most socially oriented of all Storm's works. It resembles *Der Schimmelreiter* in that it is concerned with the confrontation between an individual and a group, but differs in that the conflict is more directly relevant and contemporary — that of *Der Schimmelreiter* is pushed back a century or so. *Ein Doppelgänger* bears the familiar marks of the committed work of art: an uncompromising ethical stand on the side of humanitarian liberalism, a tone compounded of indignation and warm charity, and a message which pleads for a respectful and tolerant understanding of the capacities of each single person as an exemplar of the human spirit. It is the story of John Hansen, who leaves the army after honourable service, is unable to find employment, and more or less out of boredom commits violent crime. He is sent to prison for six years, and on his release is dubbed 'John Glückstadt', (after the jail in which he had been incarcerated); the sobriquet typifies the general attitude towards him, which is only too ready to give the dog a (literally) bad name and remains suspicious long after the reason for suspicion has gone. With considerable difficulty John gains employment; he works hard, marries and has a daughter, and in spite of public malice begins to carve out a respectable existence for himself and his family. But his employer dies and bereft of this support he is once more at the mercy of 'die liebe Mitwelt',[137] which refuses him further regular employment and reduces him to taking odd jobs. His material situation worsens, his sense of personal degradation grows, and with it his proneness to violent moods. In a quarrel with his wife he hits her; she falls, and is killed as her head strikes a projection on the stove. So John is left alone to fend for his daughter and himself. In the end, at the point of starvation, he is forced again into a criminal act. He steals potatoes from a field, but in the darkness he stumbles into a well and perishes.

Those are the bare bones of the action; but this is a Rahmenerzählung, and the curiosity lies in its framework. The frame modifies the social orientation of the story and makes the final emphasis a more personal one; the linking figure is Hansen's daughter Christine, who at the age of eight (after her father's death) is taken in by a pastor and his wife from Jena, goes back with them to their home-town and eventually marries their son, an Oberförster. She has in her mind the dim images of two men from her extreme youth: one is of her father, a kindly and loving figure, the other is of a cruel and violent man whom she remembers from further back while her mother was still alive. She cannot reconcile the two pictures, but they are clearly the two faces of the one John Hansen, aggressive and hot-tempered before his wife's death, chastened and remorseful after it. The title *Ein Doppelgänger* relates to this duality in her mind, as well as John's two names, 'Hansen' and 'Glückstadt', with all the conflicting attitudes their use implies. The concern of the framework is with the way Christine finally brings the two images together, adding the extra dimension (not without suffering) and seeing her father steady and whole for the first time. The Oberförster writes:

> seine Tochter hat jetzt mehr an ihm; nicht nur den Vater, sondern einen ganzen Menschen. (SW IV 237)

The story is told by a lawyer from John Hansen's town who makes the acquaintance of the Oberförster in Jena and then meets Christine. He reveals all the facts about Hansen's life and death to the Oberförster, who had been only imperfectly apprised of them before and who subsequently enlightens his wife, thus bringing about the coalescence of the two images about which I spoke.

But how does the lawyer know the facts in the first place? At first there is no indication; he begins by telling of the early days of his friendship with the Oberförster and of his gradual realisation that the latter's wife is the daughter of John Hansen. Then he recalls the few memories he has of times when as a boy he had encountered the ex-convict, mentioning that until now he has had no idea of the real name of the man he had known as John Glückstadt. Immediately after this, without offering, as it were, any further credentials for his knowledge, he launches into his narrative:

> John Hansen war von einem Nachbarsdorfe und hatte seine Militärzeit als
> tüchtiger Soldat bestanden . . . (SW IV 194)

The story proceeds as I have outlined it above, ending with the death of Hansen.
To a large extent it is told as if by a fictional, omniscient narrator, who is independent of the action, enters into the minds of the people involved and makes
assertions about the development of characters and events More than this, the
narrator seems to have a privileged knowledge about Hansen's end: after recounting
'what actually happened' (the fall into the well), he devotes a paragraph
(SW IV 232f.), by way of contrast, to describing the complete mystification of
everyone in the locality and the various theories which are put forward and which
he *knows* to be false. The police tried in vain, he says, to find some trace of Hansen;
in the town, some thought that he had fled the country with partners-in-crime,
others that he had committed suicide on the dykes, his body then being carried
out to sea. But the narrator knows better.

How is this knowledge compatible with the situation of a fully embodied first-
person story-teller (the lawyer) who by his own admission has only bits and pieces
of dimly remembered information to go on? The answer comes soon after this
paragraph — and here is the oddity. As the inner tale gives way to the Rahmen, we
realise that it has been given to us as a piece of total recall by the lawyer as he
stands before the window of his room in the Oberförster's house; and indeed, it
emerges as something very much more than total recall:

> Mir kam allmählich das Bewußtsein, daß ich weit von meiner Vaterstadt
> im Oberförsterhause an dem offenen Fenster stehe; der Mond schien von
> drüben über dem Walde auf das Haus, und aus den Wiesen hörte ich wieder
> das Schnarren des Wachtelkönigs. Ich zog meine Uhr: es war nach eins! Das
> Licht auf dem Tische war tief herabgebrannt. *In halbvisionärem Zustande —*
> *seit meiner Jugend haftete dergleichen an mir — hatte ich ein Menschenleben*
> *an mir vorübergehen sehen, dessen Ende, als es derzeit eintrat, auch mir ein*
> *Rätsel geblieben war. Jetzt kannte ich es plötzlich;* deutlich sah ich die
> zusammengekauerte Totengestalt des Unglücklichen in der unheimlichen
> Tiefe. (SW IV 233f; my italics.)

So that is how the lawyer knows. In a 'semi-visionary state' and through some
extra-sensory process, he has uncovered the truth about John Hansen's death and
also, we must assume, about major areas of his life as well. Other memories crowd
in now — a small boy claiming to have heard a ghostly voice calling from the field
where the well was situated, a falcon found trapped in the well and smelling of
carrion — suddenly explained by the intuitive flash. But the reservation has to be
made, the action of fantasy has to be questioned, and it is the Oberförster who
expresses the doubt:

> ich erzählte (dem Oberförster) alles, jedes einzelne, was in der vergangenen
> Nacht *mir in Erinnerung und im eigenen Geiste aufgegangen war.*

'Hm', machte der besonnene Mann und ließ seine Augen treuherzig auf mir ruhen; *das ist aber Poesie*; Sie sind am Ende nicht bloß ein Advokat!'
Ich schüttelte den Kopf: 'Nennen Sie es immer Poesie; Sie könnten es auch Liebe oder Anteil nennen, die ich rasch an meinen Wirten genommen hätte'. (SW IV 236; my italics.)

The paradox is a curious one. For all its commitment, for all its hard and glowing realism, this story rests on a factual foundation which has been established, not through the sober collation of facts or reports or experiences, nor through the privileged assertions of a 'fictional' narrator, but explicitly through the unbridled movements of a single consciousness in trance. Inevitably, the facts lose some of their quality of being steadily and implacably 'there'; the structure they constitute is balanced finely on a pinpoint of fantasy and within an ace of being broken up in uncertainty.

My second point applies more widely. In a number of stories, elements of the factual situation emerge through means other than direct narration or assertion, reaching us indirectly and in ways which we recognize as similar to our methods of gathering knowledge in everyday life. Some examples: one of the thematic turning-points of *Von jenseit des Meeres* (1863-4) is a conversation between Jenni, the central female figure, and her father (who is a planter and has brought Jenni, his illegitimate daughter by a halfcaste American woman, to Europe in order to get her away from her mother's influence). It helps to motivate and justify the father's apparent hard-heartedness in separating mother and daughter, and later, when Jenni escapes across the Atlantic to see her mother, her disillusion amply bears him out; so this point in the story is an important and prophetic one. But the conversation does not come to us as direct reporting, but as a dialogue overheard by Alfred, who tells the story and who eventually marries Jenni. Alfred, unbeknown to Jenni and her father, is in the next room, and his account repeatedly emphasizes his position:

Es mochten kaum einige Minuten vergangen sein, als ich von der Treppe her Schritte *vernahm* und bald darauf zwei Personen in das große, neben dem meinigen liegenden Zimmer *treten hörte. Eine von meinem Zimmer dahinein führende Tür . . . war zwar jetzt verschlossen; aber sie hatte ein Fenster, das von der andern Seite mit einer weißen Gardine dicht verhangen war.*
An der Stimme erkannte ich, daß Jenni und ihr Vater die Eingetretenen seien . . . Als sie sich dann näherten, wollte ich mich leise entfernen; aber die ersten Worte . . . bewirkten, daß ich regungslos und alles andere vergessend auf meinem Sitze blieb.
'Du konntest dort nicht bleiben!' *hörte ich den Vater . . . sagen . . . Ich hörte ihn* jetzt ein paarmal langsam auf und ab gehen . . . (there follow a few lines of dialogue).
Der Vater erwiderte hierauf nichts; aber *es wurde ein Fenster aufgestoßen, und an dem Geräusch bemerkte ich, wie* er den Kopf in die freie Luft steckte und mit großer Erregung sich räusperte. – Jenni hatte sich mit dem Rücken gegen die Tür gelehnt, welche die beiden Zimmer trennte. *Ich sah durch das*

verhängte Fenster den Schatten ihres Kopfes und hörte das Rauschen ihres Kleides.

Nach einiger Zeit *schien* ihr Vater in die Stube zurückgetreten zu sein . . . (more dialogue and more references to Alfred's specially conditioned knowledge of what is going on, like 'Ich sah durch die Gardine, wie . . .' or 'Der Vater schien ihre Hand zu fassen . .'; then the conversation ends).

Darauf *wurde die Tür geöffnet,* und *ich hörte, wie* ihre Schritte sich draußen auf dem Korridor nach der Treppe zu entfernten. — Ich blieb auf meinem Zimmer, bis ich zum Mittagessen herabgerufen wurde. (SW II 190ff; my italics.)

This is very like what we have seen before:[138] the crucial event drawn into the mind of an individual who experiences it, its objectivity diluted by its portrayal as a series of sense-impressions. The facts are undeniable, but the way in which they are discovered is repeatedly, meticulously, almost anxiously pointed.

Waldwinkel (1874) is prefaced and concluded with a similar sort of factual indirectness, but the method is different, and the result not nearly so certain. This is the story of a middle-aged man, Richard, who becomes the guardian of a young girl Franziska. For a time they live together as man and wife, (without actually marrying), in an isolated house; but Franziska finally deserts Richard in favour of a young forester. At the beginning there is the need to establish several things — the special position and predicament of Franziska, Richard's origins and past, and the figure of the Förster — at least in outline. Since the story is told by a 'fictional' narrator, we might expect recourse to the privileges of omniscience to satisfy this need; but we do not find it. Matters are so arranged that the facts (or approximations to fact) emerge without the narrator ever having really to abandon his standpoint of an observing stranger. The details about Franziska are conveyed through the description of a confrontation (before the burghermaster and in Richard's presence) between the girl and her erstwhile guardian, who stands convicted of considerable villainy against her. Richard himself is introduced in a scene which I mentioned earlier[139] and which contains vague references in dialogue to his former life, notably to an engagement remembered with some sadness. A little later these hints are rounded out, but the information is culled from that most unreliable of sources, pub gossip. We are allowed to hear (or overhear) a conversation between the landlord of a local inn and two of his customers, a trader and a forestry inspector. The landlord retails bits of scandal about the past life of Richard, who is newly arrived in the area — the suspicion that he had been involved in a student conspiracy in Prussia and had spent years in prison, and also the story of his wife's infidelity (Richard is supposed to have been knocked down by a carriage in which his wife was riding with her lover, and then to have killed the lover in a duel). These are in content factual assertions; but the context in which they are made lends them no great validity, as comments like this show:

Der Inspektor war inzwischen aufgestanden. — 'Schwatzt Ihr und der Teufel!' sagte er, indem er lachend auf die beiden andern herabsah . . . (SW II 447)

The inspector is hardly qualified to cast the first stone, since it is he who has previously introduced the young forester into the conversation (and, from our point of view, into the story) with highly-coloured praise of his marksmanship and dark hints about his prowess with women. Armed with these snippets, and with no other authority anywhere to confirm or deny them, we move into the action. The story ends by returning to the same setting, with the same three protagonists; and there is the same sort of mixture of fact and scandal to be sifted through. We hear of a rumour that Franziska was Richard's own flesh and blood — the landlord claims this, the trader dismisses it. From the trader we learn that it was indeed the forester who took the girl off — previously nothing has been made clear beyond the fact that she has gone. The inspector reports that Richard has also left the neighbourhood (nobody knows where he is now), and that the effects of the house where the couple had lived have been sold up. So our introductory and concluding information, such as it is, has been gained from the crisscross of talk between three old and garrulous men.

And again, *John Riew'* (1884-5) opens with a mystery that is only indirectly and incompletely cleared up. The man who narrates the story is intrigued by a new house near his home. When he tells us more about the occupants of the house (who later turn out to be John Riewe and his adopted son) he is at pains to emphasize that what he knows is culled from enquiries he has made round about: the relevant paragraphs are full of 'reporting' constructions:

> Und dennoch *sollte* das Haus bewohnt sein: ein Auswärtiger — *so hörte ich* — *habe* das früher dort gestandene . . . Gebäude . . . erworben. Wie aber das Verhältnis der . . Personen zueinander war, *darüber wußten die von mir Befragten nicht Bescheid zu geben* . . .
> Von dem Jungen freilich *ging allerlei Gerede* . . . ja, *man erzählte,* als nach einer neuen Schulstrafe der alte Herr mit liebreicher Ermahnung auf den Knaben eingedrungen *sei, habe* dieser plötzlich eine freche Gebärde nach ihm hin gemacht . . .
> *Ich frug wohl diesen und jenen,* woher denn der Mann gekommen sei; *die einen meinten:* aus Lübeck, *die andern:* aus Flensburg oder Hamburg; auch wohl, was er denn sonst getrieben haben möge, *und diese machten ihn zu einem Makler, die andern zu einem früheren Schiffskapitän.* (SW IV 8; my italics.)

Here, as in the other examples, the effect is striking: information picked up from here and there, its sources specified and acknowledged; qualified fact, fact through gossip or report or chance overhearing — never plain, unadulterated fact.

Lastly, I would draw attention to one of the most pervasive mannerisms in Storm's prose, the proliferating 'als ob' usage. It appears like a rash all over the stories, together with its cousins the constructions with 'schien' and 'wie'; one is tempted, indeed, to think of it as a kind of nervous tic. It has occurred in my previous quotations[140] (and I have talked about it) often enough to obviate the need for further examples; but it seems to me important to stress again that it is not merely a mannerism or tic but a quite definite and meaningful manifestation, in miniature, so to speak, of the hesitant attitude to matters of fact which has been my concern. There *is* purpose in a formulation like this one (from *Drüben am Markt*; Mamsell Sophie is drawing brandy from a cask):

> Aber während die Flüssigkeit hineinrann, bog sie den Kopf zurück und schüttelte sich unmerklich, *als widre sie der Dunst des Alkohols.* (SW I 547; my italics.)

Those few words in themselves imply a whole 'point of view', a narrator who is unwilling or unable to move inside Sophie and reveal what effect the alcohol has on her *in fact*. This limited observer is reduced to reporting just what he or anyone can see – the head bent back, the little shake – and to offering his own tentative suggestion of what it might mean. We are being told that our guess is as good as his, and almost every time we meet this particular type of construction, we shall discover the making of that implication, insistent and anxious.

6. ENDINGS

Hetty Sorrel, the saddest figure of *Adam Bede,* has a clandestine affair with a young squire, gives birth to an illegitimate child which she kills in her distraction, and for this crime is sentenced to death. At the last moment the sentence is commuted to one of transportation, and Hetty leaves the scene. Adam Bede, to whom she had been betrothed, is slowly restored after this shattering blow to his love and hopes, and in a year or two takes to wife Hetty's cousin Dinah Morris. Hetty is encompassed as fully as anyone else in the book by the broad sweep of George Eliot's compassion, but all the same she is made to die, a prisoner and alone, in Australia. Her death is not essential to the plot; in no sense does it relieve Adam of any residual burden or obligation, for a significant factor in his development is that he should emancipate himself from his former love and marry Dinah well within Hetty's lifetime. That Hetty *does* die this inessential death before the novel closes points, I think, to another sort of necessity. Death, says E.M. Forster, ends a book neatly,[141] and it would seem that a neat ending is obligatory. The novelist has to tie up any loose threads before concluding his narrative; we expect to be told what eventually and lastingly happens to the principal characters (whether they marry or die or whatever), so that their destinies, conditioned by the action, may be rounded off as the novel itself is rounded. A fate left unsealed is an incompleteness, in that the narrative thereby raises a question it cannot answer within its own terms of reference (we should have had to ask what effect Hetty's return might have on Adam and Dinah and Arthur Donnithorne, the squire). It is disquieting to have a limb as it were poking out from beneath the covers when we close the book. The limb has to be pushed back inside; Hetty has to die.

But Storm makes a habit of incompleteness. At the end of a round dozen of his stories[142] we lose track of one or more of the main characters. They pass before us and act out their particular drama, and then Storm relinquishes his hold on them; they drift away and disappear into a kind of limbo where all is left uncertain. This loosing of the hold is evident already in *Marthe und ihre Uhr*; the story-teller, if what he tells can be called a story, ends his reminiscences like this:

> Ob es noch so gesellig in Marthens einsamer Kammer ist? Ich weiß es nicht; es sind viele Jahre her, seit ich in ihrem Hause wohnte, und jene kleine Stadt liegt weit von meiner Heimat. — Was Menschen, die das Leben lieben, nicht auszusprechen wagen, pflegte sie laut und ohne Scheu zu äußern: 'Ich bin niemals krank gewesen; ich werde gewiß sehr alt werden'.
> Ist ihr Glaube ein richtiger gewesen und sollten diese Blätter den Weg in ihre Kammer finden, so möge sie sich beim Lesen auch meiner erinnern. (SW I 400)

We do not know whether Marthe is alive or dead — the fact that she used to predict longevity for herself perhaps tips the scales slightly in favour of the former. If she *is* alive, then we do not know whether the quality of her life is the same. The last sentence suggests the tentative hope of re-establishing contact, and that, to be strictly logical, makes it quite evident that the contact has in the first place been lost.

It is clearly relevant that *Marthe und ihre Uhr* is told by an embodied first-person narrator; the vagueness of the ending here is a ramification of the phenomenon we saw earlier,[143] total lack of recourse to narrative omniscience. A story-teller bound by human limitations, able only to record his individual perceptions, judgements and acquaintances (rather than the 'facts' about people and events), is very likely to be ignorant of what ultimately happens to the people he encounters. When they have passed out of his vision, his knowledge of their subsequent doings is dependent upon the indirect means which could be at any-body's disposal for finding out about absent friends — letters, mutual acquaintances, and so on. If no such means are available (and in the present case none appear to be, particularly since a gap of years and miles is mentioned), then he must simply admit his ignorance. This helps to motivate and make meaningful the final incompleteness; the sense of disquiet is modified, though it does remain part of one's response.

Happily, there is one story, *Der Herr Etatsrat* (1880-1) in which that very disquiet is formulated and fixed already in the text, making the reader's judgement for him. This is possible because the reader has a representative within the story, the 'junger Freund' to whom the old man (the first-person narrator) relates what he remembers of the Etatsrat, his son Archimedes (the narrator's friend and fellow-student), his daughter Phia and his decidedly villainous secretary Käfer. The weird and chilling tale, tracing the dissolution of the family and the eventual deaths of Archimedes and Phia, winds to its end, and there is a curiously cinematic return to the present as the figures, almost as though we were seeing them on a screen, gradually shrink and recede and become visibly framed once more in the old man's memory, the 'actual' context:

> Phia Sternow ruht neben ihrer . . . Mutter . . . — Eine Willi ist sie nicht geworden, nur ein verdämmernder Schatten, der mit andern einst Gewesener noch mitunter vor den Augen eines alten Mannes schwebt. — Arme Phia! Armer Archimedes!
>
> Ich schwieg. Mein junger Freund, dem ich dies alles auf eine hingeworfene Frage erzählt hatte, sah mich *unbefriedigt* an. 'Und der Herr Etatsrat?' frug er und langte aufs neue in die Zigarrenkiste, die ich ihm mittlerweile zugeschoben hatte, 'was ist aus dem geworden?'
>
> 'Aus dem? Nun, was zuletzt aus allen und aus allem wird! Da ich einst nach elfjähriger Abwesenheit in unsere Vaterstadt zurückkehrte, war er nicht mehr vorhanden. Viele wußten gar nicht mehr von ihm; auch sein Amt existierte gar nicht mehr, und seine vielgerühmten Deichprofile sind durch andere ersetzt, die selbstverständlich nun die einzig richtigen sind; Sie aber sind der erste, dem zu erzählen mir die Ehre wurde, daß ich den großen Mann mit eigenen Augen noch gesehen habe'.
>
> 'Hm! Und Herr Käfer?'
>
> 'Ich bitte, fragen Sie mich nicht mehr! Wenn er noch lebt, so wird er jedenfalls sich wohl befinden; denn er verstand es, seine Person mit anderen zu sparen'.
>
> 'Das hol der Teufel!' sagte mein *ungeduldiger* junger Freund. (SW III 338f; my italics.)

Phia is dead and safely buried, except for the occasional resurrection in the old man's mind; the same goes for Archimedes. But already with the Etatsrat things are less certain: '. .was zuletzt', etc., seems clear enough indication that he too is dead, yet 'nicht mehr vorhanden' is an oddly non-committal way of confirming it — one feels that the story-teller doesn't claim it as anything more than a reasonable deduction from the evidence he goes on to mention, general ignorance of the Etatsrat's life, abolition of his office and so on. And as to Käfer's 'after-life', that is a complete blank. It seems to me that our reaction to all this uncertainty must be of the same order as the young man's, though possibly milder in degree.

We are left equally in the air at the end of *Draußen im Heidedorf* (1871-2), the account of a legal enquiry. The tale is told by an Amtsvogt, who is called to investigate the disappearance of one Hinrich Fehse from the moorland village of the title. The facts, and the situations behind the facts, emerge (so far as they do emerge) through the testimonies of several more or less interested witnesses, and from the Amtsvogt's own recollection of having seen Hinrich once or twice some months before. The Rahmen technique is conceived and executed here with a brilliance which I take to be unsurpassed in Storm's work; report, conjecture, anecdote and gossip combine like so many brush-strokes to delineate and fill out the picture of Hinrich Fehse's fate; some areas of the canvas are clear and highly-coloured, others are more misty and ill-defined, but in the end something like the truth takes shape. The Amtsvogt, the vessel of our curiosity, probes, selects and collates, and thus we gradually come to know as much as can be known by individual human minds. The whole Rahmen element is a *tour de force*; I think it has a function and is not merely a piece of virtuoso story-writing, novelistic ingenuity in the void, but I want to leave consideration of this function for the time being; it is not immediately related to the argument here.

Hinrich Fehse conceives a fierce and enslaving passion for Margarete Glansky, a girl of volatile temperament, Slovak origins and considerable beauty, who on all these counts is unpopular with the more respectable members of the community. Margarete leaves the village, and Hinrich concludes a marriage of convenience with another woman. With Margarete's unexpected (and, for most villagers, unwelcome) return, Hinrich's feelings are inflamed again. He gives her presents and repeatedly asks her to go away with him, but she is frightened by the violence and possessiveness of his love, and refuses. Finally, in a state bordering on mental breakdown, he disappears (hence the enquiry), only to be found drowned a few days later. Is it suicide or an accident born of his distraction? The Amtsvogt cannot tell, so there already is one uncertainty. But there is also another greater one: at least we know that Hinrich is dead, but what of Margarete?

> Will man noch nach dem Slowakenmädchen fragen, so vermag ich darauf ke ne Antwort zu geben; sie soll in ich weiß nicht welche große Stadt gezogen und dort in der Menschenflut verschollen sein. (SW II 326)

'Verschollen' — the word is characteristic of the phenomenon, and it is not surprising to see it used again in the same sort of connection in *Zur 'Wald- und Wasserfreude'* (1878). Hermann Tobias Zippel's daughter Kätti fastens her affections at an early age on Wulf Fedders, who lodges at her father's house as a Primaner (later re-appearing as a student, then as a Doktor and budding scholar). Wulf is at times strongly attracted to Kätti, but ultimately chooses a much more acceptable and lucrative match with the blonde daughter of a major. When Kätti finds out, she disappears and is not seen again (like Hinrich Fehse, she runs away twice, the second time never to return). The absence of her help — she had acted as waitress and singer — hastens the failure of her father's last eccentric business venture, a spa restaurant in the forest (the 'Wald- und Wasserfreude' of the title); he goes bankrupt and, like Kätti, is consigned to oblivion. A quarter of a century passes:

> Drüben aber in der Stadt, in dem Archiv der alten Landvogtei, zu deren Bezirk die einstige 'Wald- und Wasserfreude' gehört, liegt unter den Akten über *Verschollene* ein Heft mit ganz vergilbtem Deckel; es enthält die Verwaltungsnachweise über Kättis Erbgelder, deren Zinsen längst das Kapital verdoppelt haben.
>
> Der gegenwärtige Landvogt ist Wulf Fedders, welcher bald nach seiner Verlobung alle Gedanken an künftigen Gelehrtenruhm mit der sicherer zum häuslichen Herde führenden Beamtenlaufbahn vertauscht hatte. Alle Jahre einmal, bei der Revision der Vormundschaften und Kuratelen, gehen jene Akten durch seine Hände. Dann gedenkt er plötzlich wieder der dunkelfarbigen Kätti und seiner Schülerzeit und jener Tage in der 'Wald- und

Wasserfreude'. Aber er hat gar viele Akten und zu Hause eine blonde Frau und viele Kinder; bevor er noch den Weg vom Amtslokale nach seiner Wohnung zurüchgegangen ist, haben diese Erinnerungen ihn schon längst verlassen. (SW III 183; my italics.)

Kätti has gone, and we hear no more about her. Once a year (and this is an intriguing motif), her name turns up during Wulf's work, and his memories of her are briefly revived, the girl herself is briefly resurrected; then back she goes into limbo for another year. Alive or dead? Regenerated, or still gnawed by the canker of this one rejection? No-one in the story knows, and no other means of knowing is suggested. There is a gap left at the end; Kätti slips quietly through it and escapes the confines of the story. Again the question is left unanswered, and again we are left disquieted. Our spokesman this time can be Keller, who writes to Storm about the story and gives this ambivalent judgement on its ending:

Schon seit Wochen habe ich Ihre 'Wald- und Wasserfreude' genossen, liebster Freund, und noch immer fällt es mir plötzlich ein, daß die arme Kätti ja in der Welt herumirre und wie es ihr wohl gehen möge. Dieses spurlose Verschwinden der Heldin Ihrer Geschichte ist echt tragisch und zugleich neu, auch allseitig richtig herbeigeführt; wäre der Wulf Feddersen *[sic]* etwas kernhafter und interessanter oder der Vater Zippel weniger lächerlich, so wäre der Verlauf ein anderer geworden, damit aber die Geschichte um die Pointe gekommen. Da also das alte Rätsel des Warum wieder neu illustriert ist und die Geschichte sich im einzelnen gut und kurzweilig, sogar mit Spannung liest, so hätten Sie nach meiner Meinung das melancholische Motto weglassen sollen. Dasselbe ist übrigens selbst ein gutes Zeichen; denn sobald einmal der Schriftsteller schwach wird, so wird er's erst recht nicht eingestehen und hütet sich, solche Andeutungen zu machen.[144]

The same disturbing incompleteness, then, as we have met in the other stories. But there is a difference here. *Zur 'Wald- und Wasserfreude'* is *not* told by a narrator 'in character',[145] and Storm therefore has at his disposal the resources and privileges implied in the convention of a 'fictional' entity to tell the story. Kätti may be just a name on a document for Wulf Fedders now; she may have passed entirely out of the ken of anyone we can look to in the story; but there is nothing to prevent a 'fictional' narrator from saying something like (though rather less clumsy than): 'None of her former acquaintances could tell you now what became of dark-skinned Kätti, but what in fact happened to her was this . . .' The fact that he does not do anything of the kind is a further manifestation of what I have called 'reserved omniscience', Storm's apparent unwillingness to arrogate to himself, any more than is absolutely necessary, prerogatives of knowledge beyond what is accessible to an individual human observer or participant, even when his use of a 'fictional' narrator makes such prerogatives available to him. He seems prepared to make considerable sacrifices to this unwillingness: at the outset he will use up valuable space (and in pieces as short as his, space *is* valuable),[146] in so arranging things that names, facts and relationships can be established in dialogue or by similarly devious means;[147] and at the close he will risk dispensing with clear and known fates for his characters (and I have suggested that this can be thought aesthetically, if not technically, 'necessary') and allow his people to drift out through the open end of the tale, leaving a trail of unanswered questions behind them. When the narrator is embodied and involved, the loose end, albeit disturbing, has its rationale; when he is disembodied and 'fictional', that rationale is inapplicable, and the disturbance remains unmodified.

The same is true of *Hans und Heinz Kirch*. The fictional narrator here, who at the beginning of the story lays considerable claim to omniscience,[148] nonetheless loses sight of Heinz Kirch at the end — and this time the unanswered question is, literally, a question. It is prefigured half-way through, during Heinz's first long absence and just after Hans has turned back the unfranked letter; the occasion is the mother's death:

> da die schon erlöschenden Augen der Sterbenden weit geöffnet und wie suchend in die leere Kammer blickten, hatte Hans Kirch, als ob er ein Versprechen gebe, ihre Hand ergriffen und gedrückt; dann hatten ihre Augen sich zur letzten Lebensruhe zugetan.
> Aber wo war, was trieb Heinz Kirch in der Stunde, als seine Mutter starb? (SW III 365)

These are the last words of one section; at the beginning of the next, a few years are said to have elapsed, and the narrative is concerned with quite other things; so the question is not at all a rhetorical one leading straight into an answer. It is in fact answered much later on, though certainly only in the loosest and most general way, when Heinz (if we assume that it *is* Heinz)[149] returns and gives his father a vague account of his doings overseas. But then the contact is broken once more; Heinz disappears again, and that is the last we see of him. A year or so later Hans has that sort of vision which is said to come to seamen at the death of a comrade or loved one far away. For a while he is convinced that Heinz is dead; but this sad conviction (which is at least a conviction) leaves him, and he is left to stand on the shore and throw his own agonized question out over the sea:

> 'Heinz, Heinz!' rief er. 'Wo ist Heinz Kirch geblieben?' Dann wieder bewegte er langsam seinen Kopf: 'Es ist auch einerlei, denn es kennt ihn keiner mehr'. (SW III 404)

Hans is eventually made to die in his uncertainty; part of his penance has been not to know until he passes, perhaps, into eternity. But beyond his penance and death, beyond the boundaries of the tale and beyond possible functions for this unillumined mystery, the same question insistently returns:

> Hans Adams Tochtermanne wird der Stadtrat nicht entgehen; auch ein Erbe ist längst geboren und läuft schon mit dem Ranzen in die Rektorschule; — wo aber ist Heinz Kirch geblieben? (SW III 406)

And there Storm writes *finis*. We shall never know.

A feature of the five stories whose endings I have talked about so far is that they deal with events in the more or less recent past, and at their close move right into 'the time of writing'. In stories with an embodied first-person narrator (like *Marthe und ihre Uhr* or *Draußen im Heidedorf*), this reference to the present is a logical and necessary adjunct of the point of view — the narrator is, as it were, alive to tell the tale, and thus becomes himself the link between past and present. But in stories where the narrator is 'fictional' (like *Zur 'Wald- und Wasserfreude'* or *Hans und Heinz Kirch*) the narrative scheme does not demand such a reference; so it is striking when we actually see the present tense (even the future tense) being used, when we are told what Wulf Fedders is doing and remembering *now*, or what are the successes and aspirations of Hans Kirch's son-in-law *now* (as well as being left in the dark about where Kätti Zippel and Heinz Kirch are *now*). This has one or two effects. It imparts a measure of actuality to the theme — these things are happening in our time and are relevant to our situation, part of our realities — and then it fixes the disembodied narrator in time, giving him an existence more or less contemporaneous with the events he describes, and thereby depriving him of one of the attributes of 'fictional' omniscience, namely the ability to hover over the passage of time and disregard, if he chooses, distinctions between past, present and future. Thus delimited, he begins to take on another of the bare contours of human nature (we can say 'he is a person of that time'); and we can begin to apply to him the observation I made about narrators 'in character' — that their uncertainty is in some degree motivated by their human limitation, and that our disquiet at this uncertainty is somewhat modified.

Storm seems to be taking this uncertainty as his final aim, and using that other device, the moving into present time, only as a means toward achieving it. He is *not* trying ultimately for the vivid actuality which the device might give him, *not* producing this actuality at the expense of the uncertainty which is its 'unfortunate' but necessary by-product. I am led to suggest this by reference to the endings of another group of stories, the more avowedly historical ones. In these stories, obviously, there is no question of immediate actuality; that possibility has been renounced already in the decision to set the action in the distant past. Historical narratives are by their nature the simplest to conclude neatly: centuries of hindsight ought to be enough to enable one to gather up the most recalcitrant loose ends. If uncertainty were solely a result of actuality in stories with a contemporary setting, we would expect it to disappear when actuality is not part of the plan. But it doesn't: four of these five stories[150] leave us with significant loose ends and blanknesses of various kinds. There is no doubt that the people concerned are dead — they must be by now! — but very often that is about the only thing that is not in doubt. Storm makes free use of the passing of time, the fading of memories and the decay of memorials[151] to motivate the way in which these people pass out of human ken and into oblivion, much the same sort of oblivion as swallows up Kätti Zippel or Margarete Glansky; and so we have the interesting phenomenon of *both* actuality (in the 'contemporary' stories) *and* finitude (in the historical ones) being employed to the same kind of effect, namely ignorance of what happens to the characters after the tale is over.

Aquis submersus (1875-6) sets the tone. At the end of his long confession (the story is the 'transcription' of a manuscript in his own hand), the painter Johannes tells how he finally left behind his beloved Katharina and the body of the son their negligence had killed, and walked away into the world. There the manuscript ends, and this brief conclusion follows:

> Dessen Herr Johannes sich einstens im Vollgefühl seiner Kraft vermessen, daß er's wohl auch einmal in seiner Kunst den Größeren gleichzutun verhoffe, das sollten Worte bleiben, in die leere Luft gesprochen.
>
> Sein Name gehört nicht zu denen, die genannt werden; kaum dürfte er in einem Künstlerlexikon zu finden sein; ja selbst in seiner engeren Heimat weiß niemand von einem Maler seines Namens. Des großen Lazarusbildes tut zwar noch die Chronik unserer Stadt Erwähnung, das Bild selbst aber ist zu Anfang dieses Jahrhunderts nach dem Abbruch unserer alten Kirche gleich den anderen Kunstschätzen derselben verschleudert und verschwunden.
>
> Aquis submersus. (SW II 656)

Johannes is lost to us and to everyone. We know now the part of his life described in his manuscript, but there are no answers to the questions it raises: how his experiences affect him as a personality, whether and how he eventually overcomes his guilt or whether he bears it with him till death. His early promise as a painter seems not to have been fulfilled; at least, no work of his survives. And that is the sum total of what is known about him.

Eekenhof (1879) ends even more clearly on the same note. Hennicke is finally broken in recompense for the evil and injustice he has inflicted on his son Detlev and illegitimate daughter Heilwig in his attempts to gain Eekenhof; for Detlev finally comes as a 'blonder Reiter' and carries off Heilwig, the only human being for whom Hennicke has had a spark of love. This is the last paragraph:

> Und so in seiner Einsamkeit ist (Hennicke) bis an die äußerste Grenze des Menschenlebens gelangt. Von Heilwig aber und dem blonden Reiter hat sich jede Spur verloren.[152]

And again, *Zur Chronik von Grieshuus* (1883-4) leaves a group of its characters to slip off into the mist. Magister Bokenfeld, after chronicling the last stages in the death and destruction of the house of Grieshuus, writes of the figures immediately surrounding the two main protagonists (who both die):

> Sie sind wohl itzo alle nicht mehr hienieden; denn außer zween Schreiben des Herrn Obristen, bald nach ihrem Abgang, habe ich von keinem etwas mehr vernommen. (SW III 556)

And oblivion, ignorance and loss of contact are precisely those elements of transience and finitude which seem designed to come most clearly to the fore in the Baroque lament which ends the piece:

> Auf Erden stehet nichts, es muß vorüberfliegen;
> Es kommt der Tod daher, du kannst ihn nicht besiegen.
> Ein Weilchen weiß vielleicht noch wer, was du gewesen;
> Dann wird das weggekehrt, und weiter fegt der Besen.[153]

And finally, the disembodied 'Ich',[154] the 'spirit of story-telling' who recounts the 'jäh zerrissenes Minneabenteuer' of *Ein Fest auf Haderslevhuus* (1885), ends his account of the love and death of Rolf and Dagmar by turning to his audience:

> 'Und die andern?' fragt ihr, 'was ward aus denen?'
> — Die andern? — Ich habe von ihnen weiter nichts erkunden können; es gab ja Klöster derzeit, in die hinein sich ein beraubtes, auch ein verpfuschtes Leben flüchten konnte! Was liegt daran? Die Geräusche, die ihre Schritte machten, sind seit Jahrhunderten verhallt und werden nimmermehr gehört werden. (SW IV 125)

So even this spirit, whom we heard before[155] so confident in his knowledge of Rolf Lembeck, is uncertain at the last, suddenly no longer all-knowing but a historian who has lost the facts. These dozen tales — tales of the present or of the past, tales told by natural men or created by disembodied spirits, it is all the same — lose their characters as we lose the people we no longer see. The raggedness of these endings is the raggedness of life — we recognize that — but it is not a part of living which we are used to meeting in fiction. Faced with this incompleteness, this limitation rounding off the other limitations, we remain, in the end, uneasy.

7. INTERPRETATIONS

Is there a meaningful way of drawing these various technical phenomena together? I have mentioned in passing one or two critical *aperçus* on individual facets of the problem, and more will arise later. For now, I should like to concentrate on a few interpretations which seem particularly relevant and interesting, though in the last resort they still leave us with questions. They are drawn in the main from criticism of English literature and might not normally find a place in a study of a German author; but they seem to me to be closely and surprisingly related to the problems which arise in Storm.

What of the Rahmen? Although the German Novelle (and its Romance predecessors) can claim to have exploited this technique more than any other literary form, it clearly occurs elsewhere: fascinating light is thrown on it by Graham Hough in his discussion of a full-scale English novel, Conrad's *Chance*.[156] Hough argues that Conrad is 'pre-eminently the novelist of isolation' (shades of Storm), and that all his great characters are solitaries, but then he points to the tension between

Conrad's central concern (men isolated) and his choice of genre:

> But the novelist cannot work in this mode alone. Of all writers he is the most implicated with society and the social bonds. And there is only one kind of society that Conrad had ever known intimately, had fully participated in as an adult human being — the society of a ship at sea.[157]

Conrad's lack of real intimacy with any social scheme on land leads him into difficulties when, in *Chance,* he has to describe the Fyne household and establish the figure of Flora. He gets over the difficulty by building the picture in ways very similar to the Rahmen device:

> It is handled, so far as the sheer machinery is concerned, with immense technical assurance; yet there is a slightly disturbing sense of being kept at a remove, or rather several removes from the actuality. A reconstruction by Marlow of a scene described to him by Mrs Fyne, who herself has only had a report of it from Flora's uncle, is not the same as a direct vision of Flora as an acting and suffering being. The requirement is to present Flora's life after the crash, in the house of odious relations; and I believe this elaborate series of outworks is necessary because Conrad has not the specific, intimate knowledge of the cross-currents in a dreary lower-middle-class family to portray it direct; and being the scrupulous artist that he is, he sets his subject at a distance, and relates it through a medium which he knows how to handle.[158]

Hough finds this indirectness throughout the first part of the novel (the part set on land), including the vital episode where Mrs Fyne's brother Anthony falls in love with Flora and takes her away. It vanishes in the second part, which is set on board ship: here Conrad knows all about the milieu.

Nonetheless, the 'slightly disturbing sense of being kept at . . . several removes from the actuality', and the feeling of a more sharply focussed presentation which succeeds it, are not wholly to be explained by the use or non-use of the Rahmen technique; for in the second part the same technique is still clearly in evidence ('This part of the tale is told by Marlow, freely elaborating and interpreting the account of Mr Powell: no different in narrative method, then, from the earlier part of the book'.)[159] What is the basic difference? Hough does not go into technical detail at this point; he leaves it at a 'somehow' and reverts to an explanation in terms of the plot:

> But somehow the quality of the novel seems to have changed. We cease to remember the intermediaries through whose consciousness the material has passed. We live on board the *Ferndale* as we never lived in the Fyne's house. And the reason I think is simple — we are now on board a ship.[160]

There is no mention here of exactly *how* the 'quality' of the novel changes (Hough only suggests *why*), nor of what makes us forget the intermediaries now after having been so conscious of them before. But the answer is implicit in the rest of the argument; looking back over it, I take the difference to be this: whereas in the second part of the book the Rahmen is employed on its own and without tension or scrupulosity ('*freely* elaborating and interpreting'), it is combined in the first part with *other* related devices of indirection, and conveys the impression of anxious attention to detail ('Fragments of narrative . . . observations and surmises . . . scenes, fragments of scenes, glimpses, guesses . . . this elaborate series of outworks . . . the scrupulous artist').[161] This combination of the Rahmen with related devices, together with a pervasive anxiety in their use, is just the kind of picture I have tried to draw of Storm's technical procedures; so it seems to me that Hough's explanation in terms of Conrad's vision (or the limitations of that vision) can be applied to Storm's writing in the same terms. If we do apply it, the result is odd and worrying.

Hough suggests that Conrad sets his subject at a distance because he has not 'the specific, intimate knowledge of the cross-currents in a dreary lower-middle-class family to portray it direct', and again later, because in his treatment of life on land his imagination works in a 'world insufficiently realised, insufficiently dense, without all the manifold small pressures that go to make up life as it is lived'.[162] That is a reasonable assessment of Conrad, an *émigré* writer without firm social roots or even a real native tongue (in spite of his reputation as one of the most remarkable stylists in English fiction). But Storm is commonly considered to be a strongly regional or provincial writer, securely rooted in the social patterns of his homeland (especially of his native town and province) — *too* securely rooted, it could be said, too content with the familiar and immediate portrayal of a narrow society, and lacking the imagination to move outside its physical and moral boundaries. And yet time after time, in stories set in the society Storm is supposed to know so well, we have found the indirectness of the Rahmen and associated devices, which Conrad is forced into when describing a society with which he is *not* familiar, but easily sheds when he moves into a milieu he *does* know. And the effect is the same: the limitation is scrupulously taken into account, a veil is drawn across the living reality, and we have the 'slightly disturbing sense' of being at a remove from it. Can it possibly be that Storm's indirectness springs from the same source as Conrad's? Is there conceivably a sense in which Storm could be said to lack the 'specific, intimate knowledge' of a society in whose conventions he seems utterly steeped? Or to be unable, while describing a way of life which is all the world for him, to create or lay claim to anything more than 'a world insufficiently *realised,* insufficiently dense'? Does he not *know* his world? I shall be suggesting later that something very like this is the case.

And what of the 'point of view'? Many of the phenomena I have described are closely connected with, or consequent upon, the narrative standpoint adopted, either the standpoint of a narrator 'in character' telling the story in the first person and involved in the action, or that of an observing stranger who relies on the evidence of his eyes and ears and on the tentative use of his capacity to guess and deduce. Both these standpoints are qualifications of the more normal convention of omniscience; and both receive considerable attention in Percy Lubbock's *The Craft of Fiction*.[163] In connection with Thackeray's *Vanity Fair,* Lubbock argues that any extensive appeal to the authority of an omniscient narrator is likely to defeat the coherence of the scheme; the book will seem ultimately incomplete and not really self-contained:

> there is an inherent weakness in it if the mind that knows the story and the eye that sees it remain unaccountable . . . it may seem like a thing meant to stand against a wall, with one side left in the rough; and there is no wall for a novel to stand against.[164]

To overcome this weakness, the novelist may resort to one of two methods. The first is that of the narrator 'in character' (Thackeray himself uses it in *Esmond*). The advantages of this method, Lubbock says, are clear: the picture is made salient, precise and individual by being seen through a known and defined pair of eyes; above all, it throws up no questions which cannot be answered in its own compass:

> If the story-teller is *in* the story himself, the author is dramatized; his assertions gain in weight, for they are backed by the presence of the narrator in the pictured scene. It is an advantage scored; the author has shifted his responsibility, and now it falls where the reader can see and measure it; the arbitrary quality which may at any time be detected in the author's voice is disguised in the voice of his spokesman. Nothing is now imported into the story from without; it is self-contained, it has no associations with anyone beyond its circle.[165]

This seems to me amply to refute Bernd and the clutch of authorities he invokes[166] in support of his theory that the 'fictional' omniscient narrator is a universal feature, the *sine qua non,* of story-telling.

But the method has its disadvantage too. It falls down when the story sets out to create a searching and elaborate picture of the man telling it. The narrator 'in character' must remain a shadowy figure, 'a pair of eyes and a memory',[167] and is only at his most useful when telling of things outside himself; he can give no truly cogent account of his own inner history:

> It seems, then, to be a principle of the story-teller's art that a personal narrator will do very well and may be extremely helpful, so long as the story is only the reflection of life beyond and outside him; but that as soon as the main weight of attention is claimed for the speaker rather than for the scene, then his report of himself becomes a matter which might be strengthened, and which should accordingly give way to the stronger method.[168]

The second method, the 'stronger' one, is the totally exterior mode of description, the action narrated as if by a stranger who can enter into none of the characters, reveal nothing of the true motivations behind words and actions, and make no authoritative statement about the inner meanings of events. Lubbock calls both these methods 'scenic' as opposed to 'pictorial' — that is, they both tend to narrate through a series of individual incidents and experiences (which are presented more particularly in their aspect of 'scenes' witnessed, happenings discernible to the senses of anyone there at the time), leaving the reader to make the connections; and they both relinquish the right (assumed by an omniscient narrator) to make explicit assertions about, indeed to create, 'the whole picture', the wider developments and progressions which would be accessible only to a governing intelligence behind the tale.

For the second method (narration as if by a stranger) he reserves the stricter term 'dramatic'. The formulation is Henry James', and the latter part of Lubbock's book is in essence an examination of James as the master-craftsman of fiction. *The Awkward Age* is offered as the prime example of the 'dramatic' method pure and unalloyed, and in discussing this novel Lubbock gives what seems to me a perfectly expressed and telling definition of the method itself:

> (James) chose to treat this story as pure drama; he never once draws upon the characteristic resource of the novelist — who is able, as the dramatist is not able, to give a generalized and foreshortened account of the matter in hand. In *The Awkward Age* everything is immediate and particular; there is no insight into anybody's thought, no survey of the scene from a height, no resumption of the past in retrospect. The whole of the book passes scenically before the reader, and nothing is offered but the look and speech of the characters on a series of chosen occasions. It might indeed be printed as a play; whatever is not dialogue is simply a kind of amplified stage-direction, adding to the dialogue the expressive effect that might be given it by good acting.[169]

There is a kind of drama which one could call 'realistic' or 'naturalistic'; its major distinguishing characteristic is that it avoids anything that would alienate[170] the audience from the illusion that they are eavesdropping on events taking place in 'a room with the fourth wall missing';[171] it eschews soliloquy, chorus, apostrophisation of the spectator; it attempts to show the surface quality of real life, and relies on nothing other than this surface quality to make its statements. It is plays of that kind, I think, that are recalled by the word 'dramatic' in this context; the bulk of drama (especially 'classical' drama) does not seem to accord with Lubbock's description. Assuming, then, that Lubbock is using the phrase 'pure drama' here in this rather specialised sense, one can see that 'dramatic' would be a very useful covering word to describe the common features of several of the techniques I have singled out in Storm's writing.

Watching the 'realistic' or 'naturalistic' play, we discover names only when the characters refer to or address each other by name in dialogue ('Good morning, John', or 'Here comes George; I wonder what he wants?'), and that is just what happens in Storm's stories ('Bist du jetzt immer so fleißig, Fritz?' . . . 'Richard, du bist es!').[172] In the play, we get other 'background material' — relationships between characters, their position, their origins and past and so on — in much the same way, by picking up and analysing whatever the characters let drop, what emerges in anecdote and reminiscence; and again, so it is in Storm too: 'Was hast du, Vetter Rudolf?'[173] — and the relationship is established; or this piece of conversation between the girl and the Badefrau in *Psyche,* an example of the creaking clumsiness, very like that of a bad play, into which Storm is occasionally forced in following the method:

> 'Ja, ja, Frölen, ich streit auch nicht. — Ich vergeß es nimmer — *da ich Kindsmagd bei Ihrem Großvater, beim alten Bürgermeister war* — die Angst, die ich oftmals ausgestanden; die Frau Mama — sie wird's mir nicht verübeln — war dazumalen grad nicht anders als wie das junge Frölen heute!'
> Das junge Frölen hatte die nackten Füßchen zu sich auf die Sofakante gezogen und ließ sie behaglich von dem warmen Sonnenschein beleuchten. *'Erzähl's nur noch einmal, Kathi!'* sagte sie;
> Die Alte hatte sich neben sie auf das Sofa gesetzt. 'Ja, ja, Frölen; *ich hab's Ihnen schon oft erzählt . . . Ich war die Kindsmagd für das jüngere Schwesterchen, für die Frau Tante Elsabe . . .'* (SW II 526f; my italics.)

This is terrible — does the girl really need to be told the old woman's former position, her own grandfather's rank and her own aunt's name, and does she really want to hear the story *again*? To his credit, Storm usually handles things much better; here, though, we are presented with a crop of superfluous statements which are obviously, embarrassingly designed to enlighten us and not the girl.

The play is able — or rather it is obliged — to convey certain facts or situations by visual means, where the novelist will make the direct authoritative statement: in *Howards End,* for example, E.M. Forster clears up the mystery surrounding Helen Schlegel by *telling* us that Margaret saw her and 'learnt the simple explanation of all their fears — her sister was with child';[174] whereas in the dramatized version of the same novel,[175] Helen is made to walk onto the stage and stop, sideways on against the light, to *show* her rounded figure to the audience, inviting an inference which is obvious but none the less an inference. In the same way, the two young men who appear in my quotation from *Im Sonnenschein*[176] are made to show their status by their appearance, so that the narrator is not left to tell us what they are: one is a cavalry officer, as we can see from his 'weiße festtägliche Uniform', the other is a young middle-class civilian, as we deduce from visible signs about him: 'ein junger Mann in bürgerlicher Kleidung mit sauber gepuderter Frisur'.

Or again, 'amplified stage-direction' is an extremely apt description of many of the small formulations I have mentioned — the 'als ob' constructions, phrases with 'schien' or 'wie', or emphases on the expression of an emotion rather than the emotion itself. The quotation from *Im Sonnenschein* provides several examples of this too: 'Der junge Mann lächelte, wie jemand, dem was Liebes widerfahren soll . . . als wolle er nicht bemerkt sein . . . gleichwohl schien es ihn nicht zu stören . . . ein Ausdruck brüderlichen, fast zärtlichen Vertrauens zeigte sich . . . als hätte sie sich besonnen . . . mit dem Ausdruck nicht allzu ernsthaften Zürnens . . .' All that is very similar to this series of bracketed directions drawn from a few pages of Oscar Wilde's *Lady Windermere's Fan:* '. . . looking at him with startled eyes . . . passes her hand nervously over her brow . . . with a gesture of impatience . . . with a puzzled expression on her face . . . sinks down into a chair with a gesture of anguish . . . follows her in a bewildered manner . . .'[177]

Indeed, there are times when Storm writes in an intensely theatrical way; one has the very strong sense of being in an auditorium and seeing the 'room with the fourth wall missing'. The long opening sequence of *Viola tricolor* is a remarkable case in point, another is the first paragraph of *Schweigen*, which gives the startling impression of the curtain rising on a tableau:

> Es war ein niedriges, mäßig großes Zimmer, durch viele Blattpflanzen verdüstert, beschränkt durch mancherlei altes, aber sorgsam erhaltenes Möbelwerk, dem man es ansah, daß es einst für höhere Gemächer angefertigt worden, als sie die Mietwohnung hier im dritten Stock zu bieten hatte. Auch die schon ältere Dame, welche, die Hand eines vor ihr stehenden jungen Mannes haltend, einem gleichfalls alten Herrn gegenübersaß, erschien fast zu stattlich für diese Räume. (SW III 407)

More thematically, I think it reasonable, though speculative, to suggest that one of the dominant features of dramatic spectacle is the picture of people in immediate relation with one another; the conflicts and developments are worked out first and foremost in the dialogue between one personality and another, so that what the characters say, how far they understand each other's minds, how they convey their feelings to each other and thereby to the audience, is obviously a matter of prime concern. 'The problem of communication' – the phrase I used for Storm[178] becomes, when applied to drama and especially to modern drama, a critical cliché. So again, one could talk of Storm's preoccupation with the problem as being a 'dramatic' trait.

'Dramatic', then, seems a germane and fruitful word to use. Is it possible that Storm himself was aware of the connection? We might conclude as much from the heavily quoted sentence in the withdrawn preface of 1881:[179]

> Die heutige Novelle ist die Schwester des Dramas und die strengste Form der Prosadichtung.

But it soon emerges that Storm has something else in mind, for he goes on to draw very different parallels between the Novelle and the drama:

> Gleich dem Drama behandelt (die Novelle) die tiefsten Probleme des Menschenlebens; gleich diesem verlangt sie zu ihrer Vollendung einen im Mittelpunkte stehenden Konflikt, von welchem aus das Ganze sich organisiert, und demzufolge die geschlossenste Form und die Ausscheidung alles Unwesentlichen; sie duldet nicht nur, sie stellt auch die höchsten Forderungen der Kunst.

And after this he claims that the Novelle is more or less taking the place of the drama in contemporary Germany because there simply aren't enough competent playwrights, actors and producers to maintain a flourishing theatrical tradition. This is almost the only programmatic pronouncement on the Novelle that Storm ever made; he disliked theories and theoreticians.[180] Moreover, he withdrew the preface from publication; so it seems to me questionable to read anything too positive or far-reaching into a pronouncement which he later regretted making and refused to commit to print.

The nature of the preface and of the circumstances surrounding it, together with the fact that Storm's other statements about his own work (mainly in letters) have the same inconclusiveness and are largely written as rationalisations or justifications by hindsight,[181] lead me to think that he was not really a 'conscious writer'. He sat down and wrote a story if he had time, or if he needed money, or if a likely subject crossed his path; his time was largely taken up with the demands of a large family and a full-time legal career, and it was only after his retirement in 1880 that he could build his day-to-day routine around the business of composition. He seems never to have been aware of the precise nature of his talent, nor of the conditions in which it might flourish; he felt that it was something over which he had no control,[182] and in that sense one could call him an 'inspirational' artist. He worried over his creative energy, certainly, but he could not get close to its sources, his anxiety about it is commonly expressed in vague, rather helpless terms. For instance, he tends toward the loose metaphor in describing his compositional problems: 'Meine Phantasie war ein kranker Vogel . . .',[183] or 'wenn man was auf der Staffelei hat . . .',[184] or 'Vorläufig habe ich noch einen schweren Block vor mir, der erst gewälzt sein muß'.[185] And again, his assessment of the value of his works was never very sure. Writing of *Immensee,* he delivers himself of the resoundingly trivial judgement that it is 'eine Perle deutscher Poesie',[186] and with other stories we occasionally find him unable to venture any judgement at all: he writes, for instance, that his unsuccessful attempt to recast *Ein grünes Blatt* as a verse epic has altogether destroyed his capacity to make any evaluation of the story,[187] he confesses himself 'urteilslos'[188] about *Die Söhne des Senators,* and of *John Riew'* he writes, 'Ich weiß nicht, ob's was taugt; ich hab es so, ohne umzublicken, weggeschrieben'.[189] In doubt over a series of scenes in *Schweigen,* he leaves the matter for his subconscious to work out: 'Nun, vielleicht kommt's einmal im Schlafe'.[190] His doubts about his ability at various times (especially later in his life) are often stated but not defined − '. . . es liegt augenblicklich ein solches Gefühl von Unfähigkeit auf mir, daß ich kaum wage, Bestimmtes zu versprechen',[191] or '. . . das Wollen und Wissen und doch nicht Können, damit habe ich mich in diesem letzten Sommer aufs bitterste herumgeschlagen'[192] − or else he jumps to the conclusion that his powers are failing because of ill-health and advancing age. These fears are irrational: the quality of his work was never adversely affected by age or illness, quite the reverse − he wrote *Der Schimmel-*

reiter, for example, when he was seventy years old and dying of cancer. But they are obsessive fears: as early as 1871 he is complaining, 'daß es bergab mit mir geht',[193] and thereafter his letters are full of phrases like 'die zunehmende Alters-dummheit'.[194]

Statements of that kind suggest that Storm was somehow not intimate with his own creativity, indeed that he lacked a kind of artistic self-awareness; and that is one of the reservations I have to make about the use of the term 'dramatic method' in connection with his writing. Henry James is the great practitioner of this method, but he knows precisely what he is doing. He is a highly conscious novelist, he uses the word 'dramatic' himself, and it has been said[195] that his concern with the 'technical' aspects of fiction-writing (especially with the 'point of view') is more intense even than his involvement in the actual personalities and problems of the characters he creates. In a remarkable way, Storm anticipates certain of James' techniques by many years; but of course the great original achievement of James is to have examined and employed these techniques consciously and methodically. Storm would not have thought of himself as 'following a method', and consequently he is not nearly so consistent as James in the use of the techniques. What strikes one most about Storm in this regard is that he is not so much *con*sistent as *in*sistent: I have tried throughout to convey the sense of anxiety, the almost compulsive return to special narrative modes in fleeting and insignificant moments as well as at points of tension, in the turning of a phrase as well as in the constructing of a scheme. It seems to me that Storm, without quite knowing what is happening, is driven to write in this way because of a largely unrationalised but all-determining cast of mind, a preoccupation so basic as to be unconscious.

There is another important reservation. 'Dramatic' is a descriptive term, not an explanatory one. It defines very well the common features of a series of phenomena, but it does not help us when we ask what function such phenomena perform. Why does this or that writer use 'dramatic' techniques? Not, presumably, because he always wanted to be a dramatist but never quite made the grade; James' contact with the theatre seems to have been brief, ill-starred, and abandoned without regret; Storm's was almost non-existent (all we have is the fragment of a pantomime version of the Schneewittchen fairy-tale),[196] and there is nothing to suggest that either writer was discontent with his final choice of genre. Rather than wanting to make plays out of their stories, the probability is that such writers use the dramatic method in the hope of achieving an aim which they consider essential to their chosen genre but which hitherto has only been arrived at in the dramatic form.

What aim? The answer seems obvious: Lubbock calls it 'the effect of validity'[197] or 'the look of truth',[198] Hough talks of art 'not executing its arabesques in the void' but being 'used to elucidate life',[199] and moreover he quotes[200] Henry James as saying, 'The only reason for the existence of a novel is that it does attempt to represent life', and 'Any point of view is interesting that is a direct impression of life'. The self-evident goal of fiction is verisimilitude, its greatest task is to correspond as closely as possible to life as it is in fact lived; the illusion it must create is precisely the illusion of reality.

But we still have to ask what this reality is. To claim that the dramatic method were necessary for the representation of 'the *whole* truth' about life would be to dismiss some of the greatest fiction as 'untruthful'. Surely *Anna Karenina* can be described as having the look of truth, as elucidating, representing and giving a direct impression of life; yet without a doubt its techniques are anything but 'dramatic'. It is clear that to resolve the contradiction we must abandon the idea of 'the whole truth' and think instead in terms of 'various truths'; what the novelist or story-teller offers us is not reality but *his* reality, his individual interpretation of life in the aspect turned to him, the way things seem from where he is standing. Tolstoy will give us one truth, James another; whether the truths of Tolstoy and James and a hundred others taken together will reveal *the* truth is another problem.

The particular aspect of reality illuminated by the dramatic method (and by the method of the narrator 'in character') is, it seems to me, the reality of limitation. What dramatic techniques do is to remind us just how much (or how little) we as individuals can know of life, and by what means we come to know it. They enforce the truth that in life we do not survey the world and time and people from a height, that it is not given to us to move inside the minds of other men, that knowledge is not demonstrably more than the interpretation of what our senses offer us, that we must say of our condition what is said in the troubled voice of E.M. Forster:

> For human intercourse, as soon as we look at it for its own sake and not as a social adjunct, is seen to be haunted by a spectre. We cannot understand each other, except in a rough and ready way; we cannot reveal ourselves, even when we want to; what we call intimacy is only a makeshift; perfect knowledge is an illusion.[201]

The spectre of imperfect knowledge is recognized and shown out in our two methods. The dramatic method conveys what *could be* seen and heard by one human observer — one member of an anonymous audience watching a play — and the method of the embodied first-person narrator conveys what *has been* seen, heard or experienced by one actual human character. That is the basic import of both: they bring home to us continually that the omniscient narrator *is* strictly a fiction, that the largest unit of perception we know about is the individual intelligence and sensibility in all its limitation.

In such a situation, the emphasis is bound to be on what a man cannot know rather than on what he can; the message will be, principally, that beyond a certain point things and people are not knowable to an individual mind. Curiously enough, the artist who admits as much, whose style contains the allowance that as a human being he can't know everything, comes in for a good deal of criticism. The idea of omniscience clings on tenaciously,[202] and there seems to be a blindness to any view which questions it. There is the feeling that the story-teller ought to know everything about what he relates (though he need not *tell* everything), and that if he admits or betrays ignorance he has failed in one of his essential tasks. Ernest Hemingway expresses the feeling:

> I always try to write on the principle of the iceberg. There is seven-eighths of it underwater for every part that shows. Anything you know you can eliminate and it only strengthens your iceberg. It is the part that doesn't show. *If a writer omits something because he does not know it then there is a hole in the story.*[203]

E.M. Forster, in spite of his spectre, stresses much the same point:

> And now we can get a definition as to when a character in a book is real: *it is real when the novelist knows everything about it.* He may not choose to tell us all he knows — many of the facts, even of the kind we call obvious, may be hidden. But he will give us the feeling that though the character has not been explained, it is explicable . . . (The novelist) can post his people in as babies, he can cause them to go on without sleep or food, he can make them be in love, love and nothing but love, *provided he seems to know everything about them, provided they are his creations.*[204]

And Lubbock makes certain statements grounded in the same position, like this:

> (Tolstoy's characters) are essentially familiar and intelligible; we easily extend their lives in any direction, instead of finding ourselves checked by the difficulty of knowing more about them than the author tells us in so many words.[205]

or this:

> I suppose (the writer's) unwritten story to rise before him, its main lines settled, as something at first entirely objective, the whole thing seen from without — the linked chain of incident, the men and women in their places.[206]

But those arguments are invalidated as soon as we try to apply them to the vision enshrined in the dramatic method. What happens when a writer's particular 'truth about life', the interpretation of experience which he is called upon to pursue in his art, is precisely that the part of the iceberg that shows *is* the only part that we can know or talk about; that there are certain hidden facts about other people which *nobody* can uncover; that human beings are not created but discovered, seen and heard; that the extension of their lives is not the sure exploration of intelligible entities but refined guesswork; that one does not choose to treat an entirely objective structure of character and incident in this manner or that, because lived experience does not offer such a structure? A situation of that kind is not covered by the arguments which Hemingway, Forster and Lubbock put forward. A work of fiction whose method implies something less than a perfect knowledge of its elements (and Storm's stories are like this) does not necessarily fail in any essential way; indeed, that implication may be one of its strengths. It will clearly have holes, but not the holes of aesthetic failure that Hemingway is talking about.

Wolfgang Kayser, treating specifically of Storm, attacks the same problem from the other end. He claims that Storm in fact *does* know all the things he pretends not to know, and that the uncertainty about causality, fact, incident, character and emotion is an annoying mannerism, designed to obfuscate what is really perfectly simple and obvious, not to say trivial; the reader is merely given the fun of working out the right answer, about which there is never any doubt:

> Man kann bei Storms frühen Novellen von keiner Sprunghaftigkeit sprechen. Der Zusammenhang ist ängstlich gewahrt. Wir erfahren alles, was der Dichter nur für wichtig hält. Der Leser weiß auch in jedem Fall, warum es zur Vereinsamung, zur Entsagung oder bei Anne Lene (*Auf dem Staatshof*) und Lore Beauregard (*Auf der Universität*) zum Selbstmord kam. Die Verhüllungen sind durchscheinend. Sie gewähren dem Leser den Reiz, von sich aus die letzten Gründe zu finden; aber Storm hat hinreichend gesorgt, daß kein Zweifel möglich ist.
>
> . . . Den Genuß, selbsttätig den letzten Schluß zu ziehen, überläßt der Dichter dem Leser, nachdem er ihm alle Voraussetzungen und Verbindungen gegeben hat. So wird auch in *Immensee* der Grund zur Trennung nicht unmittelbar ausgesprochen. Aber jenes an entscheidender Stelle gesungene, mit ausdrucksvollen Gesten wie Händezittern und Zur-Tür-Hinausgehen begleitete Lied mit der Zeile: 'Meine Mutter hat's gewollt' läßt keinen Zweifel. Der Deutlichkeit halber wird diese Zeile noch zur Kapitelüberschrift . . . Die verhüllte, aber genau erschließbare Motivation ist die Entsprechung zu den nur scheinbar verhüllenden Sprachgebärden des schien, des identischen wie, des es war als ob. Der Dichter hat die völlige Übersicht und schafft sie dem Leser, beide sind in jedem Augenblick klüger als die Gestalten.[207]

If that were so, then the stipulation that the author should 'know everything' would stand (and by the same token Storm's early work would probably fall). But I simply think Kayser is wrong. He suggests that there is never any doubt about the true motivations of events and actions; yet I have described[208] how, in *Immensee,* the interpretation which he considers quite obvious (the domineering mother) is only one of several possibilities, all of which are open to doubt; indeed Kayser proves the point by contradicting himself later,[209] saying that the *real* cause of the trouble in *Immensee* is not the mother but the fact that the characters subject themselves too unquestioningly to the demands of 'der bürgerliche Raum' and have not the strength to challenge it — he thereby admits that there is another layer of causality below the obvious one. He is quite certain[210] that Sophie's reason for rejecting the Doktor (in *Drüben am Markt*) is that she is physically repelled by him; this he derives from one allusive sentence, leaving out of account a whole scene (the request for a dance) where Sophie seems to be making some kind of overture to the Doktor, and ignoring several hints of a social prejudice which might affect the issue.[211] The same objection applies to his criticism of the

'Sprachgebärden': Kayser does not see that they are evidence of a real uncertainty, a real inability to assert.[212] Moreover, he confines the accusation of coy omniscience to the early stories, combining it with the rejection of these stories as being enervated by 'Bürgerlichkeit'; he reserves his praise for the later stories and their more virile concern with 'Stammestum' (his book was published in 1938, and this whole aspect of it is a bit embarrassing), and presumably considers them to be free of the artistic faults for which he criticises the early ones. But again, the examples I have quoted show the same phenomena of obscurity and uncertainty throughout; they are more marked in the early work, certainly, but are still strikingly in evidence later on; if these techniques are unacceptable at first, what is it that subsequently legitimizes them? Kayser has no answer to that, and his argument suffers by it.

One of the most enlightening and relevant comments on a formal question thrown up by Storm's work is made in passing by W.D. Williams in his recent book on C.F. Meyer.[213] Williams introduces a discussion of the Rahmen by saying that Storm's concern with isolation later develops into

> an acute awareness of the unreliable aspects of life, the fact that time by its mere passing, is continually shifting the delicate balances we set up, that there is no stable set of realities which we can grasp, our lives are lived in a shifting world of appearances. This recognition is sometimes tragic, but need not be so, and if it is predominantly melancholy, there is always a sweetness in the memory or in the expectation. It is natural that the form of his novellen continually reinforces this impression. He uses, for instance, the framework technique more frequently than any other of the writers we are considering . . .[214]

Williams then gives a slightly confusing account of the use of the Rahmen in one or two of Storm's stories, concluding with this:

> There is in fact no story as an objective series of happenings, instead we are given a version of the story, and the mood and the character of the narrator are carefully built up so that the whole is seen as an attempt at understanding the complexity of life, with no guarantee of its accuracy or validity. All this serves only to underline what is the intrinsic subject of the stories, the fact that a man can only see life from his own limited standpoint and can never be certain that what he sees appears in the same light to others.[215]

And the coalescence of the Rahmen technique and the preoccupation with the supernatural in *Der Schimmelreiter* invites, for Williams, this inference:

> Just as the fantastic or irrational is taken within the bounds of logic and rationality, so all the things we rely on, the ordinary uncomplicated things in life, reveal themselves as basically unreliable, fading away when we turn to them, or changing imperceptibly into something else and denying our expectations.[216]

One could wish (though since the book is about someone else one cannot ask) for more, and more revealing, examples to clarify these somewhat obscure formulations; and there are one or two objections to the view as it stands — I would take issue, for instance, with the assumption that 'there is always a sweetness in the memory or in the expectation'.[217] But as speculative pointers to the philosophical implications of a formal usage, Williams' remarks are fascinating. It is along these lines, I think, that we can come to a closer knowledge of what lies behind all the devices and techniques I have talked about, not just behind the Rahmen; this approach will give us the key to that 'continually disquieting element in Storm, so adroitly and unnoticeably expressed in the form of his works as well as in his actual plots';[218] and we may find a way of explaining what it is that injects the peculiar and unmistakeable anxiety into words like these from *In St Jürgen:*

> Dann sagte er: 'Auf jenem schönen Turm, der also nur in meinen Gedanken noch vorhanden war . . .' (SW II 226)

or these from *Zur 'Wald- und Wasserfreude':*

> 'Darum also; — die Tochter der Majorin meinst du?' Es klang ein plötzlich kühler Ton aus diesen Worten; die blonde Dame war auf einmal wieder in der Welt. (SW III 173)

or above all these from *Pole Poppenspäler,* where the sadness of a child's farewell is extended and deepened and turned into a world of fear:

> 'Ade! Ade!' rief das Lisei; das Pferdchen zog an, das Glöckchen an seinem Halse bimmelte; ich fühlte die kleinen Hände aus den meinen gleiten, und fort fuhren sie, in die weite Welt hinaus.
> Ich war wieder am Rande des Weges emporgestiegen und blickte unverwandt dem Wägelchen nach, wie es durch den stäubenden Sand dahinzog. Immer schwächer hörte ich das Gebimmel des Glöckchens; einmal noch sah ich ein weißes Tüchelchen um die Kisten flattern; dann allmählich verlor es sich mehr und mehr in den grauen Herbstnebeln. — Da fiel es plötzlich wie eine Todesangst mir auf das Herz: du siehst sie nimmer, nimmer wieder! — 'Lisei!' schrie ich, 'Lisei!' — Als aber dessenungeachtet, vielleicht wegen einer Biegung der Landstraße, der nur noch im Nebel schwimmende Punkt jetzt völlig meinen Augen entschwand, da rannte ich wie unsinnig auf dem Wege hinterdrein. Der Sturm riß mir die Mütze vom Kopf, meine Stiefel füllten sich mit Sand; aber so weit ich laufen mochte, ich sah nichts anderes als die öde baumlose Gegend und den kalten grauen Himmel, der darüberstand.— Als ich endlich bei einbrechender Dunkelheit zu Hause wieder angelangt war, hatte ich ein Gefühl, als sei die ganze Stadt indessen ausgestorben. Es war eben der erste Abschied meines Lebens. (SW II 415)

What is the answer? In the belief that it can be shown at its most compelling through the examination of one story which can speak for the rest by containing all the features I have described — and since the vital consideration is the congruence between theme and technique, between the vision and its expression at the level of the words on the page — I turn back to *Immensee.*

8. IMMENSEE (ii)

One of the striking features about the progressive alienation which takes place between Reinhard and Elisabeth is Reinhard's (and our) increasing awareness that he cannot really 'know' Elisabeth. She is drawn away from him, not by a quarrel or a difference of background or outlook, or by a clear exterior circumstance, but by a 'breakdown of communication' which prevents him from ever becoming clear *whether* there is a quarrel, a difference or a circumstance to be guarded against. It is impossible for him to construct a defence, for he has no information about the direction from which the attack will come, nor about the strength and nature of his enemy — if indeed there is an enemy at all. From the time he goes away to the university, he is quite unable to discover the needs, tensions and pressures which motivate Elisabeth's actions and manner; his stay at home in his first Easter vacation is characterised by his mystification about 'what is going on inside' Elisabeth. His common attitude is one of anxious, half-formulated doubt: 'Er sah sie zweifelnd an; das hatte sie früher nicht getan; nun war es, als träte etwas Fremdes zwischen sie'. Her bearing is most commonly silent; she makes no reply to his compliment as he comes to meet her, she hands back the book of poems without saying a word — she expresses herself on both occasions visually and ambiguously. What does it mean when she tries to withdraw her hand from his? What does it mean when she blushes while turning over the pages of the book of poems, what does it mean when she hands the book back to him? What is she trying to convey — or is it certain that she is trying to convey anything at all? Reinhard is constantly faced with such questions; without the answers he is powerless to make any decision or action. And Elisabeth never gives an unmistakable answer; she is indeed disastrously uncommunicative. When they talk, it is almost always at cross-purposes; the barrier between them is, as much as anything, a barrier of incomprehension.

Because Elisabeth does not (or cannot) communicate her feelings directly to him, Reinhard can make no direct reply — how does one reply to nothing? With what sword does one fight a mist?[219] His uncommunicativeness is directly consequent upon hers: '(er) konnte . . . sich des erlösenden Wortes nicht bewußt werden'. So he is forced into indirectness; he cannot cross the barrier of incomprehension, so he tries to find a way round it. His efforts usually take the form of the elliptical, heavily portentous use of words and phrases, not for their surface meaning but for the overtones of significance with which they are loaded; very often the design is to strike in Elisabeth the chords of their common experience. When, for example, he feels suspicious of Erich's attentions and wants above all to find out how suspicious he *ought* to be, if at all (such is his uncertainty), he obviously cannot say directly, 'I don't like you seeing so much of Erich'; in the first place, he has no right to determine Elisabeth's acquaintance when he has no formal engagement or understanding (unhappy idiom!) with her; and then, supposing

Erich's visits were quite innocent and undesigning (he has no positive reason for thinking that they are not)? To give vent openly to such a suspicion would be to risk embarrassment and humiliation, even ridicule; and it would anyway make Reinhard seem more 'committed' to Elisabeth than he is or has a right to be. So he turns to more neutral ground and directs the expression of his uneasiness onto the bird which Erich had given Elisabeth to replace his own, which had died. He hopes that Elisabeth will understand 'intuitively', if not intellectually, what he is hinting at, and use the neutral topic to give him an answer. If the plan works, then two things will have been achieved − first, she will have allayed (or confirmed) a doubt which he dare not express, and second, the very fact that he has succeeded in communicating at this level will be proof of a basic understanding in spite of the surface reticence. This is what happens:

> 'Elisabeth', sagte er, 'ich kann den gelben Vogel nicht leiden'.
> Sie sah ihn staunend an; sie verstand ihn nicht. 'Du bist so sonderbar', sagte sie. (SW I 423)

When Elisabeth chances to see the book of Reinhard's poems (written mainly about her), he tries to make use of the poems to reveal the genuineness and importance of his feeling for her:

> Als Elisabeth die beschriebenen Blätter sah, fragte sie: 'Hast du wieder Märchen gedichtet?'
> *'Es sind keine Märchen'*, antwortete er und reichte ihr das Buch . . .
> 'Gib es mir nicht so zurück!' sagte er. (SW I 423; my italics.)

During the walk to the coach, he realises (or so one guesses) that he wants eventually to marry her; but now is not the time to propose. He can only ask her to wait for him, and he clothes his request, again hoping she will understand, in the conventions of childhood games (for their childhood has been spent together):

> 'Was hast du, Reinhard?' fragte sie.
> 'Ich habe ein Geheimnis, ein schönes!' sagte er und sah sie mit leuchtenden Augen an. 'Wenn ich nach zwei Jahren wieder da bin, dann sollst du es erfahren . . . leb wohl, Elisabeth. Vergiß es nicht'.
> Sie schüttelte mit dem Kopf. 'Leb wohl!' sagte sie. (SW I 424f.)

Years later, when Reinhard visits Elisabeth and Erich at Immensee, he tries to find out if he still stands above Erich in her affections (whether or not he is looking for a sexual or otherwise adulterous relationship is left unsaid and anyway does not matter): one way of asserting his prior claim is to remind her that he knew her before Erich did, and once more he snatches a chance opportunity (a walk through the woods) to invoke a common memory of their childhood, the search for strawberries:

> es kam ihm plötzlich, dies alles sei schon einmal ebenso gewesen. Er sah sie seltsam lächelnd an. 'Wollen wir Erdbeeren suchen?' fragte er.
> 'Es ist keine Erdbeerenzeit', sagte sie.
> 'Sie wird aber bald kommen'.
> Elisabeth schüttelte schweigend den Kopf . . . (SW I 434)

In every case (and there are several beside the ones I have mentioned) the attempt at this kind of sub-verbal communication is a failure: Elisabeth's response is either uncomprehending, non-committal or rejecting — and even the rejections are so blurred and indecisive as to be useless. There is never a clear 'No', any more than there is a clear 'Yes'; Reinhard is lost in a shadowy world between the two. The only moment approaching genuine 'Zweiklang' comes right at the end; and ironically, the point of mutual and reasonably certain understanding is the knowledge that the relationship must finally be cut off.

We see Reinhard as an old man, casting his mind back over his youth (and we may well ask how many times he has done this before), trying once more to discover the informing rationale, the 'truth behind' what happened to him and Elisabeth; trying to discern by hindsight what signs, if any, he was given of the impending break and of the reasons for it. All he has to go on is outward indications, passing circumstances — a letter, movements of a hand, a song, news of a marriage, gestures, expressions. He can never really move behind these things; events and people have no accessible reality beyond what he sees of them. It is no accident when we hear that Elisabeth seems to Reinhard to walk 'als wenn sie von ihren Kleidern getragen würde'; (SW I 434f.) because he only sees the clothes, he is led momentarily to doubt the existence of the whole moving human body underneath. At moments like this, the received notions of reality are suddenly suspended or put into question; the moment of doubt shows up a basic assumption for the assumption it is.

And then it begins to emerge that such a doubt is not confined to questioning moments, but overshadows the whole story. Storm is not throwing out the occasional question; he is carrying the doubt through to an extreme of subjectivism, a standpoint so insistent and entrenched that I can only see it as a way of looking at all life, style become vision. The Storm of *Immensee* (and I have tried to show throughout that this is a great part of him) seems to be built in such a way that he *cannot* assume the mantle of omniscience; he cannot perform the prestidigitations that E.M. Forster asks him to perform;[220] he will not trick us into the assumption that there is a hidden but postulable truth behind the moving sense-impression which we call another person.

I want to suggest that Storm is writing this story according to a vision of the world which precludes 'inside knowledge' of any other human being; a world where absolute truth is impossible to discern (if it exists at all); where knowledge can only be based on what is perceived by the senses; where sensual impressions must inevitably pass through the distorting lens of subjective experience and personal idiosyncrasy before they reach the intellect; where there is therefore no absolutely valid communication between man and man; where, by extension, each man tends toward total isolation from other men and from the world, *having* to be an island entire in himself. Such a vision is nowhere literally expounded, but it seems to me not to need exposition; it is a basic and 'given' condition of the writing. Storm's use of the techniques determined by this vision is about as much the result of voluntary, conscious decision as the fact that he is writing in German.

First things first: *Immensee,* like every other story in the mainstream of Storm's narrative development except four, is a Rahmenerzählung.[221] The Rahmen has appeared frequently in my discussion, and I have tried to show how it is built on a variety of things: a manuscript, a legend, a place, a legal investigation, or very commonly a memory, either in the form of one person's account of experiences he has had, told to another person or directly to us, or in the form of a solitary reliving of the past, fixed on paper as the recollections come. *Immensee* is an 'Erinnerungsnovelle' of this latter kind. What is implied by the use of the Rahmen here and elsewhere? The problem is an important one, and various theories have been put forward. One of the most recent is by W.F. Mainland, who says of Storm's use of the Rahmen:

> It is a fictitious device made to overcome the idea of fiction. If the author has taken all the trouble to wrap something up, the reader will think that that something is real.[222]

That seems to me to be right so far as it goes, but it does not draw the all-important implication. The Rahmen *is* evidence of a concern to overcome fiction and express reality — but the reality is of a special kind. The fictional element which Storm is attempting to overcome is precisely that element which E.M. Forster and others[223] advocate as essential to the value of prose narrative: the fiction of omniscience, which assumes the existence of actual and absolute (though possibly hidden) truth and of accessible personal essence. And the reality thereby conveyed or aimed at is the reality that, 'in life', things always *do* come wrapped up: information about men and events outside our immediate circle of experience comes wrapped up in written or spoken report, pictures and poems, the fallible communication of the fallible perceptions of other men (we can never say, 'This is so because he tells me', but only, 'He tries to tell me what he thinks to be so'); and our immediate experience must pass through our senses and there receive its wrapping of perceptual fallibility before it reaches our understanding (never 'this is, and is so', but only, 'I perceive it, and perceive it so'). The Rahmen sets up a 'real-life' relationship between the three entities involved, the things narrated, the narrator, and the listener (or reader). *Somebody* is telling *us what* he thinks happened.

It is arguable that at the centre of *Immensee* this scheme breaks down; that there is a disembodied narrator who sees into Reinhard in an omniscient and therefore 'fictitious' way; that he presumes to a knowledge of what Reinhard is experiencing, and thus creates a situation which is impossible according to the vision of life which I suggest for Storm. To assert in the face of this argument that Storm (the narrator) and Reinhard are one and the same person, that Storm is conveying his own experience under the pseudonym of Reinhard, would not be an adequate answer, even if it were wholly true. The inconsistency is there, one cannot doubt; strangely enough, though, it is not half so large as it seems. For the fact is that the entry into Reinhard's thoughts and perceptions is always exceedingly hesitant and circumscribed. A great deal of the time, we have no more access to his personality than we have to that of any other character; even he, our centre and reference-point and summoner of the memories, must very often remain a complete stranger to us. Already in the introductory paragraph there is a forceful illustration of what I mean:

> An einem Spätherbstnachmittage ging ein alter wohlgekleideter Mann langsam die Straße hinab. Er schien von einem Spaziergange nach Hause zurückzukehren; denn seine Schnallenschuhe, die einer vorübergegangenen Mode angehörten, waren bestäubt. Den langen Rohrstock mit goldenem Knopf trug er unter dem Arm; mit seinen dunkeln Augen, in welche sich die ganze verlorene Jugend gerettet zu haben schien und welche eigentümlich von den schneeweißen Haaren abstachen, sah er ruhig umher oder in die Stadt hinab, welche im Abendsonnendufte vor ihm lag. — Er schien fast ein Fremder; denn von den Vorübergehenden grüßten ihn nur wenige, obgleich mancher unwillkürlich in diese ernsten Augen zu sehen gezwungen wurde. Endlich stand er vor einem hohen Giebelhause still, sah noch einmal in die Stadt hinaus und trat dann in die Hausdiele. Bei dem Schall der Türglocke wurde drinnen in der Stube von einem Guckfenster, welches nach der Diele hinausging, der grüne Vorhang weggeschoben und das Gesicht einer alten Frau dahinter sichtbar. Der Mann winkte ihr mit seinem Rohrstock. 'Noch kein Licht!' sagte er in einem etwas südlichen Akzent; und die Haushälterin ließ den Vorhang wieder fallen. Der Alte ging nun über die weite Hausdiele, dann durch einen Pesel, wo große Eichschränke mit Porzellanvasen an den Wänden standen; durch die gegenüberstehende Tür trat er in einen kleinen Flur, von wo aus eine enge Treppe zu den oberen Zimmern des Hinterhauses führte. Er stieg sie langsam hinauf, schloß oben eine Türe auf und trat dann in ein mäßig großes Zimmer. Hier war es heimlich und still; die eine Wand war fast mit Repositorien und Bücherschränken bedeckt; an der andern hingen Bilder von Menschen und Gegenden; vor einem Tische mit grüner Decke, auf dem einzelne aufgeschlagene Bücher umherlagen, stand ein schwerfälliger Lehnstuhl mit rotem Sammetkissen. — Nachdem der Alte Hut und Stock in die Ecke gestellt hatte, setzte er sich in den Lehnstuhl und schien mit gefalteten Händen von seinem Spaziergange auszuruhen. — Wie er so saß, wurde es allmählich dunkler; endlich fiel ein Mondstrahl durch die Fensterscheiben auf die Gemälde an der Wand, und wie der helle Streif langsam weiterrückte, folgten die Augen des Mannes unwillkürlich. Nun trat er über ein kleines Bild in schlichtem schwarzem Rahmen. 'Elisabeth!' sagte der Alte leise ... (SW I 408f.)

The standpoint from which this sequence of events is described is that of an utter stranger. We are given no information that we could not have gained by standing at the stranger's shoulder, following the old man and keeping our eyes and ears open. Every suggestion that goes beyond the mere appearance of things is (and is carefully shown to be) a tentative deduction from that appearance, not facts 'given' by an omniscient narrator.[224] Who is this old man? We don't know (we do not discover his name until the next chapter, when it is Elisabeth, *not* the narrator, who says it).[225] He seems to have been for a walk, as far as can be *deduced* from the dust on his shoes. He is looking around him — or is he perhaps gazing down into the town? Our 'observing stranger' can't quite see which it is. The old man *seems* to be almost a stranger, as far as can be *deduced* from the fact that few people greet him. He stops by *a* house; is it his? Possibly; and this becomes more likely as he walks in, gives an order to the old woman and makes his way into a room; but we are never told for certain. There is *a* table in this room, and a chair (are they *his* table and chair? perhaps, but we cannot be sure). He sits in the chair and *seems* to be resting after the walk which he *seems* to have taken.[226] A moon-beam falls on a picture; we know nothing about this picture except that it provokes the reaction 'Elisabeth!'; so it is probably (though by no means certainly) a picture of this Elisabeth, about whom, equally, we know nothing.[227]

There is a scrupulous, almost anxious concern not to overstep the boundaries of human observation. Nothing is 'given', everything is observed or deduced. Storm seems to be at enormous pains not to make any capital at all out of his privileged position as narrator. It might be objected, of course, that such an opening is a common narrative device and need not have any 'weltanschaulich' implications; its aim might simply be to create suspense and arouse interest, to make us anxious to know who this man is and what his life has been. Otto Ludwig's *Zwischen Himmel und Erde,* published half a dozen years after *Immensee,* has an apparently similar opening. (There are other similarities of course: McHaffie and Ritchie note that Reinhard and Apollonius share a certain diffidence, 'a reticence in the expression of personal emotion which paralyses the heroes of so much nineteenth-century German fiction';[228] what they share also is the galling experience of hearing by letter that the girl they loved but left behind, to whom they had never declared their love, is to marry someone else). Both introductions are descriptions of an old man preparatory to moving back into the past; both set out to show the old man 'from the outside' and reveal the minimum of detail about him. And there are sometimes close verbal echoes of *Immensee* in *Zwischen Himmel und Erde*: this passage, for example, bears an obvious and striking resemblance to the early part of my *Immensee* quotation:

> Pflastertreter hören unwillkürlich auf zu plaudern, die Kinder auf der Straße zu spielen, kommt der alte Herr Nettenmair dahergestiegen, das silberknöpfige Rohr in der rechten Hand. Sein Hut hat noch die spitze Höhe, sein blauer Überrock zeigt noch den schmalen Kragen und die bauschigen Schultern einer lang vorübergegangenen Mode. Das sind Haken genug, schlechte Witze daran zu hängen; dennoch geschieht dies nicht. Es ist, als ginge ein unsichtbares Etwas mit der stattlichen Gestalt, das leichtfertige Gedanken nicht aufkommen ließe.[229]

Ludwig's opening is followed by as omniscient a narration as one could wish to find; he moves unapologetically inside all his main characters, Fritz, Apollonius, Christiane, even the 'geschlossene Persönlichkeit' of old Nettenmair, assertively describing their inmost thoughts and motives; so a mysterious, 'observing' introduction is by no means proof of a conscientiously subjectivistic standpoint throughout the narration.

In the final analysis, though, the two introductions are very different. We soon realise that Ludwig *is* using 'just a device', and is not too worried about consistency in its use; his principal aim is to whet the reader's appetite. He has no compunctions about giving us titbits of 'omniscient' information if he thinks they will serve his ends: he tells us the old man's name, not bothering to put it into the mouth of one of the figures in the story, and he makes absolute and exhaustive judgements about character and situation:

> Es ist der Geist des Oheims, der Geist der Ordnung, der Gewissenhaftigkeit bis zum Eigensinn, der auf den Neffen ruht . . . [230]

In this way, he gradually draws back the curtain on his story (*his* story, for he creates and controls it, and, as we shall see, appears as Thomas Mann's 'Ich'),[231] completing the process in the last three paragraphs of the introduction, where we are prepared elaborately for the return to the past. The effect is one of cavalier insouciance, omniscience amounting to omnipotence:

> Die Nachbarn wundern sich, daß der Herr Nettenmair die Schwägerin nicht geheiratet hat . . . Es ist natürlich, daß die guten Leute sich wundern; sie wissen nicht, was damals in vier Seelen vorging, und wüßten sie es, sie wunderten sich vielleicht nur noch mehr . . . Denn — aber ich vergesse, der Leser weiß nicht, wovon ich spreche. Es ist ja eben das, was ich erzählen will. So blättern wir denn die einunddreißig Jahre zurück und finden einen jungen Mann statt des alten, den wir verlassen.[232]

The sense of mystery, the apparent ignorance, is consciously created and then as consciously dispelled. The narrating 'Ich' *knows*, 'was damals in vier Seelen vorging'; and to reveal this to us he cheerfully leads us back through the years, manipulating time as if it were a book's pages to be turned. The sheer *power* invested in the narrator carries us easily over the inconsistencies. Storm, on the other hand, sees the device right through to the end of his (admittedly much shorter) introduction; he is more or less completely consistent and committed to the standpoint. When he is forced, in the end, to assert his command of the narrative and create the return to the past, having to move inside Reinhard as he does so, the strain is evident; the transition is abrupt and uncomfortable:

> 'Elisabeth!' sagte der Alte leise; und wie er das Wort gesprochen, war die Zeit verwandelt — er war in seiner Jugend.[233]

Furthermore, while Ludwig never again takes up the position of a casual observer in his examination of Apollonius, Storm is constantly doing so, as if to remind us that Reinhard is, after all, another person and thus not ultimately knowable. The conventions of the introduction are actually followed again at the beginning of the chapter called 'Immensee'; the standpoint is maintained throughout the sequence, and I quote here the sections where it emerges most clearly:

> Wiederum waren Jahre vorüber. — Auf einem abwärts führenden schattigen Waldwege wanderte an einem warmen Frühlingsnachmittage ein junger Mann mit kräftigem, gebräuntem Antlitz. Mit seinen ernsten grauen Augen sah er gespannt in die Ferne, als erwarte er endlich eine Veränderung des einförmigen Weges . . . 'Holla! guter Freund', rief der Wanderer dem nebengehenden Bauer zu, 'geht's hier recht nach Immensee?' . . . der Bauer ging vorüber; der andere ging eiliger unter den Bäumen entlang . . . 'Immensee!' rief der Wanderer. Es war fast, als hätte er jetzt das Ziel seiner Reise erreicht; denn er stand unbeweglich und sah über die Gipfel . . . Dann setzte er plötzlich seinen Weg fort . . . Ein stattlicher Mann in braunem Überrock kam dem Wanderer entgegen. Als er ihn fast erreicht hatte, schwenkte er seine Mütze und rief mit heller Stimme: 'Willkommen, willkommen, Bruder Reinhard! Willkommen auf Gut Immensee!'
>
> 'Gott grüß dich, Erich, und Dank für dein Willkommen!' rief ihm der andere entgegen. (SW I 425ff.)

Who is this stranger, variously called 'ein junger Mann', 'der Wanderer' and 'der andere'? We do not know. Where is he going? We do not know, until we hear from his own lips that he wants to know the way to Immensee. What is passing through his mind? It is *as though* he were expecting a change in the road; this is deduced from the way he looks 'gespannt in die Ferne'. It is *almost as though* he has reached his journey's end, so far as can be deduced from the way he stops and looks 'über die Gipfel der Bäume'. Who is this man coming to meet him? He is as strange to us as 'der Wanderer'. It is only when the two men call each other by name that we discover who they are; and strictly speaking, there is absolutely nothing to tell us for certain that this Reinhard and this Erich are the ones we knew before. We are told exactly what a complete stranger could have seen and heard if he had been somewhere nearby, nothing more. Reinhard is as impenetrable here as Erich.

The distancing from Reinhard takes place again and again in minor ways. When he receives his mother's letter, for example, telling him that Elisabeth has accepted Erich's proposal (significantly, matters are so arranged that this fact is revealed by one of the characters, not by the narrator), we are given the text of the relevant part of the letter, reading it, as it were, over Reinhard's shoulder, but then the narrative breaks off sharply. We are told nothing of Reinhard's immediate reaction — nor indeed of any directly subsequent effects on him, for the narrative is resumed at a point years later. The same sort of thing happens again in the description of the last few minutes before Reinhard and Elisabeth meet again at Immensee. Reinhard walks along with Erich, coming nearer and nearer to the house and to Elisabeth; the passage begins with words which suggest that we are going to be taken into Reinhard's emotions, but immediately, with a 'schien', the point of view shifts outside him again, looking on and guessing:

> Reinhard wurde nachdenklich; der Atem *schien* ihm schwer zu werden, je näher sie dem Hofe kamen. (SW I 427; my italics.)

And then the veil is completely drawn over what we imagine to be Reinhard's rising tension; with the decorum of a stranger, the narrator turns away from him and concentrates on the solemn antics of a stork, Erich's remarks about the various buildings on the estate, and a description (in loving detail) of the appearance of the house they are approaching. Reinhard, for the moment, is lost to us.

The moments when we *are* allowed to 'see inside' Reinhard, rather than deduce or guess his emotions from exterior signs, are comparatively rare; and of course Reinhard is the only character in the story whose sensibility is penetrated at all — the others remain inscrutable in this sense throughout. When the omniscient step does occur, it generally takes the form of 'erlebte Rede', and its most common function is to reveal Reinhard's inability to 'see inside' anyone else, his mystification at what is going on around him; so even this one step towards omniscience is qualified by the very thing it reveals — it has the effect of reinforcing the wider impression of *not* knowing, lack of omniscience. I have mentioned one instance of this ('Er sah sie zweifelnd an . . .');[234] another occurs later in the story, during Reinhard's stay at Immensee. One evening he goes for a walk alone; on his return he sees in the garden a figure who he thinks is Elisabeth; he approaches her, but she turns and moves away:

> Er konnte das nicht reimen; er war aber fast zornig auf Elisabeth, und dennoch zweifelte er, ob sie es gewesen sei; aber er scheute sich, sie danach zu fragen; ja, er ging bei seiner Rückkehr nicht in den Gartensaal, nur um Elisabeth nicht etwa durch die Gartentür hereintreten zu sehen. (SW I 430)

Reinhard's initial puzzlement is reflected in the short, uneven phrases, as he casts around for a way of finding out, an attitude to adopt, a course to follow; then finally he seems actually to embrace the uncertainty — he decides he does not want confirmation of his doubts, and the language immediately becomes smoother and more coherent.

The relationship between character, narrator and reader is only one technical feature; almost every other technique employed in this story serves in its turn to remind us that in attempting to trace a pattern in experience we are confined to the interpretation of what our senses tell us, and that we are not very reliable interpreters. We have seen how the causality of *Immensee* is misted over, how each trail peters out so that we are forced to move back and look around for another one. We have seen also how the narrative line is hardly ever made explicit; descriptions of developments, progressions and continuing states, and overt analyses of character, are almost entirely lacking;[235] all there is to go on is a series of isolated points on a graph, which we must join up with our own curve. Most of the scenes are reported as if by a casual, occasional onlooker, who happens to be nearby now and again, for ten minutes, an hour, a day or two, and then goes away for a few years, chancing to come across Reinhard again after having almost forgotten who he is. There is only one passage left in the final version of the story which describes a relatively extended time sequence and contains any direct characterisation by the narrator; it stands out in sharp contrast to the 'scenic' disconnection of the rest. It is the opening paragraph of the chapter called 'Im Walde':

> So lebten die Kinder zusammen; *sie war ihm oft zu still, er war ihr oft zu heftig,* aber sie ließen deshalb nicht voneinander; fast alle Freistunden teilten sie, winters in den beschränkten Zimmern ihrer Mütter, sommers in Busch und Feld . . .
> (There follows a longish report of a single incident during their childhood; Elisabeth is scolded by the schoolmaster, Reinhard tries to divert the man's wrath onto himself, but in vain; afterwards he goes home and writes his first poem about Elisabeth)
> . . . — Bald darauf kam er in eine andere Schule; hier schloß er manche neue Kameradschaft mit Knaben seines Alters; aber sein Verkehr mit Elisabeth wurde dadurch nicht gestört. Von den Märchen, welche er ihr sonst erzählt und wieder erzählt hatte, fing er jetzt an, die, welche ihr am besten gefallen hatten, aufzuschreiben; dabei wandelte ihn oft die Lust an, etwas von seinen eigenen Gedanken hineinzudichten; aber, er wußte nicht weshalb, er konnte immer nicht dazu gelangen. So schrieb er sie genau auf, wie er sie selber gehört hatte. Dann gab er die Blätter an Elisabeth, die sie in einem Schubfach ihrer Schatulle sorgfältig aufbewahrte; und es gewährte ihm eine anmutige Befriedigung, wenn er sie mitunter abends diese Geschichten in seiner Gegenwart aus den von ihm geschriebenen Heften ihrer Mutter vorlesen hörte. (SW I 411f; my italics.)

Such a passage is markedly similar in nature and function to others which appear in the first version but not in the final one.[236] I am fairly sure that the character-description which it contains (and which I have italicised), brief as it is, is the *only* specimen of its kind in *Immensee*. It is in a way odd that this paragraph should have been left in while all the others like it are cut out. I can only conclude that Storm lets it stand because (like the occasional omniscient entry into Reinhard's mind) it serves to 'communicate a lack of communication' (for Reinhard, without knowing why, cannot put his own thoughts and feelings into the fairy-tales he writes down for Elisabeth) and thereby conforms to the general tenor of the narration.

If, apart from the passage just quoted, there are no explicit character-descriptions and no asserted developments or progressions, how is it that we arrive at *any* perception of what the characters are really like, or of what is actually going on? Storm's answer, I think, would be something like this: in *Immensee,* as in 'real life', the possibility of knowing what people are *really* like, or what is *actually* going on, simply does not arise. Because we are individuals and moreover prisoners of our senses, we are in no position to get at the 'truth behind' things, nor even to ascertain whether such a truth exists. All we can do is hazard our own tentative, provisional and subjective judgements about men and events from the odd snippet of outward information, gathered by the senses and assumed to be significant, though it may be purely fortuitous and meaningless.

According to such a view, when we say 'that man's character', we really mean 'our guess as to what he is like', a guess determined by our own psychopathology, other people's judgements of that man, and things we happen to hear him saying or see him doing. Erich's 'character', for example, is adumbrated in precisely this way. The first we hear of him is a mention in Elisabeth's Christmas letter to Reinhard:

> nur daß Dein alter Freund Erich uns jetzt mitunter besucht. Du sagtest einmal, er sähe seinem braunen Überrock ähnlich . . . (SW I 419)

So we are given some idea of what sort of person he is — or rather what sort of person *Reinhard thinks* he is — but no, not even that; rather what sort of person *Elisabeth remembers Reinhard saying* he *thought* he was. The clue is fantastically hedged around with provisos: we must first take the not very difficult but logically necessary step of accepting that Elisabeth has remembered rightly; then we must consider how far we can trust and defer to Reinhard's judgement, in view of the fact that Reinhard is only another character in the tale, with his own weaknesses, and that the remark was made some time in the past when he was still a boy and is therefore certainly immature and possibly no longer what he thinks of Erich.

The second clue is just as dubious in a slightly different way. It comes in a conversation with Elisabeth's mother, who says that Erich has just taken over his father's second estate at Immensee, and then delivers her own 'characterisation': 'Er ist ein gar lieber, verständiger junger Mann'. (SW I 422) Once again, we have somebody else's judgement and (taking into account the mother's possibly mercenary ambition for her daughter) an extremely partial one at that. But there is nothing else to go on so far. Next we hear that Erich has been accepted by Elisabeth after proposing three times; that doesn't help very much. The first time he appears in the flesh, rather than in other people's letters or conversations, is when he welcomes Reinhard to Immensee; here we are given one or two external characteristics. His figure is 'stattlich'; he is still wearing a brown overcoat; his face is simple and cheerful; he talks animatedly and rather repetitively; he is unfailingly attentive to Elisabeth; he smokes a 'solider Meerschaumkopf'. That is all.

Storm's doubt covers other areas beyond the idea of basic, essential character; he is suggesting that, when we talk of a 'present state of mind' or a 'present state of affairs', we really mean once again the interpretation we put on odd outward signs which might or might not be meaningful. Thus at certain times the only guide which Reinhard has (and we have) to what Elisabeth is thinking and feeling — and it may not be a reliable guide — is Elisabeth's hands. When she welcomes him at the beginning of his first vacation at home, she tries to withdraw her hand gently from his. A few days later, when there is a slight lifting of the strain, he takes both her hands, and she quietly leaves them in his. Years later at Immensee, when Reinhard reads the song 'Meine Mutter hat's gewollt', she lays her hand on one side of the page; as he reads, he feels the paper trembling imperceptibly. When the two take a boat out on the lake, he looks into her face, but she gazes past him into the distance:

> So glitt sein Blick herunter und blieb auf ihrer Hand; und diese blasse Hand verriet ihm, was ihr Antlitz ihm verschwiegen hatte. Er sah auf ihr jenen feinen Zug geheimen Schmerzes, die sich so gern schöner Frauenhände bemächtigt, die nachts auf krankem Herzen liegen. – Als Elisabeth sein Auge auf ihrer Hand ruhen fühlte, ließ sie sie langsam über Bord ins Wasser gleiten. (SW I 435)

Early the next morning, when Reinhard is about to leave Immensee secretly, Elisabeth meets him on the stairs:

> Sie legte die Hand auf seinen Arm, sie bewegte die Lippen, aber er hörte keine Worte . . . Sie ließ die Hand sinken und sagte nichts mehr. (SW I 437)

The lips frame words that do not come, and her hand has once more to be the ineffectual messenger; and at this last moment, her eyes join forces with her hands to express something like despair; she stands motionless and looks at him 'mit toten Augen'. (SW I 437)

The mind shut off from other minds and from the assurance of outer reality – that is the mind that speaks through the text of *Immensee;* the fabric of the tale is heavy with extreme subjectivism. One can take almost any paragraph and find one or other of these techniques informing it. Of course, Storm could be playing a much more extended version of the game we saw Ludwig playing in his opening pages: he could be covering tracks, creating mysteries, drawing veils, merely in order to give his reader the fun of following up the clues and discovering what is really going on. But the clues are not proper clues, because they do not lead anywhere, or rather they lead away from the whole idea of 'the truth'; the subjectivism seems to me to be too insistent, the rare departures from it too strained and obtrusive, for there to be any question of literary chicanery on a large scale. Take a sentence such as this (there are a dozen more like it):

> Dann wandte sie sich eilig ab, und Reinhard hörte, wie sie schluchzend die Treppe hinaufging. (SW I 436)

We are told, not that Elisabeth is sobbing, but that *Reinhard hears* her sobbing, so that the sobbing becomes not a fact but another subjective sense-impression. The device flits past almost without being noticed; there is no need for it to be used here, and it is highly unlikely that Storm thought of its implications as he wrote the sentence. That is precisely the point: Storm cannot help writing in this way; he does so unconsciously or involuntarily, even when there is no need. The technique is absolutely natural to him, part of the structure of his personality; that is what I meant when I said[237] that it was as much the result of conscious choice as the fact that he writes in German.

Immensee is the story of two people who are isolated from one another by the fact of their humanity, inexorably frustrated in their desire to unite or at least to communicate. Their predicament is precisely that in which Büchner places, his Danton and Julie:

Danton: Wir wissen wenig voneinander. Wir sind Dickhäuter, wir strecken die Arme nacheinander aus, aber es ist vergebliche Mühe, wir reiben nur das grobe Leder aneinander ab, — wir sind sehr einsam.
Julie: Du kennst mich, Danton.
Danton: Ja, was man so kennen heißt. Du hast dunkle Augen und lockiges Haar und einen feinen Teint und sagst immer zu mir: lieber Georg! Aber (er deutet ihr auf Stirn und Augen) da, da, was liegt hinter dem? Geh, wir haben grobe Sinne. Einander kennen? Wir müßten uns die Schädeldecken aufbrechen und die Gedanken einander aus den Hirnfasern zerren.[238]

But it is given to Danton to express the predicament and thus in some sense to transcend it; and his sense of isolation is part of a wider disillusion in which other elements come to predominate. Reinhard is denied any such expression, even though all his experience revolves around his isolation.

Furthermore, *Immensee* is cast in a prose which underlines its theme at every point, extending it into areas where the impression is of men isolated not only from other men but also from the world around them. Apprehensions of objective reality are thrown into question; the structure of 'the world outside' is precarious and not to be trusted; the only possible supports must come from within the perceptions of the individual, but they in their turn are untrustworthy because they in their turn are built from material provided by sensual fallibility. We are coming near to Büchner again, this time to the world of *Lenz;* but we are not on the edge of madness and genius but firmly within the compass of ordinary and unexceptional men — the eyes that see the precariousness of it all are 'sane' eyes. We seem close to Kleist, but again there is this difference: the 'zerbrechliche Einrichtung der Welt' is exposed and shaken, not by the violent obsessions of a sixteenth-century horse-dealer and outlaw, but by the modest velleities of a nineteenth-century Bürger. Through Reinhard, Storm tries to grasp at the shadowy entities outside the perceiving subject, but they turn to nothing in his hands. With Reinhard's voice, he challenges the cosmos to prove its substance, but all he hears is his own words coming back at him from the void:

> Reinhard rief durch die hohle Hand: 'Kommt hieher!' — 'Hieher!' rief
> es zurück.
> 'Sie antworten!' sagte Elisabeth und klatschte in die Hände.
> 'Nein, es war nichts, es war nur der Widerhall'.
> Elisabeth faßte Reinhard's Hand. 'Mir graut!' sagte sie. (SW I 415)

9. QUALIFICATIONS

The cry through the cupped hand, the apparent reply which is nothing but an echo, and hand gripping hand in fear: that image, in the compelling creative language of the artist, is as true an expression as I can find in Storm's work of his major anxiety — the anxiety that the 'real' world of objective truth, out on the other side of the senses and nowhere properly to be grasped, may after all be nothing but a figment of the individual imagination, never others' voices but only the echoes of our own. That is what seems to me to be implied in all the disparate technical features I have talked about; each of them points to that conclusion by questioning an assumption or recalling a limitation.

'What we know'[239] is what our senses tell us and what our minds make of the things told; nothing can come to us by any other route or in any other way; truth *has* to come wrapped up in its Rahmen. 'Other people' are constructs we make up out of things seen, heard and deduced; to assume that they have an existence — names, histories, characteristics — independent of the outward signs we receive, is an imaginative leap, since there is nothing else, no cross-reference, to tell us they are really 'there'. 'Physical events' are not demonstrably more than images on the retina, vibrations of the eardrum, nerve-impulses from the skin; what we actually experience is a disturbance in our mental landscape, not an external happening. Other people's minds and hearts are closed to us; as Büchner says, to discover what they think one would have to break open their skulls and tear out their thoughts — but then one would have uncovered, not a living personality, but only a mess of dead bone and flesh. The life of others disintegrates as we touch it, *because* we touch it; so all we have to rely on is the attempt at human communication, hoping to show our thoughts to others by word and gesture and to piece together others' words and gestures to find their thoughts — a process which is shown to be so tentative, fraught with difficulty and prone to failure. 'Facts' cannot be said to be true, or not true, in any objective way, for that quality is not part of them; they are real and discoverable only insofar as the individual mind registers them through sense-impression and inference; if the mind is not allowed to register them, they have no demonstrable reality or truth. And when people vanish from our lives, what can we claim to know about *their* lives afterwards? They might just as well have ceased altogether to exist 'in their own right'; when they have passed out of our ken, all that is left is dim figures in a dimming memory, threatened with extinction when the memory dies, or names on a yellowing page, read and revivified once a year; for the rest, these people are nothingness.[240] In sum, our sojourn is always within the boundaries of our senses; for Storm, it is an enforced sojourn, an imprisonment, for inside that little subjective world he is chillingly alone and terribly uncertain. He finds no answer to his questioning, and the lack of an answer is dreadful because he is asking for nothing less than proof that the world exists.

The formal philosophical theory to which all this approximates most nearly is solipsism, the view that the self is the only object of real knowledge and therefore the only thing certainly existent. The term seems not to have been coined until 1881,[241] but one of the most notable advocates of the theory was writing a century and a half before that. I mean George Berkeley, bishop of Cloyne, the victim of one of Dr Johnson's most resounding refutations.[242] Berkeley's thought, in its negative and sceptical aspect, has been summed up like this:

> Only particular things exist, and since these are only a complex of sensations, if we abstract from them that of which we have perception, nothing remains. The 'support' of ideas or sensations is percipient mind. The *esse* of material things is *percipi*. Locke's distinction between the primary and secondary qualities of objects has no validity. Both are exclusively mental.[243]

The similarity between that and the view I have claimed for Storm is clear; but the analogy cannot be taken too far. The first and most obvious reservation that has to be made is that the solipsistic viewpoint *is* only the negative aspect of Berkeley's philosophy, used by him ultimately to prove the existence of God; his scepticism is a prelude to the construction of a faith, whereas Storm's scepticism does not seem to be relieved by any such definite or optimistic end. Berkeley and Storm, then, travel only a certain distance together; Berkeley eventually goes off onto another track, Storm remains on the same one. In addition it must be said that the analogy is of course no more than an analogy: I am not making any suggestion of influence. There is no evidence that Storm ever read Berkeley; it is highly unlikely, indeed, that he had ever even heard of him (Storm was refreshingly free from over-conscious concern with *Geistesgeschichte*, 'currents of thought' and the rest).[244] So we cannot judge Storm's view in terms of whether it is a good or bad imitation of, or development from, Berkeley's; imitation doesn't come into it.

A more significant reservation, and one which points up the distinction between philosophy and literature as modes of thought, is what might be called the problem of intensity — the quality of the process by which the intellect understands a concept and the personality feels it and applies it and lives it out. As a philosophical theory, solipsism is highly cerebral and divorced from life; is principal value is as an intellectual exercise and an aid to precision in definition. Nobody takes it very seriously as a guide to practical realities, in spite of the disquieting fact that it cannot be refuted logically. It is usually rejected by appeal to the demands of experience, something like this: 'Solipsism doesn't matter because it has no effect on the way I live. Simply in order to carry on, I have to act as though the outside world *is* really there independently of my perceptions of it, as though the friend in the next room or next town *does* exist in his own right without my seeing or hearing him. If that is illusion, then we are somehow meant to embrace the illusion; it's one of the rules of the game of experience. I act as though things were really there in much the same way as I act as though the world were flat and stationary instead of being round and spinning vertiginously, as though the sky were an upturned blue basin just out of reach and not the emptiness of limitless space, as though the table were inert and solid and not a mass of diffused and dancing particles. I'm perfectly prepared to believe what the scientists (or the philosophers) say, but basically my own illusions are the things that really matter for the leading of my life.'[245] Or like this: 'It depends what you mean by 'exist'. When I say a thing exists, I mean no more that that it *is* visible, audible or tangible; when I want, or anyone wants, to see, hear or touch it, it is there to be seen, heard or touched. It is highly improbable that it should vanish just when there is no sentient being around, and even if it did vanish, it wouldn't matter, for as soon as someone goes to it again, it will be there. It is there whenever we want it to be there, and that is enough. A separation of *esse* from *percipi* is inconceivable, and quite pointless anyway'.

But supposing there were a person (and I think Storm is a case in point) to whom the solipsistic doubt is not just a logician's game, but a way in which all life is seen and felt? For such a person the appeal to 'experience' would be ineffectual; he would reply: 'But *my* experience is otherwise; it is in the living of my life, not in my idler thoughts about life, that I am brought face to face with this uncertainty, this shaking of reality and this imprisonment within the self. I honestly *don't* know whether that friend really exists now to whom I said goodbye last week; and the friend I am talking to now, how real is he and his mind?'

Or very possibly, his feelings would not reach even that stage of articulation; he would perhaps not be equipped or inclined to formulate the doubt in conceptual terms to others or even to himself; yet although (or more probably because) he did not 'think about it', the unformulated doubt might be more basic to his ways of seeing and responding to life than his conscious reflections were. So the whole position would be reversed: using the words 'intellect' and 'experience' as a convenient shorthand for the two processes I assume to be at work in the human personality, one could say that whereas the 'normal' man will intellectually accept the validity of solipsism but will experience life as though it were not valid, this other kind of man will intellectually accept the objections to solipsism (or indeed never be aware that there was such a thing as solipsism to object to) and yet basically (subconsciously) continue to experience life in a solipsistic way.

It seems to me that the difference between 'intellect' and 'experience', expressed in this way, is the essential difference between philosophy and literature. The philosophical view is directed to the understanding; it concerns itself with the intellectual apprehension of truths about existence; its guiding principle and arbiter is reason, and a theory which purports to be philosophical must stand or fall by the test of logic. The literary view, on the other hand, is directed to experience; it concerns itself with the representation or re-enactment of responses to existence; its guiding principle is emotion, and a vision which purports to be literary must stand or fall by the test of a kind of psychological impressiveness, the intensity with which it speaks and the feeling of conviction which it produces. Of a philosophical theory one asks: 'Is it grounded in logic? Is it consistent? Is its *a priori*, axiomatic element clearly recognisable as such, or are there hidden axioms claimed as deductions?' Of a literary vision one asks: 'Has it the ring of truth? When the artist creates a world in its light, am I drawn into that world, am I made to believe in its validity while I am reading and maybe for a few minutes or a few years after I close the book? Is the presented vision urgent and compelling enough to affect, albeit ever so slightly, my own vision of the way the world works, of how people act and react, of human possibility and human responsibility, of what is good and beautiful? Will I respond differently to life after I have read this book?'

Of course, the two categories are not entirely clearcut or exclusive. There are areas where they overlap, and in these areas one would place many writers and thinkers — Schopenhauer, for instance, as an intuitive, visionary, moralistic philosopher, and certainly the existentialists.[246] But that does not mean that there is no distinction to be made, any more than the existence of green means that no distinction can be made between blue and yellow. The two categories *are* different, and the difference becomes useful when we talk about Berkeley in comparison with Storm. Berkeley is a philosophical mind, and we assess him on criteria of logicality; Storm is a literary mind, and we assess him on criteria of 'impressiveness'. An inconsistency discovered in Berkeley's system might damage it seriously; an inconsistency of the same kind discovered in Storm's vision would not be so harmful. On the other hand, a lack of intensity or emotional force in Storm's presentation might lead us to reject the validity of his view, whereas the truth of Berkeley's arguments should not be affected by the way they are presented, no matter how wan or lacking in compulsion the presentation might be.[247] Or to put it another way: in the philosophical sphere the manner of the arguments is distinguishable from their matter, whereas in the literary sphere manner *is* matter, one and indivisible.[248]

And one can go a stage further than that. Storm is not just 'literary' (in the sense in which I have been using the word here) — he is very 'literary' indeed, about as far from the 'philosophical' approach as it is possible to get. I noted earlier[249] his unwillingness to commit himself to theoretical, speculative pronouncements on literature; his necessarily erratic working routine; his proneness to adopt a vaguely, helplessly 'inspirational' view of the sources of his creative energy; his uncertainty and lack of insight in making critical assessments of his own work; his irrational and obsessive fear that his powers were declining as he grew older. These things led me to suggest that Storm, in contrast to a Henry James or a Thomas Mann, was a largely unconscious writer, not intimate with his own creativity, not seeing himself as 'following a method', not really sure what was being expressed as he put pen to paper. If this is true, then he is the 'literary' figure *par excellence,* the writer whose interpretation of the world springs mostly from direct, unprocessed experience and only fractionally from cerebration. His work is not, and cannot be judged as, a kind of philosophical theory in code (if it were that, it would have been much simpler for everybody if he'd written a tract). It is the enactment, beyond consciousness, of a vision of life; it is the product of a personality which is driven almost unawares to see things in a certain way; it is powerful *because* unrationalised, compelling *because* born of compulsion.

The view of the nature of literature which I am asserting here (it is only one of several possible views, but I take it to be the most fruitful one from which to approach Storm) has been finely advocated by Penelope Gilliatt;[250] it is good to be able to turn to account here her gift for the terse formulation and the arresting image. She is talking here only of the theatre, but what she says is applicable to the other literary genres as well:

> Abstraction has always been an enemy of the theatre. The great plays are all very concrete and particular. It is audiences and textual critics, not authors, who hear the overtones that float off the top of Shakespeare or Chekhov; the authors knew nothing about them because they were at the bottom of a mine at the time, quarrying the next piece of rock . . .
> The concentration on the physical and actual that can be felt in first-rate drama is unmistakable the moment you meet it. It is blinkered and ferocious, and by comparison there is always something uneasy about a creative mind that is wandering enough to provide its own critical interpretation of a work at the same time as the work itself. Art has no need to decode itself. 'The Caretaker' is not concerned to speculate about whether it is about loneliness, or intimidation; it is about two brothers and a tramp.

Storm is precisely that kind of author, unaware of the overtones, concerned with the job in hand, the next piece of rock (and that image is close to his own rather desperate sculptural metaphor, frequently used, of the 'Block' which has to be worked),[251] uneasy and ineffectual when called upon to interpret his stories.[252] These are not *conceived* as generalities in a particular code: so far as he is concerned, they are about Reinhard or Hans Kirch or Hauke Haien. It is the critic's job to hear the overtones, to perceive the generalities, and, with as little presumption as such a presumptuous enterprise will allow, to know better than Storm what Storm was about.

My suggestion, then, is that we are dealing with a writer who not only falls into the 'literary' category but is moreover an extremely pure example of it, having almost nothing in his creative processes or statements which could remind us of the 'philosophical' approach. This point seems to me important because it anticipates and to some extent answers an objection which could be made here. For one can argue against this interpretation of Storm's view of life that it is not watertight; and that is certainly true. *Immensee* does happen to be especially dominated by these techniques, and that is why it was such a useful story to base the explanation on; but of course the picture is not always so clear. I have noted, for instance, one major series of inconsistencies, the use in seven late stories of a fictional narrator with certain of the conventional privileges of omniscience;[253] and it would be easy to find many minor lapses like the one which occurs in the opening of *Im Sonnenschein*,[254] or in my quotation from the last part of *Drüben am Markt.*[255] I have quoted hundreds of Storm's words in support of my arguments, but what of the many thousands which I have *not* quoted? It would be absurd to pretend that the passages were chosen at random — one looks for the particularly clear example, the particularly relevant formulation, and the scales are thus inevitably tipped — so it is reasonable to suppose that the great tracts of prose which have received no mention here may contain a good deal of matter which militates against my interpretation. I would claim that the examples I have cited *are* broadly representative and do give a picture that is substantially the same throughout Storm's work; but any hole in the argument, no matter how small, is enough to make valid the objection that Storm's commitment to the solipsistic view is not a consistent one.

But that is an objection in 'philosophical' terms, and as such not relevant to 'literary' works, especially works so decidedly 'literary' as Storm's are. We must assess Storm's vision by different criteria (which need be no less exacting): the realisation that it is logically ragged is not enough, simply because it is a vision or cast of mind and not a theory or system, a thing enacted and not constructed. True judgement must rest on whether the vision is sufficiently intense and impressive and affecting, not on whether its logic is sufficiently coherent.

The striking quality of Storm's techniques (as I said earlier in comparing him with Henry James)[256] is that they are *in*sistent rather than *con*sistent; in spite of lapses, the dominant impression is that he is driven to adopt this particular standpoint and write in this particular way. He seems to be most truly himself when using techniques of solipsism — and that assertion can, I think, be based on something more substantial than a vague appeal to the feel of the writing.[257] For we find him using these techniques in situations where we should *expect* a writer to be 'most truly himself'. We find him, for example, anxiously conveying physical happenings as sense-impressions when his story reaches a decisive point, when there is the need to be especially convincing, especially true to experience; surely it is likely to be at moments like these that the heart of a writer is revealed.[258] Or again, we find him slipping into the subjective mode at times when it doesn't seem to matter — the passing moment, the odd sentence here and there[259] — and using certain syntactical devices like the 'als ob' construction so freely that they become unconscious mannerisms, 'Sprachgebärden'.[260] Sentences seemingly composed quickly and without much reflection, constructions framed more or less automatically by the hand, words written when the writer is, as it were, off his guard: in these small and transient things too he may inadvertently expose himself.

So, both when Storm is trying very hard, and when he is not trying at all — the contradiction is only a surface one — we may claim to see him as he actually is; and what I have said of those two situations applies equally to the others, the choice of standpoint, the handling of communication and the rest. The mood makes itself felt all over the place; it determines the shape and development of whole stories, and it colours single sentences; it underlines some themes and modifies others; it governs the most characteristic and compelling areas of Storm's writing. That is really the only argument that has to be brought to bear in the literary context to support the thesis that the mood exists and is central. Ultimately the discovery of individual inconsistencies is not a relevant objection to the interpretation; indeed, there is a sense in which these inconsistencies could be said to be a part of the interpretation. For if, as I suggested, Storm is a highly 'literary' and predominantly 'unconscious' writer, then any vision enshrined in his work might be expected to emerge in just the way I have described: on the one hand, it invests most of his writing with a sort of subterranean anxiety and compulsion, a drive which gives it its literary value; and on the other hand, it is qualified by occasional departures, since there will be times when his conscious reflection on a story will override the less conscious and less realised drive, with the result that the drive may be sacrificed to other considerations — the desire, for example, to follow patterns set by other writers' works.[261] Storm would not, I take it, be more than very dimly aware of these occasions as departures from his creative individuality, precisely because he is not more than dimly aware of the nature of that individuality in the first place. If he doesn't quite know what he is doing, he won't know when he is not doing it.

10. DEVELOPMENTS

E.M. Forster begins his discussion of the novel by consciously constructing an untruth (or rather ignoring a truth) in order to find his way more clearly to truths which seem to him of larger interest and import. The truth he ignores is that of chronology: he asks his audience to imagine that all the novelists he is talking about are writing their novels at once, 'at work together in a circular room'.[262] So far I have ignored the truth of chronology in much the same way and for much the same reasons. I have talked about Storm's stories rather as if they were one undivided work, written in a single day; and I have tended to treat the 'vision' or 'cast of mind' that they embody as some more or less uniform, bright and steadily shining thing. The qualifications that have emerged are basically recognitions of a certain raggedness in the outline; I have not yet entertained the possibility that the outline itself could have changed from year to year and from story to story.

The possibility obviously has to be faced. There is no denying that Storm's output of prose fiction covers a period of a little over forty years, years which have their full share of incident and vicissitude. Two marriages, the first built over early adultery and the second strangely intensifying the conflicts of the first; an all-conditioning local allegiance agonized by the spectacle of bloody, protracted war across the homeland; a long period of exile, much of it spent in grinding poverty; the return home marred by the realisation that Prussia's sovereignty was no less a foreign occupation that Denmark's had been; the ruin and death of an eldest son; the strains and honours (and the varied experience) of a distinguished legal career; the final years spent in the shadow of cancer and in speculation on death which for him was at best a torturing enigma[263] and at worst extinction: if a man is changed by what happens in his life, then all that[264] surely changed Storm, and if a writer's work moves as his life moves, then surely Storm's work will have shifted its ground. So there is a strong case to be made out for seeking to establish some sort of development, a change (or perhaps several changes) of direction through these fifty-odd works. I want to look at this problem on three levels, and to suggest that significant changes and developments are discernible on the first two, while on the third, the level at which this part of my study mainly operates, there is not so much change, so that the neglect of chronology may not be such a definite untruth after all.

My first and shallowest level is that of the choice of subject-matter; here the facts are quite simple and the instruments of reasoning quite crude. There is no doubt that a number of Storm's stories provide a chronicle of the forty years of life from which they spring, and one can go into much easy detail. When Storm was young and unhappily in love, he wrote stories about unhappy young love.[265] When he was in exile, he wrote a couple of stories about exile.[266] When his first marriage belatedly blossomed into full passion, he wrote a story about the belated blossoming of married love.[267] When his second wife suffered the strains inherent in her position as substitute wife and mother, he wrote a story about the tensions of a second marriage from the woman's point of view.[268] When his eldest son caused him tribulation, he wrote some stories about painful relationships between fathers and sons.[269] As a lawyer he was able to base the occasional story on experience and anecdote from his professional life.[270] As a lover of his homeland he tended generally to set his stories in the places with which he was most intimate.[271]

Connections of that kind are correct enough, but they do not take us beyond the truism that writers usually write from experience, finding their raw material in things that happen to them or things they come across. If we tried to elevate that truism into a first principle and use it as our guiding light in exploring the genesis of literary creation, we should be led into absurdity: for instance, it would follow that two writers faced with the same experience would produce works essentially indistinguishable from one another. Moreover, we should be making an assumption which leaves out of account many other factors which might decisively condition a writer's work — the nature of his intellectual inheritance, the circumstances and relationships of his early years, the books he reads, the people he knows, and so on. Reference to biographical data of mature experience may tell us why he treats certain subjects, but it cannot tell us how he treats them. The 'why' in this case is a shallow and catalytic one; it is the 'how' that might give us more profound and interesting insight into a writer's creative uniqueness. Or again, what makes a man a writer in the first place? Why does one person feel the need to encompass an experience in this peculiar way, while another will let the experience go by, forgotten after the immediate and transient response? Questions like those cannot be discussed at this first level either.

Then there is a second and deeper level; and here I would place elements which seem closer to the sources of literary art, elements described in terms like 'theme' or 'concern' or 'morals'. Are there developments to be found at this level in Storm's work? Clearly there are, and a number of critics have tried in various ways to classify the stories according to some pattern of change. Usually the classifications are chronologically based; Pitrou's, indeed, is almost purely chronological: conditioned as he is by the biographical shape of his work, he is content to draw lines at decisive points in Storm's life, and thus produces four groups of stories — those written before the exile (up to 1853), those written in exile (1853-64), those written after the return to Husum (1864-80), and those written in retirement at Hademarschen (1880-8). He does not draw any conclusions from this grouping, but confines himself to the odd comment pointing out a development in a particular story from an earlier one.

Stuckert's book is constructed differently from Pitrou's; he separates life from works and is thus able to devote a self-contained section of four chapters to discussion of the stories. This ought to have freed him from too much preoccupation with chronology, but he wastes his advantage by drawing lines just as Pitrou does, only at different dates.[272] Then he invites objections by attaching a definite thematic label to each of the four groups he establishes. The first group he calls the 'Situationsnovelle' (1847-56); that is reasonable, an illuminating name for a fairly unified category. The second group he calls the 'psychologische Problemnovelle' (1857-67); but does that really throw light on *Im Schloß*, or suggest any essential connection between, say, *Späte Rosen* and *Drüben am Markt*? The relevance of the category is made more questionable by the fact that out of the eleven stories he discusses under this heading, Stuckert has to make reservations about no less than seven, calling them works of transition or relating them more or less closely to stories in other groups. And the series of *Märchen* and *Spukgeschichten* written in the early 1860's are another embarrassing excrescence here. Groups 3 and 4 are two halves of the same category, the 'tragische Schicksalsnovelle'; the years 1871-9 are designated as 'Aufstieg zur Meisterschaft' and 1880-8 as 'Höhe des Schaffens'. Again, the rule seems more honoured in the breach than the observance: *Beim Vetter Christian, Viola tricolor, Pole Poppenspäler, Ein stiller Musikant, Zur 'Wald- und Wasserfreude', Die Söhne des Senators, Schweigen* and *'Es waren zwei Königskinder'* were all written between 1871 and 1888. Of course, Stuckert does not claim that his classification is any more than a rough and ready one; but it seems to me *too* rough and ready to be really useful, since it does not do justice to a large proportion of the works in his last three categories.

Böttger's study, like Pitrou's, is a 'critical biography', and he is thus faced with the same problem of folding his examination of the works into his narration of Storm's life. But he proceeds more freely than either Pitrou or Stuckert and is able to produce an argument which accords more satisfactorily with the complicated reality. He suggests that a line of development is discernible in the broad movements of these forty years: there is a social concern which is at first only implicit (hidden beneath the surface of apparently quite personal works like *Immensee*), but which then becomes an overtly liberal, democratic and progressive view, shot through with religious scepticism and advocacy of independence for Schleswig-Holstein (in *Auf dem Staatshof, Im Schloß, Veronika* and *Abseits,* for example), followed by a long period of political and personal disillusion (emerging in *Waldwinkel, Der Herr Etatsrat* and the 'father-son' stories), which in its turn is translated into a more optimistic and generalised humanitarian ideal, the specific concerns being with questions of social motivation and justice (stories like *John Riew', Ein Doppelgänger* and *Ein Bekenntnis*). *Der Schimmelreiter,* in Böttger's judgement, is at once typical and untypical, belonging and yet not belonging to the general current he discerns:

> Die Novelle 'Der Schimmelreiter' nimmt im Gesamtschaffen Storms eine Sonderstellung ein. Sie ist nicht nur formal der krönende Abschluß, sondern sie zieht auch im Gehalt die Summe aus dem gesellschaftlichen Denken eines ganzen Lebens. Im Gegensatz zu allen anderen Erzählungen dieses Dichters tritt sie aus der privatmoralischen Sphäre heraus und behandelt das öffentliche Wirken in einer Deichgenossenschaft.[273]

That is the main line of development proposed, with *Der Schimmelreiter* as its ambiguous climax. For the rest, Böttger argues that at certain points along this line there are groups of stories which constitute reactions of one kind or another. The *Märchen* and *Spukgeschichten,* he says, are an attempt at a 'Flucht aus dem Unbehagen an der kriegerischen Wirklichkeit während der Mitte und des siebenten Dezenniums des 19. Jahrhunderts';[274] or more positively, they arose from the conviction 'daß ein solcher Ausflug ins freie Land der Phantasie die Kraft gibt, um die Kämpfe der Zeit besser zu bestehen'.[275] And he sees the series of

Chroniknovellen from 1875 onwards as Storm's way of expressing his attitude to the political power which he felt to be crushing him and destroying all that he thought valuable:

> Zwar eignete er sich nicht zum Rebellen. Aber eine einigermaßen anständige, konsequente Haltung war ihm Selbstverständlichkeit. Von seiner Meinung über das Junkertum, über die mit ihm verbundene Orthodoxie und die Bismarcksche Politik ging er nicht mehr ab. Sobald es ihn drängte, seine antifeudale, radikalliberale Gesinnung künstlerisch zur Geltung zu bringen, wich er darum in die Vergangenheit aus . . . Diese Novellen sind für Storm 'Urbilder von Begebenheiten, die aus der Vergangenheit in die Gegenwart hereinragen und die zugleich aus dem Erlebnis gegenwärtiger Junkerpolitik erhellt werden'.[276]

In the same way, smaller groups of stories, like those concerned with art and those which are comic in conception, are claimed to be aberrations or excursions which are nonetheless related, as reaction or manifestation, to the principal development.

Böttger does not try to make things seem tidier than they are, and the pattern he produces seems to me therefore to be a valuable one. I would take issue with his emphases — does the concern with social issues, particularly those of class, *really* predominate throughout? — and with his argument about what he calls the 'Desillusionsnovellen', because he does not adequately show how these stories, which almost always examine the failure of closely individual relationships, could have sprung from a political as well as a personal disenchantment. Those things apart, Böttger's study is illuminating; and even though in the end one is inclined to reject his strongly sociological approach, one can be grateful for the stimulus it provides.

Understandably, it is mostly these longer, monographic studies that seek to establish complex or multiple categories for Storm's works. Other less prolix writers tend to confine themselves to making simple comparisons between early and later stories — a 'two-stage' development — and there is a large measure of agreement on these comparisons. Walter Silz, in his discussion of *Der Schimmelreiter,* is representative of the agreed view:

> Under the stress of experience, especially private sorrow, Storm's art matured and deepened toward the end of his life. The writer of soft, sentimental idylls, perfumed with faded flowers and blurred by hopeless reminiscence, became a tragic poet who coped, in strong, sharp-lined, cogent Novellen, with the bitter realities of life . . .
> Two of Storm's most characteristic tendencies reach perfection in his final work: his 'Stimmungskunst', no longer an end in itself or a lyrical self-indulgence, as in his early tales, but creating the atmosphere and background for vigorous action; and his 'Heimatkunst', which limited itself to the small patch of the world that he knew well, but within these limits plumbed ultimate depths . . .
> In place of the frail, passive heroes and heroines of Storm's earlier tales, who end in wistful resignation and whose fate evokes in us pathetic rather

than tragic emotions, we meet in the later Novellen more resistant protagonists.[277]

That, I think, is substantially the same as what E.K. Bennett says:

> Speaking to Heyse in the later years of his life, Storm regrets that a
> common acquaintance of theirs did not live to see 'die zweite Periode meiner
> Novellistik'. To which Heyse replied, 'Ja, als du in Öl zu malen anfingst' . . .
> And this distinction between Storm's earlier and later work as that between
> water-colour and oil-painting describes with some accuracy the difference
> between the two styles. The earlier Novellen deal with sentimental situations
> from which the maximum of Stimmung is obtained; the later Novellen deal
> rather with problems — though still problems within the range of family
> affections — and are written with much greater intensity of feeling. The
> difference between the earlier and the later Novellen is as Heyse's metaphor
> suggests a difference of colouring; a greater depth and richness is apparent in
> the later works, though the subject matter has not essentially changed, but
> remained what it always was: the affectional life of the individual within the
> family. Only that in the later works this affectional life is exposed to and
> jeopardized by much intenser dangers than those of mere sentiment.[278]

And Wolfgang Kayser's view is markedly similar, though couched in superficially
different terms:

> So war der Weg des Dichters nicht geradlinig, und die frühen Novellen
> enthalten nicht schon im Keime alles, was sich später nur geläutert und
> reifend vollendet hätte. Sein Werk gehört zwei getrennten geistigen Sphären
> an; dem Bürgertum und dem Stammestum. Die Trennung vollzieht sich
> keineswegs als glatte Ablösung. Oft stoßen beide Welten in ein und derselben
> Novelle aufeinander. Wohl aber läßt sich sagen, daß seit den ersten Durch-
> brüchen des Stammestums das Spätwerk überwiegend von daher geformt
> wird.[279]

If we leave aside the labels 'Bürgertum' and 'Stammestum' (and I imagine that
Kayser would have expressed himself differently if he had been writing at another
time), the argument that emerges from Kayser's book is fairly typical of the conventional judgement: that between Storm's early and late stories there is a development from weakness to strength, from sentimentality to intense and authentic
emotion, from narrowness to breadth of scope, from the 'pathetic' to the 'tragic'
(whatever those words may mean), and, evaluatively speaking, from bad to good.
Opinions seem to vary only on the question of how much of stage 1 remains at
stage 2; evidently, Bennett thinks the same bass-notes are sounded throughout,
Silz sees the final flowering of what is already there, and Kayser thinks the change
is a fundamental one.

As something to set beside these views,[280] I would offer three tentative
approaches to a classification. All three are simple, distinguishing between 'early'
and 'late' works, and all make the division somewhere in the mid-1870's. The first
approach (its simplicity containing a good deal of complexity) is in terms of range.
In the earlier work we find the stories written around a number of preoccupations

which seem to shade into one another. Insofar as one can say at all that a particular story is dominated by a single preoccupation, the distribution is something like this. There are stories of loneliness and failed relationship; these commonly deal with intense attachments that are thwarted for no definite, discoverable reason; the failure leads to a lifetime of solitude (the contours of which are carefully described) and anxious brooding on 'what went wrong'.[281] Then there are stories with a girl or woman at their centre; these trace the destinies of women who succumb to, or overcome, clear or obscure forces which threaten their fulfilment or even their lives.[282] Then patriotic stories, usually very short pieces, expressing in a muted way the love of homeland, the devotion to a received way of life, and the bitterness of exile or existence under an occupying power.[283] Then, fairy-tales and ghost-stories.[284] Then (something of a ragbag) stories portraying the happy resolution of highly specific and peculiar difficulties.[285]

The later work displays a different set of preoccupations; these seem to be a little more distinct from one another than the earlier themes. There are stories dealing with the threatened (and sometimes actual) collapse of family life; these mostly revolve around conflicts between fathers and sons.[286] Then there are historical tales (or *Chroniknovellen*), looking back into the history of Schleswig-Holstein and reconstructing personal destinies from myth or historical document.[287] Then, stories with a strongly contemporary and social orientation; these (frequently overlooked in discussion of Storm) examine a variety of issues and problems, some of them anything but genteel — class distinction, prejudice and superstition, mental illness, alcoholism, the effects of heredity, the position of the ex-convict, medical ethics; the outlook that emerges from them is uncompromisingly humane, liberal and 'modern', and some of the themes prefigure the concerns of the Naturalists a decade or so later.[288] That leaves *Der Schimmelreiter*, which we can best treat as being in a category by itself, or rather as entering more than one category: it could be said, for example, to be at once a historical tale and a socially committed work.[289]

My second approach is concerned with the question of what might be called balance, in a thematic rather than aesthetic sense. In the early stories, the weight of interest is commonly thrown onto purely personal concerns, men and women as individuals in search of relationship with other individuals. Social motivation and outward pressures are like the background hum of traffic, present but hardly ever heeded; sometimes the mind is alerted to these forces, when the guess is hazarded that they might be conditioning the individual destinies enacted before us, but the guess is usually found to be inadequate, and the forces move once more into the background. *Immensee* certainly gives this impression, and *Im Sonnen-schein, Drüben am Markt, Im Schloß* and *Auf der Universität* (as well as several others) seem to me to do so as well. The role of the 'outside world' in these stories is discreet; its significance is ambiguous, never wholly demonstrable and always likely to elude the grasp; Böttger is wrong when he makes the quiet hum into a roar. But he is more justified in the later works; here the balance shifts, and more often now the absorbing confrontation is not between individual and individual, but between an individual and a group or external situation. John Hansen, Franz Jebe, Hauke Haien and the heroes of the historical tales are brought face to face with their society and their world, and are asked to make a general commitment or engage in a general conflict, in a way that the central characters of the early tales are not. What Silz calls the 'more resistant protagonists' are different from the 'frail, passive heroes' not so much because of their character as because they are given something solid to resist. The early work draws us inward and down into personality, the later work is a turning outward and through a broader arc of experience.

The third approach is an ethical one. Some of the late stories contain the suggestion of a certain freedom of choice, men in at least partial control of their circumstances and therefore bearing a measure of responsibility for what they do and suffer; in the earlier stories, that kind of freedom is absent, and we have the spectacle of men acting and suffering as they do for no other reason than that they *are* men. My introductory and concluding chapters, seen in each other's light, are essays in this contrast. I have tried to show that Reinhard and those other early figures inhabit a world where being alone is a state of nature, the norm and consequence of 'the way things are'; the desire to achieve relation with another, above all in love, is human but humanly impossible (or nearly so). These people fail because they have attempted something outside an almost all-encompassing limitation on men, and that is like attempting to defy gravity; we cannot really say it is 'their fault' or their inadequacy if they have failed to achieve something which (in Storm's world at this time) it is not given to men to achieve; Storm would not want them blamed for being unable to fly. On the other hand, I shall suggest that Storm's world has changed in this respect by the time he comes to write his last stories: now, encounter with and commitment to others *is* a human possibility, indeed a duty and necessity; Franz Jebe and Hauke Haien are given their chances, but they do not take them, and we can thus assign to them a large part of the responsibility for their failure. By choice or temperament, they cut themselves off; it is because of the way they are, rather than 'the way things are', that they do not achieve what is shown to be humanly possible; and so there is an acceptable moral justice in their going under. The changes discerned by the approach in terms of 'balance' and by that in terms of 'ethics' seem to me to be the significant ones. We think of them as changes for the better, as advances in the grasp of values; for we are jealous of our realities and our freedoms.

And so to the third level, the level of what I have habitually called vision. It is fairly artificial to draw a firm line between this and the level of 'themes, concerns and morals', but there is some use and justice in the division. My concern here is with the 'how' of Storm's writing, the question which reaches further than the 'why' of subject-matter[290] or the 'what' of theme. By discovering how the story is told, how the scenes and situations are acted out, and how particular words and even mannerisms merge into each other to imply a special point of view, we can discover how Storm's eyes see the world; and to know that is to have come close to the creative source, the thing which urges him to write and which makes his art uniquely and distinctively his own.

As the years pass, are there changes in the vision, which is the same as saying in the techniques which embody the vision? The turning outward at the thematic level is likely to imply a development away from entire subjectivism; for if Storm concerns himself with confrontations between individuals and external entities (social groups or the forces of nature), then surely he must consider these entities to be as independently real as the individuals who are brought up against them; there can be no proper struggle unless both protagonists fight in the same arena, on the same plane of substance. Reinhard's call comes mockingly back at him from the void;[291] but when Hauke Haien cries out, his words are taken up and whipped away by powers which bear in and assault him from without and which seem violently and implacably 'there':

> Ein Schrei, ein Verzweiflungsschrei brach aus der Brust des Reiters: 'Elke!' schrie er; 'Elke! Zurück! Zurück!'
> Aber Sturm und Meer waren nicht barmherzig, ihr Toben zerwehte seine Worte; nur seinen Mantel hatte der Sturm erfaßt, es hätte ihn bald vom Pferd herabgerissen . . . (SW IV 399f.)

A change like that leads one to expect other developments in the vision, developments signified by changes in the techniques I have been discussing; and the search for such changes yields some result. Since the question of narrative standpoint has been central to the argument throughout, special weight will have to be given to any phenomenon of standpoint which speaks against the 'solipsistic' interpretation; and sure enough, we have already seen a significant phenomenon of this kind, moreover one which argues strongly for a chronological contrast and development. I talked earlier about a series of seven late stories[292] in which Storm employs the standard device of a 'fictional' narrator with omniscient qualities; it emerged that in these stories the names of the characters are 'given' by the narrator rather than discovered or overheard in dialogue, and that this mechanical sign of specially privileged knowledge is paralleled by other less tidy but more important indications: the narrator moving inside several characters, telling us what these people are really like (as opposed to how they would appear to an observing stranger), knowing and detailing their past histories — and all the time supporting his assertions with no other credentials than his status as the traditional story-teller who knows everything about his characters because he has effectively created them out of thin air. From 1877 onwards, every story by Storm which is not told by an actual embodied narrator bears the marks of narrative omniscience, whereas every story of the same kind written before 1877 seems to be largely told by an intelligence which is imperceptible to any of the characters (and thus 'fictional') but otherwise comparable in its limitation with a normal human observer.[293]

If the limitations of Storm's fictional narrators before 1877 are to be admitted as evidence *for* the claim that the vision is a solipsistic one, then it has to be accepted that the measure of omniscience the narrators achieve after 1877 operates *against* that claim. According to the arguments I have been using, the use of the omniscient convention implies a belief that things are ultimately and conclusively knowable in life in the way that a story-teller knows them in the story, that we can say a thing exists and mean more than merely that we perceive it, that people have an objective reality in themselves and an essential character beyond our speculations on who they are and what they are like — in short, a belief in the existence of absolute and independent truths.

That being so, it seems as though we can say that the solipsistic anxiety is an early phenomenon: somewhere in the 1870's the cast of mind is somehow remoulded, and the mature Storm is rewarded in his search for substance in the world outside him. Reasons could be found in the richness of his experience: the following of conscience in war and revolution, the physical deprivations of exile, the having and rearing of many children (and the anguish of spirit this sometimes involved), the thousand encounters of professional life — these things could be said to have brought him to an apprehension of outward realities that *could* not be denied or doubted, so insistently and uncompromisingly did they force themselves upon him. Or again, this abundance of things done and suffered may perhaps have left him less and less time and room for his doubts; if one only finds the solution by ceasing to look for it — and solipsism is that kind of problem — then Storm may have been led willy-nilly to achieve Hume's benificent state of 'carelessness and inattention',[294] finding that the world existed simply because he had to live unquestioningly as though it did. All that is a sensible argument for a decisive change in the nature of Storm's vision, and it is the more promising because the grasping of reality at this level blends so perfectly with that 'turning outward' which we find in the themes of his later stories.

But there is a great deal to be said on the other side as well; I have mentioned much material in Storm's later work which argues against a radical change or development. Even within these seven stories we have seen passages and situations which indicate strong doubts about the notions of absolute truth and objective existence, doubts which qualify the claims to omniscience which the stories seem at first to make. In four of them, the narrator loses track of his characters at the end, seemingly unable to say what finally happens to them in consequence of the enacted events.[295] In *Hans und Heinz Kirch*, communication between human beings is shown in all its fallibility and examined with anxious, 'problematic' concern;[296] and in the same story, the question around which all the latter part of the action revolves — who is the man who has returned claiming to be Heinz? — is never properly answered; the narrator seems to have been deprived of his authority to make the conclusive, omniscient statement; he has to weigh the evidence and draw his private conclusions from it, much as his characters have to.[297] *Zur 'Wald- und Wasserfreude'* contains the disquieting image of one character bringing another to life merely by thinking about her,[298] and reaches its uncertain end with a strikingly similar image.[299]

And the evidence for a continuing solipsistic doubt, discoverable already within this series of stories, increases as soon as we move outside them and look at the other late work. Between 1877 and the end of his life, Storm admittedly writes seven stories whose 'fictional' narrators are endowed with a certain amount of privileged knowledge; but in the same period he writes *ten* stories which have no 'fictional' narrator at all — all of these are told by one of the characters in the tale, and we are constantly reminded thereby of the limitations of insight and impartiality to which these individual and normal human observers are necessarily subject.[300] And then there are the other phenomena. The raging elements through which Hauke Haien takes his last desperate ride across the dyke are largely drawn inside Hauke's consciousness; they exist and are strong only to the extent that he sees, hears and feels them.[301] The facts and situations and conflicts which go to make up *Ein Doppelgänger* seem at first 'true' enough, yet ultimately they are revealed as an extraordinary combination of dimly remembered incident and unfettered, semi-visionary intuition in trance.[302] *John Riew'* opens with an anxious detailing of the devious and unreliable ways in which the story-teller gleans information about the mysterious occupants of the new house near his home;[303] he acknowledges the sources of his information and reminds us yet again of what Storm's stories seldom let us forget — that knowledge is learned, picked up, inferred, guessed, but *not* dropped whole and perfect from heaven. And finally, the use of 'als ob' and similar constructions is still very frequent in the later stories, with the undiminished function of stressing that what goes on inside people is compounded not of truth but of tentative comparisons in the observer's mind.[304]

So there is evidence for and against change, probably rather more against. There is one more thing to be said, though, in favour of some kind of evolution: in the main, the examples I have picked out for close discussion have been drawn from stories written before the late 1870's, and this in itself suggests that the material is not so abundant (or at least not so clearly susceptible to my method of treatment) after that time. Nonetheless, there *is* still a lot of material there, and any conclusion will have to take that into account as well as the rest. I would therefore suggest this: late in his life and late in his writing, Storm more frequently achieves a measure of certainty about the existence of the world beyond his own sensibility; that world assumes an independence and force which impinge upon him ever more urgently and reassuringly; turning outwards, he is able to grasp and be supported by its reality. But the old ghost is never properly exorcised; time and again, he is led to question his new apprehensions, and the apparently solid world becomes once more insubstantial; other men and other minds are hidden again behind the barrier of perception, or disintegrate in his fear that they may be either closed off from him or merely shadows thrown by his own thoughts. From beginning to end his work is apt to ask what reality is, and to find no more than an anxiously provisional answer; there is a reference both backwards and forwards in that moment from a work written in the middle of his creative life, that shaking of the foundations at the end of *Aquis submersus:*

> Indem ich aber eintrat, wäre ich vor Überraschung bald zurückgewichen; denn Katharina stund mir gegenüber, zwar in schwarzen Trauerkleidern und doch in all dem Zauberschein, so Glück und Liebe in eines Weibes Antlitz wirken mögen.
>
> Ach, ich wußte es nur zu bald; was ich hier sahe, war nur ihr Bildniß, daß ich selber einst gemalet . . . — Aber wo war sie selber denn? (SW II 653)

11. LITERARY CONNECTIONS

Fontane's wry and harassed affection for Storm, recorded in the fourth section of his autobiographical work *Von Zwanzig bis Dreißig,*[305] was compounded of a number of conflicting elements: an admiration, amounting almost to reverence, for most of Storm's lyric poetry, a more qualified (though still considerable) respect for his stories, a ready sympathy with him in the sufferings engendered by his pursuit of conscience and political integrity, a delight in memories of hours spent with him in discussion of literature, a warm personal fondness — and yet, at the same time, a regretful awareness that his long friendship with Storm never really ran deep, a characteristic suspicion of what he felt to be Storm's somewhat highfalutin' notions of 'the poetic life' and his proneness to posing, and a lasting sense of irritation at Storm's provincialism in all its aggressiveness and, what was worse, its clumsiness. Storm in Berlin had more than a little of the yokel in the big city; he was vociferous in praise of his homeland and in criticism of his hosts the Prussians, he was tenacious in the almost ritual observance of the customs of the way of life he had been forced to leave behind him (Fontane comes down especially hard on the matter of tea-making); and he blundered about the Berlin *haut monde* with that lack of style which was for Fontane the cardinal social sin.

It was this backwoods, isolationist quality that annoyed Fontane more than anything else. He expresses it in wonderfully apt coinages like 'Husumerei'[306] and 'Provinzialsimpelei',[307] and tells (half against himself) the hilarious story of a visit he and Storm paid, on the latter's insistence, to the elegant Café Kranzler in Berlin;[308] he records his agonies of embarrassment as Storm (blissfully unconscious and absorbed in a discussion of Mörike) drew the attention of everybody in the place with a variety of conspicuous *faux pas* — wearing all the while an immensely long and grotesquely superannuated scarf with dangling tassels. With his sure sense for the comically appropriate detail, Fontane picks on that scarf as the emblem of Storm's provincialism, his inability to negotiate respectably or respectfully with a world beyond his own remote and circumscribed provenance.

It is possible to view this narrowness of range and values as a limitation on Storm's work as well as on his social demeanour; the concerns he cherished could be thought of as parochial and aberrant, losing their force and validity when they are seen in the light of the wider developments in the literature and thought of his time. Indeed, there is a temptation to regard him almost as a sort of primitive, a man ensconced in his little provincial backwater and letting the world pass him by, untouched by artistic tradition and unschooled in received techniques, writing for the love of it, and therefore producing work of which the quality is mixed in the way one might expect — occasionally (that is, inadvertently) original and powerful and relevant, usually picturesque in its local atmosphere and colouring, often dropping into quaintness, commonly in danger of cliché (for the primitive won't know if what he is saying has been said a thousand times before), and fundamentally naive in a neutral sense.

That is of course not wholly, nor even largely, true. Storm was conscious of being a part of German literature, and anxious about his position in its hierarchy; he knew that he was a better poet than, for example, Geibel, and a better Novellist than Heyse, but equally he knew that he would only occupy a 'Seitenloge'[309] in literary history. He was in constant touch with the work of other contemporary German writers, both major and minor — his friendships and voluminous correspondence with Fontane, Keller, Mörike, Heyse and a host of others (as well as with Turgenev across the linguistic frontier) testify to that. His stay in Berlin showed up his social limitations, certainly, but in more essential ways it was a pronounced success: he arrived as an established and respected poet and was brought into contact with artists and literati of all kinds, being stimulated by, and stimulating, the talk and atmosphere of the literary circle known, weirdly, as 'Der Tunnel über der Spree' (and its more select offshoot, the 'Rütlikreis');[310] if Berlin can be said to have had a metropolitan cultural pulse in the 1850's, then Storm felt that pulse as much as anyone. His reading was wide and his judgement sure:[311] his enthusiasm for the work of, say, Keller, Fontane, Meyer, Ludwig and, strangely enough, Kleist, is not reflected in the conventional assessments of the day, but has been clearly vindicated since, as have his doubts about Geibel, Freytag and Heyse.[312] That is a suggestion of his literary involvement; and as for the political and historical realities, it is surely arguable that to have lived in Schleswig-Holstein when Storm did is *not* to have been moored in some secluded backwater — the currents of mid-nineteenth-century history flowed across that piece of Europe as strongly as they did across most others, and Storm was decisively and cruelly caught up in them.

And yet, when all that is said, we still in the end have a sense of his distance and independence, a certain freedom from the forces which moved other men of his generation; and it seems to me that we feel this because we know him to have been isolated, not from contemporary 'literature' or 'history', but from the contemporary movement of what is commonly called 'thought'.[313] He did not sit at the feet of a Feuerbach as Keller did; and he was largely unaffected by the controversies raging around Darwin and Darwin's German disciple Ernst Haeckel. These men cannot be regarded as specific sources for his occasional positivistic excursions,[314] nor for his flirtations with the new views of heredity and scientific determinism;[315] what little there is of such things he seems to have worked out more or less by himself. At the level of conscious reflection Storm's contact with the 'thought', the 'Geistesgeschichte' of his time, is inconsiderable as a constituent of his work. If we are to see him against a cultural background or as part of a cultural development, our justification can only be the appeal to vague concepts like the 'Zeitgeist'. The claim that his vision fits into a larger vision, the context of nineteenth-century literature, is speculative and impressionistic; there is no chapter and verse to quote from letters or theoretical writings, there is no all-changing encounter or dominant influence.

For the claim can be made; we can indeed see ways in which the particular vision 'fits in', even though to explain *why* it fits we might have to be vague and talk about 'something in the air'. I want to place my conclusions about Storm beside the conclusions of two major general studies which have recently appeared. Comparison with the first suggests that Storm's modes of expression are at once characteristic of his age and distinctly precocious; and comparison with the second suggests that his work is a significant attempt to formulate and encompass a common German experience.

Richard Brinkmann's *Wirklichkeit und Illusion*[316] explores a progression which the author discerns in German narrative literature of the nineteenth century; the argument rests on the analysis of three works, Grillparzer's *Der arme Spielmann* (1847), Ludwig's *Zwischen Himmel und Erde* (1856), and Keyserling's *Beate und Mareile* (1903). Brinkmann's conclusion is that, under the pressure of the literary concern and approach known as 'realism', the at first unquestioned distinction between the terms 'subject' and 'object', between the 'subjective' and 'objective' modes, begins to break down, so that eventually the two concepts become interchangeable, each signifying itself *and* the other. At one point the conclusion is summed up like this:

> Wir haben gesehen, wie sich Dichter im 19. Jahrhundert eben bei dem Versuch, das 'Objekt' als 'Objekt' zu isolieren, Wirklichkeit illusionslos als konkrete, 'objektive' Tatsächlichkeit zu sehen und darzustellen und über die 'Subjektivität' der romantisch-idealistischen Poesie hinauszukommen, in die individuelle Subjektivität verstricken. Das Jahrhundert der exakten Naturwissenschaft, der quellentreuen und wahrhaftigen Historie, des Positivismus, das Jahrhundert, das nicht nur in der Geschichtsschreibung das 'Selbst gleichsam auslöschen' wollte, um 'nur die Dinge . . . reden zu lassen*' und zu sehen, 'wie es *eigentlich gewesen*' sei oder ist, kann das 'eigentlich'

Gewesene, das was 'eigentlich' ist, das Tatsächliche doch nur als subjektive Illusion begreifen und darstellen. Das gilt auch und, auf Grund ihrer Seinsweise, in besonderem Sinne für die erzählende Dichtung dieser Epoche.[317]

In *Der arme Spielmann* we see (so the argument runs) the first signs of the loss of the Goethean assurance, which can discover the ideal in the real, 'im Besonderen das Allgemeine ergreifen'.[318] We no longer find the assertion that the individual example can lead us to universal truth; the universality the example enshrines is the esoteric one of 'inwardness'. This 'inwardness' is only accessible through the individual soul, and so its representation demands the concentrated portrayal of the individual case in all its isolation, 'aus dem Zusammenhang eines idealen Ganzen gelöst und auf sich selbst gestellt'[319] — a portrayal, moreover, which is true to the accessible actuality of its object (and Brinkmann shows here the 'authenticating' detail of the Rahmen, the declaration of the sources of the narrator's knowledge, like what we have seen in Storm but less insistent and still coloured by the feeling of narrative 'Souveranität' or omniscience).[320] But the reproduction of 'objective' reality leads to the dim recognition of how 'subjective' that reality is, and so the process of disintegration begins:

> Eine differenzierte Darstellung der 'Wirklichkeit', des 'Tatsächlichen', scheint es nur unter der Bedingung einer stärkeren Beteiligung des Subjekts zu geben. Es sieht so aus, — und dafür spricht die genauere Betrachtung der kleinsten Einzelheiten wie auch die Einsicht in die Struktur des Ganzen der Erzählung — als ob sich das individuelle, besondere Einzelne, so wie es 'wirklich', 'tatsächlich' ist, der Möglichkeit einer objektiven Darstellung entzöge; als ob es umso mehr die Form der Subjektivität annehmen müßte, je vollständiger es die Darstellung wiederzugeben, je mehr sie seiner, des 'Tatsächlichen' habhaft zu werden versucht, je näher sie es heranholt, um ihm 'auf den Grund' zu gehen.[321]

In *Zwischen Himmel und Erde,* says Brinkmann, the process has gone further. Ideal and real are irrevocably separated, the individual case no longer implies even an indirect universality — "Es gibt durchaus nur noch den 'individuellen Fall' ".[322] 'Innerlichkeit' is replaced by individual conscience, 'Gutheit, Gutmütigkeit in einem psychologischen, meist sentimentalen Sinn'.[323] The characters are not motivated[324] by an all-encompassing human condition or by general human qualities; they are seen only as products of their own particular and narrow environment, and moreover as shut off from each other's qualities. And again, the narrative technique reinforces the sense of a lost general apprehension of truth:

> Das Besondere, Individuelle, Tatsächliche in seiner 'objektiven' Beschaffenheit scheint in dem Maße die Form der subjektiven Bestimmungen anzunehmen, mit denen der Erzähler es vorstellt und darbietet, wie die Darstellung es als Objekt isoliert und es dicht heranholt, um es in seinen differenzierten Einzelheiten zu fassen. Das gilt für die Dinge und Geschehnisse und vor allem für die Menschen.[325]

And *Beate und Mareile* represents the provisional extreme to which the other stories have been moving. The moral individuation is complete: what had been 'Innerlichkeit' and became 'Gutheit' with its attendant recognition of the demands of conscience, is now only discernible as a vague sense of guilt. Personal isolation is total; each human being is irrelevant to his fellows, relating to them only in a tangential, glancing way. And that is all inseparably bound up, as cause or effect or both, with the manner in which reality is seen:

> Was ist wirklich? — so kann die Frage für Keyserling und seinesgleichen nicht mehr lauten. Sie kann nur lauten: Was sieht, was erlebt, was empfindet der Einzelne; *wie* sieht, erlebt, empfindet der Einzelne und wie reagiert er darauf? Welt, Wirklichkeit gibt es nicht an sich, gibt es nicht für *den* Menschen. Welt, Wirklichkeit gibt es nur für gewisse geschichtlich gebundene Gruppen, für gewisse Kollektive der Gesellschaft, ja im Grunde nur für den Einzelnen. Wenn es überhaupt noch eine 'objektive' Wirklichkeit gibt, so ist es eben diese Tatsache, daß es Welt und Wirklichkeit nur in der Form der Subjektivität gibt, einer Subjektivität, die weit hinausgeht über die 'transzendentale' Subjektivität Kants und aller seiner legitimen Nachfolger . . .[326]

There is no doubt that the process here described does exist in nineteenth-century German literature; and Brinkmann's subtle and illuminating arguments throw great light on the creative sources of that literature, as well as showing by implication that there is a definite ground here from which the more radical twentieth-century 'experiments with reality' can be said to have sprung. My only objection is to his choice of *Zwischen Himmel und Erde* to illustrate the 'median' of the process. Ludwig's story was published in 1856, only nine years after *Der arme Spielmann* but forty-seven years before *Beate und Mareile,* so that it constitutes nothing like a half-way house chronologically; we have two points close together on one side of the graph, and we can draw any curve we like to join them to the third over on the other side. More important: although thematically the story is without doubt narrowed down and particularised, it still seems to me basically 'objectivist' in its technique and approach: as I suggested earlier,[327] Ludwig retains much of the 'Souveranität' which is associated with the traditional posture of narrative omniscience and which implies a belief in an absolute and absolutely knowable truth about things — the easy movement back and forth in time, the entry into the minds of different characters, incident surveyed from a height. I would put *Zwischen Himmel und Erde* before, not after, *Der arme Spielmann* on Brinkmann's line of development, in spite of the chronological fact. The middle stage of the process could perhaps have been better exemplified by a piece of fiction from the 1870's; there are plenty to choose from there.[328]

But the process itself stands, and what I have claimed for Storm clearly makes him part of it. In his efforts to be 'objective', to portray only what is true to the facts of experience, he is necessarily forced into the 'subjective' mode, for the fact of experience that exercises him most is precisely the fact that experience *is* subjective. But what is also clear — and this is a measure of his precocity — is that the results of this compulsion in Storm's writing bring him closer to Keyserling than to Grillparzer or Ludwig. *Immensee,* written a full half-century before *Beate und Mareile,* [329] contains many of the features which Brinkmann observes in the later story. The similarity emerges, for example, when Brinkmann discusses a brief moment between Beate and Günther, and concludes:

> daß diese Worte und Handlungen Beates kaum eine eigene und selbständige Aktivität bekommen. Sie sind vielmehr das, was Günther hört und sieht, als das, was Beate spricht und tut. [330]

It emerges also in the analysis of the first chapter of Keyserling's story, where the world is seen continuously through Günther's eyes, with the result that his 'Erlebnis-Realität' is presented as the only 'objective' reality; [331] and in the conversation where Mareile is first referred to and introduced into the action, a conversation from which we have to pick up the odd fortuitously mentioned detail and draw our own tentative conclusions about her character; [332] and in the way a character will take up and talk about other people and things ('the outside world') only insofar as they reflect his own inner states and feelings. [333] And Brinkmann could be talking about Storm when he writes:

> Gewiß fühlen die Menschen ihre Einsamkeit — und das gehört zu den intensivsten Eindrücken der Erzählungen Keyserlings —, aber sie haben nichts in der Hand, was sie darüber hinausführen könnte. Es gibt keine wesenhaft verbindende Wirklichkeit. Jeder hat nur seine eigene, und wirklich ist sie nur, wie und insofern der Einzelne sie sieht und als wirklich an sich selbst spürt. [334]

Brinkmann sees Keyserling's vision as something extreme and (in 1903) new; [335] but there is Storm coming close to the extreme already in 1850. What is more, by the 1880's Storm is experimenting with possibilities of transcending the 'realistic' dilemma, of finding substance in the outer world by a faithful commitment to it; he can be said to have lived out, and to have found at least a tentative answer to, the problem before Keyserling's work ever poses it.

Of course, the similarity between the two writers, particularly in technique, is far from being total; there are differences which place Storm clearly 'before' Keyserling on Brinkmann's scale or on any other. The most notable of these differences is that Storm does not wholly share what Brinkmann calls Keyserling's 'Resignieren des Realismus im Sinne des 19. Jahrhunderts'. [336] Keyserling resigns fairly cheerfully: when his Mareile says, 'Eine Wolke ist auch nur so für den da, der sie gerade sieht', she is not expressing a gnawing anxiety but making a languid, unconcerned affirmation; up to a point she is quite happy to live life in the cocoon of subjectivity, and her mood is representative of Keyserling's world in general, where 'die lustvolle Hingabe an das Leben gibt zeitweise das Gefühl genußreich-heiterer Ungebundenheit'. [337] Storm, on the other hand, is never so contented; he represents an earlier sense of the world in his need for solidity in external reality and in the equation of that solidity with stable and positive living. The need is not fulfilled in his experience and so cannot be fulfilled in his work; but the unfulfilled need is in his eyes a frightening condition which unbends the springs of action. So he continues to search without ever wholly resigning; he continues to explore possible hopes, answers, proofs and assurances; and he continues to record the anguish that comes when the search is fruitless. His expectation is disappointed; but that he cherishes the expectation at all is an indication that he has not reached Keyserling's stage of emancipation.

That apart, much of Storm's work seems to me surprisingly 'modern' in its tone and implications. His unostentatious yet profound qualifications of the traditional notions of reality take him beyond his time and anticipate the harsher revaluations seen in our own century. Erich Auerbach talks of a case

> wo der Schriftsteller zuweilen den gedachten Eindruck dadurch erzielt, daß er sich selbst als Zweifelnden, Fragenden und Suchenden hinstellt, als ob ihm die Wahrheit über seine Personen nicht besser bekannt sei als ihnen selbst oder dem Leser. Das Ganze ist also eine Frage der Einstellung des Schriftstellers zur Wirklichkeit der Welt, die er darstellt; welche eben ganz verschieden ist von der Haltung solcher Autoren, die die Handlungen, Zustände und Charaktere ihrer Personen mit objektiver Sicherheit interpretieren; [*sic*] wie dies früher allgemein geschah; Goethe oder Keller, Dickens oder Meredith, Balzac oder Zola teilten uns aus ihrer sicheren Kenntnis mit, was ihre Personen taten, was sie dabei dachten und fühlten, wie ihre Handlungen oder Gedanken zu interpretieren seien; sie wußten genau über ihren Charakter Bescheid . . . es blieb stets der Schriftsteller mit seiner Kenntnis einer objektiven Wahrheit als übergeordnete, führende Instanz erhalten.[338]

It comes as something of a shock when we realise that Auerbach is contrasting the conventional procedure of these traditional writers, not with the work of some minor nineteenth-century lawyer and sentimentalist, but with the originality of Virginia Woolf.

Now to the second and more important comparison. At the beginning of *Re-interpretations,* J.P. Stern expresses what I take to be his major premiss like this:

> I have called this book Re-interpretations for two reasons. First, because I see the prose-works which I have here considered as attempts at re-interpreting the world — at creating worlds — from points of view other than that of the common and commonly explored social certainties of their age; the world itself being presented in these writings not so much as a thing final and indisputably real but rather as in itself an 'interpretation'. And since the works discussed here do not readily adopt the mode of realism as that age (and largely also ours) conceived of it — sometimes the realism is directly challenged, sometimes it is silently by-passed, sometimes the writings are defeated by it — I have tried to suggest criteria, alternative to the common notion of realism, according to which the value of these writings, their especial charm and the weaknesses to which they are prone, may be more justly and fruitfully estimated.[339]

And a little later he states the problem again:

> The situation of nineteenth-century German literature is one in which the literary imagination is but indifferently sustained by the worldly world. Quite often we shall notice, in that situation, a certain lack of feeling for the hard and ineluctable finality of experience — for the deed done that cannot be undone, the word said that cannot be unsaid.[340]

Dr Stern examines the ways in which a number of writers try to overcome or at least circumvent this alienation from the 'real', which is at its clearest in their relations with the *worldly* world, the social certainties — what he calls 'the realm of Leviathan'[341] — but which is no less present in their contact, or lack of it, with the generality of the objective world, the world outside. Their individual records of this relation, and the alternative values they offer when it is found wanting, are shown to be the things that distinguish them from one another; while the fact that the relation *is* inadequate, and the need to offer alternatives, emerge as something specifically German, marking these men out from writers of other cultures:

> We shall see how different are the ways in which different authors convey to us their experience of the worldly world as 'merely' an interpreted and fundamentally unsteady world, with what different other worlds they contrast it, and how often a poignant evocation of its unsteadiness is an author's last word.[342]

The world of *Der arme Spielmann* is just such a world, where the two values quietly posited, the will to goodness and the commitment to art, both fail to make any impact on objective experience — the one vitiated by impracticality and the evil with which it is surrounded, the other made absurd by the cacophony which results from the attempt to objectivise that beautiful commitment in actual sound. In the end we are left with the suggestion that the worth of art can only be affirmed by the narrative achievement in which it is shown to be *in*validated — the story as an artistic triumph in its portrayal of the defeat of art — and the worth of pure good will only in a world beyond the world, in a religious solution; and both affirmations remain implicit and tentative.[343]

Grillparzer's 'interpretation' I assume to be characteristic of (though by no means the same as) the 'interpretations' and 'solutions' offered by the other writers Dr Stern discusses;[344] elsewhere, for example, he talks of 'Stifter's strange and relentless *will* to harmony and perfection, a will that shrinks from self-knowledge and replaces the true consequences of experience by a made-up world'.[345] The central theme of *Re-interpretations* is the disconnection, brilliantly traced, which exists in the creative German mind between the individual sensibility and the world outside it — usually and explicitly the social world, but also often and by implication the whole world of objective reality. The dominant question of the study is not how any of these authors treats the reality which is common to us all, but

> what kind of reality an author has in mind, or rather not 'in mind' only, but in the very fibres of his being, the very movement of his pen.[346]

It seems clear to me that the cast of mind I suggest for Storm is absolutely at one with the preoccupations of these other writers. He is faced with that very disconnection; his writing is conditioned and his realism modified by it at every point, and I have argued before[347] that this conditioning is not consequent upon reflection and analysis ('in mind') so much as upon more basic and less accessible structures (the 'fibres of his being' and the 'movement of his pen'). Storm writes thus, not through choice or decision, but because that is the way he is made.

Storm's work points again and again to that disconnection, that uncertainty about the substance of the objective world; in his quiet way he leads us more directly to the edge of the chasm between subject and object,[348] and makes us more strongly aware that we are on the edge, than perhaps any other writer of his time. His writing is *about* the chasm, and his fundamental concern is to show and drive home the fact that it exists and is frightening; for the most part he does not create a world of his own away from the edge, nor claim to propose sure ways of throwing a bridge (illusory or effective) across to the other side. He does, it can be claimed, offer provisional values to set against his ultimate doubt, but I do not think we have the sense that he is ever deceived by what he offers, ever satisfied, in a way unsatisfactory to us, that any of these values really provides a final solution. What values are they? There is the fact of his art, the achieved formulation somehow resolving or transcending the condition formulated — giving the answer by the fine enactment of the question —, but that is impalpable and ambiguous, and meaningful only to us and not to him, because it only operates when we contemplate him contemplating the condition. There is the recurring delight in the impressions gained from the very senses that block his way to genuine contact with reality — delight, as it were, in the shape and colour and proportions of the prison bars, in the patterns of shadow they throw; that seems to me to be implied in our appreciation of characteristic perfect 'plastic' moments like this one from *Die Regentrude:*

> Dann ging er an den Wagen, der eben abgeladen wurde; er zupfte eine Handvoll Heu heraus, führte es an seine breite Nase und lächelte so verschmitzt, als wenn er aus dem kräftigen Duft noch einige Krontaler herausriechen könne. (SW I 320)

or this one from *Der Schimmelreiter:*

> er nahm das vor ihm liegende Messer und klopfte wie liebkosend auf das Gerippe der armen Ente. 'Das war mein Leibvogel', setzte er behaglich lachend hinzu; 'Sie fraß mir aus der Hand!'[349]

But so often, as in the 'als wenn' and the 'wie liebkosend' here, and in the stress on what is heard in my quotation from *Hinzelmeier,*[350] the delight is qualified at the centre by the uncertainty, and we are reminded that the shapes and sounds and smells *are* after all still prison bars. Then there is 'Husumerei', the refuge in local tradition and received custom, the rattle of the *Teekessel* lid[351] trying to drown out the voices of insistent doubt; but where in his work (as opposed to his life) do we find the fabric of convention giving any great promise of protection and not shot through with the darker tones of anxiety? And there is the alleged consolation, much discussed and criticised, of clinging to the past, either by reminiscence or by the preservation of memorials to the past in the present; but Storm always shows these things in their painful deficiency,[352] and I am sure that he never considers them seriously as possible answers. And lastly, there is the nearest approach he makes to a real solution, the turning outwards which I have mentioned:[353] the engagement on equal terms between an individual and the forces of society or nature is in some sense a leap across the chasm, taking it on trust that the ground on the other side is firm. And yet even this later intimation of assurance is tainted with the old doubt: the social forces which press in on John Hansen are yet deprived of substance by being products of dream and memory, and the natural forces which whip away Hauke Haien's voice are yet shown largely to be motions on his mental landscape.[354]

I have said that Storm's work takes us to the fact of disconnection, not trying to avoid it or offer illusory answers; and in that respect he differs, in a way that crystallises his distinctive achievement, from his friend Gottfried Keller. The difference emerges clearly from the discussion of Keller in *Re-interpretations.* Talking at first generally, Dr Stern says:

> Indeed, a whole literary genre, the *Bildungsroman,* is at least partly conceived as an imaginative means of taking the sting of finality out of experience by making experience repeatable. The genre is fundamentally solipsistic. It leads the young hero from self-absorption into society, as though social life were a problematic task rather than a natural condition, the given thing; and his journey, inevitably, is more fascinating than his arrival.[355]

And later,[356] moving to a closer examination of *Der grüne Heinrich,* he mentions various elements in the novel which have the effect of 'taking the sting of finality out of experience': he cites, as an instance of how the real external consequences of Heinrich's actions strive to make themselves felt, Judith's condemnation of Heinrich's behaviour towards Römer:

> 'Weißt du wohl, Heinrich, daß du allbereits ein Menschenleben auf deiner grünen Seele hast?'

but notes that, although this indictment strongly presses 'the irretrievable nature of past experience . . . the finality of wrong-doing', its force is vitiated by the way Heinrich dockets the experience away as a lesson to be learnt, a thing of value only insofar as it helps *his* education: 'Die Geschichte soll mir zur Warnung dienen', he says, and a little later, '. . . es gehört zu meiner Person, zu meiner Geschichte, zu meinem Wesen, sonst wäre es nicht geschehen!' And Dr Stern discerns this same feeling — things having substance only by virtue of being connected with the hero — in the figures of Anna and Judith, of whom he says that 'they don't exist outside Heinrich's emotional and moral need of them, and even on that premise they don't come to life'.[357] The general conclusion on the nature of Heinrich's experience is that "all *comes* at him, scarcely anything *is*, 'in and by itself' ".[358]

I would go further and suggest that the root of this sense of unreality is not so much in the genre Keller chooses here as in the narrative methods he habitually employs here *and* elsewhere; for we find distinct traces of this unreality in his Novellen as well. Indeed, some of the Novellen have the air of scaled-down Bildungsromane and are subject to the same sort of deficiency, a deficiency which is if anything aggravated by Keller's handling of the shorter form. One of the clearest examples is the framework which surrounds and 'authenticates' the first three tales of the *Züricher Novellen*. The process at work here is precisely one of 'education' or 'maturing'. Young Herr Jacques confides to his godfather the secret (and evidently naive and immature) wish he cherishes to become 'ein Original'. The old man, in order to show Jacques that his views on 'originality' are misguided and that one cannot order one's life with such ambitions in view, tells him three stories[359] about 'originals' from the annals of Zürich's history. The anecdotes have their desired effect: Jacques is shaken out of his youthful dreams, and promises, suitably chastened, to be content with an apparently unexciting future:

> Über dem sorgfältigen Abschreiben vorstehender Geschichte des Landvogts von Greifensee waren dem Herrn Jacques die letzten Mücken aus dem jungen Gehirn entflohen, da er sich deutlich überzeugte, was alles für schwieriger Spuk dazu gehöre, um einen originellen Kauz notdürftig zusammenzuflicken. Er verzweifelte daran, so viele, ihm zum Teil widerwärtige Dinge, wie zum Beispiel fünf Körbe, einzufangen, und verzichtete freiwillig und endgültig darauf, ein Originalgenie zu werden, so daß der Herr Pate seinen Part der Erziehungsarbeit als durchgeführt ansehen konnte.[360]

Jacques mends his ways; his conceptions about life and what is valuable in life are re-formed; the 'Erziehungsarbeit', in part at least, is 'durchgeführt'. But the indirectness, the separation from reality, is obvious: Jacques learns not from experience but from anecdote, which is experience selected and predigested for his benefit. He has in no sense come up against life; it is not what happens to him that reshapes and redirects him; he is merely talked out of error before he ever actively slips into it. Being protected from the possible consequences of his mistaken values, gaining experience at second hand (or rather at third hand, since he learns from another man who teaches by the example of yet other men), is a learning less real even than that which the hero of Keller's Bildungsroman undergoes – at least things actually *happen* to Heinrich Lee.[361]

Just the same is true of *Das Sinngedicht*. No matter how accomplished and organic the artistic whole, no matter how perfect the fusion of the tales and their encompassing frame (and so far as that goes, the work is an absolute *tour de force*), the fact remains that Keller has left the centre empty. In courting and winning Lucie, Reinhart has to forget the epigram with which he starts on his quest, for that epigram is the symbol of his initial, crude and innocent view of love. He has to be stripped of his belief that all one has to do is to find the woman, make sure that she is suitable and then marry her; he has to learn that she must have the right to measure him as he measures her, that her acceptance of him, as well as his of her, is the precondition of success. But Reinhart's 'education' is an immensely contrived thing, without teeth or claws; his ordeal is unreally safe, because he goes through it not in experience, which can damage and humiliate him, but in fictional anecdote, which cannot. The vital lesson he learns, the autonomy and rights of women in the area of love and marriage, is not learned through what actually happens to him; indeed, his actual and active preliminary encounters with the toll-keeper's and then the parson's daughter can surely do nothing but confirm him in his illusion that the whole choice is his. He learns only through the exemplary, doctored events of stories told round the fire; the issues are worked out on the neutral ground of fiction. And if Lucie's tales have the effect and intention of affirming and substantiating her reality and independence, then her character and situation do precisely the opposite: for the 'fact' is that ever since the first approach of womanhood she has lived the life of a recluse with her guardian, tucked away in their remote house (of which the isolation is constantly emphasised). There is an overwhelming impression that her existence, just like that of the other two women he kisses, depends upon Reinhart, that her life has consisted merely in waiting for him to arrive. One begins to feel that she has no other validity than as the object of *his* affection, the product of *his* loving imagination. Her independent existence, proudly asserted in her words and tales, is a chimaera; she almost literally does not exist without him.[362] The whole effect is of reality tidied up, insulated, made safe, and thereby invalidated; experience simulated and thereby bereft of life.

Add to that the weaker places in *Die Leute von Seldwyla* – the lion that is not a lion but a cure for sulking,[363] the too symmetrical, too well-ordered experiences (as if chosen by his mother) to which Fritz Amrain is subjected on the way to mature and responsible citizenship,[364] the contrived ordeal which Wilhelm is made to undergo in order to prove that he has learned his lesson, the lesson being true human values, which can seemingly only be taught when Wilhelm is *isolated* from humanity[365] – and a fairly striking picture emerges. In the situations I have talked about, Keller is refusing to make any kind of approach to the 'real' world, the 'world outside', refusing to take account of the problem of whether it is steadily and independently and intractably 'there' (and thus whether the values he posits have any more than a purely subjective application). For the convenience of his message he skirts the problem and *arranges* reality as he pleases; he creates a world to suit himself, and the penalty he pays is that all reality is drawn inside the individual's consciousness and subordinated to the individual's development. Of course this is necessary, to some extent, in a moral tale: if the tale is not to be boring and in-effectual, real life has to be 'arranged' a little to make the moral clear and amusing. But there is always this danger: the point may come (and I think it does come, now

and then, in Keller) where the arrangement is so divorced from life   at the moral
is no longer relevant to us, since it operates in a world other than the one we know.

I would call this aspect of Keller's work a happy solipsism; he is cavorting about
far from the edge of the chasm, cheerfully renouncing the hope of connection with
reality. To put it crudely, he seems to start by saying, 'All the world is in my own
mind; I control my mind, and so I control the world and can make it do anything I
want it to'. He may know that he is ignoring the disconnection — maybe we cannot
ask him to show it, because that would do violence to the character of his work —
but as it stands, his answer to the question raised by the 'German experience' is an
easy answer, the result of no creative questioning. That the world he paints is his
own world, absolutely created and controlled, is the charm and strength of his
writing — and yet also its greatest weakness.

Storm's solipsism is unhappier. He walks constantly to the edge and looks across
the chasm and knows that he is imprisoned in the small subjective world this side
of the disconnection. His achievement is more considerable than Keller's in this
respect (though in other ways it is of course less so), not because it is unhappier
but because it is informed with greater rigour and less illusion. The consolations
that suggest themselves to him are less than properly consoling, and he knows
and shows that. At the last, the one genuine and possible escape he proposes — an
escape that is not 'escapist', because it is a movement into reality and not away
from it, out of the prison and into the world — is the more valuable for being
qualified and not claimed as a panacea; the more valuable also in that it is the
result of an honest quest. He is characteristic of his own day and relevant to ours,
yet at the same time his contribution lives originally and on its own. The best of
him is in his quiet delineation of the prison, and in the integrity with which he
portrays what, for him, is our condition.

III RESPONSIBILITY ON A SPLIT LEVEL

1. INTRODUCTION

So war sein Leiden denn zu Ende. — Ob eine solche Buße
nötig, ob es die rechte war, darüber, mag ein jeder nach
seinem Innern urteilen; daß mein Freund ein ernster und
ein rechter Mann gewesen ist, daran wird niemand zweifeln.
(Ein Bekenntnis).

in seinem Kopfe wühlten die Gedanken: Was hatte er für
Schuld vor Gottes Thron zu tragen?
(Der Schimmelreiter).

Ein Bekenntnis and *Der Schimmelreiter* are Storm's last two complete stories; after
finishing them, he made preliminary studies and wrote odd scenes for another tale,
Die Armesünderglocke, and set to work, at the persuasion of his children and
friends, on a series of autobiographical sketches. But neither the tale nor the
autobiographical work came to anything; in July 1888, four months after completing
Der Schimmelreiter, Storm was dead.

During the last three years of his life, Storm's manner of work changed somewhat. He had previously been in the habit of writing his works one after the other,
waiting until one story was completely off the stocks before starting on the next.
But *Der Schimmelreiter* was different. The idea of such a story had been with him
for years already, and by 1885 he was ready to begin work on it. First notes were
made in February 1885,[366] and he hoped to write the story down in 1886;[367] but
various factors intervened to postpone the final composition. His health was
deteriorating, and he was often gravely ill; he was shattered by the death of his
beloved but profligate son Hans in December 1886; and he seems to have felt a
curious apprehension about the material of *Der Schimmelreiter* and his own ability
to treat it. Whenever a less demanding or more malleable theme came his way, he
turned to it almost with relief and left *Der Schimmelreiter* in order to write another
story. This is how *Ein Fest auf Haderslevhuus, Bötjer Basch, Ein Doppelgänger* and
Ein Bekenntnis came to be written.

In October 1886, Storm fell ill with pleurisy. By December he was on the road
to recovery and able to get up, but he suffered a serious relapse on hearing the news
of his son's death in Aschaffenburg, and was prostrate well into the New Year. By
March 1887 he was feeling fitter, and he spent the next two months on the
composition of *Ein Bekenntnis* (dictating the first part to his daughter, since

initially he was unable to write). In May the family practitioner, Dr Brinken, revealed to him that he was suffering from stomach cancer, 'die Krankheit unserer Marschen'.[368] After the first shock, Storm felt that he would be able to reconcile himself to this and face it with a measure of equanimity; but as the days went by he slipped into a melancholia which rapidly became deep depression, and he lost all will to engage in any sort of activity, let alone to write. His brother Aemil decided to act, and carried out, with the cooperation of the rest of the family, a brilliant little campaign of deception. He got his son-in-law, one Professor Glaeveke, to make a mock examination of Storm and diagnose another, lesser illness; Dr Brinken pretended to agree that he had made a mistake in his own diagnosis, and Storm was completely taken in. His mind was eased, and his urge to write returned. It is largely to this deception that we owe *Der Schimmelreiter.*[369]

These two last stories, wrested so strangely from the failing energies of a man in the grip of fatal and ghastly disease, fill their place at the end of Storm's creative life with a certain appropriateness. Each in its particular way manifests and acts out a concern which is recurrent in his later work — the concern with 'responsibility'. The term covers a widish range of preoccupations. At one end of the scale, the examination of responsibility is to all intents and purposes a morally neutral examination of causality: 'Why did this happen? How *could* it happen? Was it inevitable? If so, at what stage did it become inevitable? If not, were the possibilities of avoiding it reasonable and human ones?' At the other end, the moral problem has become paramount: we are faced with areas of guilt, penance and possible redemption. The issues in the stories tend to be worked out somewhere on the scale between these two extremes, the pure causality and the pure ethics of responsibility; usually both aspects are present, shading into one another and becoming virtually indistinguishable — 'How did this happen?' comes to mean the same as 'Who or what is to blame for this?'

These questions are fairly clearly asked; but the answers are folded into the action in such a way that it is frequently difficult, and occasionally impossible, to find them. This, as I have tried to show throughout this study, is in the nature of Storm's art and vision. In his anxiously subjectivistic world, the 'real' causes of things are felt ultimately to be as inaccessible as the 'reality' of the things in themselves. We find no absolute and given answer; we are left to provide our own, and we do not necessarily arrive at it by the use of reason: '. . . darüber mag ein jeder nach seinem Innern urteilen'. Thus in *John Riew'* (1884-5), a disaster occurs: a girl, Anna, becomes addicted to drink, is seduced while drunk, gives birth to an illegitimate son and soon afterwards commits suicide out of shame and her sense of degradation. How did this happen? Who is to blame? Various possibilities are suggested. Does the fault lie with Anna's mother, Riekchen, who is such a formidable amalgam of all the trivial virtues that she becomes an ineffective and tittering drag on her family, driving her husband to drink and an early grave, and failing to see the danger confronting her daughter? Can we blame heredity, in the form of alcoholism passed down from father to daughter? Can we blame the old captain, John Riewe, who encourages Anna at an early age to take sips from his grog and thus perhaps activates her latent tendency to alcoholism? (John, who tells the story, takes the guilt upon himself and tries to atone for it by bringing up the illegitimate child to be a valuable member of society.) Can we blame the seducer, the Baron, a member of that feckless class of minor aristocratic ne'er-do-wells which in Storm's eyes is a blight on society and without which the world might be a better place? Is Riekchen guilty of the principal error when she assumes this man to be honourable by virtue of his honourable title and entrusts her daughter to him? Or is it just simply Anna's fault — does she not get exactly what she deserves for what may after all be called profligacy and wantonness? It is a measure of Storm's complexity, causal penetration and great human charity that 'sin', in this crude and cruel 'one-for-one' sense, is the last possibility we think of and the one we are ready at once to discount.

The answer is hidden; or perhaps there is more than one answer; or perhaps there is none. I incline towards the second or third of these possibilities. I think Storm may be saying: 'I tell you this as it happened (or: I tell you life as it happens); I may have my own ideas about the root or roots of this disaster, but there again I may not. Can *you* find a thread to draw these things together? If you can, is it only your own thread, or should it be everybody's? I leave you to judge'. And so we return to our basic formula: 'Darüber mag ein jeder . . .'

Something like this problem is present in most of Storm's stories, from the earliest onwards; part of our response to them depends continually on how we see the workings of causality. We are constantly called upon to separate root causes from catalysts, the 'Ursache' from the 'Anstoß'. This act of separation may lead us into deeper water than we think, and it is difficult to maintain that any one interpretation is more 'right' than another; all seem to veer towards the purely subjective and intuitive. *Immensee,* the first and apparently the simplest of Storm's full-scale works, has produced an extraordinary range of varying judgements about its causality. Pitrou sees the root of the trouble in Reinhard's pusillanimity;[370] Kayser sees it in Elisabeth's domineering mother;[371] Stuckert sees it (since the motivation is inadequate in psychological terms) in the workings of an inevitable 'Schicksal';[372] Böttger sees it in the 'Widerspruch zwischen dem bürgerlich-humanistischen Ideal und der reaktionären bürgerlichen Praxis;[373] McHaffie and Ritchie see it in 'the Curse of Silence'; I see it in a view of the world which says that being alone is part of the human condition, and that something will nearly always intervene to prevent people coming fruitfully together in love. If we were all put together in a room, we should no doubt all be saying, 'No, no, the rest of you have the catalysts; I have the cause'.

The problem is there, then, at the start; and it is there, if anything more intensely, at the end. In *Ein Bekenntnis* and *Der Schimmelreiter,* we seem at first to be faced with a fairly clear set of causal and moral responsibilities ('This happened because he did this and was at fault in that') and an associated moral problem ('Did he really deserve all he got?'); but I want to suggest that in both these stories severally something else is going on at the same time, operating on another level of responsibility, at variance with the surface issues, unexpected, practically unnoticed, maybe even 'unintended', but nonetheless present and active and capable of isolation through a study of the text.

If this other operation does exist, then it affects the conventional assessments of *Der Schimmelreiter* perceptibly and those of *Ein Bekenntnis* radically. The fact of the incongruity — between the apparently 'intended' interpretation and what emerges from the text — brings yet more clearly into focus the problem which seems to be raised by so much of Storm's work: the problem of the 'unconscious' artist, the man not intimate with his own creativity, the writer who doesn't quite know what he is writing. And finally, the presence of the operation marks a decisive advance over the stories I talked about in the first part of this study: there we saw a kind of fatalism functioning regardless of human will, making relationship impossible, but here there is a measure of choice and an element of responsibility, and we see men 'punished' for failing to make a commitment which is *not* beyond human possibility.

2. EIN BEKENNTNIS

The 'confession' is made by Franz Jebe, a doctor, to Hans, an old and close friend from the university whom he meets again by chance after many years. The substance of it is this: as a boy in his last year at school, Franz has a dream in which he sees

> die Gestalt eines etwa dreizehnjährigen Mädchens; ein schlichtes aschfarbenes Gewand zog sich bis an ihren Hals hinauf, wo es mit einer Schnur zusammengezogen war. Schön war sie eben nicht; ein etwas fahlblondes Haar lag ein wenig wirr auf ihrem kleinen Kopfe, aber aus den feinen durchsichtigen Zügen ihres Antlitzes blickten ein Paar lichtgraue Augen unter dunkeln Wimpern in die meinen, unablässig, sehnsüchtig, als solle ich sie nie vergessen; und mit unsäglichem Erbarmen blickten sie mich an: eine verzehrende Wonne überkam mich, ich hätte unter diesen Augen sterben mögen. (SW IV 246)

This vision obsesses him for months, and remains with him, unobtrusive but ineradicable, during his medical studies at the university (he is a brilliant, rather solitary student, with a reputation for arrogance). After completing his studies, he sets up in practice as a gynaecologist, and is quickly successful. One day, at the house of friends, he meets a Swiss girl, Else Füßli; she is the incarnation of the girl in his vision. He falls deliriously in love with her, and she with him; they marry and live together for three years in blissful happiness, clouded only by the fact that Else is terrified of physical pain and cannot stand the spectacle of suffering in others (an unfortunate weakness in a doctor's wife, one might think). In the fourth year of the marriage, Else falls ill; Franz examines her and finds that she has cancer of the womb, at the time an incurable and invariably fatal disease involving unspeakable final agonies. Her attacks of pain grow steadily worse, and she implores him to put her out of her misery; finally he does so, administering a quick and painless poison, and she dies peacefully and gratefully. Months later he picks up a periodical which he had received before Else's death but had tossed aside in his distraction at her illness; in it there is an article by a former professor of his in whom he has implicit faith; the professor reveals in the article that he has found a fairly effective (three successes from five) surgical cure for carcinoma uteris. If Franz had read this article as soon as he received the periodical (as had always been his practice before), he might well have saved Else.

After two and a half years (during which time, shattered by his grief and guilt, Franz has worked on like an automaton rather than a human being) he is called to the house of the Etatsrätin Roden, whom he examines and finds to have carcinoma; his mind is in a whirl, but the presence of the Etatsrätin's pretty daughter Hilda makes him feel suddenly calm and capable of action. He suggests surgery, and the Etatsrätin agrees; he performs the operation, and it is a success. Mutual attraction has sprung up between him and Hilda, and he knows that he would be well received if he asked for her hand. But he feels he cannot do this, and so he comes away to Reichenhall; this is where he meets Hans and is finally able to get the story off his conscience. After confessing to his friend, he resolves to go away and work among primitive peoples. For nearly thirty years he leads a life of selfless service in East Africa, practising his medicine for the benefit of the natives, and eventually dies there, after spending this last half of his life in terrible solitude and longing for death.

In 1884 Paul Heyse had written a Novelle, *Auf Tod und Leben,* on roughly the same theme. Storm read it when it came out, but deliberately refrained from referring to it when he came to write his own story (for which, in fact, he had first had the idea some time *before* 1884).[374] There is an interesting correspondence between the two writers about these stories, and I shall be talking about this later; first, I want to mention the sort of confusion which arises when a critic (in this case Stuckert)[375] examines *Ein Bekenntnis* by comparison with *Auf Tod und Leben.* Stuckert's evaluation of the two works is unobjectionable (or at least the objections to it need not concern us here); he considers *Ein Bekenntnis* to be on balance better than *Auf Tod und Leben,* and no doubt it is. But when he comes to talk of the 'moral' content of the stories, something, it seems to me, goes wrong. He makes two preliminary assertions: first, that Heyse is treating the moral theme, 'is euthanasia right?', and second, that on the contrary Storm's problem is (and here he quotes from the correspondence), " 'Wie kommt einer dahin, sein Geliebtestes zu töten?' *und* 'Was wird aus ihm, wenn er das getan hat?' " But then, more or less in the same breath, Stuckert claims that Heyse sees the problem from a social viewpoint; for him, redemption takes the form of reintegration into society, after the lifting of the load of guilt by the understanding and forgiveness of a loving person; the problem for

Heyse is in fact the redemption, *not* the morality of the act. One volte-face to Stuckert; and he rapidly becomes two up when he argues Storm's greater profundity and universality. He claims that the circumstances in which Franz kills Else (the fact that a cure *is* possible and that he overlooks it) only sharpen the conflict and are not basic to it. Franz's real crime, says Stuckert, is that he has offended against the 'Heiligkeit des Lebens'; for Storm this is the basic religious sin, which can only be atoned for by 'immerwährendes Opfer im Dienste dieses Lebens'; church and justice are inadequate to acquit, let alone redeem him — he must take his guilt alone before God (Storm's 'protestantischer Grundzug' coming out here, Stuckert says). But surely this is saying precisely that *Storm* and not Heyse is treating the moral theme, 'is euthanasia right?'? Leaving aside for the moment the question of what *is* actually going on in these stories, I am compelled to conclude the following: Stuckert thinks Storm is writing about what he (Stuckert) asserts that Heyse is writing about, and he (Stuckert) thinks Heyse is writing about what he (Stuckert) thinks Storm is writing about. And to make matters worse, Storm and Heyse themselves, in their correspondence on the stories, often seem ready to take their own spin on this lunatic carousel.

As soon as we enter the ambience of responsibility, this sort of chaos seems to engulf us. In what follows I shall try to suggest a way out of the confusion — a way out which receives strong support from the text and very little from any other quarter. The text has to be paramount, I think; ultimately it must be elucidated from within itself, with its own words as the final arbiter. That, I hope, affords some justification for my adding one more voice to the chorus of answers to the questions 'Why did it happen?' and 'Who is to blame?'

On the 21st June 1887 Storm sent the proofs of *Ein Bekenntnis* to Heyse for his comments. Heyse returned them on the 25th June, with a letter setting out his criticisms. One of these was that Storm had not specified Else's illness:

> Bedenklicher noch ist mir die Krankheit selbst in ihrer namenlosen Unbestimmtheit, die Dir freilich zweckmäßig schien, da Du auch eine ganz unbestimmbare neue Heilmethode einführen wolltest. Ich weiß nicht, ob ein Arzt, der die Novelle liest, nicht stark den Kopf schütteln wird.

Storm was in full agreement with this; he consulted a gynaecologist, who suggested that cancer of the womb would fit the bill (by a fantastic irony, the gynaecologist involved was none other than Glaeveke, who at exactly this time made the mock examination of Storm and pretended to reject stomach cancer in his diagnosis). Storm wrote the change into the story;[376] it is an unqualified improvement and need detain us no further.

Another of Heyse's objections, and one which will concern us a good deal, was this:

> In das sehr einfache Problem: ob man einem Unheilbaren zum Tode helfen dürfe, hast Du ein fremdes Element hineingetragen: die Möglichkeit des Irrtums über die Hoffnungslosigkeit des Falles. Eine solche bleibt ja in allen menschlichen Dingen . . . Wir können doch nur nach unserm redlichsten Erkennen handeln, gleichviel, ob eine spätere höhere Erkenntnis uns, was wir im einzelnen Fall für sittlich zulässig, ja notwendig gehalten, als ein Irrtum aufzeigt . . . Daß (Franz) dieses Zuspät einen lebenslangen Kummer verursacht, ist natürlich. Aber sein Leben zerstören durfte er nicht.

Storm replied:

> Dein Problem: 'ob man einem Unheilbaren zum Tode helfen dürfe?' war nicht das meine. Ich wollte darstellen: 'Wie kommt einer dahin, sein Geliebtestes zu töten?' *und* 'Was wird aus ihm, wenn er das getan hat?' Auf diesem einfachen Wege fanden sich die beiden Tatsachen ganz natürlich ein: die Erschwerung seines Bewußtseins durch die, jetzt so merkwürdig stimmende, von ihm übersehene Entdeckung der Möglichkeit einer Heilung; und die Abweisung einer sich nahenwollenden neuen Liebe.[377]

This criticism and this reply provide a useful starting-point for an interpretation of *Ein Bekenntnis* on the 'intended' level. In this context, it is evident that Storm is *not* all that interested in the moral problem (so Stuckert is right in his assertion and wrong in his interpretation, paraphrased earlier). He is not concerned about the objective guilt or otherwise of Franz's action — he leaves that for the reader to judge. He merely wants to examine the mental state and decisions of a man who is racked with guilt; the fact that the man *feels* guilty is enough to make the examination worth while: 'Ich wollte *darstellen* . . .' The motif of the unread article is a device of intensification, another ingredient added to the mixture to make more interesting the experiment which is being carried out on Franz's psyche. Let us see then what we are 'shown'.

Franz kills his beloved wife, and finds later that he need not have done so. He summarizes his own indictment like this:

> 'Daß ich meiner Elsi den Tod gegeben, während ich nach dieser neuen Vorschrift vielleicht ihr Leben hätte erhalten können, das liegt nicht mehr auf mir; es ist ein Schwereres, an dem ich trage — so mühselig, daß ich, wäre es möglich, an den Rand der Erde laufen würde, um es in den leeren Himmelsraum hinabzuwerfen. Laß es dir sagen, Hans, es gibt etwas, von dem nur wenige Ärzte wissen, auch ich wußte nicht davon, obgleich ihr mich zum Arzt geboren glaubtet, bis ich daran zum Verbrecher wurde . . . Das ist die Heiligkeit des Lebens . . . Das Leben ist die Flamme, die über allem leuchtet, in der die Welt ersteht und untergeht; nach dem Mysterium soll kein Mensch, kein Mann der Wissenschaft seine Hand ausstrecken, wenn er's nur tut im Dienst des Todes, denn sie wird ruchlos gleich der des Mörders!' (SW IV 284f.)

This is the burden of Franz's guilt (and I repeat that Storm's concern, and ours for the moment, is to see how he carries it, not to decide whether it is just that he should carry it at all). The major part of the story is given over to an examination of his attempts to expiate his crime. Several possibilities of expiation are proposed, but each is rejected in its turn, for one reason or another. The following is a schematised account of these possibilities and rejections; I should mention that they are woven skilfully and subtly into the fabric of the story and are not pinned on to the action like a row of paper flags, as might appear from this.

At first, Franz considers whether he should surrender to authority (the law and the church) and acquiesce in society's punishment for his crime. But he cannot:

> nein, Hans, ich bin ein zu guter Protestant, ich weiß zu wohl, weder Richter noch Priester können mich erlösen; mein war die Tat, und ich allein habe die Verantwortlichkeit dafür; soll eine Sühne sein, so muß ich sie selber finden. Überdies — bei dem furchtbaren Ernst, in dem ich lebte, erschien's mir wie ein Possenspiel, wenn ich mich auf dem Schafott dachte. (SW IV 276)

This is deadly dubious, of course; but let us accept it provisionally as sincerely meant and not a rationalisation of cowardice. Another possibility is the resumption of former relationships, a gradual reintegration into the social scheme. Franz's friends Wilm and Käthe Lenthe (almost his only friends in the town) invite him to come to them again as he had done when he was single; he comes, and tries to recreate that old way of life, but in vain:

> Ich setzte mich stumm auf meinen alten Sofaplatz, aber es war jetzt trübe auch im Haus meiner Freunde. (SW IV 277)

A third possibility is the resumption of Franz's proper function in the community, reintegration through his profession. After Else's death, he withdraws from his practice and leaves his assistant to run it; but there is an epidemic, the assistant is worked half to death, and Franz realises that he is bound to give his own service to the community; he does so, and after the epidemic has been eliminated he continues in his practice, working as well and successfully as ever; but this has no good effect on him:

> Ich tat, was ich mußte oder auch nicht lassen konnte, aber ohn Anteil oder wissenschaftlichen Eifer. (SW IV 277)

Then there is a psychological possibility, the hope contained in a sort of trauma: Franz cures the Etatsrätin of the disease from which his wife had died. We feel that this reliving of the experience, in a way that is different in that he can now play a healing role with greater knowledge and a recipe for action, might in some sense purge him. But this seems doomed to failure as well — a failure measured by Hilda's response when Franz tells her that her mother is on the way to recovery:

> gleich einer Trauerkunde haben Sie die Himmelsbotschaft mir verkündet! . .es tut mir so leid, daß Sie nicht froh sein können. (SW IV 283)

Fifthly, redemption might come from the building of a new love relationship: Hilda is willing to marry Franz, and he feels strongly attracted to her. She offers him sympathy and confidence and another possibility, that of purging himself by confession to her:

> 'Ja, ja, ich weiß', erwiderte sie, plötzlich still werdend, 'Sie haben Ihre Frau so sehr geliebt und haben sie verloren!'
> 'Es war die Krankheit Ihrer Mutter', fügte ich hinzu; 'ich vermochte sie nicht zu retten' — — nur zu töten! hätte ich fast hinzugesetzt, denn mich überkam ein fast unabweisbarer Drang, diesem jungen Wesen meine Seele preiszugeben, ihr alles, was mich zu Boden drückte, bloßzulegen, so wie ich es heute vor dir getan habe. — Aber ich bezwang mich; sie hätte darunter zusammenbrechen müssen. (SW IV 283)

So he will not confess to her; neither will he marry her, since he feels that this would be a denial of her humanity:

> pfui, pfui! Dies edle Geschöpf zum Mittel einer Heilung zu erniedrigen, es würde nur ein neues Verbrechen sein! (SW IV 285)

Nonetheless, Franz still feels that confession might be the best balm for his tortured soul; when he meets his old friend Hans at Reichenhall, he reveals everything to him; and this does produce a kind of liberation:

> Daß Du zur rechten Zeit mich fandest, daß ich zu Dir das Ungeheure von der Seele sprechen konnte, hat meinen Geist befreit. (SW IV 287)

But even that is not sufficient: confession has not cleared his conscience, it has only cleared the ground for a decision as to what he must do to redeem himself; and thus he hits upon the seventh means of expiation: a life of total self-sacrifice in the service of others:

> ich gehe fort, weit fort, für immer, nach Orten, wo mehr die Unwissenheit als Krankheit und Seuche den Tod der Menschen herbeiführt. Dort will ich in Demut mit meiner Wissenschaft dem Leben dienen; ob mir dann selber Heilung oder nur der letzte Herzschlag bevorsteht, will ich dort erwarten. (SW IV 287)

And so he goes away to East Africa and works there for thirty years. All the information we have about these years is a short note to Hans which Franz writes on his death bed, with a covering letter from the local Catholic missionary. We cannot know whether this drastic means of redemption 'works' or not; we are not told its results, but only its symptoms, a hard life and desperate solitude. We discover that in the midst of this seventh possibility Franz has rejected an eighth and a ninth, that of entry into the Catholic Church ('. . . obwohl er den rechten Weg des Heils verschmähte . . .' writes the missionary), (SW IV 287) and that of suicide:

> Ich habe ehrlich ausgehalten; mitunter nicht ohne Ungeduld, so daß mir die Gedanken kamen: Was bist du doch der Narr? Der Weg hinaus ist ja so leicht! — Aber ich hatte damals noch die Kraft, mich abzuwenden, daß ich an mir selber nicht zum Frevler würde. (SW IV 288)

But at the end he longs for death, calling it 'das Tor zur Freiheit'. (SW IV 288) Perhaps in the last analysis it is death, with its hope of reunion with Else, (SW IV 288) that will provide the final solution; but of course we cannot know. To his last breath, Franz's destiny is in the balance.

Whether Franz 'expiates', whether he is 'saved' or 'redeemed', we do not know. What we do know is that he suffers, that he is in a way 'punished', or punishes himself. The punishment is a characteristically Stormian one: he is made to be alone. The sentence begins while Else is still alive; after her penultimate attack, the curse is already laid:

> Ich . . . ging . . . in mein Zimmer hinab, wohin die Magd mein *einsâmes* Frühstück gestellt hatte. (SW IV 268; my italics.)

His first reaction to Else's death is to withdraw from all contact with others:

> ich scheute mich vor den Menschen, ich vermied sie und lebte wie ein Einsiedler . . . Und niemand störte mich in dieser Vereinsamung. (SW IV 273)

The possibilities of regaining relationship in community, friendship and love are all thwarted; he works without involvement in his patients, his friends' house is a sad place for him, and he cannot marry Hilda.[378] The basic ingredient of his years in Africa is absolute solitude; he denies himself the comfort of the only available formal relationship (the Catholic one) with God, and his loneliness is so ghastly that death comes as a release:

> Jetzt endlich geht die Zeit der furchtbaren Einsamkeit, in der ich hier die zweite Hälfte meines Lebens hingebracht habe, ihrem Ende zu. (SW IV 288)

Solitude, the removal of contact with other men, is Franz Jebe's punishment; *but is it not also his crime*? This is where we begin to move away from the recognition of intention into the perception of what I have called the split level of responsibility. The interpretation set out above is, I think, a reasonably fair approximation to what Storm 'intends' us to see; but there is something vaguely disquieting about it, something is wrong. We have the odd indication: one I have already mentioned is Franz's dubious reason for refusing to give himself up to the law — 'Ich bin ein zu guter Protestant', etc. This is strongly reminiscent of what seems to me a most extraordinary piece of special pleading in Hebbel's *Agnes Bernauer:* König Ernst decides he must have Agnes put to death, and he dismisses the suggestion that he could separate Agnes and Albrecht, put her away in secret and give out that she is dead. This is the reason he gives:

> Und ich sollte ihm das zweite Weib geben, während das erste noch lebt? Nein, Preising, das Sakrament ist mir heilig.[379]

That, so far as I can see, puts the sin of divorce above that of murder, and it rings the most peculiar bells. Anyway, Franz's protestations smack oddly of mock-heroics, and the same strange taste is present in the tone of what he says in rejecting the possibility of marrying Hilda.[380] I shall return to these and other oddities later. It should just be said now that they tend to estrange us from Franz when we are obviously 'meant' to be in full sympathy with him.

Then the central inadequacy of this 'intended' interpretation hits us: it leaves entirely out of account the relationship between Franz and Else. The story is fifty pages long;[381] this relationship, from the first meeting until Else's death, accounts for twenty-three pages; (SW IV 250-72) its antecedents (the 'Vision' and its effects) take up another five. (SW IV 245-50) Thus, over half the narration is devoted to it; and yet this interpretation says next to nothing about it, except by implication to assert that it is blissful and perfect, and that its perfection has the function of accentuating Franz's grief, guilt and loneliness when it ends. If this is its only function, then one must infer that Storm has devoted over half his story to what is no more than a device of intensification, that there is more seasoning on the plate than meat. No, Storm is far too good a cook to do that kind of thing; it is undeniable that towards the end of his life he was a highly skilled literary craftsman, and would not make a mistake like that; he could not, even if he wanted to. And with that provocative statement we begin a walk on very thin ice.

The other major criticism which Heyse makes about *Ein Bekenntnis* (in his letter to Storm of the 25th June 1887) is concerned with the motif of the 'Vision'; he objects to

> das visionäre Element, das dem Charakter des hellblickenden Naturkundigen fremd sein sollte, zumal es mit dem Verlauf der Geschichte nichts Wesentliches zu schaffen hat. Ich würde dringend raten, diese Partie in der Buchausgabe zu streichen. Sie erweckt Erwartungen, die nicht erfüllt werden. Denn auch zur Charakteristik der sensitiven jungen Frau ist sie nicht nötig, während sie für den Arzt störend erscheint.

And a few weeks later he writes again:

> Warum soll die visionäre Vorgeschichte stehenbleiben? . . . Wie leicht ist sie herauszuschälen; bei der Operation fließt nicht ein Tröpfchen Blut, und Du hast die Komposition um einen unkünstlerischen Nebenschößling erleichtert, der nicht bloß überflüssig, sondern störend war.[382]

Storm is half agreed on this:

> Wie sollte ich verdrießlich über Deinen Brief sein, lieber Freund; hatte ich Dir doch die Bogen grade geschickt, um zwei Prinzipaleinwände zu hören, die ich mir selbst gemacht hatte. Der eine war der, daß die visionäre Vorgeschichte zu stark war, um nicht für den Leser auf Grund derselben die Entwicklung erwarten zu lassen. Bei aufmerksamem Lesen wirst Du bemerken, wie ich im Verfolg bemüht gewesen, dies abzuschwächen. Zu ändern ist das für mich nicht mehr. Es ist ein Jugenderlebnis, das mich unglücklicherweise reizte, es hineinzuweben.[383]

So Storm himself is uneasy about the relevance of the 'Vision'; it is a youthful experience which he merely wishes to perpetuate somewhere; and he subsequently tries, he says, to weaken its effect on the story as a whole. But 'Zu ändern ist das für mich nicht mehr'[384] — he does leave it in, even though (as Heyse rightly says) it could be cut out with no great difficulty. And furthermore, it is just not true that he makes any extensive attempt to correct the impression that the vision is important. The only paragraph in the whole story which could be construed in this light is one spoken by Franz just after he has recounted his first meeting with Else:

> 'Ich habe dir', unterbrach sich Franz, 'von meinem jugendlichen Traum-gesicht, das sich vielleicht nur aus dem Eindruck des damaligen großen Sterbens und einer kaum geahnten Sehnsucht nach dem Weibe erzeugt hatte, nur gesprochen, um dich es mitfühlen zu lassen, wie tief der Anblick der Fremden mich erregen, wie eigen und innig eine Ehe mit ihr sich gestalten mußte; denn wenn es für unser Leben etwas Ewiges geben soll, so sind es die Erschütterungen, die wir in der Jugend empfangen haben. Sonst freilich war es eben nichts Außerordentliches, daß ich einmal einem Weibe begegnete, welches mich so lebhaft an meine Traumgestalt erinnerte, daß ich im ersten Augenblick und noch in manchen späteren beide nicht voneinander zu trennen vermochte. Jedenfalls, auf mich hatte dieses erste Sehen einem elektrischen Schlage gleich gewirkt; und', fügte er leiser hinzu, 'was wissen wir denn auch von diesen Dingen!' (SW IV 251f.)

One paragraph seems to me insufficient to wipe out, or even play down, the effect of the previous five pages; for the rest, not only is no effort made to play it down, but (I would submit) every attempt is made to play *up* the visionary, magical, super- or non-human element. I still want to leave aside the question of whether this 'playing-up' is intentional or not; I wish simply to take the text as it stands, and examine what is there precisely *because* it is there, by virtue of its existence before us on the page. I want to look closely at the relationship between Franz and Else, and at the vision which heralds it, because together they take up over half the story; and I suggest that this examination will show up the relationship in a very different light — it will emerge as a thing of dreams and magic, unreal and un-human, and thus incapable of invoking our human sympathy for the bereaved partner when it ends — and will make of Franz a very different sort of man, a man unwilling or unable to make any kind of extensive contact with other human beings, afraid of relationship but rationalising his fear in other ways, with chosen solitude as his crime and enforced solitude as his punishment.

Storm says, "Ich wollte darstellen: 'Wie kommt einer dahin, sein Geliebtestes zu töten'".[385] To become involved in this situation as something valid and illuminating to our experience, we need to be convinced of the reality of this relation between Franz and 'sein Geliebtestes', and to see in Else a recognizable personality capable of becoming somebody's (maybe even our) 'Geliebtestes'. But what is Else, and what is the relation? We look in vain for an encounter between two real and rounded human beings; all we find is a fairy-tale romance beyond the human possibility, insubstantial, Romantic, and slightly sinister and worrying; it recalls above all Hoffmann (I am thinking particularly of *Der goldne Topf*: Anselmus marries Serpentina and is perfectly happy, but we are 'worried' and slightly repelled by the idea of a young man sitting in Atlantis with a snake, and enjoying it). Else seems to have little, if any, fleshly existence: she is a waif, a transient spirit, surrounded by the grey shrouds of death and the supernatural, pre-eminently a figure in a dream. This is borne in on us over and over again; I can show it by simply listing fourteen quotations (there are more), leaving them to speak for themselves except insofar as the italics are mine:

(Käthe introduces Franz to) 'Unsere Freundin Else Füßli . . . aus der Familie, der auch Heinrich Füßli angehörte, dem zuerst die Darstellung des *Unheimlichen* in der deutschen Kunst gelang'. (SW IV 250)

Es war wie damals auf der Treppe unserer alten Gelehrtenschule: alles um mich her war vergessen, aber vor mir im hellen Lampenlichte sah ich die Augen und das blasse Antlitz meines *Nachtgesichtes*. (SW IV 251)

Ich hatte nun *mein Nachtgespenst geheiratet* . . . es war ein Glück! . . . ich hatte einst den Fouquéschen Ritter Huldbrand beneidet, wie er mit einer *Undine* seine Brautnacht feiert; ich hatte *nicht gedacht, daß dergleichen unter Menschen möglich sei* . . . Mein Glück ging *über jeden Traum hinaus.* – Es war so manches *Eigene, Fremdartige* an ihr, das mich *im ersten Augenblick verwirrte und mich zugleich entzückte.* (SW IV 252)

da wir uns Aug in Auge trafen, sah ich, daß sie mir entgegen*fliegen* wollte . . . (there follows a description of Else coming towards Franz, a butterfly settled in her hair and a snow-white kitten at her side) . . . Ein *Märchenbild;* das Seltsame war nur, *daß es in einer Reihe von Tagen sich ganz in derselben Weise wiederholte.*
    'Was machst du für Faxen, Elsi!' rief ich endlich lachend; 'Bist du eine *Undine,* eine *Elbe,* eine *Fee*? Was bist du eigentlich? . . . Du bist so *unergründlich!*' Da *flog* sie in meine Arme: 'Dein bin ich; *nichts* als dein! . . .'
    Aber der Schmetterling aus ihren Haaren war davongegaukelt. (SW IV 253)

(Else tells Franz) 'mein Leib hat nie von Schmerz gelitten, so daß ich, wenn andere klagten, mir oft als eine fast *Begnadete* erschienen bin'. (SW IV 255)

Immer wieder tauchte von Zeit zu Zeit *von dem nur ihr so Eigenen* auf, aber es war stets anmutig, und wenn ich eben *aus der nüchternen Welt zurückkam,* so war mir oft, als stamme es *aus andern Existenzen.* (SW IV 258)

'Herein, holde *Elfe!*' rief ich, und da stand sie vor mir . . . 'Ja, Elsi . . . du bist schön, *zu schön fast für ein Menschenkind!*' (SW IV 259)

(Franz is called away from a ball to attend a gravely ill patient) Als ich spät . . . in den Tanzsaal zurückkehrte, *flog* Elsi mir entgegen: '*Wo stand der Tod*?' frug sie ernst . . . (SW IV 260)

Und wir tanzten miteinander; nur dies eine Mal in unserem Leben . . . jetzt war mir, als würden meine Füße *beflügelt, als ströme eine Kraft, die Kunst des Tanzes, von meinem Weibe auf mich über,* und dennoch – mitunter befiel mich Furcht, als könne ich sie *nicht halten,* als müsse sie mir *in Luft zergehen* . . . Ich ließ das alles wie einen *stillen Zauber* über mich ergehen. (SW IV 261) ja, ich habe nie bemerkt, daß überhaupt gehaushaltet wurde; es war, *als ob die toten Dinge ihr gegenüber Sprache erhielten* . . . Es war *wie im Märchen*. (SW IV 261)

(A long description of how Franz comes home one day to find Else in a trance, uttering strange premonitions) . . . diesen *halbvisionären Zustand*. (SW IV 262f.)

(After Else's penultimate attack) wie eine welke Blume lag sie mir im Arm, an meiner Brust, *blutlos, ohne alle Schwere des Lebens* . . . Wie ein *Irrsinn* flog es mich an: 'Ist *etwas in ihr*, das sie nicht sterben läßt?' . . . denn ich liebte sie ja so grenzenlos, so *wahnsinnig*, daß ich auch jetzt, trotz meines vielgerühmten Scharfsinns, nicht lassen konnte, sie immer wieder *über das Menschliche hinauszuheben*. (SW IV 266f.)

Da schrie sie plötzlich auf: wie von *Dämonen*, die aber *kein sterblich Auge sah*, fühlte sie ihren Leib in meinen Armen geschüttelt; mir war's, als wollten sie *die Seele heraushaben* und als könnten sie es nicht. (SW IV 270)

(Franz gives Else the poison) . . . es mag ja *Täuschung* gewesen sein, mir aber war es, als säh ich in das Antlitz *meines Nachtgesichtes*, wie es einstmals verschwindend von mir Abschied nahm; jenes und meines Weibes Züge waren mir in diesem Augenblicke eins . . . Das Abendrot brach durch die Scheiben und *überflutete sanft die Sterbende* und alles um sie her. (SW IV 271)

It is impossible to ignore so many statements of such intensity; it is myopic to dismiss them, and the 'Vision', as a piece of literary misjudgement by the author; it is disproportionate to lump them all together and call them a device of intensification which does not come off — impossible, myopic and disproportionate, that is, if we look only at the text and leave out of account the author's intentions. Heyse claims that the vision 'erweckt Erwartungen, die nicht erfüllt werden', and Storm agrees;[386] but they are both manifestly wrong. The expectations aroused by the vision are admirably fulfilled in the quotations I have set down here; their fulfilment involves conclusions that I can see no way of avoiding; and these conclusions, gained from our response to the text as it stands, give us a progressive illumination, from Else via Else-Franz to Franz, and indicate a new causality, another level of responsibility.

Else is more, or less, than human; she has no faults, except that she cannot stand pain or the spectacle of pain and is thus withdrawn from the human possibility of enduring and overcoming suffering (and this is perhaps the major possibility we look for when we read a work of literature). She runs the household perfectly, she is always generous, loving and faithful. The individual peculiarities she reveals from time to time never irritate, estrange or frighten Franz; they leave him 'verwirrt' but 'zugleich entzückt' (SW IV 252); they may be strange, but they are 'stets anmutig'. (SW IV 258)

So the relationship is impeccably blissful from start to finish. It is never tested; it never deteriorates or improves; it never even changes. It merely gets more and more impossibly idyllic and less and less human as time wears on. It is all too good to be true, or rather too good to be real and affecting in the way that it was 'intended' to be. We cannot be touched by the problem Storm says he is examining, because it hardly exists; ultimately, Franz has not killed his 'Geliebtestes' — he has killed a dream.

The situation is so 'dreamlike' that an absurd possibility suggests itself. Could Franz perhaps be making it all up? Could it be that he never even married anyone, let alone killed his wife? Of course not; but the suggestion is absurd only because we are not given a *dénouement* saying that this was indeed so. If there *were* such a *dénouement,* if we were told at the end that Franz had in fact never married and never killed, then everything would fall beautifully into place; Else's insubstantial, dreamlike quality, her identification with the girl in the vision, and the fairy-tale bliss of the marriage — all these things would become meaningful as the inventions of an impoverished personality, bent on wish-fulfilment and the evasion of real human action and experience. The story would be entirely successful as a psychological oddity. Is that perhaps one of the expectations which Heyse says are aroused but never satisfied? All this is of course a wildly speculative interpretation, but it is worth mentioning because it is the kind of interpretation to which the study of the text seems to be leading us. It is absurd but it is illuminating, and between it and the more conventional 'intended' interpretation there is a psychological no-man's-land where we can perhaps place Franz, seeing him as a man who has indeed married and indeed killed his wife, but whose real tragedy (unknown to himself) is that he has never achieved a real human relationship with her or anybody else. This is what I mean when I say that Franz is not killing 'sein Geliebtestes' but a dream; and I think this is the only really satisfactory interpretation one can put on the character of Franz or on the story as a whole.

Franz is nearly seventy when he dies; he had his vision at the age of seventeen or eighteen. The whole of his adult life is centred on that dream and on its realisation in four years of marriage to Else, four years out of fifty or more. He spends fifty years either in contemplation of the dream, or in experience of its realisation, or in atonement for the sin of destroying it. He indulges this obsession because it relieves him of the necessity of relating to any other human being; it is a means of escape whenever he is confronted by the possibility of a real relationship. Once we begin to look at Franz in *this* way, all the inadequacies and oddities in the story and all the inconsistencies in Franz's character become resolved and meaningful.

First and foremost, we have an explanation for Storm's apparently capricious insertion of the 'Vision' motif, his refusal to remove it, and the 'unintentional' impact it has on the whole atmosphere and theme: it is the armour, heaven-sent, by which Franz can defend himself against the onslaught of all other living personalities. Then we can fully understand our disquieting impression that something is basically wrong,[387] that from first to last we seem to be witnessing an attempt to present Franz as a rather more admirable person than we feel him in fact to be. The clue is in the Rahmen situation, in the character of Hans, the friend who reproduces Franz's confession for us. Hans, recalling his student friendship with Franz, says:

> Was mich mit ihm verbunden hatte, war zum Teil ein von wenigen bemerkter phantastischer Zug in ihm, *dem in mir etwas Ähnliches entgegenkam.* (SW IV 240; my italics.)

So Hans himself, the apparently impartial listener, is also apt to take refuge in a fantasy life; that being so, he is likely to see the 'phantastischer Zug' not as a weakness but as a virtue, and in consequence he will be more sympathetic to Franz than a 'normal' observer might be. That gives the whole narrative a colour which could well be very misleading; it certainly casts doubt on the respectful judgement of Franz which forms my head-quote — for that judgement is given by Hans, not by Storm or anyone else.

Almost everything in Franz's experience now appears in a new light. To begin with, another of Hans' recollections from student days shows how Franz had then used academic superiority as a pretext for keeping himself from contact with others:

> *Nähere Freunde besaß er, außer etwa mir, fast keine.*
> Die meisten, welche seiner Fakultät angehörten, schien es zu drücken, daß er so schnell und ruhig mit seinem Urteil fertig war, während sie noch an den ersten Schlußfolgerungen klaubten. Einen einfachen Menschen, in dem aber ein tüchtiger Mediziner steckte, frug ich eines Tages: 'Was hast du gegen Franz Jebe, daß du ihm immer aus dem Wege gehst? . .'
> 'Er ist hochmütig!' versetzte er; 'das sind keine Leute für mich . . .' (SW IV 240f; my italics.)

and as Franz himself takes over the narrative ('confessing himself' to Hans), we are given a whole series of signs indicating his fear of human encounter. The memories of his childhood are already shot through with this fear; after going home after school, he says, he always used to turn (or flee?) to animals, going into:

> einen großen abgelegenen Hühnerhof . . , der . . . übrigens außer dem gewöhnlichen Federvieh von mir mit Meeresschweinen und Kaninchen, gezähmten Möwen und Bruushühnern, auch wohl mit gefangenen Ratten und Feldmäusen und anderem unheimlichen Geziefer bevölkert zu werden pflegte; *nach der Schulzeit war das meine liebste Gesellschaft.* (SW IV 244f; my italics.)

At the university the dream stands him in good stead; it becomes more real than reality, and he uses it to avoid involvement with women:

> der Eindruck jener kindlichen Luftgestalt, die ich nur im Traum gesehen hatte, lag unverrückbar im Grunde meiner Seele; keine der halb- oder vollgewachsenen Schönen, die meinen Mitstudenten das Hirn verwirrten, konnten ihn erschüttern . . . mein eigen Nachtgesicht barg ich . . . im Innersten meines Lebens, gleich einem heiligen Keim, den ich vor aller Störung meiner Zukunft zu bewahren hatte. (SW IV 249)

When Franz sets up in practice, the demands of his profession become an excuse for isolating himself:

> Bald mußte ich mir die schwarze Doktorkutsche, bald genug einen Assistenzarzt zulegen;[388] ich wurde der erste Arzt der Stadt und bin es vielleicht auch

jetzt noch. Unter solchen Umständen konnte von einer Teilnahme an geselligem Verkehr nicht viel die Rede sein. (SW IV 250)

He does indeed become friendly with Wilm and Käthe Lenthe, but after Else's death he severs contact with them as well.[389]

I have already indicated how unreal the figure of Else seems, the fleshless incarnation of a dream, and how unsatisfactory the marriage is as a valid human relation. Else and the marriage are indeed facts of Franz's experience (if we dismiss the possibility that he might have invented them); they have happened, and to that extent they are 'real'. But they are right on the edge of reality, always threatening to dissolve into the world of the visionary and fantastic. They are utterly characteristic of Franz as we are seeing him now; they are the nearest he can come to our emotional realities; they constitute his extreme, his boldest, in fact his only venture into what we think of as human experience. His one positive decision and act is to kill his wife; within weeks, he discovers that he need not have done so — so even that one action proves invalid and useless, even killing is reduced almost to an empty gesture.

His reaction to the disaster is quite typical; he withdraws even more completely from the community. Then onto the stage steps the Etatsrätin's daughter, Hilda Roden. Else had always been a misty figure, a spirit rather than a person, generally surrounded with some sort of mystic aura and filling Franz with ecstatic supernatural joy. Hilda forms a contrast so entire that Storm *must* be inviting us to make a comparison. He portrays her briefly but with care, and she emerges as an intensely 'real', full-blooded girl, capable of offering warmer comforts than ecstasy or wonderment:

> Ein junges Mädchen von etwa achtzehn Jahren kam mir bei meinem Eintritt entgegen; frisch, aufrecht, ein Bild der Gesundheit . . . Ein leichtes Rot überzog sekundenlang ihr Antlitz; sie schloß ihre weißen Zähne aufeinander und schüttelte so lebhaft den Kopf, daß der dunkle Zopf, der ihr im Nacken hing, zu beiden Seiten flog; und dabei zuckte aus den braunen Augen, die je zur Seite des feinen Stumpfnäschens saßen, ein fast übermütiges Leuchten . . . Mir war, als flösse aus diesen einfachen Worten ein Strom von Mitleid zu mir herüber, so warm war ihre Stimme . . . Dann fühlte ich einen kräftigen Druck ihrer Hand in der meinen . . . (SW IV 278ff.)

The words are few, and it is hard to find anything remarkable in them individually; yet in the hands of Storm they take on the most wonderful graphic and sensuous significance. The girl rises from the page; we can see her clean beauty and almost smell her freshness; she is indubitably and eminently 'there'. What is poor Franz to do in the face of someone so overwhelmingly real and alive? He is in just the kind of situation which he finds most intolerable.

The attraction is present so obviously as to make even third parties think of a possible match here. Franz takes the way out which is entirely in accordance with what we know of him, the way of rationalisation. And thus we see what is behind the disturbingly mock-heroic tone we saw him adopting when giving his reason for refusing to marry Hilda:

> pfui, pfui! Dies edle Geschöpf zum Mittel einer Heilung zu erniedrigen, es würde nur ein neues Verbrechen sein! (SW IV 285)

The sentiment is noble, but the motive is spurious.

So Franz goes away to Reichenhall; he spends four weeks there before meeting Hans. His life during this tiny period has no narrative significance; it is a mere lull in the action and could easily have been passed over without comment or description. But Storm does not pass over it. He gives us one fact about it, namely that Franz has had no company but that of a pet jackdaw; Hans records:

> zu mir sich wendend, setzte er hinzu: 'Die arme Kreatur ist eifersüchtig; sie hat in den vier Wochen, die ich hier nun zugebracht habe, mich mit niemandem als mit ihr selber reden hören — und die Unvernünftigen haben feinere Ohren als wir Menschen!'
> Ich sah ihn an: solche Intimität zu Tieren hatte ich nie bei ihm vermutet; er mußte sehr vereinsamt sein. (SW IV 248)

So we have come full circle: just as he had done when a child, Franz turns now to animals and away from men. One more brush-stroke is added to our picture of him.

Franz's final escape is to Africa;[390] I call it an escape because the manner in which he announces his decision suggests that he is thinking in terms of going 'away from here' rather than 'to somewhere specific'. He prefaces his announcement with the words, 'Ich gehe fort, weit fort . . .' And we subsequently discover that his life in Africa is characterised above all by solitude, the absence of human contact.

I have listed, more or less in the order in which they appear in the text,[391] nine rejections of real human relationship, or rather eight plus the marriage, which seems to me to be, in its unreality, a rejection in itself. I would think that in their various ways they add up to a complete and convincing picture of Franz as I have suggested him to be. They are too numerous to be dismissed as a creative accident or coincidence which can be left out of account; and what is more, they have a genuine and striking symmetry. Set down just as headwords, in the form of an arrow with the marriage at the point, they look like this:

1. University solitude
　2. Animals
　　3. University girls
　　　4. Solitude of practice
　　　　5. Marriage
　　　6. Solitude of work
　　7. Hilda
　8. Animals
9. African solitude

There is a clear parallelism between 1 and 9, 2 and 8, and so on, and I would claim that this is not something which I have engineered. One might be prepared to accept one coincidence, but it strains credulity to say not only that these rejections (all nine of them) have appeared by accident, but also that they just accidentally happen to have appeared in a pattern. And even if by some extraordinary chance the whole thing *were* an accident, the fact remains that the rejections are there and the pattern is there, and there is nothing Storm or anyone can do about them, short of mangling the text beyond recognition.

We are left, then, with two interpretations of *Ein Bekenntnis:* one on the 'intended' level of responsibility, concerning itself ultimately with the first half of the quotation which heads this chapter:

> Ob eine solche Buße nötig, ob es die rechte war, darüber mag ein jeder nach seinem Innern urteilen . . .

and the other on this odd and new level, casting doubt in effect on the apparently uncontroversial assertion in the second half of the quotation:

> daß mein Freund ein ernster und ein rechter Mann gewesen ist, daran wird niemand zweifeln.

This other interpretation suggests that Franz may be 'ernst', but he is anything but 'recht' — that is, he makes no just estimate of his own inadequacy and therefore does not accord other people their rightful reality. His real fault lies in his nature, not in any criminal or sinful or otherwise immoral act that he may have committed. His 'crime' is that he cannot face the demands of relationship with others and does all he can to avoid such relationship; he is 'punished' for this in that his failings cause the possibilities of human encounter to become progressively fewer and more remote, until even the small encounters he *could* face and be enriched by are denied him. In short, solitude is 'punished' by solitude; to desire it is the crime, to be compelled to suffer it is the penalty. That is the nature of Franz's penance in Africa.

The first interpretation is supported by some external evidence in the shape of letters, and by the surface narrative contained in the text. The second is supported by no external evidence of that sort, but rests on what I think are very powerful indications at all levels in the quality of the text as it stands. Which are we to choose, and what does our choice imply? With those questions in mind, I come to *Der Schimmelreiter,* which seems to me to contain, though in a lesser degree, the same kind of ambiguity.

3. DER SCHIMMELREITER

I shall have less to say about this, Storm's last and longest story. This is partly because there is no obvious 'intended' interpretation by which one can measure one's own ideas (I shall mention in a moment one or two of the interpretations which have been made); and partly because it is not my concern here to offer an exhaustive analysis of *Der Schimmelreiter* — I just want to isolate one thread in the narrative which may have passed unnoticed. This thread has two things in common with the element which seems to me to inform the whole of *Ein Bekenntnis:* first, it suggests a level of causality and responsibility different from the one on which the story seems to be moving; and second, it tends to define this responsibility as arising out of the central character's inadequate relationship with his fellow-men. Hauke's 'crime' is not quite what it appears to be: he errs in that he turns away from other men, and he is 'punished' in kind, by being forced to turn further and further away; and this, partly at least, is what eventually destroys him.

If, in connection with *Der Schimmelreiter,* one asks 'how did this happen and who is to blame?' one gets a variety of answers. Pitrou is content to adopt the judgement of the narrator, the enlightened Schulmeister, though with the proviso that Hauke Haien's work is not invalidated by his destruction:

> Ainsi, une ultime fois, Storm reproduit les motifs dominants dans son oeuvre de prose: il les continue en une puissante synthèse, il les baigne dans le sel rajeunissant de la mer natale. Une ultime fois, il remet aux prises, comme le 'Grüner Heinrich' de Keller, comme Auerbach, Freytag, Spielhagen, Heyse, l'individu supérieur avec une collectivité stupide, et les forces de bien, d'amour que celui-ci incarne triomphent, au moins dans une gloire posthume, de la routine, de la sottise et de la méchanceté grégaires.[392]

Böttger, the East German, puts on his doctrinal spectacles (though elsewhere in his book he takes a sly glance over the top of them now and then) and sees the whole thing in socio-historical terms, as the clash between two great eighteenth-century forces embodied in the Deichgraf and the people. I quote at length what he says, because it is interesting as a phenomenon and also because it contains scattered and passing references to the problem I shall be discussing:

> Der Gegensatz ist ein typischer der Zeit. An ihm enthüllt sich, daß die wissenschaftliche Aufklärung im 18. Jahrhundert keine das ganze Volk umfassende Bewegung darstellte, sondern bloß die mehr oder minder zufällige Errungenschaft vereinzelter Persönlichkeiten. Der Gegensatz zwischen körperlicher und geistiger Arbeit war so groß, daß die Entfremdung zwischen den natur-wissenschaftlich-technisch Gebildeten, die sich zur Durchführung ihrer Pläne vor allem auf die Landesherren und deren Bürokratie stützten, und den Bauern beinahe unerträglicher scheint als die zwischen Feudalherren und Leibeigenen. Auf dem Gegensatz von rationalistischer Einstellung zur Arbeit und traditionalistischem Schlendrian, zu dem auch das Beharren im Aberglauben gehört, ruht der Konflikt der Novelle. An dem riesenhaften Problem der Manufakturperiode, breite Volksschichten, die nur allzusehr an gemütliche Arbeitsverhältnisse und Gleichgültigkeit gegenüber öffentlichen Aufgaben gewöhnt waren, zu Arbeitsdisziplin, Unterordnung und Verständnis für neue technische Methoden und Ziele zu erziehen, scheiterte Hauke Haien. *Freilich fallen auch Schicksal und Charakter des Deichgrafen ins Gewicht.* Aber der ganze Arbeitsstil ist eben der der Zeit, wo nicht überzeugt, sondern vor allem befohlen wird. Er treibt den Deichgrafen in völlige Vereinsamung, die Dorfgenossen in um so finstereren Aberglauben . . .
> In Wirklichkeit ist Hauke Haien ein Mensch des 18. Jahrhunderts, in dem Storm etwas von seiner eigenen Problematik gespiegelt hat; er verkörpert in dieser Hinsicht die Vereinsamung der Intelligenz innerhalb der deutschen

Misere im allgemeinen, der achtundvierziger Intelligenz innerhalb des Bismarck-
reiches im besonderen. *Sein Schicksal zeigt, daß eine Loslösung vom Volk am
Ende zum Untergang führt.* Darin sehen wir aber weniger eine persönliche
Schuld als den Widerspruch einer Gesellschaftsordnung, die an der Bildung
der bäuerlichen Menschen nicht das geringste Interesse hatte, die es nicht
fertigbrachte, die innere Teilnahme an einem großen Gemeinschaftswerk zu
wecken, *und die die Intelligenz in eine volksfremde Isolierung trieb.*[393]

Stuckert is more circumspect.[394] Admittedly, he starts with a purple passage,
claiming that the principal figure in the story is not the living Hauke but the
ghostly Schimmelreiter, and investing this ghost with the most awesome significance:
it is wholly real and yet above reality, 'Hier vollzieht sich die Verwandlung der
Wirklichkeit in den Mythos', all the natural elements combine to form this Wodan-
like god-hero figure, it is indisputably real and active, even the schoolmaster
recognizes its existence, and so on. Then he closes off the flow of rhetoric and
concerns himself with the problem of where the guilt lies. Storm leaves Hauke's
personal guilt in the air, he says; is it that Hauke forbids the new dyke to be
broached? or that he consented to inadequate repairs (this is how Hauke himself
sees his guilt)? or that he did not allow a living thing to be buried in the dyke? or
that he offended man and God by initiating the work in the first place? Stuckert
concludes that there is no explanation on the human or psychological level; he
thinks that Hauke Haien's whole being is an 'uranfängliche Schuld', and that his
death is thus meaningful as a kind of sacrificial gesture. He does not give up his
life only because he cannot bear to live on without his wife and daughter; he
realises that he has offended against a human and superhuman order, and that
that order can only be restored by the sacrifice of his life; he makes this sacrifice
by an act of will, not an act of resignation, and thus in death he is still a free man.
In death also he fulfils the old condition that a living thing must be thrown into the
dyke if the dyke is to hold. But death is not the end for Hauke; his dyke lives on,
and so does he, serving the community by his ghostly appearances. This immortality
has been achieved, not by his service, but by his sacrifice; this is the law of life, its
'absolute Tragik'.

Thus Stuckert on responsibility. He has much more to say, of course, and at one
point[395] he looks in a different way at the processes at work in the story. He sees
Hauke as engaged in three different but intermingling battles. The first is 'der
Kampf gegen die übermächtige Gewalt des Draußen', the age-old struggle of the
Frisian with the sea and its power. The third is 'der Kampf mit dem, was *ihm* als
Schicksal verhängt ist' — that is, the range of personal threats and disasters which he
must face: Elke's illness after giving birth to their daughter Wienke, Wienke's feeble-
mindedness, his own illness and weakening will; it is out of these things that Hauke's
destruction comes — he is broken, not by the sea, but by the death of his wife and
child.

The second battle (and I have left it till last because it points to what I have to say) is a battle against 'die menschliche Gemeinschaft'. In his fight against the sea, Stuckert says, Hauke is working for the community; but he must also work through it, and in so doing he offends against its order; society needs him but cannot bear what he *is*. This is the thread I want to isolate; and if it requires a name, we may call it the thread of Hauke's egocentricity.

In his whole career as Deichgraf, Hauke Haien is guilty of one piece of professional misjudgement. In the summer before the great flood, he rides along the dykes, inspecting them as he goes. The new dyke is intact, but the old one, at the point where it joins the new, is eaten into by the sea and riddled with rodent-burrows. He knows that extensive repairs will be needed if the dyke is to hold, but when he recommends these repairs to his colleagues (especially to his chief opponent Ole Peters) he meets with stubborn resistance and objection to the cost. In his weakness (he has only just risen from his sickbed) Hauke agrees to minor running repairs.[396] On the night of the flood, it becomes evident that the repairs were insufficient, and the old dyke is in danger of being washed away. Ole Peters gives orders for a breach to be made in the new dyke, so as to relieve the pressure on the old one. Hauke finds the men carrying out these orders, and yells for them to stop. They do so, but this causes the pressure to become too great, and the old dyke breaks:

> 'Herr Gott! Ein Bruch! Ein Bruch im alten Deich!'
> 'Euere Schuld, Deichgraf!' schrie eine Stimme aus dem Haufen: 'Euere Schuld! Nehmt's mit vor Gottes Thron!'
> Haukes zornrotes Antlitz war totenbleich geworden . . . in seinem Kopfe wühlten die Gedanken: Was hatte er für Schuld vor Gottes Thron zu tragen? — Der Durchstich des neuen Deichs — vielleicht, sie hätten's fertiggebracht, wenn er sein Halt nicht gerufen hätte; aber — es war noch eins, und es schoß ihm heiß zu Herzen, er wußte es nur zu gut — im vorigen Sommer, hätte damals Ole Peters' böses Maul ihn nicht zurückgehalten — da lag's! Er allein hatte die Schwäche des alten Deichs erkannt; er hätte trotz alledem das neue Werk betreiben müssen: 'Herr Gott, ja, ich bekenn es', rief er plötzlich laut in den Sturm hinaus, 'ich habe meines Amtes schlecht gewartet!'[397]

That, then, is where *Hauke* thinks his guilt lies: in his weakness in consenting to inadequate repairs. But this one error is only the last link in a more complex chain of causality stretching back into Hauke's childhood. He makes this error because he is ill and tired and no longer has the strength to resist the weight of opposition to his plans, opposition crystallised in the figure of Ole Peters. This opposition springs not only from the fact that Hauke's projects are expensive and demanding on the community, but also from Hauke's personal unpopularity. True, Hauke is hounded by the malice of Ole and by superstitious rumour, but the ground for the malice and rumour is already prepared by his unpopularity; and the basis of his unpopularity is a fault or cluster of faults within him, centring round a sort of overweening Ichbezogenheit.

Hauke has a unique talent for angering fate[398] and his fellows by his arrogance and single-minded ambition. The mantle he wears most easily, even when a boy, is the mantle of scorn: when he believes himself in the right, he dogmatizes with total disregard for his own inexperience or the feelings of others. One day he comes home extra late from the dykes, and his father is angry with him:

> 'Du hättest ja versaufen können; die Wasser beißen heute in den Deich'.
> Hauke sah ihn trotzig an.
> — 'Hörst du mich nicht? Ich sag, du hättst versaufen können'.
> 'Ja', sagte Hauke; 'ich bin doch nicht versoffen . . .
> Aber . . . unsere Deiche sind nichts wert! . . die Deiche, sag ich! . . sie taugen nichts, Vater!' (SW IV 296)

And the scorn this small boy pours on the achievements of other men is matched by the way he despises the powers of nature. He mocks at the waves as they crash ineffectually but ceaselessly against the dykes:

> 'Ihr könnt nichts Rechtes', schrie er in den Lärm hinaus, 'so wie die Menschen auch nichts können!' (SW IV 297)

Later, when he comes to work for Deichgraf Volkerts, Hauke stirs up a hornets' nest when he tells his master the names of all the people living by the dykes who have neglected the maintenance work demanded of them. Even the fat and lazy Deichgraf is annoyed at this presumption on the part of his Kleinknecht, and his anger is only diverted when one of Hauke's complaints coincides with a personal grudge of his own. (SW IV 313) Nonetheless, Hauke inevitably treads on many toes in exposing the shortcomings of certain members of the community:

> und die, welche früher im alten Schlendrian fortgesündigt hatten und jetzt unerwartet ihre frevlen oder faulen Finger geklopft fühlten, sahen sich unwillig und verwundert um, woher die Schläge denn gekommen seien. Und Ole, der Großknecht, säumte nicht, möglichst weit die Offenbarung zu verbreiten und dadurch gegen Hauke . . . in diesen Kreisen einen Widerwillen zu erregen. (SW IV 314)

With such a foundation of bad feeling (and such a perfect centre of malice in Ole Peters), it is only natural that the circumstances of Hauke's marriage to Elke and appointment as Deichgraf should be widely interpreted as a piece of opportunism; and in a rather odd way, this malicious interpretation is not far off the mark.

What I mean is that Hauke seems rather more preoccupied with being Deichgraf than with building dykes, less concerned with doing the best for the community than with justifying his appointment to his fellows, and to himself. Certainly, he gives distinguished service to the community; but this service is only a means for him; his ends and his motives are strange and dubious.

This desire for self-justification emerges clearly in the plan to build the new dyke. Hauke first conceived the idea long ago; but the final formulation and the decision to act upon it are a *direct* reaction to Ole Peters' taunts about his marrying

Elke in order to get the Deichgraf's job:

> 'Es muß gehen!' sprach er bei sich selbst. 'Sieben Jahr im Amt; sie sollen nicht sagen, daß ich nur Deichgraf bin von meines Weibes wegen!' (SW IV 341)

And again:

> 'Du sollst mich wenigstens nicht umsonst zum Deichgrafen gemacht haben, Elke; ich will ihnen zeigen, daß ich einer bin!' (SW IV 344)

And later, when Ole accuses him not only of getting the post by marriage rather than merit, but also of building the dyke in order to get more land for himself, Hauke replies:

> 'und willst du Weiteres wissen, das ungewaschene Wort, das dir im Krug vom Mund gefahren, ich sei nur Deichgraf meines Weibes wegen, das hat mich aufgerüttelt, und ich hab euch zeigen wollen, daß ich wohl um meiner selbst willen Deichgraf sein könne; und somit, Ole Peters, hab ich getan, was schon der Deichgraf vor mir hätte tun sollen'. (SW IV 361)

He does what is necessary — what the Deichgraf before him should have done — but this is almost accidental; his real reasons, as he admits himself, are quite different.

Hauke must justify himself to himself as well as to others; he is an Emporkömmling figure, endowed with knowledge and ability but lacking the slowly acquired capacity for wearing the mantle of authority with assurance and calm. His attitude to his power is always coloured by uneasiness; at one point Storm conveys this with absolute economy and wonderful visual effect:

> Er hatte sich in den Lehnstuhl des alten Deichgrafen gesetzt, und seine Hände griffen fest um beide Lehnen. (SW IV 343)

Hauke is seeking strength and confidence from the chair; by assuming this one trapping of authority he is trying to convince himself of his total authority and worth.

As with the chair, so with the dyke. Leaving aside for the moment the symbolic functions of the dyke for us as readers, I want to indicate the peculiar symbolism with which Hauke himself seems to be investing it. He wants it to 'mean' his own validity and success as a man, even his immortality. His name and value, he thinks, will last as long as the dyke stands. If the dyke succeeds in its physical function and protects the community from the sea, then it will also protect Hauke from the charge of failure. His whole life, in fact, is made to depend on it. But this dependence proves ultimately to be mistaken, or misdirected: when disaster comes, it comes from an 'irrelevant' source, a breach in the old dyke. So Hauke's symbol withstands while Hauke himself succumbs; and there is more than a breath of absurdity in that.

All through, Hauke's attitude to the dyke, like his attitude to the position of Deichgraf, is strangely distorted. He wants it to do more for him than it can reasonably be expected to do; he attributes to it powers of emotional and spiritual assurance and protection, when its only possible protectiveness is physical. From the start he sees the dyke as more than it is: normally a sober, clear-sighted man, he is led into an attitude of passionate, intoxicated pride in its success, a pride which tempts fate and alienates his fellows. He can never weigh up its pros and cons with complete sobriety; as he stands on the shore and envisages the prospect of fertile new land created by the projected dyke, we read:

> Wie ein Rausch stieg es ihm ins Gehirn. (SW IV 342)

Later, when he hears the land behind his dyke called, for the first time, the 'Hauke-Haien-Koog', his reactions are described in this extraordinarily 'hybristic' passage:

> In seinen Gedanken wuchs fast der neue Deich zu einem achten Weltwunder; in ganz Friesland war nicht seinesgleichen! Und er ließ den Schimmel tanzen; ihm war, er stünde inmitten aller Friesen; er überragte sie um Kopfeshöhe, und seine Blicke flogen scharf und mitleidig über sie hin. (SW IV 374)

And some time after that, he rides out over the dyke with his daughter Wienke; she is frightened by the sea:

> 'Es tut mir nichts', sagte sie zitternd, 'nein, sag, daß es uns nichts tun soll; du kannst das, und dann tut es uns auch nichts!'
>   'Nicht ich kann das, Kind', entgegnete Hauke ernst; 'aber der Deich, auf dem wir reiten, der schützt uns, und den hat dein Vater ausgedacht und bauen lassen'. (SW IV 379)

He is delegating to the dyke the responsibility for protecting himself and his family; and more than this, there is again a sort of hybris in the way he assumes practically sole credit for the creation of the dyke — the word 'lassen' is the only concession he makes to the fact that it is not his own unaided achievement.

I have said that Hauke's whole life depends on the dyke. There is a brief and quiet echo of this idea, and a premonition of the disaster to come, in the scene where Hauke surveys the damage and erosion in the old dyke. He imagines what the only solution would be in the event of a storm-tide:

> Hauke fühlte sein Herz stillstehen, sein sonst so fester Kopf schwindelte; er sprach es nicht aus, aber in ihm sprach es stark genug: Dein Koog, der Hauke-Haien-Koog, müßte preisgegeben und der neue Deich durchstochen werden! (SW IV 385)

The prospect of his dyke being robbed of its effectiveness is enough to rob Hauke momentarily of *his* intellectual effectiveness (his head spins), and even of his capacity to live (his heart stands still).

Even at the end, all Hauke's emotions are subordinated to an almost hysteric joy that his dyke is holding and will always hold:

> sein Deich aber — und wie ein Stolz flog es ihm durch die Brust —, der Hauke-Haien-Deich, wie ihn die Leute nannten, der mochte jetzt beweisen, wie man Deiche bauen müsse! . . 'Der soll schon stehen!' murmelte er, und wie ein Lachen stieg es in ihm herauf. (SW IV 396)

Ein unwillkürliches Jauchzen brach aus des Reiters Brust: 'Der Hauke-Haien-Deich, er soll schon halten; er wird es noch nach hundert Jahren tun!' (SW IV 399)

Hauke, it seems to me, relies too much on his dyke for his 'salvation', which, as a thing of earth and straw, it cannot give him. He imagines that his validity among men, his success as a social being, can rest solely on this inanimate creation. But this is not so; and here we have arrived at the same problem as is present in *Ein Bekenntnis*. The community requires more; it demands from Hauke something he is not prepared to give: a committed entry into the lives of those around him, partly manifested in mundane things like simple sociability, tolerance for others' views, respect for others' reality. Hauke is willing to *serve* the community, but for one reason or another he cannot *engage* himself in it. His service is invalidated if he despises those whom he serves (and there are strong indications that he does)[399] and will not identify himself with them. He never achieves this identification; whether through circumstance or inclination he is always more or less isolated from his fellows. The text is full of references to this isolation: it is present already in his boyhood:

> Und der Junge karrte; aber den Euklid hatte er allzeit in der Tasche, und wenn die Arbeiter ihr Frühstück oder Vesper aßen, saß er auf seinem umgestülpten Schubkarren mit dem Buche in der Hand. Und wenn im Herbst die Fluten höher stiegen und manch ein Mal die Arbeit eingestellt werden mußte, dann ging er nicht mit den andern nach Haus, sondern blieb . . . (SW IV 295)

> Stand eine Springflut bevor, so konnte man sicher sein, er lag trotz Sturm und Wetter draußen am Deiche mutterseelenallein. (SW IV 297)

> Mit denen zu verkehren, die mit ihm auf der Schulbank gesessen hatten, fiel ihm nicht ein; auch schien es, als ob ihnen an dem Träumer nichts gelegen sei. (SW IV 298)

> So für sich, und am liebsten nur mit Wind und Wasser und mit den Bildern der Einsamkeit verkehrend, wuchs Hauke zu einem langen, hageren Burschen auf. (SW IV 300)

And when Hauke grows up and becomes (in theory) a full member of the community, there is still no contact. The causes are different, but the effect is the same:

> Sein Verkehr mit anderen Menschen außer in Arbeit und Geschäft verschwand fast ganz; selbst der mit seinem Weibe wurde immer weniger. (SW IV 345)

> es war doch trotz aller lebendigen Arbeit eine Einsamkeit um ihn, und in seinem Herzen nistete sich ein Trotz und abgeschlossenes Wesen gegen andere Menschen ein. (SW IV 367)

> Fortan lebte er einsam seinen Pflichten als Hofwirt wie als Deichgraf und denen, die ihm am nächsten angehörten; die alten Freunde waren nicht mehr in der Zeitlichkeit, neue zu erwerben war er nicht geeignet. (SW IV 375)

This absence (or avoidance) of contact combines with Hauke's alienating criticisms, plans and manner to put him outside the society he serves. It is probably his greatest flaw; it renders his life's work useless because it produces a resistance to his plans which results in their coming to nothing. And more than this, it is — as we saw it to be for Franz Jebe — at once his crime and his punishment; for he seems dimly to feel his solitude and sense his inadequacy, and he seeks comfort increasingly in his relationship with his wife and child, most strikingly with Wienke:

> an der Wiege seines Kindes lag er abends und morgens auf den Knien, als sei dort die Stätte seines ewigen Heils. (SW IV 367)

> 'So, mein Wienke' — und das Kind vernahm wohl nicht den Ton von heftiger Innigkeit in seinen Worten —, 'so, wärm dich bei mir! Du bist doch unser Kind, unser einziges. Du hast uns lieb . . . !' Die Stimme brach dem Manne; aber die Kleine drückte zärtlich ihr Köpfchen in seinen rauhen Bart. (SW IV 383)

This, as much as his death, is the penalty Hauke pays; he is sentenced to the realisation of his loneliness. It is a calamity that his daughter is feeble-minded; but it is a greater calamity that all Hauke's desire for relationship for himself and Elke must be concentrated into this one weak vessel, which Stuckert with rare perception calls the "letztes und höchstes Erzeugnis von Storms Überzeugung der 'Geworfenheit des Menschen' ".[400] 'Du hast uns lieb' — nobody else does.

I want to take one more look at the dyke as it appears to us from this other level of responsibility, and to point out a parallelism. Hauke's new dyke and the old one meet end to end and form a continuous wall. At the place where they meet there is a Priel, a natural sandy channel through which the sea-water had originally run round the old dyke. The joining of the two dykes involves the blocking-up of the Priel, and this is the greatest technical problem Hauke has to face in building his new dyke. There is a superstition among the people that the Priel will reopen unless something living is thrown into it as it is blocked. Someone throws in a stray dog; Hauke is furious, rescues the dog and orders that nothing of the kind be repeated. The damage and erosion in the old dyke (which I have frequently mentioned) is in fact situated at the point where the two dykes meet, and is largely caused by the reopening of the Priel. This is where, on the night of the storm-tide, the old dyke bursts after the attempt has been made to broach the new one. Elke and Wienke are drowned by the water rushing through the breach, and Hauke throws himself and his horse into it.

All that seems to me strikingly symbolic of the tragedy of Hauke Haien. He is the new dyke, the community is the old. He and the community stand side by side; their common safety and mutual usefulness depend on how they are joined. Hauke's greatest difficulty is in grafting himself onto the community; he will not accept the community's demand that he cement the join by throwing *himself*, his own living personality, into it. He tries to make do with a patchwork join, a relationship based on professional service, authority and force (he will serve, and serve well, but he will not commit himself). But it is a woefully weak connection, constantly eroded by old differences and present strains. When the great emergency comes, the community finds itself endangered by Hauke's very existence; it tries to destroy him, but Hauke will not be destroyed. The only thing left is for the relation to be severed, for Hauke to be cast off. The floods of loneliness and alienation stream in between Hauke and the community, and in them the man and his whole family go under. Hauke dead can no longer possibly achieve any human relation with the community; but he can still serve, in a manner comparable in its limitation to his service while alive: his dyke stands, and his ghost acts as a sentinel for posterity.

So once again we have a split level of responsibility, two[401] sets of answers to the questions 'How did this happen and who is to blame?' As I said, it is not as easy to discern a clear 'intended' interpretation here as it was with *Ein Bekenntnis*; but we can be reasonably sure that Storm 'means' us to see the story more or less in the way that Pitrou (*pace* the Schulmeister) sees it:[402] as the tragedy of the strong, clear-sighted individual who is marked off from society by his intelligence and enlightenment, and steadily ground down by the mob forces of superstition, malice and gossip. This other interpretation calls the mob 'the community' and sees it in a warmer light; it suggests that Hauke's isolation and downfall are born of his weakness and inadequacy, not of his strength; it is a fault, not a virtue, that he cannot integrate himself into the social order. I would claim again for this interpretation that it is there in the text and can be arrived at without too free or too perverse a use of the imagination; that there can be a genuine response on this level; and that it raises much the same problems as were raised in my examination of *Ein Bekenntnis*. As before, I see no way in which recognition of these problems can be avoided, save by mangling the text or simply ignoring large chunks of it.

4. CONCLUSIONS

In the picture which has emerged from this discussion of *Ein Bekenntnis* and *Der Schimmelreiter*, there are two features in particular that relate closely to certain arguments contained in the rest of my study. I want to end by isolating these features and drawing one or two more conclusions from them about the nature of Storm's art.

The first feature, obviously is the difficulty of finding more than a very tenuous link between the author's apparent intention in these stories and the reader's (or rather my) response to them as they stand. How does this dichotomy arise? Looking back at *Ein Bekenntnis* (since it is the clearer case), I would suggest that the process is something like this. We arrive at what seems to be an 'intended' interpretation by looking at the evident facts of the story, then by turning to biographical sources — in this case Storm's correspondence with Heyse — which might tell us what the author had in mind at the time he was writing, whether he feels he has been successful in expressing what was in his mind, whether he has had any second thoughts about it since, what influences or considerations he was moved by, and so on. The facts of the story and the statements of intention in the letters more or less coincide. But the interpretation into which they coalesce is somehow not satisfactory: there are too many loose ends, inconsistencies and false tones. So we put aside the letters and the summary of the action, and go to the text itself, moving around in it and trying to find what is there. After a while a pattern begins to emerge, and in this pattern we find a new psychopathology for Franz, a different characterisation of him. When the story is looked at in this light, it becomes (so it seems to me) illuminating and enriching in a number of ways: we gain an insight into the workings of the minds of men like Franz and into the nature of the suffering that may befall them because of their inadequacy; we find a literary satisfaction in the way Franz is subtly and insistently revealed for what he is, through his own words and the judgements of his biased confessor; and we have a formal, 'stylistic' pleasure in the symmetry with which his various rejections and escapes are presented. And yet a disquiet remains. It would be so much better if we could find something which proved that this is what Storm *meant* us to see in his story; but we can't, and the only credentials we have for persisting in our interpretation are faith in our own judgement and appeal to the text.

Ein Bekenntnis raises once again, and in very acute form, the problem which has beset me through this whole study of Storm's fiction — the problem of justifying, by the available external evidence, conclusions which suggest themselves insistently in the stories as absolute entities. Each of my three chapters is in its particular way an instance of the difference between what seems to have been intended and what is in fact achieved (with the rider that I have found the achievement usually much more considerable than the intention). The bleak world of the early stories — the chronicle of attachments whose failure is seemingly inevitable, the doubt about the efficacy of human will and action, the grey and sterile life of solitude which is these people's, and somehow all people's lot — that world is nowhere described in letters, theoretical writings or known conversations (indeed, one would be quite hard put to it to find Storm giving substance in his own words to the critical cliché that his early work is 'about' loneliness). The solipsistic vision — the breaking-up of received notions of reality, the imprisonment within the self's consciousness, the mocking echo which is the only answer to the anxious call for assurance — that vision is nowhere set out as a logical system or even as a conscious way of looking at life. The second level of responsibility — the efforts of Franz Jebe and Hauke Haien vitiated by their inability to recognize, respect and foster the reality of (to 'love') their fellow human beings — that level cannot be shown to have been in Storm's mind when he wrote his two last stories. And yet that world and that vision and that level *are* there (that, at least, is my claim); and they arise clearly out of the living and immediate relation between the reader and what is read, and they become part of what I take to be a fundamental literary experience — that of seeing an existence, and possible ways of living in that existence, created and acted out in an achieved artistic whole and in a manner relevant to life as we know it.

It is hard to believe that the whole effect could be accidental (particularly hard in view of the formal qualities of *Ein Bekenntnis*), and I don't think my interpretations are based on a wholesale misreading of the texts. So, putting those two possibilities aside, we seem to be left with another two. First, Storm could have kept deliberately and completely quiet about his real preoccupations, confiding them to no letter or journal, no friend or relative. If this were so, we should have to treat the views he actually does express as conscious attempts to cover the trail or lay a false one. We could perhaps put this construction on certain statements of the kind I have mentioned here and there, statements answering correspondents' criticisms of his work: the vague and unfulfilled promise to recast,[403] or the regretful refusal to do so because 'it's too late now'.[404] This could be Storm's mild-mannered way of saying, 'The point you object to is all part of my intention, and I shall certainly not change it; your criticism shows that you do not really understand what I am driving at'. Perhaps also he could have left his 'real' intentions out of his journal *Was der Tag gibt* because he wanted his stories to speak entirely for themselves without their author's mediation. But all that is improbable: the thought of him systematically keeping his own counsel for forty years is not consonant with what we know of this gregarious, 'other-directed'[405] and voluble man.

The second possibility is that with writers like Storm we may have to postulate some deeper level of intention, a coherence and unity which their work displays but which they themselves do not consciously recognize. This is presumably what is meant by saying that a certain writer is not a good critic of his own work. I have several times drawn attention to what seemed to me to be indications of a lack of artistic self-awareness on Storm's part, indications that certain modes of writing come to him so naturally that he hardly knows he is using them.[406] This must be fairly common in literature; why else should, for example, Thomas Mann or Henry James stand out as writers of a specially 'conscious' creativity? With Storm, certainly, one usually has the feeling that he 'gets his story right' by relying on some internal barometer whose mechanism he does not understand and is not really concerned about, so long as it keeps working. And as for 'interpreting' his own works or discussing their 'meaning', his reaction seems to be rather like that of lyric poets as T.S. Eliot describes them, men who write a poem as a kind of formulating exorcism, and then say to what they have created: 'Go away! Find a place for yourself in a book — and don't expect *me* to take any further interest in you'.[407]

I have been principally concerned with what Storm's barometer points him towards, and have found only marginal need to ask *why* the barometer should be as it is and point the way it does. For that, I suppose, one would have to go to Storm's life and situation, and look for social, economic, political or historical reasons, or for an early trauma or for Dilthey's 'Grunderlebnis'. Such an approach might well lead to the same conclusions as I have reached about Storm; if it did, then we could perhaps say that the external evidence *does* after all coincide with the textual interpretation — the point being that, here at least, in looking at letters and statements of intention, we happened to be relying on the wrong sort of evidence.

The other feature that is contained in the picture I have drawn of Storm's later world, the world of ambiguous responsibility, is the notion of 'responsibility' itself. The fact that the word has been at all meaningful in this context is already an indication that the picture in these stories is subtly but decisively different from the one we saw in those earlier works, *Immensee, Drüben am Markt* and the rest. Storm's early stories, I suggested, portray a world more or less dominated by a force, rather like gravity only stronger, which draws men apart from their fellows and down as far as they can go, that is, to the state of being alone (only death, I imagine, can take the process of division and dissolution further). This force is somehow absolute in its operation: it seems at first to prevail within a logical scheme of cause and effect (that is, we think we can see sensible reasons why this or that relationship fails), but ultimately it is shown to prevail independently of that scheme (that is, the reasons turn out to be not quite adequate, or even 'absurdly' inadequate), and we are left with an axiom, a proposition beyond which rational reflection has no place — the axiom that the force prevails because it *must* prevail. To say, as I have done before,[408] that this is a kind of fatalism, is strictly correct, but the word is misleading in its tone: the immense merit of Storm's art is that it almost always leads us to think, not about 'Fate' or the 'World-order' but about 'the way things are', not about 'Man' but about 'people', not about 'Life' but about 'living'; the whole posture is unheroic.[409] A modest sort of fatalism, then; and it implies, both logically and in the practice of the stories, that the way of things is something about which not much can be *done*. The force is likely to override individual will;[410] a man has little control over the shaping of his life; he can offer little resistance and plan no effective defence, because the power that opposes him does not play to the rules (works, that is, independently of discoverable cause and effect). That is why it is wrong to complain that Reinhard, or Fränzchen, or the Doktor, or Ehrhard, or Agnes,[411] should have got up and *done* something about their situation; the great trouble is that they can hardly be said to have a 'situation' in the normal sense, except that of not knowing, and being unable to find out, what is going on. The forces ranged against them are mostly nebulous and shifting and shown (if shown at all) not to be susceptible to conquest by human action; that is what changes Reinhard from a boy who doesn't believe in angels and wants to catch lions into a 'passive' and ineffectual man, or what changes Fränzchen from an energetic and independent young woman into a wasting, silent, uncomplaining figure. And because, for example, the characterisation of Reinhard and Elisabeth is so sparse as to accord them hardly any important distinguishing feature beyond the fact that they are human, a general implication is made; we have the sense of being told, not 'This is what happened to Reinhard and Elisabeth', but 'This is what happens to everyone'.

But now, in discussing *Ein Bekenntnis* and *Der Schimmelreiter,* we can talk about responsibility and we can say 'This is what happened to Franz and Hauke (not everyone), and this is perhaps why it happened'. These two men are built in a particular way, with individual virtues and shortcomings, and it is their personal response to a well-defined situation that determines, to some degree, the course of their lives. That is as much as to say that the response of some other kind of personality to the same situation would have caused things to turn out differently, and therefore that the shaping of events and destinies is at least partly dependent on the nature of the individual involved in them.

This is not evidence for a simple 'belief in free will'. Franz and Hauke are not, it seems to me, entirely at liberty to decide which way to act at any given point. What they do is largely conditioned by what they are, and there is little chance of their changing their temperament by an act of will. They are of course not 'passive'; both of them are full of drive; but I mean that they cannot do much to affect the source and direction of their drive. Part of the achievement of these two stories is in the conviction they press that Franz and Hauke could not be conceived of as adopting any course of action other than the one they do adopt. If they acted differently, they would be quite different people; and to that extent what happens to them is inevitable and not a matter of untrammelled will.

But there is a kind of choice. Franz and Hauke could not be conceived of as acting differently, but other human beings could; and that indicates a real human possibility. The suggestion that these particular men are cut off from committed contact with their fellow-men does not carry with it, as the earlier 'fatalistic' view did, the implication that this kind of contact is out of human reach. It *can* be achieved, and the fact that these two do not achieve it is due to their particular inadequacy, not to a general limitation on men. The forces tending to separate people from each other are no longer seen as insuperable; the wall is lower now[412] (or men are taller), and human beings adequately equipped can get across it. And when I talk of the issue being a 'moral' one, of Franz and Hauke being 'to blame' for their misfortunes, bearing 'responsibility' or being 'punished for their crime', I mean that their equipment for living is shown to be less than adequate, that their humanity falls short of what is demonstrated to be possible. Given their temperament, which is not changeable by their will, they have no choice but to act as they do and to fail; but a 'better' temperament could have led another man to act differently and to succeed. It is not 'their fault' — and yet the fault lies in them. It is no longer a fault that need be in every one of us, no longer a deficiency of all human nature.

This paradox of conditioned choice is matched by that turning outwards which I have suggested is present in Storm's later work in general, as a hesitant, provisional answer to the solipsistic doubt.[413] The commitment that Franz and Hauke will not make is precisely the leap across the chasm; and the fact that they will not make the leap suggests that now the leap can and ought to be made. And that change, from an unsteady world of human powerlessness to a more stable world where human beings have a measure of control, constitutes an advance in the estimate of the worth of men and the value of living. For by transcending the bounds of that early world, Storm gives hope that our impotence is less than total, that it *does* matter what we are and what we do. And that hope is the finer for having been carved out of hopelessness.

APPENDIX A

I would divide the 46 stories which Goldammer calls 'Novellen' (rather than 'Märchen' or 'Spukgeschichten') in the following way (NR = not a Rahmenerzählung):

	'Mainstream'		'Departures'
	Marthe und ihre Uhr	NR	Im Saal (political idyll)
	Immensee	NR	Posthuma (psychological freak sketch)
	Im Sonnenschein		Ein grünes Blatt (political idyll)
	Auf dem Staatshof	NR	Angelika ('subjective' in special sense)
	Drüben am Markt	NR	Wenn die Äpfel reif sind (comic)
	Im Schloß		Späte Rosen (happy resolution, 'literary')
	Auf der Universität	NR	Veronika (religious theme)
	Abseits	NR	Unter dem Tannenbaum (political idyll)
	In St Jürgen		Von jenseit des Meeres (happy resolution)
	Eine Halligfahrt		Eine Malerarbeit ('Künstlernovelle')
	Draußen im Heidedorf	NR	Beim Vetter Christian (comic)
	Pole Poppenspäler	NR	Viola tricolor (happy resolution)
NR	Waldwinkel	NR	Psyche ('Classical', happy resolution)
	Ein stiller Musikant	NR	Die Söhne des Senators (happy resolution)
	Im Nachbarhause links	NR	Schweigen (happy resolution)
	Aquis submersus	NR	Bötjer Basch (happy resolution)
NR	Carsten Curator		
	Renate		
NR	Zur 'Wald- und Wasserfreude'		
	Im Brauerhause		
	Eekenhof		
	Der Herr Etatsrat		
NR	Hans und Heinz Kirch		
	Zur Chronik von Grieshuus		
	'Es waren zwei Königskinder'		
	John Riew'		
	Ein Fest auf Haderslevhuus		
	Ein Doppelgänger		
	Ein Bekenntnis		
	Der Schimmelreiter		

There is a clear correlation between stories 'in the mainstream' and those that are Rahmenerzählungen.

APPENDIX B

The 46 'Novellen' can be divided into two groups:
(a) those narrated by a fully embodied person who is involved in the action, and
(b) those narrated, at least in part, by a fictional intelligence.

Group (a)	*Group (b)*
Marthe und ihre Uhr	Im Saal
Ein grünes Blatt	Immensee
Auf dem Staatshof	Posthuma
Späte Rosen	Im Sonnenschein
Auf der Universität	Angelika
Von jenseit des Meeres	Wenn die Äpfel reif sind
In St Jürgen	Drüben am Markt
Eine Malerarbeit	Veronika
Eine Halligfahrt	Im Schloß
Draußen im Heidedorf	Unter dem Tannenbaum
Beim Vetter Christian	Abseits
Pole Poppenspäler	Viola tricolor
Ein stiller Musikant	Waldwinkel
Im Nachbarhause links	Psyche
Aquis submersus	Carsten Curator
Renate	Zur 'Wald- und Wasserfreude'
Im Brauerhause	Eekenhof
Der Herr Etatsrat	Die Söhne des Senators
Zur Chronik von Grieshuus	Hans und Heinz Kirch
'Es waren zwei Königskinder'	Schweigen
John Riew'	Ein Fest auf Haderslevhuus
Bötjer Basch	
Ein Doppelgänger	
Ein Bekenntnis	
Der Schimmelreiter	

The first paragraph of *Der Schimmelreiter* makes it an ambiguous case, but since it contains two fully-embodied narrators beside the 'ich' of that paragraph, it seems fair to make it a part of group (a).

APPENDIX C

The 21 stories which are narrated, at least in part, by a 'fictional intelligence' (group (b) of the previous appendix) can be divided thus, according to the way the names are established:

Names discovered in dialogue	*Names 'given' by omniscient narrator*
	1848 Im Saal
1849 Immensee	
1850 Posthuma	
1854 Im Sonnenschein	
1855 Angelika	
1856 Wenn die Äpfel reif sind	
1861 Drüben am Markt	
1861 Veronika	
1861 Im Schloß	
1862 Unter dem Tannenbaum	
1863 Abseits	
1873 Viola tricolor	
1874 Waldwinkel	
1875 Psyche	
	1877 Carsten Curator
	1878 Zur 'Wald- und Wasserfreude'
	1879 Eekenhof
	1880 Die Söhne des Senators
	1882 Hans und Heinz Kirch
1883 Schweigen	
	1885 Ein Fest auf Haderslevhuus

Im Saal is a very early and minuscule family/political idyll, hardly a story at all. In *Schweigen,* only one name is discovered, the rest are given.

Apart, then, from these two exceptions (both of which have an element tending to disqualify them as exceptions), the chronological division is absolutely consistent: in *all* stories of this kind written before 1875, the names are discovered in dialogue; and in *all* stories of this kind written after 1877, the names are given by an omniscient narrator. And of course, this chronology applies fairly closely also to the other indications these stories give (how character, relationship, provenance, etc., are established) which imply omniscience, or lack of it, in their narrators.

APPENDIX D

David Hume's scepticism, pursued with conscientious and to this day unrefuted logic, led him beyond Berkeley to a point where all reason for living and thinking vanished. He saved himself, as it were, only by commitment to priorities other than logical truth. Towards the end of the first book of his *Treatise of Human Nature*, he expresses the somewhat stunning opinion that the only justification for the study of philosophy is the pleasure it affords to those with a predilection for it. 'Nay', he says, 'if we are philosophers, it ought only to be on sceptical principles, and from an inclination we feel to be employing ourselves after that manner'. And again: '(If I abandoned philosophy) I *feel* I should be a loser in point of pleasure; and this is the origin of my philosophy'. (*Treatise*, Book I, part iv, sec. ii; Hume's italics).

The second book of the *Treatise* deals with passions, and the third with morals — evidence enough that Hume ultimately commits himself to the living of life, the practical realities of experience, no matter how shaky the logical foundation for those realities might be. He dismisses his solipsistic scepticism very much in terms of 'being meant to embrace the illusion' or following 'the rules of the game of experience' (cf. above, p. 138). Bertrand Russell (in his *History of Western Philosophy*, London 1946, n.e. 1961, p. 644f) quotes, in addition to the sentences above, the following three passages, which seem to me classically to sum up the position of 'rejection by appeal to experience' (Hume's italics throughout):

> Nature, by an absolute and uncontrollable necessity, has determined us to judge as well as to breathe and feel; nor can we any more forbear viewing certain objects in a stronger and fuller light, upon account of their customary connection with a present impression, than we can hinder ourselves from thinking as long as we are awake, or seeing the surrounding bodies, when we turn our eyes towards them in broad sunshine. Whoever has taken the pains to refute this *total* scepticism, has really disputed without an antagonist, and endeavoured by arguments to establish a faculty, which nature has antecedently planted in the mind, and rendered unavoidable.
>
> (*Treatise*, Book I, part iv, sec. i).

> The sceptic still continues to reason and believe, even though he asserts that he cannot defend his reason by reason; and by the same rule he must assent to the principle concerning the existence of body, tho' he cannot pretend by any arguments of philosophy to maintain its veracity ... We may well ask, *what causes us to believe in the existence of body*? But 'tis vain to ask, *whether there be body or not?* That is a point, which we must take for granted in all our reasonings.
>
> (*Treatise*, Book I, part iv, sec. ii).

This sceptical doubt, both with respect to reason and the senses, is a malady, which can never be radically cured, but must return upon us every moment, however we may chase it away, and sometimes may seem entirely free from it . . . Carelessness and inattention alone can afford us any remedy. For this reason I rely entirely on them; and take it for granted, whatever may be the reader's opinion at this present moment, that an hour hence he will be persuaded that there is both an external and internal world.

(*Treatise*, Book I, part iv, sec. ii).

This third passage is particularly interesting in the present context, for it accords very closely in mood and content with the much-quoted words from the conclusion of Storm's cycle of ghost stories, *Am Kamin* (1861):

'Wenn wir uns recht besinnen, so lebt doch die Menschenkreatur, jede für sich, in fürchterlicher Einsamkeit; ein verlorener Punkt in dem unermessenen und unverstandenen Raum. Wir vergessen es; aber mitunter dem Unbegreif-lichen und Ungeheueren gegenüber befällt uns plötzlich das Gefühl davon; und das, dächte ich, wäre etwas von dem, was wir Grauen zu nennen pflegen'. (SW I 319)

That little speech is a critical favourite; it pops up time and again in works on Storm and usually seems to be quoted in order to 'prove' that he didn't like being on his own. Seen in a 'solipsistic' light, though, it takes on a new relevance. 'Wenn wir uns recht besinnen' — there is the use of reason; 'jede für sich in fürchterlicher Einsamkeit' — there is the sceptical anxiety about the existence and accessibility of other minds; 'in dem unermessenen und unverstandenen Raum' — there is the doubt about the external world, its nature and causalities; 'Wir vergessen es' — there is Hume's 'chasing it away' and seeming sometimes 'entirely free from it' and the 'carelessness and inattention' he is so dependent on; 'mitunter . . . befällt uns plötzlich das Gefühl davon' — there, with opposite emphasis, is Hume's 'sceptical doubt' which 'must return upon us every moment'; 'Grauen' — there is Hume's 'malady which can never be radically cured'.

Strictly speaking, there is no justification for claiming that the passage necessarily represents Storm's own attitude: it is spoken by an 'alter Herr', a character in the Rahmen, and another character rejects it immediately as 'Unsinn!' — whose side, then, is Storm on? There is nothing to tell us for certain. I only suggest that it *is* a true expression of his attitude (and incidentally one of the very few explicit 'philosophical' pronouncements that appear anywhere in his work) because all the other evidence I have talked about points in the same direction.

BIBLIOGRAPHY

An almost complete bibliography up to the mid-1950's can be obtained from the use of the following three sources in conjunction:

E.O. Wooley, *Studies in Theodor Storm*, Bloomington, Indiana 1943.

C.A. Bernd, 'Die gegenwärtige Theodor-Storm-Forschung, eine Bibliographie', in *Schriften der Theodor-Storm-Gesellschaft*, 3 (1954), p. 60ff.

H. Gebauer, 'Beitrag zur Storm-Bibliographie' in *Schriften der Theodor-Storm-Gesellschaft*, 5 (1956), p. 60f.

The bibliography which follows is confined to works referred to in my text and notes.

1. STORM'S WORKS

Theodor Storm, Sämtliche Werke in 4 Bänden, hrsg. P. Goldammer, Berlin 1956.

2. CORRESPONDENCE

Th. Storm, Nachgelassene Schriften, hrsg. G. Storm, Band I, 'Briefe an seine Braut', Brunswick 1915.

Th. Storm, Briefe an seine Frau, hrsg. G. Storm, Brunswick n.d. (1915).

Th. Storms Briefe in die Heimat aus den Jahren 1853-64, hrsg. G. Storm, Berlin 1907.

Th. Storm, Briefe an seine Kinder, hrsg. G. Storm, Brunswick n.d. (1915).

Th. Storm, Briefe an Dorothea Jensen und an Georg Westermann, mitgeteilt von E. Lüpke, Brunswick 1942.

E. Esmarch, *Aus Briefen Th. Storms, ein Beitrag zu seinem Leben und seinen Schriften* (in 'Monatsblätter für deutsche Literatur', hrsg. A. Warneke, 7.Jg, 1902/3).

Th. Storm, Briefe an seine Freunde Hartmuth Brinkmann und Wilhelm Petersen, hrsg. G. Storm, Brunswick 1917.

Storm-Fontane, Briefe der Dichter und Erinnerungen von Th. Fontane, hrsg. E. Gülzow, 1948.

Th. Storms Briefe an Klaus Groth, hrsg. C. Jenssen, in *Schriften der Theodor-Storm-Gesellschaft*, 4 (1955).

Der Briefwechsel zwischen Paul Heyse und Th. Storm, hrsg. G. Plotke, Munich 1917-18. (2 vols.).

Der Briefwechsel zwischen Th. Storm und Gottfried Keller, hrsg. P. Goldammer, Berlin 1960.

Briefwechsel zwischen Th. Storm und Emil Kuh, hrsg. P. Kuh, *Westermanns Monatshefte*, Bd.67, 1889-90.

Th. Storms Briefe an seinen Freund Georg Lorenzen, hrsg. C. Höfer, Leipzig 1923.

Briefwechsel zwischen Th. Storm und E. Mörike, hrsg. H. Rath, Stuttgart n.d. (1919).

Blätter der Freundschaft. Aus dem Briefwechsel zwischen Th. Storm und Ludwig Pietsch, mitgeteilt von V. Pauls, 2.Auflage, Heide in Holstein n.d. (1943).

Th. Storm, Ein rechtes Herz, sein Leben in Briefen dargestellt von B. Loets, Leipzig n.d. (1945)

3. MONOGRAPHS

C.A. Bernd, *Theodor Storm's Craft of Fiction*, Chapel Hill, N. Carolina 1963.

F. Böttger, *Th. Storm in seiner Zeit*, Berlin n.d. (1958).

W. Kayser, *Bürgerlichkeit und Stammestum in Th. Storms Novellendichtung*, Berlin 1938.

E.A. McCormick, *Th. Storm's Novellen*, Chapel Hill, N. Carolina 1964.

R. Pitrou, *La vie et l'oeuvre de Th. Storm*, Paris 1920.

Therese Rockenbach, *Th. Storm's Chroniknovellen*, Brunswick 1916.

G. Storm, *Th. Storm, ein Bild seines Lebens*, 2 Bde., Berlin 1912-13.

F. Stuckert, *Th. Storm, sein Leben und seine Welt*, Bremen 1955.

L.W. Wedberg, *The Theme of Loneliness in Th. Storm's Novellen*, The Hague 1964.

4. SHORTER PIECES, ARTICLES ON STORM

M.A. McHaffie & J.M. Ritchie, "Bee's Lake, or the Curse of Silence — A Study of Th. Storm's 'Immensee' ", *German Life & Letters*, N.S. 16 (1962-3), 36-48.

W.F. Mainland, 'Theodor Storm', in *German Men of Letters*, ed. A. Natan, vol. I, London 1961.

Thomas Mann, 'Theodor Storm', in *Gesammelte Werke in 12 Bden*, S. Fischer Verlag 1960, Bd. IX, p. 246ff.

J.W. Smeed, 'Theodor Storm and his Reading Public, Some Cases of Editorial Interference', *Durham University Journal*, June 1960, p. 125ff.

5. BOOKS ENCOMPASSING STORM

E.K. Bennett, *A History of the German Novelle*, 2nd edn., rev. H.M. Waidson, Cambridge 1961.

E. Feise, *Xenion, Essays in the History of German Literature*, Baltimore 1950.

Th. Fontane, *Von Zwanzig bis Dreißig* (Gesammelte Werke, Jubiläumsausgabe, Berlin 1920, 2.Reihe, vol. ii).

F. Martini, *Deutsche Literatur im bürgerlichen Realismus* 1848-98, Epochen der deutschen Literatur, 1962.

W. Silz, *Realism and Reality, Studies in the German Novelle of Poetic Realism,* Chapel Hill, N. Carolina 1954.

R. Taylor & M. Hamburger transl. *Three German Classics* (Immensee, Lenz, A Village Romeo and Juliet), London 1966.

B. von Wiese, *Die deutsche Novelle von Goethe bis Kafka,* 2.Bd, Düsseldorf, n.d.

W.D. Williams, *The Stories of C.F. Meyer,* Oxford 1962.

6. OTHER WORKS

E. Auerbach, *Mimesis, Dargestellte Wirklichkeit in der abendländischen Literatur,* Berne 1946.

R. Brinkmann, *Wirklichkeit und Illusion, Studien über Gehalt und Grenzen des Begriffs Realismus für die erzählende Dichtung des 19. Jahrhunderts,* Tübingen 1957.

T.S. Eliot, *The three Voices of Poetry,* London 1953.

E.M. Forster, *Aspects of the Novel,* London 1927.

P. Gilliatt, a review of Barry Bermange's 'No Quarter' (*The Observer,* 18.10.1964, p. 24)

Sir P. Harvey ed., *The Oxford Companion to English Literature,* Oxford 1932, 3rd edn., 1946.

'An Interview with Ernest Hemingway', *Paris Review,* Spring 1958.

G.B. Hill ed., *Boswell's Life of Johnson,* rev. L.F. Powell, Vol I, Oxford 1934.

Graham Hough, '*Chance* and Joseph Conrad', *The Listener,* 26.12.1957, p. 1063ff.

Graham Hough, 'Henry James' in: I. Watt et al., *The Novelist as Innovator,* BBC London 1965.

Gottfried Kellers Gesammelte Werke in 4 Bden., Insel-Ausgabe, Leipzig 1922.

P. Lubbock, *The Craft of Fiction,* London 1921, n.e. 1954.

Otto Ludwigs Werke, hrsg. V. Schweizer, Meyers Klassiker-Ausgaben, Leipzig n.d.

Thomas Mann, *Der Erwählte,* S. Fischer Verlag 1956.

D. Riesman with N. Glazer and R. Denny, *The Lonely Crowd,* Yale 1950.

B. Russell, *History of Western Philosophy,* London 1946, n.e. 1961.

J.P. Stern, *Re-interpretations, Seven Studies in 19th Century German Literature,* London 1964.

Oscar Wilde, *Plays,* Penguin 1954.

NOTES

1 F. Martini, *Deutsche Literatur im bürgerlichen Realismus 1848-98*, Stuttgart 1962, p. 630ff.; and W. Kayser, *Bürgerlichkeit und Stammestum in Theodor Storms Novellendichtung*, Berlin 1938.
2 L. W. Wedberg, *The Theme of Loneliness in Theodor Storm's Novellen*, The Hague 1964.
3 Apart from a fairy-tale, *Hans Bär*, which he wrote for Berta von Buchan in 1837.
4 Gertrud Storm (*Theodor Storm, Ein Bild seines Lebens*, I. Band, Berlin 1912, p. 158) records that the old lady was very annoyed at having been made the subject of the story.
5 SW I 395; the italics in all quotations from this story are mine.
6 See below, p. 48, esp. note 79.
7 See above, p. 3f., for the intense, 'present' reality with which Marthe seeks to invest her memories.
8 Storm to Constanze, 24.12.1845. This gives the lie to the much more sentimental account of the old woman given by Storm's daughter (Gertrud Storm, I 158): "Sie gehörte zu den einsamen Menschen; ihre Eltern waren lange tot, die Geschwister verheiratet. So kehrte sie gern in der Erinnerung in die Zeit ihrer Jugend zurück. – Tante Brick wußte Storm sein Heim wohnlich und behaglich zu gestalten. Mitunter, in der von Storm so geliebten Dämmerstunde, erzählte sie ihm von ihrem einfach verflossenen Leben. Daraus entnahm der Dichter den Stoff seiner ersten Novelle, 'Marthe und ihre Uhr' ".
9 F. Stuckert, *Theodor Storm, Sein Leben und seine Welt*, Bremen 1955, p. 242.
10 R. Pitrou, *La vie et l'œuvre de Theodor Storm*, Paris 1920, I, 3, 4.
11 F. Böttger, *Theodor Storm in seiner Zeit*, Berlin n.d., p. 118.
12 In this play, a man is driven into hysteria, and then comatose acquiescence, by his terror of two men who are pursuing him; we are never told the reason for the pursuit, and there is never any need to know it.
13 This poem, which Storm wrote in 1851, is called *In böser Stunde*; SW I 87.
14 'Bee's Lake, or the Curse of Silence. A Study of Storm's "Immensee" '; *German Life & Letters*, NS 16 (1962-3), p. 36f. My quotation appears on p. 48.
15 McHaffie and Ritchie suggest (p. 37) that something similar has happened already, during the incident described in the first paragraph of "Im Walde": "Reinhard's inability to deflect the schoolmaster's anger from Elisabeth contrasts markedly with the idealised picture he has of himself as her protector".
16 The linnet is later replaced by a canary, Erich's gift to Elisabeth.
17 This is the second occasion when Reinhard's awareness of his feelings and desires is associated with his inability to express or realise them (cf. above, p. 10f.).
18 A biographical incident is often quoted in support of the theory that maternal domination is the key to *Immensee*. Paul Schütze (*Theodor Storm, sein Leben und seine Dichtung*, Berlin 1907, quoted in SW I 656f.) describes the incident thus:
> Nicht ohne Anregung durch einen wirklichen Vorgang hat übrigens der Dichter *Immensee* geschaffen. Eines Tages – so hat er selbst mehrfach erzählt – befand er sich in einer Gesellschaft, in der man eine junge Dame erwartete. Sie erschien aber nicht, und es wurde dann erzählt, ein älterer, reicher, als nüchtern geschäftsmäßig charakterisierter Mann habe um sie angehalten, und diese Verlobung sei ein Werk der Mutter. Unter der Anregung diese Vorfalls erschien am nächsten Tage das Lied "Meine Mutter hat's gewollt".

But one has to be very wary of using this piece of evidence in any analysis of the story (rather than just the poem); Schütze continues:
> Ob er die Novelle selbst schon früher begonnen hatte oder erst von diesem Liede aus darauf kam, darüber ist er sich selbst später nicht sicher gewesen.

19 That is, the first published version, in Biernatzki's *Volksbuch auf das Jahr 1850*.
20 That is, the Buchausgabe of 1851, in the collection called *Sommergeschichten und Lieder*.
21 SW I 417f. I am indebted to Goldammer's excellent and exhaustive notes (SW I 657ff.) for knowledge of these and other variants. E. A. McCormick also details all the variant

readings of *Immensee* in his book "Theodor Storm's Novellen" (Chapel Hill, N. Carolina 1964, p. 22f.).

22 Storm sent a copy of the Biernatzki text to Tycho Mommsen, who returned it with some sharp and cryptic comments in the margin ("Lebende Bilder, tote Kunst" and suchlike). This is what principally decided Storm to embark on an extensive revision of the story.

23 Böttger, *op. cit.*, pp. 121f., 125.

24 See above, p. 9f.

25 The milestones in which were: in 1837 an abortive engagement to one Emma K.; from 1836 to 1842 an intense, painful and rather odd affection for Berta von Buchan, who was only twelve when he first conceived a passion for her, and whose mother seems (naturally enough) to have played a considerable part in ending the affair; in 1846 marriage to his first cousin Constanze Esmarch, a marriage founded only on a certain mutual cousinly affection; and only a year after the wedding, a passionate, requited, but obviously impossible love for Dorothea Jensen. One other point: the water-lily episode is a fairly accurate record of what Storm himself actually did one night in Berlin in 1838 (cf. Gertrud Storm, I, p. 137).

26 This is the opinion of, for example, Pitrou and McHaffie and Ritchie.

27 I shall be returning to these things later (below, p. 67ff.).

28 Cf. below, p. 257ff.

29 Fritz Martini (p. 641) sums up something of what I have been saying, like this:
> Leitmotive und Bildsymbole. . .schaffen die Suggestion eines aus verborgener Determination ablaufenden Geschehens. Ein Gewebe aus Kausalem und Irrationalem, das niemals in allen Faktoren ergründet werden kann, baut das Tragische in Storms Novellistik auf. Der Schauer dieser Gefangenschaft wird dadurch erhöht, daß das vorgezeichnete Geschick auch nicht durch die Fürsorge und Liebe gelöst werden kann, daß es keine Brücke vom Ich zum Du gibt.

But he also says (p. 635):
> . . .Storms Dichtung spricht angesichts von Einsamkeit und Tod aus einer tiefgreifenden Verstörung des Weltverhältnisses.

He seems to be implying here that solitude, for Storm, is a *disturbance* of the natural state of things, and not a norm. That I would not accept.

30 Cf. SW I 662f., and McCormick, p. 35ff.

31 In talking of reminiscence in Storm's work, critics usually seem to imply that he uses it somehow to protect us from reality, to make life seem less nasty than it is, to deceive us into ignoring the 'lachrymae rerum'. Thus Benno von Wiese (*Die deutsche Novelle von Goethe bis Kafka*, II. Band, Düsseldorf n.d., p. 219) writes of Storm: "Wie gerne war der Leser bereit, (die Täuschung einer . . . im poetischen Dämmerschein der Stimmung zerfließenden Welt) mit der wirklichen Welt zu verwechseln, zumal dann, wenn die Unerbittlichkeit des Tragischen durch eine zarte poetische Schwermut und den Goldton der Erinnerung gemildert wurde". Ernst Feise (*Xenion, Essays in the History of German Literature*, Baltimore 1950, p. 226) writes: "Immer zieht Storm den Stoff in sein Ich hinein, formt ihn aus rückschauender Erinnerung und legt so über das furchtbare Geschehen den lindernden Schleier der Zeit, der diesem Geschehen. . .die Härte des grellen Lichtes nimmt". And Therese Rockenbach (*Theodor Storms Chroniknovellen*, Brunswick 1916, p. 74) writes: "Die Form der Erinnerungsnovelle trägt dazu bei, über die oft tragischen Ereignisse einen mildernden und versöhnenden Schleier auszubreiten". C. A. Bernd (*Theodor Storm's Craft of Fiction*, Chapel Hill, N. Carolina 1963, p. 94) quotes these last two observations and finds Feise's "excellent" and Rockenbach's "also quite correct". I find all three meaningless when applied to *Immensee* and most of Storm's other stories.

32 This predicament, of course, is just like Marthe's (cf. above, p. 4f.).

33 SW I 439-42. Since the story is so short, I shall not give page-references for my quotations from it.

34 This is recalled by Ludwig Pietsch in a letter to Storm dated 19.12.1869.

35 Cf. below, p. 177.

36 Böttger, p. 153.

37 Heyse to Storm, 26.11.1854.

38 Storm to Heyse, 8.5.1855.

39 Heyse to Storm, 26.11.1854.

40 See above, p. 9.

41 Böttger (p. 161f.) gives a good account of the class problem as it appears in *Im Sonnenschein*, and infers a certain anti-Prussian feeling here (Storm wrote the story during his first unhappy years in Potsdam) from the fact that the officer class is *not* represented as "der erste Stand des Staates".

42 Kayser (p. 24) criticises this gap in the motivation: "Man empfindet, oft mitten beim Lesen, daß man 'nicht mehr mit kann'. So hakt trotz aller Einsicht gerade bei den Motivationszusammenhängen die Bindung an den Dichter aus. Der Leser kann ihre Bündigkeit nicht anerkennen. Er soll etwa in 'Immensee' bzw. in der Novelle 'Im Sonnenschein' glauben, daß die Mutter bzw. der Vater es so gewollt haben und daß damit alles begründet sei". Kayser goes on to claim that this is a weakness caused by Storm's inability to see the dictates of "der bürgerliche Raum" as anything less than absolute. I think the gap signifies something beyond that, and certainly that the reader *isn't* asked to think that everything is grounded in parental domination.

43 SW I 459. This occurs in my quotation on p. 26 above.

44 SW I 559ff. I shall be returning to this passage in another connection later (below, p. 78ff.) For various reasons, incidentally, the two friends are better known by these professional titles than by their names, so I have used the titles throughout. It is hard to think of the Doktor as "Christoph" or of the Justizrat as "Eduard".

45 Kayser (p. 16) is quite sure that this interpretation is the only possible one: "Wenn es in 'Drüben am Markt' von der Bürgermeisterstochter, die den Doktor betrachtet, heißt: 'In ihrem Gesichtchen zuckte es wieder wie vorhin, da sie vor dem Branntweinfäßchen kniete', so wissen wir aus dem 'vorhin', daß ein Ekelgefühl sie erfaßte. Für uns ist denn auch das 'Ich kann nicht', mit dem sie später die Werbung des Doktors ablehnt, nur scheinbar verhüllt und nicht unerklärlich wie für die Gestalten der Novelle". If this is obvious, why do the other critics offer different and conflicting interpretations? (cf. below, p. 30 note 47, p. 32 note 50). And anyway, it is just not true; Kayser completely ignores the many other signs, just as 'significant' as this one, which point in quite other directions.

46 I talk of some of these indications in the next few paragraphs.

47 This is Pitrou's view (II, 2, 4).

48 I have made this point more fully above, p. 17f.

49 The Justizrat reports (SW I 560): "Es war in unserem Garten, hinten an dem Steintischchen ...was die kleine Hand in der weißen Manschette dort auf die Marmorplatte mag geschrieben haben, das hab ich freilich nicht entziffern können, aber gesprochen hat sie nichts hierüber".

50 Böttger (p. 326) claims that this is the real reason, though he makes an interesting reservation about calling it purely a 'class' issue: "Die Liebe zur Tochter des Bürgermeisters scheitert zwar nicht an einem Stände- und Klassengegensatz, aber doch an der unvollkommenen Erziehung des Plebejers, die ihre wirtschaftlichen und sozialen Ursachen hat, am Gegensatz und lächerlichen Kontrast von unentwickelten und entwickelten Formen des menschlichen Umgangs und Verhaltens". Stuckert's judgement is similar but confused. He says (p. 265) that there can be no lasting relationship between the "kleinbürgerlich", uncouth Doktor, and the charming patrician Sophie; the doctor realises this too late, but remains under the happy illusion that Sophie has rejected him for social, not personal reasons. But surely then, this is not an illusion? Stuckert is implying that the doctor is uncouth *because* "kleinbürgerlich" and that Sophie is charming *because* patrician – and therefore that the reasons are social rather than (or before being) personal.

51 See above, p. 31f.

52 See above, p. 29.

53 I shall be returning to this obscurity later (below, p. 77ff.)

54 Pitrou (III, 1, 4) and Böttger (p. 247) both point out the similarity between Agnes (the central figure of *In St Jürgen*) and Marthe (of *Marthe und ihre Uhr*). Böttger also remarks on the early, "biedermeierlich" quality of the work, as does Stuckert (p. 295). Moreover, Storm took as his model a story which he had known for many years (*Das Heimweh*, an anonymous tale which appeared in Biernatzki's *Volksbuch auf das Jahr 1849*); this in itself suggests a return to earlier preoccupations.

55 I shall be examining this moment more closely later (below, p. 63f.).

56 Kayser, p. 36f. Stuckert (p. 293f.) also, though less pungently, makes the point both about Harre's weakness and the sentimentality of the closing scene.

57 Storm to Pietsch, 8.11.1867.

58 Storm to Groth, 5.3.1868.

59 Kayser, p. 62.

60 See below, p. 116ff., p. 139ff.

61 See above, p. 16f.

62 Or rather, the part of the gallery that I have talked about. There are many more figures that belong there: Anne Lene (of *Auf dem Staatshof*, 1856); Anna (of *Im Schloß*, 1861); Lore (of *Auf der Universität*, 1862); Meta (of *Abseits*, 1863); and a dozen others in stories written after *In St Jürgen*.

63 Cf. below, p. 47ff.
64 In this she resembles Marthe; cf. above, p. 4.
65 E.g. E. K. Bennett, *A History of the German Novelle*, 2nd edn., rev. H. M. Waidson, Cambridge 1961, p. 162f.; and von Wiese, p. 217f.
66 E.g. W. D. Williams, *The Stories of C. F. Meyer*, Oxford 1962, p. 10. Cf. also my quotations from von Wiese, Feise and Rockenbach above, p. 20 note 31.
67 E.g. Stuckert, p. 240f.; Böttger, p. 123f.
68 E.g. Kayser, p. 18, 20; W. Silz, *Realism and Reality, Studies in the German Novelle of Poetic Realism*, Chapel Hill, N. Carolina 1954, p. 117. Böttger (p. 122) rightly repudiates this when he says of *Immensee* "Am Ende steht nicht die Resignation, sondern die Qual einer Liebe, die nicht mehr leben, aber auch nicht sterben kann".
69 E.g. Stuckert, pp. 240, 255, 295 etc. etc.; McHaffie and Ritchie, p. 37.
70 E.g. Kayser, pp. 25, 31; McHaffie and Ritchie, p. 37.
71 E.g. Stuckert, p. 293f., Pitrou, I, 3, 6.
72 E.g. von Wiese, p. 217.
73 In SW.   Of the seven stories Goldammer calls "Märchen und Spukgeschichten", four have at least the rudiments of a Rahmen. Indeed, one of them, *Am Kamin*, pushes the technique to its limit: at one point the position is that the narrator tells us that Alexius tells the company that a relation told him that a Medizinalrat had told him. . .! (SWI 316ff.)
74 I notice that Graham Hough uses a similar phrase, calling the traditional type of narrator "the wire-pulling puppet-master", in his talk on Henry James (published in: Ian Watt et al., *The Novelist as Innovator*, BBC London 1965, p. 71).
75 E. M. Forster, *Aspects of the Novel*, London 1927, p. 87ff. Cf. also below, p. 118ff.
76 Thomas Mann, *Der Erwählte*, Fischer 1956, p. 8.
77 See Appendix B.
78 In the last five of this list of stories, the situation is doubly enforced: a fully-embodied person tells us what has been conveyed to him by the principal protagonists, who are self-evidently embodied and involved.
79 For example, I talked earlier (above, p. 41) of the way the full extent of Agnes Hansen's suffering in *In St Jürgen* is probably hidden because the narrator's imaginative entry into her predicament seems less than total. And I shall be suggesting later that the "phantastischer Zug" which the narrator of *Ein Bekenntnis* admits as a part of his nature makes us suspect that the picture he draws of his friend Franz Jebe may be misleadingly sympathetic; for Franz is stated to have this "phantastischer Zug" too, and I claim that the basic and invalidating limitation of his character can be quite precisely defined in terms of "das Phantastische" (See below, Chap. III, sec. 2, esp. p. 180f.).
80 I owe some of the formulations, particularly the terminology, of the problem of the narrator to Bernd, but my conclusions are opposite to his.
81 Bernd, p. 4. For the sake of simplicity, my quotation of the passage (above, p. 47) follows Bernd's exactly in its omissions.
82 Bernd, p. 7.
83 Bernd, p. 77. It is not easy to see just what Bernd means by this formulation.
84 Not very much further, in fact: everything I discuss here is contained in the introductory section of the novel, which makes it more difficult to understand why Bernd has ignored it.
85 Mann, *Der Erwählte*, p. 11.
86 Mann, p. 11f.; my italics.
87 Mann, p. 12; my italics.
88 Mann, p. 12.
89 Mann, p. 13; my italics.
90 Kleist, Kafka and Robbe-Grillet, for instance, tend to give their characters initials rather than names; thus the Marquise von O. ., K., and A and B.
91 It is worth mentioning also that in these stories which have a fully-embodied first-person narrator, an elaborate account is often given of the way the narrator *became* acquainted with the character(s) whose story he is telling: that is, the processes of acquaintance are treated in a manner which suggests that they are thought to be in themselves interesting, 'problematic' and worthy of detailed attention (Cf. especially *Im Nachbarhause Links*, *"Es waren zwei Königskinder"* and *John Riew'*, which latter story I discuss in this connection below, p. 100f.)
92 At the end of the story (SW I 560) his friend does in fact call him "Christoph", but this is the only time.
93 See Appendix B.
94 Indeed, in two early stories, *Posthuma* (1850) and *Wenn die Äpfel reif sind* (1856), the characters' names never emerge at all.

95 See Appendix C.
96 The assertion that these are Dutch coffee-cups looks like a lapse in standpoint — the narrator is 'giving' us something a stranger would have no means of discovering; unless, as is possible, Dutch cups are at this time associated with high quality in china; then the inference would be reasonable for a stranger to make. So far as I can see, this is the *only* lapse (if it is one) in the whole of the opening section.
97 See above, p. 54f.
98 But they only *tend* to do so; even in these stories, there are certain significant reservations which relate to my theme and which I shall be discussing later.
99 SW III 7. Editions agree on the penultimate word. This use of 'erholen' (as a slightly intensified 'holen') is presumably an archaism that survived in dialect..
100 See above, p. 49ff.
101 See above, p. 48f.
102 This same situation frequently appears in Thomas Mann's early work: *Der Wille zum Glück* (1896), *Der kleine Herr Friedemann* (1897), *Tristan* (1903) and *Tonio Kröger* (1903) are all concerned with artist figures who at one time or another are unhappily in love with girls who, like Gertrud, have a "blondes Köpfchen" and a "heitere Natur" (she is described in this way in SW II 244). Friedemann, indeed, is uncannily like Brunken, hunchbacked but with fine eyes and a face that is "beinahe schön zu nennen".
103 See above, p. 70.
104 I shall be talking more of this later (below, p. 84ff).
105 Cf. SW IV 315f., 318f., 322f., 324f., 332f.
106 SW IV 389; cf. also p. 345, 367, 385f., 387, 388f.
107 In *Ein Bekenntnis*; cf. below, p. 169ff.
108 In *Der Schimmelreiter*; cf. below, p. 184ff.
109 *John Riew'* comes up again in this connection below, p. 167f.
110 See above, p. 10.
111 See above, p. 51ff.
112 See above, p. 60ff.
113 In section 4 of this chapter, above, p. 67ff.
114 And of course the situation of *Angelika*.
115 5.5.1875; my italics.
116 Heyse to Storm, 21.10.1875; Heyse's italics.
117 Storm to Heyse, undated; Storm's italics.
118 In *Veronika, Waldwinkel, Aquis submersus* et al.
119 In *Von jenseit des Meeres, Aquis submersus* and *John Riew'*.
120 In *Eekenhof* and the poem *Geschwisterblut*.
121 In *Schweigen*.
122 In *John Riew'*.
123 In *Ein Bekenntnis*.
124 Like the grotesque exhibitionist Etatsrat (of *Der Herr Etatsrat*) or the near-nymphomaniac murderess Wulfhild (of *Ein Fest auf Haderslevhuus*).
125 Cf. J. W. Smeed, 'Theodor Storm and his Reading Public, Some Cases of Editorial Interference and its Effect', *Durham University Journal*, June 1960, p. 125ff.
126 See above, p. 67ff.
127 See below, p. 94.
128 See above, p. 59f.
129 SW III 371; in this and all the subsequent quotations from *Hans und Heinz Kirch*, the italics are mine.
130 From this point on, for simplicity's sake, I use the term 'Heinz' (in single inverted commas) as a convenient shorthand for 'the man who has returned, claiming to be Heinz'.
131 There is a single exception to this: 'Heinz' is once called by name ("hatte sich Heinz", SW III 381).
132 That is, the conversation I have just discussed (above, p. 90f.).
133 See above, p. 90f.
134 This is what I meant when I said (above, p. 85) that our 'prejudices' are relevant as well as those of the narrator or characters.
135 In this regard, it is interesting to note that in the real-life situation on which Storm closely modelled his story, the family concerned *never found out* for certain whether the returned wanderer was genuine or a fraud. Storm sketches the outlines of this real-life situation as part of the entry for 5.10.1881 in his journal *Was der Tag gibt* (quoted by Gertrud Storm, II, p. 211ff.).
136 Forster, p. 88.

137 SW IV 233; this is the phrase of a kindly though somewhat ineffectual Bürgermeister, whose comments throughout presumably reflect Storm's attitude.
138 See above, p. 61ff.
139 See above, p. 54.
140 Cf. particularly the extracts from *Im Sonnenschein* (p. 55f.), *Der Schimmelreiter* (p. 65ff.), *Eine Halligfahrt* (p. 72), *Drüben am Markt* (p. 79) and *Hans und Heinz Kirch* (pp. 74, 92, 93).
141 Forster, p. 74. He also talks (p. 77f.) about love and marriage as convenient endings, stressing that the unproblematic permanence a novelist attributes to these is an illusion which we *want* a book to encourage us in.
142 It happens most clearly in: *Marthe und ihre Uhr, Eine Halligfahrt, Draußen im Heidedorf, Waldwinkel, Ein stiller Musikant, Aquis submersus, Zur "Wald- und Wasserfreude", Eekenhof, Der Herr Etatsrat, Hans und Heinz Kirch, Zur Chronik von Grieshuus,* and *Ein Fest auf Haderslevhuus*; and in one or two other stories there are more ambiguous examples of the same phenomenon.
143 See above, p. 48ff.
144 Keller to Storm, 25.3.1879.
145 Percy Lubbock uses this phrase in *The Craft of Fiction*, London 1921, n.e. 1954, e.g. p. 126.
146 Cf. above, p. 61. It is sometimes said (e.g. Lubbock, pp. 74, 142) that the renunciation of omniscience is easier in short works of fiction than in long ones. I should have thought just the reverse to be true, particularly in view of the 'space-saving' properties of omniscience.
147 Cf. above, p. 51ff.
148 See above, p. 59f.
149 Cf. p. 84ff.
150 The exception is *Renate*.
151 C. A. Bernd traces the appearance of these elements of transience in *Aquis submersus* and *In St Jürgen*; as might be expected, his argument holds up better for the former (and by extension for the other historical pieces) than for the latter.
152 SW III 252. When the story was first published (in the *Deutsche Rundschau*, XXI, October 1879), it had a different ending. There was a concluding section (quoted by Goldammer, SW III 610f.) which tells of a couple, brother and sister, who lived together in Norway till their death and who were rumoured to belong to a noble German family (the implication being, of course, that they were none other than Detlev and Heilwig). For the first *Buchausgabe* (1880), and in all editions thereafter, Storm cut out this section and replaced it with the closing sentence which I quote here. He doesn't say anywhere why he did this; one imagines that he relied on some internal barometer which told him that the first ending did not 'feel right'. Vague as that original ending appears, was it nonetheless perhaps *still* too conclusive for Storm? I suspect so.
153 SW III 557; Storm seems to have written this himself.
154 See above, p. 59ff.
155 See above, p. 59ff.
156 Graham Hough, '*Chance* and Joseph Conrad', *The Listener*, 26.12.1957, p. 1063ff.
157 Hough, p. 1063.
158 Hough, p. 1064.
159 Hough, p. 1065.
160 Hough, p. 1065.
161 Hough, p. 1064.
162 Hough, p. 1065.
163 Percy Lubbock, *The Craft of Fiction*, London 1921, n.e. 1954.
164 Lubbock, p. 116.
165 Lubbock, p. 251f.; his italics.
166 Bernd, pp. 3, 5 and notes 1, 2 and 3.
167 Lubbock, p. 130.
168 Lubbock, p. 144f.
169 Lubbock, p. 190.
170 One recalls the Brechtian ideas of "alienation", and especially Brecht's distinction between 'epic' and 'dramatic' theatre.
171 The phrase is Strindberg's, from his preface to *Miss Julia*.
172 See above, p. 54.
173 See above, p. 54.
174 *Howards End*, chap. XXXV.
175 By Lance Sieveking and Richard Cottrell, directed by Toby Robertson, 1965.
176 See above, p. 55ff.
177 Oscar Wilde, *Plays*, Penguin 1954, p. 38ff.

178 See above, p. 67ff.
179 SW IV 622f. The preface was originally intended to introduce the 11th volume of the Gesamtausgabe of Storm's works. He wrote it "Im ersten Zorn" (letter to Heyse, 1.8.1881), after reading a newspaper report that Georg Moritz Ebers had claimed that the Novelle was a thing a novelist might dash off as a recreation from the serious business of writing novels. The report grossly misrepresented what Ebers had actually said, and Storm, on the advice of Heyse, Keller and possibly Erich Schmidt, wisely withdrew the preface. Ebers was a Jew; in a letter to Keller (14.8.1881), Storm let slip an anti-Semitic comment (which was uncharacteristic of him); Keller wrote a sharp reply (18.8.1881), and Goldammer (ed. *Der Briefwechsel zwischen Theodor Storm und Gottfried Keller*, Berlin 1960, p. 16f.) picks on this unfortunate episode as emblematic of the growing strains in the long pen-friendship between these two "Peripherie-Germanen". The preface was first published in 1913 by Fritz Böhme, in a supplementary volume to his edition of Storm's works.
180 In a letter to Keller (14.8.1881), Storm refers to his own theorisings about literary genres as "dergleichen dummes Zeug, was keinen andern Grund hat, als daß man selbst nichts machen kann".
181 For example, his observations on the element of the grotesque in *Der Herr Etatsrat* were all written *after* the story had been published (August 1881) and in reply to comments from friends (letters to Margarete Mörike, 23.8.1881; to Erich Schmidt, September 1881; to Ernst Esmarch, 4.7.1882).
182 Gertrud Storm (I, p. 128) reports Storm as saying (apropos of the force which usually sparked off his stories): "Es formulierte sich oft fast ohne allen Willen, es kam von selbst und wurde von mir festgehalten".
183 Letter to Heyse, 20.6.1876.
184 Letter to Keller, 8.8.1882, apropos of *Schweigen*.
185 Letter to Lorenzen, 23.5.1877, apropos of *Carsten Curator*. Cf. also letters to Heyse, 17.10.1881, apropos of *Hans und Heinz Kirch*, and 29.8.1886, apropos of *Der Schimmelreiter*, which Storm calls "ein böser Block".
186 Letter to his parents, 27.3.1859. Cf. also his letter to Brinkmann, 11.9.1852, where he writes of *Immensee*: "Ich weiß jetzt auch, worin sein Wert und seine Bedeutung liegen. Es ist eine echte Dichtung der Liebe und durch und durch von dem Dufte und der Atmosphäre der Liebe erfüllt. Von diesem Gesichtspunkt aus muß jede Beurteilung ausgehen". That is not exactly an epoch-making insight.
187 Letter to Fontane, 23.3.1853.
188 Letter to Petersen, 23.4.1880.
189 Letter to Heyse, 7.2.1885.
190 Letter to Keller, 8.8.1882.
191 Letter to Westermann, 6.10.1876, apropos of *Carsten Curator*.
192 Letter to Heyse, 3.11.1878.
193 Letter to his son Ernst, 22.5.1871.
194 Letter to Petersen, 14.3.1883. Cf. also letters to Kuh, 6.7.1876; to Petersen, 9.9.1877.; to Heyse, 3.11.1878; to Heyse, 2.5.1879 and 15.11.1882; to his daughter Lisbeth, 6.5.1883; and to Keller, 5.5.1883.
195 By Graham Hough in 'Henry James' (*The Novelist as Innovator*, p. 72ff.).
196 SW I 249ff. Storm was also quite keen on amateur dramatics (cf. Stuckert, p. 437f.).
197 Lubbock, p. 116.
198 Lubbock, p. 126.
199 Hough, p. 75.
200 Hough, p. 69.
201 Forster, *Aspects of the Novel*, p. 88.
202 I made this point briefly above, p. 47.
203 'An Interview with Ernest Hemingway', *The Paris Review*, Spring 1958, p. 84; my italics.
204 Forster, p. 88; my italics.
205 Lubbock, p. 48f.
206 Lubbock, p. 74.
207 Kayser, p. 22f.
208 See above, p. 9ff.
209 Kayser, p. 25.
210 Kayser, p. 16.
211 See above, p. 29ff.
212 Kayser's argument is distorted here by the fact that he begins (p. 15) his discussion of the "als ob" type of construction by giving two untypical examples. He quotes (from *Immensee*, SW I 421) "Nun war es, als träte etwas Fremdes zwischen sie", and (from

Angelika, SW I 486) "Er schrak zusammen, als sei hinter ihm die Tür seines Glückes zugefallen". He says that the turn of phrase is pointless: "Denn tatsächlich ist etwas Fremdes zwischen sie getreten, tatsächlich ist die Tür des Glückes zugeschlagen". But these cases are specialised: the two sentences he quotes are clearly pieces of "erlebte Rede", similes or comparisons made *in the mind of the character himself*, not tentative deductions about possible states of mind made *by a stranger looking on*. My quotation from *Drüben am Markt* (above, p. 101) should make the difference clear, as should the many examples of the construction contained in my quotation from *Im Sonnenschein* (above, p. 55f.).

213 W. D. Williams, *The Stories of C. F. Meyer.*

214 Williams, p. 10.

215 Williams, p. 11.

216 Williams, p. 12.

217 Cf. above, p. 4, 20, 43.

218 Williams, p. 12.

219 Reinhard is beset by Hamlet's predicament, forced into a position where he must "take arms against a *sea* of troubles" — what arms to take against a sea?

220 See above, p. 119.

221 See Appendix A.

222 W. F. Mainland, 'Theodor Storm', *German Men of Letters*, ed. A. Natan, London 1961, p. 162.

223 See above, p. 118ff.

224 Possible exceptions are: (a) the use, twice, of the word "unwillkürlich", and (b) the identification of the old woman as "die Haushälterin". These are cases so near the border-line between omniscience and non-omniscience that they are not worth arguing about. But McHaffie and Ritchie (p. 36) make another point: "It is only his dark eyes, which contrast so strangely with his snow-white hair, which point to a concealed tragedy ('Augen, in welche sich die ganze verlorene Jugend gerettet zu haben schien'). This is perhaps more than the casual observer in the street could possibly see. . ." I would take issue with this: why should the old man's youthful eyes point to a concealed tragedy? McHaffie and Ritchie seem to have misunderstood the meaning of the words they quote, especially the word "verlorene". Surely the phrase is a perfectly reasonable (though imaginative) image which a "casual observer" might well choose to describe how the man's youth seems (and again we have a 'schien') to have all drained into his eyes, leaving the rest of his body old?

225 The same goes for all the other names in the story.

226 At this point we have been brought to the extremes of caution enjoined by the military mind and splendidly satirised by Henry Reed in his poem *Judging Distances*, in terms which reflect Storm's standpoint with surprising accuracy:

> . . .and lastly
> That things only seem to be things.
>
> A barn is not called a barn, to put it more plainly,
> Or a field in the distance, where sheep may be safely grazing.
> You must never be over-sure. You must say, when reporting,
> At five o'clock in the central sector is a dozen
> of what appear to be animals; whatever you do
> Don't call the bleeders *sheep*. . .
>
> . . .The still white dwellings are like a mirage in the heat,
> And under the swaying elms a man and a woman
> Lie gently together. Which is, perhaps, only to say
> That there is a row of houses to the left of arc,
> And that under some poplars a pair of what appear to be humans
> Appear to be loving.

227 McHaffie and Ritchie (p. 36f.) notice some of the uncertainties I have mentioned, but they preface their account of these uncertainties by saying: " 'Immensee' is almost pure 'Stimmung' with all sorts of things hinted at but nothing stated explicitly"; and they conclude it by noting: "How 'Biedermeier' the whole situation is. . !" To attach these labels to this particular phenomenon seems to me to beg the questions. Of course Storm's early work is full of "Stimmung" (so many people have said it that I suppose it must be true), and of course one can see him as a writer in the Biedermeier tradition; but in what way do these two terms illuminate the actual individual problem here, the problem of narrative uncertainty? Is such a problem the monopoly of the Biedermeier mode or the *Stimmung* technique? Surely not.

228 McHaffie and Ritchie, p. 47.
229 *Ludwigs Werke,* hrsg. V. Schweizer, Meyers Klassiker-Ausgaben, Leipzig n.d., 3. Band, p. 11f. The use of the word "unwillkürlich", the reference to the gold/silver headed cane, and the observation about a "vorübergegangene Mode", are extraordinary coincidences in these two very similar scenes.
230 Ludwig, III, p. 12.
231 See above, p. 47ff.
232 *Ludwigs Werke,* 3. Band, p. 13ff.
233 SW I 409. All the temporal transitions in the story have this same terse, strained quality: "Sieben Jahre waren vorüber" (SW I 412); "Es war im Juni; Reinhard sollte am andern Tage reisen" (SW I 412); "Weihnachtabend kam heran" (SW I 417); "Als es Ostern geworden war, reiste Reinhard in die Heimat" (SW I 421); "Fast zwei Jahre nachher saß Reinhard. . ." (SW I 425): "Wiederum waren Jahre vorüber" (SW I 425).
234 See above, p. 123f.
235 There are indeed one or two longish passages of such description in the first version; significantly, Storm extirpates them for the Buchausgabe (cf. SW I 657ff., McCormick, p. 22ff.).
236 See above, p. 131, note 235.
237 See above, p. 126.
238 *Dantons Tod,* Act I Scene 1.
239 In what follows, of course, I am referring back in turn to the half-dozen technical elements examined earlier (pp. 45-122) and showing them in the 'solipsistic' light.
240 There are strange affinities here with the blind Argentinian writer Jorge Luis Borges, in whose extraordinary stories one often finds moments like this one: "Things duplicate themselves in Tlön. They tend at the same time to efface themselves, to lose their detail when people forget them. The classic example is that of a stone threshold which lasted as long as it was visited by a beggar, and which faded from sight on his death. Occasionally, a few birds, a horse perhaps, have saved the ruins of an amphitheatre". (J. L. Borges, *Fictions,* ed. A. Kerrigan, London 1965, p. 29).
241 According to the Oxford English Dictionary.
242 Boswell records: "After we came out of the church, we stood talking for some time together of Bishop Berkeley's ingenious sophistry to prove the non-existence of matter, and that every thing in the universe is merely ideal. I observed, that though we are satisfied his doctrine is not true, it is impossible to refute it. I never shall forget the alacrity with which Johnson answered, striking his foot with mighty force against a large stone, till he rebounded from it, 'I refute it *thus*' ". (*Boswell's Life of Johnson,* ed. G. B. Hill, rev. L. F. Powell, Oxford 1934, p. 471).
243 This admirable résumé is from *The Oxford Companion to English Literature,* ed. Sir P. Harvey, Oxford 1932, 3rd edn., 1946, p. 82.
244 Cf. Stuckert, p. 144f.
245 This is essentially the position which David Hume adopts, as the only antidote to the annihilating consequences of his own sceptical thinking, which is more consistent and far-reaching even than Berkeley's, especially in the matter of the logic of causation. See Appendix D.
246 Another writer who seems to me to inhabit, now and then at least, the borderland between the 'philosophical' and the 'literary' — and to achieve distinction there — is John Wisdom. One finds the solipsistic doubt (and the possibility of transcending it) beautifully expressed in his book *Philosophy and Psycho-analysis,* Oxford 1957, esp. p. 169f.
247 I say this purely for argument's sake and imply no criticism of Berkeley, who is well-known as a delightful stylist incapable of wan presentation.
248 Cf. above, p. 67.
249 See above, p. 116ff.
250 In a review of Barry Bermange's *No Quarter (The Observer,* 18.10.1964, p. 24.
251 See above, p. 116, note 185.
252 See above, p. 116f.
253 See above, p. 58ff. I shall be returning to this inconsistency later (below, p. 150ff.).
254 See above, p. 56, note 96.
255 See above, p. 80.
256 See above, p. 117.
257 It was from this appeal that I started (above, p. 45), but I hope to have defined more closely since.
258 Cf. above, p. 161.
259 Cf. for example, my quotations from *Hinzelmeier* (above, p. 62) and from *Immensee*

(above, p. 131).

260 See above, p. 100f., 120ff.
261 This is only a hypothetical point; I have no desire to take up the question of specific influences, since to do so cannot really contribute to any elucidation of the aspects discussed here.
262 Forster, *Aspects of the Novel*, p. 25.
263 "Das quälende Rätsel des Todes" is a phrase Storm used in a letter to Mörike (3.6.1865) just after Constanze's death.
264 Since all this is perfectly well-known, I find it hard to understand what prompts judgements like the one with which Ronald Taylor begins the introduction to his translation of *Immensee* (*Three German Classics*, transl. R. Taylor and M. Hamburger, London 1966, p. 9): "The stories and the lyrical poetry of Theodor Storm are as unproblematical as their author's life was uneventful". (As it happens, that is literally true: Storm's life was *not at all* uneventful, and his work is unproblematical to exactly the same extent, i.e. not at all).
265 *Immensee* (1849), *Posthuma* (1850), *Im Sonnenschein* (1854), *Angelika* (1855).
266 *Unter dem Tannenbaum* (1862), *Abseits* (1863).
267 *Späte Rosen* (1859).
268 *Viola tricolor* (1873).
269 *Carsten Curator* (1877), *Hans und Heinz Kirch* (1881-2), *Bötjer Basch* (1885-6).
270 Notably *Draußen im Heidedorf* (1871-2).
271 Rather more than two-thirds of Storm's works are set in Schleswig-Holstein.
272 A much more glaring example of this kind of mistake is to be found in L. W. Wedberg's *The Theme of Loneliness in Theodor Storm's Novellen*. Cf. my review of this book in *German Life & Letters*, n.s. Vol. XIX, No. 2, January 1966, p. 119ff.
273 Böttger, p. 352.
274 Böttger, p. 231.
275 Böttger, p. 231.
276 Böttger, p. 298f.
277 Silz, p. 117.
278 Bennett, p. 171.
279 Kayser, p. 64.
280 The main arguments of this study show where and how and how strongly I disagree with these critics; I would want to dissociate myself particularly from Silz.
281 *Marthe und ihre Uhr, Immensee, Posthuma, Im Sonnenschein, Angelika, Wenn die Äpfel reif sind, Drüben am Markt, In St Jürgen, Eine Halligfahrt, Draußen im Heidedorf, Waldwinkel, Ein stiller Musikant, "Es waren zwei Königskinder", Die Armesünderglocke* (unfinished).
282 *Auf dem Staatshof, Veronika, Im Schloß, Auf der Universität, Von jenseit des Meeres, Im Nachbarhause links, Zur "Wald- und Wasserfreude".*
283 *Im Saal, Ein grünes Blatt, Unter dem Tannenbaum, Abseits.*
284 *Hans Bär, Der kleine Häwelmann, Hinzelmeier, Am Kamin, Die Regentrude, Bulemanns Haus, Der Spiegel des Cyprianus.*
285 *Späte Rosen, Eine Malerarbeit, Beim Vetter Christian, Viola tricolor, Psyche, Die Söhne des Senators.*
286 *Carsten Curator, Der Herr Etatsrat, Hans und Heinz Kirch, Bötjer Basch.*
287 *Aquis submersus, Renate, Eekenhof, Zur Chronik von Grieshuus, Ein Fest auf Haderslevhuus.*
288 *Pole Poppenspäler, Im Brauerhause, Schweigen, John Riew', Ein Doppelgänger, Ein Bekenntnis.*
289 It can be seen from this classification that the facts ascertained at the shallow level of subject-matter can be of some help at the deeper level of theme.
290 See above, p. 143f.
291 See above, p. 136.
292 See above, pp. 54f., 58ff.
293 See Appendix C.
294 See Appendix D.
295 See above, p. 104f.
296 See above, p. 73ff.
297 See above, p. 84ff.
298 See above, p. 122.
299 See above, p. 104ff.
300 See above, p. 48f.
301 See above, p. 65ff.
302 See above, p. 97f.
303 See above, p. 100f.

304 See above, p. 100f.
305 Th. Fontane, *Gesammelte Werke*, Jubiläumsausgabe, 2. Reihe, 2. Band, p. 224ff.
306 Fontane, p. 233.
307 Fontane, p. 242.
308 Fontane, p. 246f.
309 Storm uses this word in a letter to Emil Kuh in 1872; but this time he had written only about half his stories, and hardly any of his finest ones, so that his opinion of himself may have risen subsequently.
310 Fontane (*loc. cit.*) gives an interesting account of all this.
311 Much surer on other people's work than on his own.
312 Cf. Stuckert, Chap. 13, esp. p. 438ff.
313 Martini (p. 640) points to "das Autochthöne seiner Natur, das ihm fremden Bildungs-einflüssen wenig zugänglich machte", and Böttger (p. 121) notes: "Ganz auf sich gestellt, half sich der Erzähler als reiner Autodidakt voran, dem das Erbe nichts, die selbständige Verarbeitung der erlebten Wirklichkeit alles bedeutete". Cf. also Stuckert, p. 144f., 443f.
314 Notably at the end of *Viola tricolor.*
315 In later stories, especially *Aquis submersus, Carsten Curator* and *John Riew'.*
316 Tübingen 1957. The subtitle is: "Studien über Gehalt und Grenzen des Begriffs Realismus für die erzählende Dichtung des neunzehnten Jahrhunderts".
317 Brinkmann, p. 314; author's italics. The two quotations I have asterisked are taken from the writings of Ranke.
318 Brinkmann, p. 303.
319 Brinkmann, p. 303.
320 Brinkmann, p. 130ff.
321 Brinkmann, p. 144f.
322 Brinkmann, p. 304.
323 Brinkmann, p. 305.
324 Brinkmann takes the belief in a binding, universal causality as one of his criteria for the 'objectivist', 'absolutist' view of the world. In this connection it is worth remembering that one of the main planks of David Hume's scepticism is the problem of proving cause and effect.
325 Brinkmann, p. 214.
326 Brinkmann, p. 308; author's italics.
327 See above, p. 128ff.
328 Raabe, Meyer, Keller, Freytag, Fontane, and of course Storm, all published novels or stories between 1870 and 1880.
329 And, incidentally, between *Der arme Spielmann* and *Zwischen Himmel und Erde* in point of time.
330 Brinkmann, p. 216; cf. above, p. 134.
331 Brinkmann, p. 243f.
332 Brinkmann, p. 252; cf. the characterisation of Erich in *Immensee* (above, p. 133ff.).
333 Brinkmann, p. 287f. I think this is precisely the nature of, for example, the various functions in *Immensee* of the strawberries, the yellow bird, the book of poems, the folk-song collection and the water-lily.
334 Brinkmann, p. 306f.
335 Brinkmann, p. 243f.
336 Brinkmann, p. 308.
337 Brinkmann, p. 306.
338 E. Auerbach, *Mimesis*, Bern 1946, p. 476f.
339 J. P. Stern, *Re-interpretations*, London 1964, p. 2.
340 Stern, p. 10.
341 Stern, p. 31.
342 Stern, p. 76f.
343 Stern, pp. 61, 76f.
344 The remaining writers are Büchner, Schopenhauer, Heine, Stifter, Fontane and, in passing, Keller.
345 Stern, p. 291; author's italics.
346 Stern, p. 101.
347 See above, pp. 117f., 125, 134ff., 139ff.
348 Apropos of Brinkmann's study I talked (above, p. 155ff.) of the breaking down of the distinction between 'subject' and 'object'; that I now talk of the 'chasm between subject and object' is only an apparent contradiction. The conflict is between two metaphors, each imperfectly describing aspects of the same phenomenon and each useful in its context.

Neither 'breaking-down' nor 'chasm' have any self-contained validity.

349 SW IV 308. I am indebted to Mr T. D. Jones of Jesus College for first drawing my attention to this passage.

350 See above, p. 62.

351 Fontane (*op. cit.*, p. 242) picks out this revealing detail.

352 Bernd draws this conclusion from *Aquis submersus*, where the deficiency is very clear, and from *In St Jürgen*, where it is less so. For the inadequacy of memories as an escape, see above, pp. 4, 20, 41, 42f.

353 See above, pp. 149, 150f., 151f., 152f.

354 See above, p. 65ff.

355 Stern, p. 10.

356 Stern, p. 303f.

357 Stern, p. 307.

358 Stern, p. 306.

359 In fact, the Pate tells Jacques the first two (*Hadlaub* and *Der Narr auf Manegg*) and gets him to copy the third (*Der Landvogt von Greifensee*; the Pate has written his own version of this, not being satisfied with the common account).

360 *Gottfried Kellers Gesammelte Werke*, Insel-Ausgabe, 4. Band, Leipzig 1922, p. 236.

361 Jacques is rather closer to the central figure of Stifter's *Der Nachsommer*, Heinrich Drendorf, who learns not from his own present mistakes but from his mentor's past ones, and who lives by a received, not an experienced, wisdom.

362 And in this respect she accords perfectly with what Dr Stern says of Judith and Anna in *Der grüne Heinrich* (cf. above, p. 162ff.).

363 In *Pankraz der Schmoller*.

364 In *Frau Regel Amrain und ihr Jüngster*. "Regel" is short for the mightily symbolic name "Regula" (as if the abbreviation weren't symbolic enough). There is, it is true, a passage in this story (Keller, *ed. cit.*, 3. Band, p. 180ff.) where Fritz goes off to war with a mob of Seldwyler, and finds at the end of the day that what had at first seemed to him a splendid jaunt, a game of soldiers, has turned into grim and bloody reality, with dead and wounded comrades strewn about him. There the outside world *does* clamour to be heard, and the consequences of the hero's stupidity are real and terrible. But ultimately the implacable actuality of the scene is pushed away, and the experience becomes just another lesson, one more stage in the process of 'becoming' – in this case, becoming a responsible lad.

365 In *Die mißbrauchten Liebesbriefe*. The educative capacity of Nature, from which Wilhelm is made to benefit during his period of solitude and regeneration, seems to me one of the most dubious propositions in Keller's whole scheme of "Bildung".

366 Letters to his daughter Lisbeth, 20.2.1885, and to Schmidt, 3.2.1885.

367 Letters to Heyse, 4.12.1885, and to Gebr. Paetel, 5.12.1885.

368 This is how Tede Haien describes cancer in *Der Schimmelreiter* (SW IV 328).

369 Thomas Mann gives a splendid brief account of this deception in his essay on Storm (Th. Mann, *Gesammelte Werke* in 12 Bden., S. Fischer Verlag, IX. Bd, 1960, p. 266f.). I owe the biographical details of the preceding paragraphs to Stuckert, pp. 112f., 394, 399.

370 Pitrou, I, 3, 6.

371 Kayser, p. 22ff.

372 Stuckert, p. 244f.

373 Böttger, p. 125.

374 Letters to Heyse, 4.12.1885 and 25.5.1887.

375 Stuckert, p. 394f.

376 Letter to Heyse, 15.7.1887.

377 Ibid., Storm's italics.

378 See above, p. 174.

379 *Agnes Bernauer*, Act IV, Scene 4.

380 See above, p. 174.

381 SW IV 239-88; the pages are large, and the print is small.

382 17.7.1887.

383 Storm to Heyse, 15.7.1887.

384 The regretful, mock-resigned way in which Storm rejects the idea of changing the story is reminiscent of his tone in my quotations from his letters apropos of *In St Jürgen*, and could perhaps be explained by the construction I put on those quotations (See above, p. 39).

385 See above, p. 172.

386 See above, p. 176.

387 See above, p. 175f.

388 A significant zeugma, this, relegating even a colleague to the status of a coach. Franz cannot treat his assistant as a person; he is a thing which is necessary, like the coach, for the efficient running of the practice. There's many a true word spoken in syntactical jest.

389 See above, pp. 173, 175.

390 This appears to have been something of a fashion; Fontane draws attention to the desire, and roundly dismisses it for what it is, in the 35th chapter of *Effi Briest* (there is nothing to suggest that he is commenting here on *Ein Bekenntnis*, though he would certainly have read the story before he came to write his novel). In the relevant passage, Instetten says: "Und da hab ich mir denn, weil das alles nicht geht, als ein Bestes herausgeklügelt: weg von hier, weg und hin unter lauter pechschwarze Kerle, die von Kultur und Ehre nichts wissen. Diese Glücklichen. . !" To which Wüllersdorf replies: "Ach was, Instetten, das sind Launen, Einfälle. Quer durch Afrika, was soll das heißen? Das ist für 'nen Leutnant, der Schulden hat. . ."

391 The exception is the jackdaw episode, which I have moved from its place early on in the text to its proper chronological position in Franz's life.

392 Pitrou, p. 725.

393 Böttger, p. 354ff; my italics. One wonders whether such "technisch-wissenschaftlich Gebildete" as Böttger describes did in fact exist at all in the 18th century; and also whether Böttger is not projecting into a historical context the problem he himself is faced with in present-day East Germany. I owe these points to a conversation with Dr J. P. Stern.

394 Stuckert, p. 399ff.

395 Stuckert, p. 400f.

396 The foregoing is described in SW IV 384ff.

397 SW IV 398. The last sentence is an echo of the biblical injunction, "Hat jemand ein Amt, so warte er des Amtes" (Romans 12, 7 in the Luther version).

398 I talk more about the element of 'hybris' below, p. 190f.

399 For instance, my quotations above, p. 188f.

400 Stuckert, p. 406.

401 Or rather one and a half.

402 See above, p. 185.

403 Apropos of *Im Sonnenschein* (see above, p. 25).

404 Apropos of *In St Jürgen* (see above, p. 39 and of *Ein Bekenntnis* (see above, p. 176f.).

405 The term was coined, I believe, by David Riesman (D. Riesman with N. Glazer and R. Denny, *The Lonely Crowd*, Yale 1950, especially the later chapters).

406 See above, pp. 39, 116ff., 125ff., 134ff., 139ff.

407 T. S. Eliot, *The Three Voices of Poetry*, London 1953, p. 18; author's italics.

408 See above, pp. 28, 43, 169.

409 *Der Schimmelreiter* is almost the only story which encourages us to make free with capital letters.

410 Of the early stories I discussed, only *Posthuma* comes close to implying any condemnation of its central character (and therefore positing the existence of will or moral choice); but there, the young man is not condemned for inactivity, and apart from this, I think the dominant mood of the story is 'fatalistic' (see above, p. 21ff.).

411 In *Immensee, Im Sonnenschein, Drüben am Markt, Angelika* and *In St Jürgen* respectively.

412 Cf. above, p. 19f.

413 See above, pp. 149, 151, 152f., 162f., 165.

INDEX

The page-references given below indicate only the more important discussions of the works listed.